仅以此书献给我们的同事兼朋友——
美国旧金山大学利玛窦中西文化研究所
的吴小新博士

We dedicate this book to
Dr. Xiaoxin WU
Colleague and Friend

目　录

TABLE OF CONTENTS

前　言

　　学者们早就发现只要有人存在的地方就有宗教活动的存在。宗教跟人类语言有很多相似之处，宗教行为的独特性在于它对人类是有意义的；宗教觉悟是人类建构意义能力的一部分，让人类有更加充分的理由生活在这个世界上；个人宗教性的能力表现为既创造文化，同时又受到文化的塑造；因此，在漫漫的历史长河中和丰富多彩的文明里，宗教通过不同的形式加以展现。

　　本书是以学术研究的视角来看待宗教，并探讨宗教和宗教性在当代世界的经验。本书作为宗教社会学的专门著作，希望为在中国高校学习的本科生和研究生修读宗教研究课程时提供必要的帮助，同时也希望帮助其他更多的对宗教感兴趣的读者深刻理解宗教在当代文化（东方和西方的）中扮演的角色。

　　本书具有很多独特之处，相信会使读者从中受益。首先，本书包括中文和英文两个版本；其次，本书关注于宗教性和文化间通行的互动，而不是某一个特定宗教传统的历史发展；第三，三位作者来自不同的学科——社会学、社会心理学、宗教历史，这些学科都是对宗教进行科学性研究的重要领域；他们共同努力成就了这一跨学科研究的著作；最后，这部书带有很强的跨文化研究色彩，范丽珠博士是对传统中国文化和宗教社会学有深入研究的中国人，她对当代中国民间宗教表现形式的开拓性研究已经赢得国际学术界的广泛认可，James D. Whitehead 博士和 Evelyn Eaton Whitehead 博士是土生土长的美国人，长期在美国大学主要教授天主教和基督教方面的课程。从 1998 年开始，他们每年都会到中国的高校授课，所走过的地方包括上海、杭州、南京、香港。

本书的第一部分介绍了宗教性的几个基本因素：意义建构或在生命较深层面对意义的需要，以及超越或寻找那些值得为之生、甚至为之死的价值。开篇章节部分包括对西方宗教和宗教性学术传统的概述，同时论证了这些精神的皈依就存在于中国民间信仰与实践文化传统的核心部分。

第二部分吸收了某些现代宗教意识相关主题，从曾经产生巨大影响而今受到广泛质疑的世俗化（世俗化假设预言在现代化进程中，宗教的命运是不可避免地消亡）假设开始。讨论随后转向作为中西方现代化内在动力的相同性和相异性，并分析了在晚现代文化中宗教的位置和宗教性的表现方式。

第三部分提出宗教在中国未来发展趋势的几种观点。第九章和第十章讨论了中国传统遗产的信仰与实践，作为中国在 21 世纪发展的潜在资源。最后的这两章，思考了中国宗教和宗教性对世界文明和平发展可能的贡献。

在过去的五年中，本书的三位作者一直保持着愉快的合作关系，他们的研究主要关注在飞速发展情况下中国社会的宗教性。每年他们都安排一定的时间一起工作，或在中国、或在美国，他们深深地感受到认真而又深入的跨文化研究为彼此带来的益处和挑战。这一持续性的合作研究，首先是由美国旧金山大学利玛窦中西文化历史研究所（Ricci Institute for Chinese－Western Cultural History at the University of San Francisco）主任吴小新博士率先倡议并始终支持下进行的，本书的出版是利玛窦中西文化历史研究所长期支持中西方学术对话、文化理解系列项目的部分成果。

范丽珠
写于上海逸仙路文化花园寓所

第一部分　建构意义

第一章　宗教性与建构意义

　　本章将讨论宗教性的问题。宗教性是人类希望生活
富有意义的需要与愿望的表现，全世界的宗教传统都是
在回答人类所面对的终极问题：人类的起源和归宿，忍
受痛苦与死亡的经验等等。

　　"由其根本的属性决定，人类渴望知识"。这段著名的话是出
自二千多年前希腊著名哲学家亚里士多德的《形而上学》。那时西
方哲学家非常关注人类如何认识这些问题：怎样区别观点与特定
的知识？如何区别科学与智慧？人们很少注意到激励好奇心是知
识与科学的基础。本章将思考人类如何展示出对理解其生活世界、
领悟生活意义与目的深切的渴望与持久的期望。

　　人类学家格尔茨（Clifford Geertz）发现："建构意义的动力来
自于生活经历，在一定的形式和秩序下，如我们熟悉的生物需求
一样，表现出明显的真实与迫切。"[1]宗教体现在与这种愿望和能
力密切相关的思考形式和行动方法中，特别是跟这种欲望所要表
达的想法一致。用格尔茨的话说，就是"无知、痛苦和不公正的
无法避免性"。[2]

　　调动能力，我们通过认识世界的形式，并创造性地规范生活中那
些数不胜数的细节来使之富有意义。我们发现了世界的秩序：四季轮
转，年复一年，和人类生活并存。我们还接受了一个加诸于我们的世
界秩序：一个星期为七天，一年之中还包括各种各样的节日。这种发

现与发明的结合就存在于人类建构意义的核心部分。

哲学家里科（Paul Ricoeur）发现："我们为了认识而创造，用创造性的力量来建构意义，以领悟我们的存在和我们世界的特征。"伦理学家施韦克（William Schweiker）评价里科上面的话时说："人类创造道德的、宗教的、文化的、科学的和诗歌的意义，以便掌握他们生活世界和生命的真实。"[3]

里科笔下的创造（invention）不是不着边际的虚构（fantasy），他所指出的是：创造性的努力展现于人类致力的所有领域中——道德、文化、科学、宗教——通过设计目标的模式来让我们的生存具有意义。我们每个人都存在于社会生活中，而这个社会生活对我们来说是早就存在的：语言、法律、文化理念和道德规范等构成了意义层的内容，这些是我们先人的创造，其目的都是使我们居住的世界具有"人性化"。

社会学家马克斯·韦伯（Weber）这样描述这个世界：人类兼具发现者和创造者的双重角色，当一个人观察时，"就如同一个悬挂在自己编织的意义网中的动物一样。"[4]蜘蛛网的形象是那么生动而又引人入胜：网既是蜘蛛生活的舞台，又是它编织的、与物质形态相异的家。千百年来，人们将存在的社会世界作为一种客观的事实，或者是作为上帝的礼物，不假思索地接受了。一旦人类意识到我们建构了社会结构以至于我们的道德理念，于是就要对我们精心塑造的道德、文化、宗教的世界承担责任。[5]

一、建构意义：讲故事

人类是如何像他们寻找发现其生存目的和方向那样"建构意义"呢？我们往往通过讲故事来表述并建构意义。在故事中，我们试图揭开罩在痛苦、死亡和命运上的神秘面纱。这些故事的结构填充物是各种象征符号（symbols），带着神秘，半显半掩地衬托出新的意义。其中一些故事会不断地讲下去，成为经典文本，甚至代表性地形成了某些宗教传统的核心，如佛教、基督教。

喜欢讲故事在人类社会中是非常普遍的事情。我们在床上哄孩子时讲故事；我们听爷爷、奶奶讲他们年轻时的经历和那些冒险的传奇。当我们讲故事的时候，我们会把经历过的各种迥然不同的情节编入一个故事场景中；生活中许许多多的细节有的忘记了，有的还栩栩如生，被当作故事讲述出来。个人的生活或社区的往事就这样成为了故事。

我们对故事的痴迷好像永远不会停止。阅读名人的传记——包括政治领袖、军事英雄、圣人或各种明星——从中既可以了解他们生活中的一些轶闻趣事，同时更能获得某些领悟，以便对我们自己的生活有所启发。故事有助于我们体会生活的意义，阅读别人的故事常常会让我们自己对生命奥秘的体悟清楚地显示出来。

一个国家或民族也不断地讲故事。毛泽东领导的震惊世界的万里长征是一段英雄的史诗，至今仍然吸引着千万读者。哥伦布（Christopher Columbus）发现"新大陆"的航行是美国诞生故事的一部分。文化故事都具有"创始神话"的功能，比如在百姓中流传的历史中，那些重要的事件既有夸张叙述的成分又能和正式的记载相吻合。

语言、意义建构和神话

20 世纪早期，西方哲学家出现了将语言作为人类中心部分进行更深刻理解的主张。如哲学家维根斯坦（Ludwig Wittgenstein）和海德格尔（Martin Heidegger）关注于语言在人类创造生命意义中所扮演的角色，海德格尔以其典型的晦涩难懂的方式表示："语言是存在的栖身处（Language is the house of being）。"哲学家特雷西（David Tracy）概括了对语言的这种新的兴趣："语言不是可以随意拿起或放下的器物；它永远在那里，包围着并进入我所经历、感觉、判断、决定、行动的一切。我属于我的语言、而远胜于语言属于我。"[6]

不管是和朋友聊天、给孩子讲故事还是推敲阐发一个哲学理论，人类都是运用"现成的"的语言。每一种语言都有其特别的历史以及表示各种意思的词汇，每种语言都是长期文化历史的产物。我们从孩童开始学着用包含丰富想象和象征符号的语言说话，运用这套充满色彩、表达细微差异的语言系统编排故事，在一定程度上可以帮助我们理解生命的状态与运动。故而，人类生活中没有完全私人的故事，因为语言作为一种象征充分地展示了我们生活在其中的文化。

讲故事会涉及到被学者们称作神话部分的创世纪。这里神话并不意味着是虚构的或者是骗人的故事，相反，通过讲故事，神话反映出人类领悟生命的"大问题"。这样的神话不是单纯的历史记载，它们是人类在寻求意义的想象力的表现。哲学家玛丽·米雷（Mary Midgley）这样定义神话，"它们是想象的形式，有影响力的象征符号系统，用以表达理解这个世界的特别方式。"[7]在希腊语中，神话意指故事场景——具有固定目标和方向的故事。社会学家贝拉（Robert Bellah）提醒我们，"神话并不是要描述真实，描述真实是科学做的事。神话更希图改变事实，于是它就为个人和社会提供了道德和精神的意义。"[8]

希腊剧作家埃斯库罗斯（Aeschylus，公元前525—公元前456年）的《普罗米修斯之禁锢》，是在其创作二千五百年后迄今仍然表演的著名悲剧。在这个神话故事中，作者叙述了一个关于神普罗米修斯将神火送给人类作为礼物的故事。其他的众神确信火具有危险性，必须由神来掌控，故判决普罗米修斯必须为他的行为承担终生的惩罚。

这个神话并没有任何历史事件作为依据，相反其作者借助故事来解释人的超凡能力。在文学层面上，这个故事告诉我们人们能够使用、控制火是一个重要的文化成就，火的使用极大地改善了人类生活。但这个戏剧性的故事让我们正视神话的特点：故事里火的意义超过文字本身的意义。剧作家将火作为一个符号象征，吸取这个形象的多方面意义来探索人类能力的多重性，以便获得深刻意识和道德领悟。神话故事承认理性意识包含着意义和危险性，因为它具有强大的力量，并在超验领域中找到了源泉。

在希伯来圣经（Hebrew Bible）中，我们找到一则关于人类起源的故事。当然这个故事也是个神话，不是因为它的情节而是因为作者们的意向——用里科的话说，这个故事企图"抓住（人类起源的）真相"。

在《创世纪》（Book of Genesis）的记载中，这个神话描述了人类出现的伊甸园——亚当和夏娃与可爱的始祖耶和华神一起在这里快乐地生活着。但是在伊甸园还住着一条蛇，蛇在这个神话中扮演着一个象征性符号的角色。这个具有毒性的动物，是生活在沙漠中的希伯来部落尽人皆知的危险物，是恶魔的象征。这个故事提醒我们：邪恶——神秘、破坏性的力量会损害人类的团结并摧毁人与人的关系——在人类早期的经验中已经显示出来了。

在这个古代希腊和以色列的神话中，我们领略到戏剧力图展现人类想象力的作用，戏剧极力地使人类生活中的神秘面向具有意义——神话到底是表现了人类社会中理性多重力量的存在？抑或是邪恶在人类早期历史令人难以琢磨的显示？下面我们就要看看象征符号作为有影响力的因素是如何在神话中发挥作用的。

二、象征符号和丰富的意义内涵

象征符号的影响力——如上面提到的火和蛇——不仅存在于字面上，更在于它们被赋予的超乎寻常的意义中。对我们来说，火包含很多意思：提供温暖，点燃光明，致命的摧毁。在西方人的想象中，蛇象征着危险的处境、恶毒的企图、突然的死亡。里科写道，象征符号具有"丰富的内含"。[9]由于象征符号具有记忆储存的特质，下面我们会继续从故事、神话和经典中发现新的意义。

中国古代圣人庄子讲了一个"庖丁解牛"的故事。庖丁技艺高超且动作熟练，所以根本不需要磨刀。后来，这个戏剧性的故事在连环画中就演变成这样的情节：屠夫由于手持带有神力的刀，其力量远远超出实际生活中的常人。小孩子听了这个神话后，会着迷于屠夫超凡的力量。后来，少年长大以后重温这段故事时，就有新的心得，原来这个故事告诉我们若要获得与众不同的技艺，一定要经过多年的勤学苦练。于是，屠夫的故事也就不再只是一个神话。事实上，不是故事本身有什么变化，而是读者本人的辨识能力有了增长，有能力从故事中体悟出更深奥的意义。结果，从同一故事中他有了"更多"的发现。

再后来，他作为一个成年人的读者，重温这个故事，故事的另一个因素变得更有意义。经过时间的历练，屠夫知道如何辨识牛骨间那些细微的缝隙，在看不见的空间游刃有余，所以屠夫从来不需要磨刀。透过想象的跳跃，读者领悟到新的意义：也许在各种挑战与困境中——不论是面对客观世界中强大的阻力，还是在人际关系中遭遇的令人苦恼的矛盾——都会找到某种"空间"，而这"空间"就是使问题得到妥善解决的突破口。实际上，这个故事本身并没有任何的变化，而是读者对故事含义的认识一再扩展。这个故事中的象征符号——恰如每一个神话中的情节——展示着意义本身被不断地丰富。这种丰富，如里科所说的，在"实际感悟层面上，是取之不尽、用之不竭的。"[10]

象征符号、神话和经典

在无数我们听过的故事中，大概只有一两个能够被记住。那些特别令人着迷的故事，我们会一遍又一遍反复地听。因此，打动人心的故事总是具有一种特别的魅力穿越时空的限制，一代一代地传下来。这种经久流传的故事我们称作为经典。

特雷西（David Tracy）定义经典为"这些内容都有助于建立或形成一种特别的文化"[11]，被吸收进经久流传的故事中的象征符号与理想一道成为文化和宗教的基本内容。古代史诗《伊利亚特和奥德赛》将那个时代的希腊文化一直保存到今日。其他经典，如希伯来圣经、伊斯兰教的可兰经、佛经等——仍然是具有影响力的传统宗教存在的基础。

我们称作经典的故事，都具有激起人兴趣和好奇心的特点。首先是它们共同具有特殊性与普遍性。也就是说，每个故事都是在特定的地点、特定的时间、用特定的语言写就的（当然，圣经的许多卷本，是在数百年间由不同的作者来完成的。但是现在它作为一本整体著作，被视为希伯来人在以色列时期完成的）。经典故事都是那么引人入胜，得到其他文化和其他时代的人的认可与欣赏，翻译成不同的语言，于是经典故事的影响也就能够穿越时空的限制。如，道家的《道德经》在美国几乎每年都有新版的英文翻译。

其次，这些经典具有文字本身的含义以及超越字面的意义。通常故事的文本没有变化，只是提供了一个固定的基础。但是，当在新的环境或新的翻译中阅读时，同一个故事常常会发展出新的解释，于是新的含义就从旧有的情节上发展出来。正如里科所表达的那样：社会和经典中的象征符号具有"向读者展现新的可能性：世界延伸的视野和个人无限的能力"的作用。[12]

数个世纪以来，宗教文本已经被广泛地理解为历史事实的记载。只是在近几十年，一些学者才普遍认识到，这些大量的记载与历史并没有关系，而不过是为了建构意义。这些经典致力于发现、检视并反映生活中各个方面那些始终难以解答的问题——来自痛苦和死亡的困惑、爱之天赋的奥秘、了解个人命运的挑战……人类学家格尔茨观察到："作为一个象征的、想像的、找寻意义的动物，人类的观点打开了一个全新的路径——通向宗教的分析。"[13]

三、生命的"有限处境"

人类为意义而斗争显示在对有限性的特别关注。里科认为"那些有限处境，……包括孤独、错误、痛苦和死亡……在人类的不幸与伟大相互对峙之处"。[14]格尔茨指出，对人最根本的挑战是那些无意义的混乱状况和道德上的困境。"混乱——事情的混乱缺乏的往往不仅是解释，而是可解释性——之所以有打乱人生活的威胁存在，在于其分析能力的有限性，在于其忍耐力的有限性，在于其道德领悟力的有限性。"[15]

人类的痛苦提供了一个不断重复的有限性的证明。由于认识到痛苦似乎是不可避免的，人类努力地想表达痛苦不是简单的不合理的存在。我们不顾一切地想发现——或者创造，如果需要对我们所忍受痛苦的一些解释。世界上存在着的这些伟大的宗教都试图面对人类的痛苦，有时告诫人们通过某些方式缓解痛苦，更多地强调那些更有意义的存在实际上具有超越于痛苦本身的价值。

人类意识中具有一种本能，即在痛苦中去发现道德意义。比如，很多文化都相信痛苦来自于惩罚。在天主教和基督教普遍接受的新约中，耶稣的朋友们给他看一个天生失明的孩子，问他这种缺陷是否应看作其父母的"罪"。印度教和佛教所理解的"业"（karma）就是将眼下遭遇的痛苦与过往的道德行为联系起来。这种解释在中国民间信仰的"报应说"中得到发展。把大千世界中道德的报偿将忍受的痛苦与以前的恶行连在一起。令人不解的是，为什么痛苦会持续存在呢？于是，人类努力地通过宗教的或非宗教的途径为其所遭受的痛苦找出合理的解释。

死亡引起第二个限制。人类的经验证实死亡是极其正常的事情，因为每个生命都会有结束的时候。历史记载中充满了人类如何渴望逃避死亡，或努力抢在死神前面以便能超越个体的死亡，继续拥抱生命。死亡不仅是生存、而且是理解的藩篱，我们不能洞察其奥秘也无法领悟其意义。于是，人们始终在问相同的问题：为什么我们会死？死亡是不可避免吗？什么东西能免我于死？

每种文化都努力地缓和由死亡所造成的恐怖。最生动的例子是葬礼，葬礼的仪式和习俗被人类学家视为人类宗教行为的最早证明。在悲伤与崇敬中埋葬了父母，墓地中树起了墓碑，亲人定期会到这里来祭祀，通过象征性仪式对亡者表示感激和别无选择地接受天人相隔的事实。在特别时期由于专注于死者的葬礼，生者的生活被打乱了。不同的文化有不同的葬礼习俗，但表示对死者的尊重是普遍的。在很多地方，这种尊重包括感觉死者继续存在，并对活着的人有影响力。

"宗教性"这个词指涉使生活富有意义的不懈努力，特别是面对这些"受限制的处境"。社会学家贝格尔（Peter Berger）观察到"宗教的冲动，寻找超越于这个世界有限空间的经验存在之意义是人类永恒的特质"。[16]宗教的能力在于必须要面对着人类的特性：生活充满了疑惑，却常常无从解答。对于大多数人来说，疑惑和迷惘本身就是寻找解脱和释然的动因。对人类状况的思考，尽管不可能令人避免于死亡，但在一定程度上会起到丰富人性的作用。

四、我们存在的"终极条件"

社会学家贝拉（Robert Bellah）将宗教定义为："关于人存在的终极条件的一套象征形式和行为。"[17]这些终极条件包括：宇宙的起源，世界的秩序和人的命运。

建构意义的宗教能力使人们关注于生命的起源。我们怎样解释存在的事实？世界难道仅仅是一个偶然的事件，抑或是一个大布局的部分？宇宙学家能够解释很多关于世界进化的问题、首先是宇宙的起源。难以想象的凝缩、突然扩张导致出现人们常说的创世"大爆炸"，科学家能够带我们回到爆炸开始的第一毫微秒。可是我们还想知道：在爆炸开始前的那一瞬间到底发生了什么？关于这一最为关键的"终极条件"，科学家始终缄默不语。

很多宗教的条件，包括对起源问题的解释，通常被编造进开天辟地的传说故事中。事实上，希伯来圣经包括两个创世纪的记载证实了面对人类起源奥秘，不同宗教想象力的存在。这些不是严格意义上的历史记载，没有任何人可以证实这一创世事件。如里科描述那样，这些虚构的文学，其价值在于"领悟我们存在的特征"，并"把握（我们生命）的真实"。

引起宗教冲动的第二个终极问题是在这个世界极其重要的道德秩序。我们注意到物质世界的存在和按照普遍一致法则运行的生物世界。法则与道德秩序究竟是相似的，抑或有很大的差异性？

天主教思想家一直想澄清这样的"自然法则"，是否有一种普遍的准则（universal code）（"不杀人、不说谎、不偷盗"）存在于我们人群中？中国文化早就意识到"道"或自然/道德结构的存在并掌控着世界的运转（一种尊重并顺从的模式），从而产生了大同的理想。孔子曾说："朝闻道，夕死可矣。"孟子提出辨识良知可能性的问题。在某些特别的时候，良知组成人的道德特质。孟子希望人们体会这种良知的存在，于是他建议特别要留心，清静的夜晚和忙碌的白天之间那短暂的时刻，只有在远离喧嚣的时候，人性中分辨善恶的良知才能苏醒。但是孟子意识到这种良知本性非常容易受到损伤，因为人若沉湎于日常事务就会失去与生俱来的善的悟性。

第三个终极关怀的问题是关于人类命运的奥秘。人类生命是否可以简单地视为进化的一个偶然结果：稍纵即逝的彗星？每个生命都有些持续的目标？人生轨迹是否是命中注定的，一如命运？

人生的每个阶段都是在我们自己手中把握的吗？无论哪种情况出现，个人怎样来回应呢？命运是固定的还是可以改变的？命运是禁锢我们的监牢，还是帮助我们的精神得到解脱？这些就是宗教信仰要回答的问题。中国人对命运的信仰和基督徒相信上帝的意旨，都表现了宗教对人类命运困境的回答。

五、宗教的回应——个人的与文化的

宗教的圣人，如佛祖和耶稣，代表着来自宗教深刻的觉悟。他们令人景仰的经历既独特又打动人心，成为不断演进的精神信仰的基础。当这些宗教的天才谈及他们独一无二的经历时，他们使用的语言和意象都是来自于自己的文化。释迦牟尼的经历用印度的巴利文（Pali）及梵文（Sanscrit）记载下来，同时还伴有莲花和大象的形象。耶稣使用的是阿拉姆语（Aramaic），夹杂着希伯来的方言，还有摩西五书的形象和词汇，犹太教的经文。他的话语被新约圣经用希腊语言记录下来，在文化意象和细微之处无不体现出当地的习俗。所有个人的经历通过作者自身拥有的文化语言来传递，从而与宗教的经验连在一起。一个人对天或真主或上帝强烈的感受往往是非常个性化的，一旦要表达出来只有借助其自己所处文化的语言。如社会学家格利立（Andrew Greeley）观察到的那样："我们总是用那些来自我们继承和接受的文化隐喻来诠释生活。"[18]社会学家贝拉（Robert Bellah）补充道："宗教的悟性要透过象征符号化来展示，以便能跟经验一样具有完整性。"[19]

每个人的宗教经验总是会从其文化传统的习惯用语和意象中获得滋养——如果这个经验有足够的说服力——便会被吸收到共同的故事库和象征符号中。文化的精神遗产（spiritual heritage）通过不同的制度性宗教表现出来，如伊斯兰教、基督教；有时则通过文化形式，如精神探索和寻求宗教意义，表现为比较散漫的特征。正如我们在第四章要讨论的那样，中国是一个非常值得关注的例子，中国人的精神信仰传统就散布于整个文化之中。

六、文化符号（Cultural Codes）：掌握一个文化的表达方式

任何文化都包括丰富的象征符号，这些象征符号就承载了人们的价值和理想。如在中国文化中，"龙"和"道"就体现出核心的象征意义。研究文化符号学的学者都重视这样的象征核心。施雷德（Robert Schreiter）概述了文化符号学的方法："文化作为传播形式是要结合过程来研究的，并关注在通过文化路径中各种符号（*semeia in* Greek）所承载的信息。"[20]

龙和鱼　符号（codes）是解释性的系统，为我们提供文化象征的各种微妙含义。在西方基督教文化中，龙象征的是邪恶势力。人们熟悉的圣·乔治（St. George）画像提醒西方观察者，文化符号赋予这个动物特别的意义。在圣经创世纪的故事中，龙与蛇类似。但是在中国文化中，龙是正面的形象，表现为超凡的力量；而舞龙是很多文化节日中典型的部分。在全世界表现观音慈悲情怀的艺术品中，观音移动时被想像成骑在一条大龙身上。因此透过不同文化符号的视角，同一种具有符号意义的动物会被理解成截然不同的意思。

一种宗教传统会将不同的意义（符号）赋予单一的象征符号。在基督教的复活节（Easter）中，纪念耶稣的复活，火扮演了重要的角色。仪式开始于只有火光的夜晚，人们手中举着燃烧着的巨形蜡烛，火光闪耀，进入教堂，将教堂照亮。在基督教信仰的另一部分，火象征的不是启蒙而是惩罚，地狱的痛苦是由永远不息的火来代表的。

任何一个文化的符号都有意无意地流露了"周遭发生的事情怎么会是这样的"想法。这些符号作为某一文化思想或信仰的一部分，自然而然地被其成员所理解，每个人对其含义都心知肚明，根本不用说就是这样了。因为符号所代表的意思作为这个文化的核心而存在。只有熟悉了这套东西，才能了解领悟这个文化。

在中国文化中，"鱼"具有丰富的象征意义。这是因为"鱼"这个字与"裕"同音的关系。外人若不了解中国文化的符号，无论如何也不能理解在中国宴会的餐桌上为什么盛着鱼的那道菜会显得特别重要。

作为象征符号的食物　文革期间，毛泽东主席在接见全国工人代表的时候将芒果赠送给工人代表。于是这个普通的水果就代表了党和伟大领袖对工人阶级在社会主义建设中所做贡献的高度赞赏。很快，得到领袖"赐福"的芒果便被赋予了重要的象征意义。腊制的芒果被广大人民群众摆放在家里，供在毛主席像旁边。一个新的象征符号进入共产主义世界，为工人及全国人民提供了精神意义。

在更深的层面，所有中国的食物都和中国文化重要的象征符号"阴"和"阳"有着某种关系。因为每种食物都毫不例外地具有"热"或"寒"的属性。在中国文化中身体平衡和健康远非热量吸入的问题，而是强调不同食物的阴阳协调。中医的原理就是极其关注这一深层次的营养均衡问题。

玉　艺术评论家霍兰·科特（Holland Cotter）注意到中国文化对玉的欣赏和热衷远胜于西方。"在西方人的眼里，玉不那么引人注目。它的表面看起来不那么生动，其颜色也不那么鲜艳，很难形容。"但是这种特殊的石头在中国文化中被赋予多方面的含义。"玉在中国有着丰富的内容，包含着道德和精神的意义。它是鲜活的，用手触摸的时候很柔和，又很光滑……儒家赋予玉以道德的含义，玉象征着正直、忠诚、毅力等气节。"[21]

夜晚　是充满危险抑或养精蓄锐的时刻？正如玉一样，夜晚在东西方的经典中代表着不同的意义。在《创世纪》中，读者看到英雄雅各（Jacob）在夜晚受到危险的对手威胁（《创世纪》第32章）。雅各与无法确知的对手搏斗，直到黎明到来的时候，他才意识到对手原来是自己神秘的神。在这个令人着迷的古代故事中，夜晚代表着充满危险的时间段，在黑暗中人们无法辨识危险的存在，也无法避免突然遭到的袭击。

我们在《孟子》中读到关于黎明的一段生动描述。黎明，"其日夜之所息，平旦之气"。在这一宝贵的、安静的瞬间所察觉感悟的东西，很容易在白日无数令人烦扰的琐事中流逝。于是，孟子补充说，即使"夜气不足以存，然其日夜之间，亦必有所生长。故平旦未与物接，其气清明之际，良心犹必有发见者"（孟子，告子上）。[22] 这个故事显示，在儒家文化中，夜晚是人们养精蓄锐的最佳阶段。

中国文化受到"阴阳"信仰的影响，强调昼与夜周期的轮转。于是，中国人对夜晚象征意义的想象完全是正面的。而在西方文化中恰恰相反，西方文化普遍流行二元对立：好与坏、肉与灵、夜与昼。故，夜晚的象征意义在西方人眼里就完全等同于危险和昏暗的愚昧。

面对人们难以领悟的各种奥秘——痛苦与死亡、生命起源和命运，每个文化都创造了宗教信仰和活动来获得解释和安慰。因为宗教经典和仪式只能在自身存在的语言、意象中找到表述方式，所以宗教和文化形成了一种特别而又复杂的关系。在接下来的章节中，我们会检视宗教在人类生活中的地位及其与文化的关系。

注释

[1] Clifford Geertz, *The Interpretation of Cultures*, p. 140.

[2] Geertz，格尔茨将建构意义的挑战描述作"确认或者至少是认识到，人类面临的无知、痛苦和不公正是不可避免的，同时否认这些不合理的

存在作为世界整体的特征。"

[3] See p. 79 of William Schweiker's essay, "Understanding Moral Meanings: On Philosophical Hermeneutics and Theological Ethics, in *Christian Ethics: Problems and Prospects*. Ricoeur's observation appears in *Interpretation Theory: Discourse and the Surplus of Meaning*.

[4] Max Weber, quoted in Geertz, *Interpretation of Culture*, p. 5. 格尔茨又说:"我把文化置于这些网络中,在分析过程中我不是把它们当作寻找规律的实验科学,而是寻找意义的解释。"

[5] See p. xi of *Meaning and Modernity: Religion, Polity and Self*. 赵文词是这样评价我们对道德价值和宗教真实发展承担的认识,"不是找到理由来放弃,而是提醒我们我们对其负有责任。"

[6] David Tracy, *Plurality and Ambiguity*, pp. 49—50.

[7] Mary Midgley, *The Myths We Live By*, p. 1

[8] Robert Bellah, *Broken Covenant*, p. 3

[9] 里科在他的著作很多处都讨论了象征符号和经典中的 "surplus of meaning"。参考 *Freud and Philosophy*, p. 19 and also p. 5 of Mark Wallace's introduction to Ricoeur's *Figuring the Sacred*.

[10] Paul Ricoeur, *Figuring the Sacred*, p. 5

[11] David Tracy, *Plurality and Ambiguity*, p. 12

[12] Paul Ricoeur, *Figuring the Sacred*, p. 8

[13] Clifford Geertz, *The Interpretation of Cultures*, p. 140.

[14] Paul Ricoeur, "Toward A Hermeneutic of the Idea of Revelation," *Essays on Biblical Interpretation*, p. 86.

[15] Clifford Geertz, *The Interpretation of Cultures*, p. 100. 格尔茨称这些境遇是:"困惑、痛苦、难以弄清楚的道德矛盾,……本质的挑战……任何宗教…希望存在下去,就要考虑如何来克服它们。"

[16] Peter Berger, *Desecularization of the World*, p. 13.

[17] Robert Bellah, "Religious Evolution," in *Beyond Belief*, p. 21

[18] Andrew Greeley, *Religion as Poetry*, p. 25.

[19] Quoted in Robert Ellwood, *Introducing Religion from Inside and Oatside*, p. 8.

[20] Robert Schreiter, *The New Catholicity*, p. 30

[21] Holland Cotter, "The Jade of China, Alive with Meaning Yet Glossily Elusive," *New York Times*, (Friday, Aug. 6, 2004), p. 31

[22] Mencius 6A 8. "The restorative influence of the night" is James Legge's translation. See his *The Works of Mencius*, p. 408.

第二章 宗教与超验

这章将讨论超验问题。人类渴望超越普通和平凡，在它们的深层发现那些比生命本身更重要的价值，以便面对身边各种不同的遭遇。

人们渴望获得的不仅仅是更多的财富，更期待着意义和目标的实现，以便使生命具有更丰富的价值。通览中西历史、穿越各种文化，除了在那些战乱的年代，人们始终渴望得到一个好的世界。对于获得更多实惠的渴望，以及那些无法企及的东西的渴望，显示了人们对超验的向往——追求"超越"那些对普通和平凡的限制。

宗教哲学家约翰·希克（John Hick）以对超验的渴望来定义宗教：

> 宗教（或特别是宗教传统）以觉悟为中心，回应超越于我们自己和我们世界的事实，告诉我们超验路径在何处：是在宇宙之外，还是在其中，或两者兼有。[1]

约翰·希克的定义包括四个因素：觉悟、回应、事实、超越。宗教始于觉悟——一种省察或对事实的意识或自觉的信仰。这种觉悟即是一种回应，经常表现为对世界宗教传统的信仰、仪式和实践。宗教传统印证了这种觉悟不是荒诞或幻觉，而是对现实的认知。事实上，一种来自对现实世界超验方面的认知，为我们在熟悉经验世界里开启了更多的可能。探索超验现象将使我们对宗教性获得更丰富的理解。

一、超验的暗示

在公元前四世纪的希腊，苏格拉底作为一个声名远播的大师，或用现代名词说，他作为一个公共知识分子，和雅典贵族青年进行着饶有兴味的讨论，提出关于社会现存的规则和他们生命深层意义的问题。市政府的权威受到这些讨论的挑战，于是有人要求苏格拉底停止和青年的讨论。苏格拉底拒绝接受这项命令并继续他的教学，结果他被告上法庭，法庭要求他说明拒绝停止具有潜在破坏性讨论的理由。

如柏拉图（Plato）在其经典《忏悔录》记载的那样，苏格拉底向法官解释他不能接受命令的理由。苏格拉底认为一个较高的权威是来自良知、发自内心的声音，良知和内心的声音才是他个人最忠实的表达。面对死亡威胁，苏格拉底重申了他必须按照自己良知行事的意愿。于是，他被宣判死刑，被迫喝下有毒的东西。这一幕成为西方道德觉悟的前奏，标志着个人良知高于一切的境界，即便这种内在良知会与社会规范相冲突，个人也不会放弃追求。

在为良知献身的过程中，苏格拉底保持着一个超越其自身生命的价值。他的选择是超越意识的典型。苏格拉底坚信的不仅是构成真实生命的价值——值得为之生的目标，而在那个道德选择的重要时刻，他更保持着死得其所的价值——一个完整的为人之道：超越或超验于个人安全与保障的普通生活目标。

同一个世纪的晚期，中国的圣人孟子描述了相似的超越信仰。他写道：

生亦我所欲也，义亦我所欲也；二者不可得兼，舍生而取义者也。生亦我所欲，所欲有甚于生者，故不为苟得也；死亦我所恶，所恶有甚于死者，故患有所不辟也。[2]（《孟子·告子章句上》）

从表面上看，对人类来说生命就是最大的价值，而死是最大的恐怖。但如何回应有关生死的问题，并非容易之事。今天我们很多人可以想象在什么情景下会非常理智地需要"超越"个人安危，那些价值包括我们孩子的生命、家庭的荣耀、保卫我们的国家、个人的名誉及自尊心等。为了这些，我们愿意牺牲自己的生命。那么我们该如何解释这些价值？这些价值又来自何方？在这里超验的问题是宗教与宗教性讨论的一部分。

无论是苏格拉底还是孟子都不属于任何宗教。他们也都没有信仰一个超越的神，或将超自然的境界作为其道德献身的动力。但是他们都认为，活在世界上就要使生命和追求的价值保持一致。由此可见，价值本身就直接反映了人类所具有的超越能力。

二、超验于"尘世"

在苏格拉底和孟子之前数百年，印度的宗教人物清楚地勾勒出了一个道德景象，即超脱苦海。公元六世纪前，佛祖乔达磨（Siddhartha Gotama）昭示其信徒，要认识到人类生活充满了贫困、疾病和死亡。如果这样的痛苦是人类经验最根本的状况，那么什么是消解的方法呢？佛祖相信，如果人类能够发现其不幸的缘故，认识其痛苦的根源，他们就能够处理这一切。人类就以这样的方式，超越于人类生活的普遍困境。

在佛教中，通向这一目标的途径就是要认识到人类自己是在作茧自缚。人类的所作所为是因为错误地假设每个人是分别与独立的存在。如果能够认识到真相——我们是唯一宇宙意识或自我的所有部分——我们就会摆脱疯狂的斗争和令人烦躁的竞争。在这个状态下，肉体上的痛苦也就被认为没有任何终极的价值。

于是佛祖和他的追随者们幻想一个和谐又文明的境界，超越这个痛苦现实、超越世俗生死轮回，这就是涅槃（*nirvana*）[3]。一旦达到涅槃，所有痛苦只不过是暂时的，就像闪烁的烛光一样，很容易熄灭。最后的状态是一个完全彻底的和平世界，展示的是经由佛祖——"觉悟者"所感悟到的通过冥想的方式来获得平静和满足的境界。

从佛祖的洞察力发展出来的宗教传统，就是一套旨在获得平静和觉悟的信仰方式。首先要求人们不要沉迷于世俗生活那些烦杂忙碌的事情，寻找思想觉悟的人应该脱离家庭到寺庙修行，在那里人们会不受干扰专心修练，最终修得正果。后来，当佛教传入并成为中国文化的部分时，"出家"就成为一个特别的词，特指那些离开世俗生活专门修行者的生命方式。

在释迦牟尼五百年以后，耶稣的追随者面对着来自现实生活的挑战：人应该怎样活着才能完全领悟耶稣的教诲？人必须放弃什么以便追求超越罪恶和死亡的生活道路？是否有超越现实存在的理想和价值？

耶稣的第一批追随者们生活在罗马帝国，罗马帝国的文化根本就和基督教的信仰与实践势不两立。由于要保持对信仰忠诚就意味着要面对死亡的威胁，这些耶稣早期的追随者在循道过程中意识到，人完全可以超越其眼下痛苦与被迫害。于是，他们祈祷将来和上帝永远在一起，想象天堂是一个死后没有痛苦的、平静的乐土。

如同佛教文化一样，早期天主教的传统发展出一套道德原则和信仰方式来帮助人们进入天堂。人们相信每日的祈祷和慈善的工作都会有助于个人超越生死从而获得永生。这些变化会纯洁灵魂，以便进入到上帝的天国。对于很多信徒来说，天堂是"真正的家"，而在尘世的生活只不过是要经历的必要考验而已。

和佛教相同，早期基督教根据尘世日常生活的情况来估价超验的世界。在《新约圣经》约翰第一书中写道：

> 不要爱世界和世界上的事。人若爱世界，爱父的心就不在他里面了。(I John 2：15)

这样的劝诫引起了很多耶稣信徒像佛教的和尚一样藏身于远僻荒凉之地，或建立与世隔离的修院进行修行，以避免受到凡间琐事的干扰。[4]

在这些历史传统中，超越理想的吸引人之处在于摆脱凡间琐事的纠缠。由于敏感地意识到人类的痛苦和社会的不公正，佛教和基督教都试图转移人们对人类社会现实生活痛苦的注意力，从精神上挑战造成这些苦难根源。不过，透过宗教理念进入到超验世界，并不是鼓励人们积极地改变现实社会生活的状况。

三、"现世"超越

佛教和基督教，包括新教和天主教，至今对整个世界还具有深远的影响。在历史进程中，在每一个宗教传统中，从宗教超越的本质中都会发展出信仰的新内容。而这些信仰新的面向，都有助于该宗教被中国文化接受。

在佛教传统中出现了菩萨的偶像，佛教菩萨是指上求佛法，下化众生的圣人。菩萨标榜大慈大悲，普渡众生。菩萨放弃了到涅槃世界，宁可选择留在世上忍受痛苦来拯救世人。"所有的世人在苦海中，我要将一切痛苦和罪孽承担下来；我要将所有悲伤接受下来，因为我要解救众人。"[5]

在佛教传统中，另一新发展显示超越的意义得到扩大。在公元纪年开始初期，一部新的佛教经书向我们介绍了一个新菩萨维摩诘。维摩诘是梵语 Vimalakirti 之音译，也译作"毗摩罗诘"，译曰"净名"、"无垢称"，意即以洁净无染污而著称者，俗惯以"维摩"略称之，是大乘佛教中一位颇为著名的在家菩萨。这位圣人的修行方式不是以脱离尘世或是进入寺庙来寻求解脱，而是充分享受世间的快乐及对世界的关怀。维摩诘所作的一切，重新解释了佛教的"出家"理想。维摩诘坚持寻求精神觉悟，并从那些表面的关怀转向内心的修炼。[6]按照这种新的理想，佛教徒可以在现实生活中寻求超越：若菩萨欲得净土，当净其心，随其心净，则佛土净。这种对佛教全新的诠释强调了慈悲心的重要性。时至今日，佛教的慈善活动都可以追溯到维摩诘对此世超越的肯定。

基督教传统形成了一个类似的对超越的重新诠释。耶稣在讲道会堂宣布他的使命是寻找神的领地或王国，这一理想通过公正与爱得到了改变。在这个世界里，穷人得到关怀，敌人得到宽恕。由于这样的想法与基督徒生活的社会现状截然不同，神的国度最初被理解为一种指定的超越现实存在的允诺。多数基督徒认为神国存在于天堂，是在死后才能享受的。于是有理由离开尘世期待进入天堂神的领地。

几百年过去了，基督教在世界各地传播开了，基督徒思想家发现在耶稣的教诲中有关于神的王国的一些新解释。人们记得耶稣说："我的国不在这个世界。"但在另一个章节中，他说："神的国就在你们中间。"当有人问神国降临的迹象，回答是："瞎子看得见，瘸子能走路，……穷人得到福音。"

天主教与基督新教的神学家开始谈到神之国的两种可能性——"现世"和"尚未完全实现的"。公正与爱的超越理想并不意味着简单地作为一种报偿而感觉到天堂的美好，而是一种挑战，激励耶稣的信徒们努力地超越其生活的社会。神之国在这里是"现世的"，不管什么地方，都能满足怀着美好愿望者的现世的需要。同时，神之国又是"尚未完全实现的"，因为宗教的理想似乎永远都无法在此世完全实现。

佛教徒和基督徒以及其他宗教的信徒投身于慈善公益活动中，意在消弭痛苦并完善这个世界。今天，多数宗教仍然保持着超越的理想，引导信徒对现实生活中复杂问题进行深层次的思考，并全身心地为问题的解决做出贡献。这就是宗教的超越，这种超越必然会使人们在这个尘世中被体验到。

四、中国："入世"的超越

在以色列和印度的古代文化中，宗教创始人这样来描绘生活方式：认识到超越尘世的价值，接受这些价值，并对正义和悲天悯人的行为产生影响，他们向往着一个更好的世界。在古代中国，与西方截然不同的是，超越在现实世界中得以实现，孔子也意识到了佛祖和耶稣共同感受到的人生烦恼与苦难。孔夫子为人类设想了一个更好的形式去活着，一种要胜过现实一切的生活方式。用中国思想史专家施瓦茨（Schwartz）的话来说，孔子已经意识到"在理想的社会秩序和现实状况之间有着不可逾越的鸿沟"。[7]但是对于孔子来说，这种至高无上的理想在中国古代王朝曾经存在过。作为一个中国人，孔子没有幻想其他的那些不着边际、远离现世生活的理想，尽管他致力于追求一个更好的生活。但是超越对于他和他的弟子们来说是"一种内在的超越"。[8]

也许宗教取向（spiritual orientation）在中国文化中最有说服力的宗教性超越是祖先崇拜的习俗。施瓦茨（Schwartz）注意到在中华文明中"我们称之为祖先崇拜的信仰无处不在"，他提醒我们，祖先崇拜就是这个文化宗教整体的一部分。[9]从远古时期，中国人就以家庭作为宗教的中心，家庭培养了道德与忠诚，个人道德修养就是从家庭开始的。当古希腊文化普遍地将公共场所作为启发个人和公民的道德之处时，中国人则首先关心的是家庭。对孔圣人来说：

> 人们是在家庭中学会如何维持社会道德伦理的，家庭就是权威产生的领域。权威被接受及其运作不是依赖物质上的强迫，而是通过结合宗教力量、以家族关系纽带为基础的道德情感来实现。[10]

祖先崇拜仪式强调，家庭的关系超越了个体生命结束的本身，任何个体生命的终结都不会影响家庭的延绵。在中国文化中对祖先崇拜极为重视。祖先崇拜表明死亡"不是简单地死去离开人世，因为家族就包括了死去的祖先灵魂传递以及生者的世界"，这是一种神圣的"生物"承续，个人与其祖先神圣的承续超越了"生死界限"。仪式的意义在于：

> 亡灵与活着的子孙继续保持着系统性关系。由于家庭成员跨越生与死的界限，他们在其群体内继续扮演相同的角色……[11]

由于对祖先灵魂的重视是如此地"以现实生活为中心的，尽管超越的事实是与祖先崇拜密切相关，但是儒家学者倾向于用人文主义来解释祖先崇拜"。[12]

超越和人文主义

另一种"此世"的超越是比较现代、典型的西方式，表现为通过人文主义方式来改变世界的各种努力。哲学家玛萨·努斯鲍姆（Martha Nussbaum）所赞成的那种超越，并不是将我们的注意力远离现世人生，而是不断养成超越普通人生的内在冲力。[13]她将此称之为"一种内在的、人性化的超越"。[14]

天主教哲学家查尔斯·泰勒（Charles Taylor）赞同人文主义将我们的关注点放到"对普通生活的肯定上"，把"美德的重要性置于日常生活、生产和家庭的中心"。[15]但是查尔斯·泰勒反对那种否认超越眼前任何"一切"价值和信仰的人文主义。他指出对于现在的很多人来说，他们所拥有的人文主义的关怀受到宗教价值的塑造——或基督教，或佛教，或印度教。对于这些人来说，人类超越的能力与宗教信仰是相一致的，"生命无法将事物的每一点都穷尽透彻地加以展现"。[16]查尔斯·泰勒坚信："尽管痛苦和死亡都是负面的，因为与存在和生命的毁灭有关，但是我们可以从痛苦与死亡中得到一种领悟，即还有某种境界肯定超越生命的价值存在。"[17]

对于诺贝尔奖得主、诗人谢默斯·希尼（Seamus Heaney）来说，艺术与诗歌同样凸显了超越的问题。他写道："诗歌具有达到某种高度的潜力，使人能够成为一个可能改变、或发展的因素，要在想象中对更光彩、更丰富的生活充满渴望。"[18]在谢默斯·希尼看来，诗歌在寻找"一个转瞬即逝的可能，一个潜在的启示，而这个启示由于会受到客观状况的否定、以至于饱受威胁"。[19]艺术和诗歌追求"透视"寻常和平凡，渴望着那些常常被否定或忽视的人类生活。

人文主义与超越相遇在生命价值的问题上。难道人生的意义就在于为个人的生存而奔波？如果答案是肯定的，那么痛苦和死亡的影响显然就只是负面的，或许还应该有些"其他的"。价值赋予人生意义，即便是面对死亡和痛苦，也不会减损人生价值。像卡尔·拉内（Karl Rahner）[20]、史维克（William Schweiker）[21]和查尔斯·泰勒那样的宗教学者坚持认为，一个人既可以是人文主义者，同时又可以信仰超越的价值。

五、超越：走近地平线

地平线是一个人们熟悉的景象。每天黎明我们看见太阳从天和地之间的地平线上升起；每天黄昏我们又会发现太阳落山就好像掉到地平线下面去了。地平线是我们视线范围的标记，是我们视力所及的最远端。它是个奇特的界限，比如我们在地平线附近发现一棵树，但是当我们企图走近时，会发现地平线其实还在更远的地方。我们很快意识到，人们永远都无法真正地接触到地平线。因为我们每向前走一步，地平线就往后倒退一步。

地平线阻隔了我们看到视线以外的东西，即使这些东西与我们有关联，并确实在超出视线范围内的某个地方存在着。探究地平线以外的景象作为永恒的动力，激励着水手、诗人以及科学家和宗教思想家产生了无穷的想象力。

地平线的这些特点在于既非常普通又具有象征性，对宗教学者来说更是很有吸引力的隐喻。和我们在第一章讨论的"有限的状况"和"终极问题"有关，地平线象征着人类的理性理解力所不能超越的界线。

里科这样描述地平线，"把它看作一件从不曾拥有的事物的隐喻"[22]，地平线就在我们视线的最远端，不断提醒着有很多超越我们知识的屏障存在，而这些存在往往是我们根本无法企及的。意识到这点也许会使我们变得沮丧，或者产生敬畏之心。对一些人来说，就像里科所观察到的那样，"这是地平线，我们视力所及的景象并非全面或包罗万象，我们所能做的只是对在远处静静横亘在那里的一切表示致意。"

作为一个象征，地平线在某种程度上标志着了解人类生活全貌的愿望遇到障碍。故而，我们关于痛苦和爱、关于死亡和命运的问题难以找到答案。为什么人要忍受痛苦？死亡难道仅是简单的个人生命的消失，抑或对生命会有"更多"其他的启发？个人如何理解自己的命运——她是谁，她会变成谁？这些问题迷失于没有完满答案的困境中。当然人们会继续活下去，并从中受到鼓励和刺激去"再想想"。

我们知识的界限和意义的关系这些问题，不断地考验着我们对生命目标的完整领悟。但是地平线不仅仅反映了人类面对的困境，而且还是人类情感的所在。这两者都十分的引人注目，值得我们思考。

疑惑与渴望

由于知识的有限性，我们都经历过产生好奇心的冲动情绪。传统上好奇心被视为哲学开端，同时也可能是宗教的起点。我们眼花缭乱，因为我们常常要面对日出日落，被世界上那些难以解释的疑团所困挠。星光熠熠的宇宙和浩瀚无垠的大海是那么巨大，在面对这些自然现象时，我们深切地感到自己的渺小和微不足道。正如学者拜纳姆（Caroline Bynum）观察到的那样："我们自问，在人的精神范围内什么东西是无论如何不能包括和消解的？我们惊叹于神奇的奥秘和那些似是而非的隽语。"[23]好奇心与敬畏心非常相似，人类常常伴随着十分浓厚的好奇心，经过多年的训练最终趋向科学的发明与发现。好奇心同样也会产生故事、神话和仪式，并构成宗教生命的重要部分。

在希腊悲剧《安蒂格妮》（Antigone），女主人公赞美奇迹："有很多令人惊奇的事情，但是没有任何东西比人类更加奇妙，……人类可以做任何选择……唯独面对死亡时，她表示没有任何可以逃遁的途径。"这使我们惊讶于人类心智的能力及其限制。好奇心在爱的礼物、新生婴儿的奇迹、艺术的光辉或艺术品中产生出特别的鉴赏能力。好奇心提醒人类尽管我们可能无力解决现实生活中的所有问题，但是我们还是会细细地品味体会它们。

第二种产生于人类境遇限制的情绪是渴望。当理性洞察力遭遇到障碍时，会促使人们对生活奥秘萌发更丰富的遐想。我们渴望克服阻隔彼此的空间距离；我们渴望去除痛苦和不公正；我们渴望自由和健康，虽然灵魂方面的状况或许很难由我们个人来安排。以上罗列的内容无法穷尽人们的渴望——长寿、永不枯竭的爱情、更丰富的意义。好奇心常常会使我们心怀感激，迫切地探索希望。一个希望会鞭策我们向前、使我们的地平线向前扩展。

穿越地平线

好奇心和诸多渴望激励我们超越各种樊篱限制。16 世纪欧洲的探险家，在好奇心的驱使下，跨洋过海去发现远方那些神奇的一切。今天的宇航员进入了曾经是人类禁地的太空，探寻我们宇宙的奥秘。带着想象和希望，人类继续寻找超越地平线之限的途径。在舟船之类的交通工具上，在故事和幻想以及宗教仪式上，无一不凝聚了人类试图超越与生俱来的知识限圈的梦想和憧憬。

有些超越的行为近似于逃避现实。比如我们创作的童话故事或科学幻想小说，都只是带着读者短暂地穿越凡俗世界的界限，但是当故事结束了，读者又得回到他们熟悉的日常生活当中。

而人类其他想象活动则产生了不同凡响的结果。在佛教想象的世界里，人们远离暴力，对所有的生物都要保持慈悲、关怀和公正的心。基督教对"上帝之国"的想象是，人类群体的希望在于更多的关怀与正义，酝酿出宽恕和慈善的行动来改变人们的生活。在每个文化中，艺术的形象和宗教的活动已经跨越了普通人理解力的界限，挑战——如果只是相对于时间——那些常见的将人与人、人与人的美好希望分隔开的各种限制。

在地平线：破晓之际

每天黎明，破晓之际让我们看到了地平线。天亮是一个每天发生的事情。但是，就如地平线一样，破晓是一个重要的符号性暗示。因为天亮了，我们走出黑暗，我们又获得了光明。破晓标志着启蒙的瞬间。但是，光明与想象力是一种天赋，而远非个人的成就。在很多文化中，人们将破晓的自然景象与内心的省悟联系起来。在英文中，会说，"它让我开始明白了（it dawned on me)"。在中文，"晓"包含着知识的意思。

传统宗教和文化将此隐喻转为表述觉悟是如何成为一种天赋的过程，告诉人们新的希望和信仰如何跨越界限进入我们的世界，它们的莅临又如何扩大和丰富了这一切。

在第一章，我们回顾了雅各与未名攻击者之间在夜晚的搏斗。这个故事始于一个不祥的声明："只剩下雅各一人。"（旧约 32）夜晚有一个人来和他摔跤，直到黎明。由于两人是在夜间摔跤，雅各在黑暗中受伤。那人说，天黎明了，容我去吧。雅各说，你不给我祝福，我就不容你去。由于受到了祝福，雅各意识到那个人是神，说"我面对面见了神，我的性命乃得保全"。故事的结局是："日头刚出来的时候，雅各经过毗努伊勒，他的大腿就瘸了。"这个神话故事，或许是早在公元前九世纪就已经出现了。危险的夜晚搏斗与破晓带来启蒙这两种情形，可谓是鲜明的对比，结合了充满了搏斗、受伤的痛苦记忆、解脱和省悟的幸福记忆。

在中国经典中，从孟子开始，便以破晓的隐喻来描述易于失掉的良知："其日夜之所息，平旦之气，其好恶与人相近也者几希，则其旦昼之所为，有梏亡之矣。"（《孟子·告子章句上》）[24]这种特殊的良知恰恰产生于清静的夜晚和忙碌的白天之间那短暂的时刻。

对中国学者和圣经的作者来说，天亮是获得真理启示的象征。觉悟作为天赋的品性，在特别时候进入人的处境。海德格尔（Martin Heidegger）让我们意识到希腊语"真实"是 *a/letheia*"不再隐瞒"，他还进一步注意到"真实"不是人类通过努力思考而成就的东西，而是被证实的。在艺术中，如同宗教的意识，悟性和灵感常常作为天赋使那些被隐蔽的东西呈现出来。在夜与昼交替的瞬间，在夜的黑暗或昼的嘈杂中，那些被模糊的真实有机会显露出来。在这稀少而特别的时候，人类会超越其平常的知识界限，产生对人类生命及其意义更深刻的理解。

超越的能力植根于人类对美好生活的向往，存在于人类宗教性的核心之处。好奇心和渴望引导人类超越其常理的界限，进入神秘的省悟，而这就是宗教存在的实质。

注释

[1] John Hick, *An Interpretation of Religion*：*Human Responses to the Transcendent*, p. 3.

[2]《孟子·告子章句上》

[3] See G. C. Pande, "The Message of Gotama Buddha and Its Earliest Interpretations," in *Buddhist Spirituality*.

[4] See Peter Brown's discussion, in *The Body and Society*, *of this inclination to leave the city and society in search of personal salvation*.

[5] See *Sources of Indian Tradition*, edited by William DeBary, p. 161.

[6] The Chinese translation of the *Vimalakirti Sutra* appears in Number 475 in volume 14 of *Taisho Shinshu Daizokyo*（大正新修大藏经）. Vimalakirti's remarks about "leaving home" are at p. 358a.

[7] Benjamin Schwartz, "Transcendence in Ancient China," *Daedalus*, (Spring, 1975), p. 61.

[8] Ibid. , p. 63.

[9] Benjamin Schwartz, *The World of Thought in Ancient China*, p. 20.

[10] Ibid. , p. 70

[11] Ibid. , p. 21

[12] 杜维明是人文主义儒学颇具影响力的拥护和推动者，不过是宗教性的人文主义，"完善的人文主义是不会否认或轻视天的"。参见 p. 149 of his essay in *Our Religions*.

[13] Martha Nussbaum, "Transcending Humanity," *Love's Knowledge*, p. 376.

[14] Ibid. , p. 379

[15] Charles Taylor, *A Catholic Modernity*? p. 22.

[16] Ibid. , p. 20.

〔17〕 Charles Taylor, *A Catholic Modernity?* p. 20.

〔18〕 Seamus Heaney, *The Redress of Poetry*, p. 114.

〔19〕 Ibid. , p. 4.

〔20〕 Karl Rahner, "Christian Humanism," *Theological Investigations*, Vol. 9.

〔21〕 William Schweiker, "Theological Ethics and the Question of Humanism," *The Journal of Religion*, Oct. 2003, vol. 83, no. 4, pp. 539—61.

〔22〕 Paul Ricoeur, *Freud and Philosophy*, p. 526

〔23〕 Caroline Bynum, Metamorphosis and Identity, p. 52

〔24〕《孟子·告子章句上》See James Legge's translation in *The Works of Mencius*, p. 408.

第三章　西方的宗教研究

本章将讨论西方学者在宗教学术性研究中所使用的五种方法，并定义几个中心词汇：宗教、宗教性、信仰以及神圣。

一、西方宗教的学术性研究方法

今天宗教是社会科学领域的一个重要题目，涉及到社会学、心理学、人类学、历史和政治学，还有哲学家、神学家及批判理论家也参与到这一研究中来。不同领域的学者认识到宗教是多元化的现象，任何一个学科都无法单独对宗教进行全面性的研究。

西方对宗教的学术性研究可以归类为五种方向。事实上，这些不同类型间并非差异巨大。因为某些学者经常会使用几种不同的方法来理解宗教复杂的事实。当然这五种方向不足以完全体现所有重要学者在此领域的贡献。但是，这样的概述可以为开始涉猎宗教研究者提供一个框架。

我们从基本的描述开始。在西方的学术传统中，宗教研究的是：

一个由群体共有的思想、感情、行动的体系，为其成员提供一个信仰的主体；控制个人和社会行为的伦理准则；个人与组织及其宇宙间关系的参照模式。[1]

即使宗教在日常需要和希望的层面上接触人类生活的时候，

它也关注自身超越日常生活普通意识的那些部分。通过肯定神圣存在的事实，宗教仍然触及到人类经验的深层领域。如丹妮斯·卡莫迪（Denise Carmody）注意到，宗教承认："在人类生活的终极方面，个人与社会是相同的，信仰往往处于核心部分。"[2]

表一　西方关于宗教的学术性研究方向	
A. 宗教经验	在与终极存在关系方面的个人省察
B. 宗教制度	宗教团体的结构与功能
C. 宗教传统	世界智慧传统的（比较）研究
D. 宗教在历史上的角色	宗教思想与制度的积极与消极影响
E. 宗教研究	对符号象征话语意义的公开调研

A. 宗教经验——对终极真实性关系的个人省察

在第一章和第二章，我们探讨了宗教作为人的产物——包括故事、道德戒律、仪式活动、组织性团体等这些人类宗教的部分。但是，宗教研究的学者所呈现给我们的宗教信徒所报告我们的事实，都不是宗教的"全部"。因为，这些内容是宗教的结果而并非其来源。在其本质核心，宗教是人类对其经历过的大于人性的现实世界的回应。

詹姆士（William James）这样表述这一伟大的现实世界："在人类意识中似乎有对真实存在的感觉"，也就是对我们称之为"某些事情"的感知能力，它比由现代心理学假定的用以展示现存世界的"感觉"更深刻、更普遍。[3]

宗教意识承认现实世界比有直接证据的经验更丰富。这里有存在的层面、意义的层面、有价值的层面，都超越或超验于我们平时所进入的境界。由宗教领悟力所强化的现实世界层面，其内容在我们日常生活经验中是看得见摸得着的，是天地万物的真实基础。

借助历史，人类早就意识到现实世界的范围超越了日常存在的普通特性。这种超越的程度是极为重要的，因为它是所有现实世界之源、生活的支撑者以及最深层的价值。人类的社群通过有意识的努力回应超越来深化对它的理解（通过不断编纂故事、经书和神学体系），并加强与神圣事物的联系（通过信徒在这个世界虔诚的行动、祈祷、道德行为和慈善公益服务）。

对于所有接受这种超越事实意识的人来说，宗教就是活着的东西，不仅仅是信徒要遵从的经典和参与的组织，还要认识到现存的宗教包括修炼的部分，以便与终极世界沟通。在天主教和基督教的词汇中，终极世界是宗教的信仰或灵性，即个人对上帝存在现实的回应。[4]

西方的宗教传统，以犹太教为典型，天主教、基督新教和伊斯兰教都采取了对话的方式。这些主要的西方宗教常常会归类为"经卷的宗教"，因为每个宗教都有一部经典文本作为神的福音。对犹太人来讲，是摩西五书；对天主教和基督新教徒来讲，是圣经；对穆斯林来讲，是可兰经。这种关系很深厚，这些宗教都尊崇古代近东的宗教人物亚伯拉罕作为其信仰创始人之一。另外，圣经被天主教和基督新教徒使用，成为包含了大量的希伯来经文（旧约圣经）与以耶稣生活和语言为中心的新约圣经。而可兰经承认犹太人先知摩西和宗教人物耶稣作为其传统的一部分，结果是先知穆罕默德的出现。

在西方宗教意识中，信仰生活与所有现实世界的伟大源泉有着深厚的个人联系。这是一种卓然存在的现实和终极的奥秘。耶和华之名与犹太人、上帝之名与天主教和基督新教徒、安拉之名与穆斯林，把人与伟大的宇宙之源形成的密切关系同人与人之间互爱互助结成的纽带相比较，它们既相同又相异。在西方通过各种宗教经验，逐渐意识到人的不完整性（或罪）。而这一认识在信徒中扮演了重要的角色，从而使皈依变得有意义了。

东方智慧的传统，如印度教和佛教，连同某些神秘的思想脉络也被编织进西方宗教的结构中，它强调宗教经验的一致性。这些传统培养出对普通意识幻觉差异的认知，并非与至高无上（及个人）的其他事物有一种密切的关系。差异的存在——自我/他人、心理/身体、好/坏，掩盖了难以发掘的现实世界整体。在这些共同的传统中，宗教经验获得了对自我或绝对真理真实确定的价值，并消除了自我单独存在的意识。

当东方宗教信仰呈现出广泛的多元性，一些共同的原则获得了普遍的确认。首先，东方传统强调神圣具有超越宇宙的特性，并存在于万事万物中无处不在的奥秘中。在绝大多数东方传统中，精神追求的目标是认识个体的相异性，因为人和宇宙是合一的。东方的传统最感兴趣的是个人的转变和象征性的意识，而非揭示信仰的真相和神学。和犹太教、基督教、伊斯兰教不同的是，在东方传统中没有唯一真神的出现。普世超越的信仰在大量人格化崇拜中被广泛接受，并在仪式活动中呈现出多样性的特征。印度教的多神信仰和中国民间寺庙中无可胜数的神祇就是这种宗教经验的最好例证。最后，以代替个人的罪恶，这种方式强调幻想和自我麻痹，在皈依方面更强调对现实世界的整体服从。[5]

宗教经验的分析是宗教学术性研究的基础。但是对宗教和宗教性的研究需要拓展到探索复杂人类现象的其他方面。如人类学家格尔茨（Clifford Geertz）所观察到的那样，"我们透过对情感与行动的了解，发现经验本身似乎不再能确实地勾勒出我们称呼的宗教"，换言之，人性的其他方面，如意义、认同和权力，"必须和我们捕捉生命中宗教信仰旋律的过程相关联。"[6]

B. 宗教制度—— 观察宗教团体与组织的结构和功能

在现代西方社会，特别是欧洲和北美，宗教常常通过既有的教义和道德原则来推动组织性的社会运动。宗教社会学关注这些宗教组织本身，研究宗教团体及其与社会之间的互动。在西方社会学理论中，宗教通常被描述为一种具有共同的世界观和道德观的社会组织。

社会组织　宗教作为有可识别的成员和明确的领导人员的社会团体而存在，人们自愿地加入其中。也就是说，成员们认为自己的参与是出于个人的选择，当然也不排除文化传统和其他的社会因素的影响。典型的是，在宗教团体成员间发展出来的密切关系，会促使成员们彼此支持，并产生相互忠诚的强烈感情。

共同的世界观　成员间共同分享对生活的一种全面理解，这种理解是植根于其宗教传统的经典文本（理解为"神圣的经典"）和基本教义之上。那些有价值的信仰被普遍地接受。这些信仰有关个人命运（如受宿缘观念的操纵，或天的影响，或天意的左右）、天地万物（如被耶和华或安拉创造的）、社会（受到神的自由意旨和隐含在创世纪的"自然法"的指引），由受过特别训练和经过任命的神职人员组成的、得到认可的权威组织来定义并管理核心信仰，并借助一个明确的领导体系来发挥作用。宗教世界观的功能像一个透镜，是一个透过明确评价成员经验的不同侧面来解释的架构。

共同的道德观和"生活方式"　个人和社会行为的标准源于群体的核心信仰。共有的价值决定了成员对价值的辨别力：我们是谁和我们该怎样做？这些道德感通过日常生活中祈祷和崇拜仪式等宗教活动以及伦理道德行为表现出来。宗教团体通过不断地强化个人祈祷和公共崇拜的仪式来加强信仰者与神、或现实世界中神圣/超验方面的关系。宗教团体鼓励道德规范和持续的道德承诺，以便在同情他人、公正、和谐与和平等行为方面引导信仰者。

社会学家已经对宗教团体内部结构作了大量的观察，这些调查提供了关于宗教成员情况的信息。例如，团体成员年龄跨度和其社会经济地位，男性与女性的比例，同时还提供了对团体生活的分析。例如，成员中个人奉献的程度，他们参加团体的最初动因，他们继续参与的理由，成员在团体中的持续时间及为何有些人不再继续参加团体的活动等等。

社会学家和其他领域的专家们也对宗教制度和大规模社会在功能方面的关系进行了探讨。他们研究发现，宗教团体在人类社会中扮演了各种不同的角色。在积极的方面，宗教团体经常会在道德价值、社会稳定以及社会所需的公共福利服务方面有所贡献。在消极的方面，宗教团体是道德偏见、民族内部的冲突以及社会歧视之源。

宗教社会学的主要关注点一直围绕着这个有争议的问题——世俗化假说，它明确地肯定面对社会现代化，宗教制度不可避免地失去其社会重要性。我们将在第五章讨论这个不断争论的世俗化理论。

C. 宗教传统——世界文明传统的比较研究

几个世纪以来，人类学家和其他社会科学家以进行田野研究来证明不同种族社区和民族文化的信仰和仪式活动。这些研究最初集中于行为者，描述日常生活的活动和社会交换，记录当地民众对为什么会发生某些事情的解释。多数这些解释是用来追溯宗教的世界观和共同的信仰，同时还普遍地存在于该群体所认可的宗教故事和象征符号中。

对宗教传统最有影响的定义出自文化人类学家格尔茨（Clifford Geertz），他的定义成为宗教研究的典范。在《作为一种文化系统的宗教》一书中，格尔茨描述宗教作为：

（1）一套信仰体系

（2）通过对现存的普通秩序观念和

（3）在人心中建立起强有力的、普遍持久的情绪和动机

（4）并使这些情绪和动机看起来似乎是唯一实在的。[7]

格尔茨的宗教定义在当代社会科学家中被广泛地用于解释文化基础。格尔茨在自己所做的田野研究中，比较了印度尼西亚和现代摩洛哥村庄文化中伊斯兰教流行的习俗。中国拥有丰富的文化传统，不少学者对中国人的信仰和仪式活动进行了各种不同的研究。下一章和第三部分，我们将讨论对中国传统宗教研究的进展及其宗教传统在当代中国的表现。

对不同宗教传统的认识要通过比较来研究。比较宗教研究领域为有效的对话提供了环境，对话的主题是普遍地围绕着人类家庭的不同信仰和仪式习俗展开的。

对宗教进行理性的比较研究只是在近年来才出现。印度教和神话学的德国学者缪勒（Max Muller）率先将这样的研究称为"宗教的科学研究"。1870 年，缪勒认为外国语言的研究和考古学与神话学研究方法的进步，使得对世界主要宗教进行分析与系统性的研究成为可能。在 19 世纪以后的几十年，宗教科学研究学系（不同于西方大学中传统的基督教神学研究学系）在欧洲大的学术机构建立起来。

在 20 世纪中期，出现了第二波对世界宗教比较研究的热潮。1951 年在美国只有三个教授职位专门从事宗教学术研究，到了1970 年代增加到 30 个职位。1957 年，伊利亚底（Mircea Eliade）进入芝加哥大学，1964 年，史密斯（Wilfred Cantwell Smith）在哈佛大学成立了世界宗教研究中心。正是通过这两个教授的努力，世界宗教比较研究的合法性学术地位才终于在美国高等教育体系中获得了承认。

四年后，英国第一位宗教研究教授史玛德（Ninian Smart）在其就职演讲中倡导宗教的比较研究，其中包括五个领域：宗教历

史、宗教现象学（对不同传统中习俗和信仰的分析描述）、宗教社会学（考察信仰传统和其周围文化的关系）、宗教哲学和神学。

今天，不仅宗教学者感兴趣于在世界不同宗教传统中建立联系，而且作为一个国际会议每五年举行一次的世界宗教议会，已经成为来自不同国家和不同宗教背景的人相聚和沟通的场合。长达一星期的会议不仅为思想交流提供了平台，而且在那些表现其广泛宗教感的人群中，也分享人类生命的经历和共性的信仰。

最早的宗教议会是 1893 年在芝加哥举行的，很大程度上是基督教徒倡导发起的。其切入点是欢迎信仰内部的对话，但基本的心态是反映一种"实践"神学观，即所有其他宗教传统的真理和价值都能在基督教中得到满足。1993 年第二次会议，也就是宗教议会一百周年的时候，宗教内部对话的态度有了一个戏剧性的改变。将基督教视为最基本的、甚至是唯一的、真正宗教模式的时代已经一去不复返了，替而代之的是新的愿景，多数世界宗教都更重视宗教领袖和普通信徒的共同努力，来提升对神圣超验的感悟，以使世界成为人类温馨美好的家园。

D. 宗教在历史中的角色——宗教思想和制度在文明中的积极与消极影响

宗教与社会间的关系既有积极的互动，同时也兼具矛盾对立的一面。学术界对这种关系始终有很大的兴趣，其中关于宗教负面作用（特别是基督教）最有影响的理论是马克思和恩格斯提出来的。马克思看到宗教是"虚幻意识"的形式，在历史过程中将男人和女人束缚住了。按照马克思主义理论，历史进步的决定因素在于经济，故宗教的功能要从属于主导性的经济体系。在他们生活的时代，马克思和恩格斯认为基督教给予人民群众的希望是虚假的，宗教使人们忍受资本主义经济体系的不平等。"宗教是这个世界（资本主义世界）总的理论，……是它的热情，它的道德上的核准，它的庄严补充，它借以安慰和辩护的普遍根据。……宗教是人民的鸦片烟。"[8]

其他社会科学家考察了宗教在人群和文化中显示的积极作用。挑战马克思主义经济决定一切的思想，德国社会学家韦伯强调宗教思想和价值在建构社会中的积极作用。他最有影响的著作《新教伦理与资本主义精神》描述了基督教道德规范（或者准确地说，改革后的加尔文主义伦理思想）如何为资本主义在欧洲的兴起做出积极的贡献。

涂尔干（Emile Durkheim）同韦伯一样是宗教社会学现代原理的创始人，他强调宗教的角色是社会共同道德价值的资源。这些价值能够将信仰者整合在一个道德群体，一个社群经常要为道德秩序提供支持，有时候会作为社会控制的力量。很多西方学者强调宗教对社会稳定的贡献。帕森斯（Talcott Parsons）发现宗教信仰和行为是以形成社会凝聚力，将教会成员整合进大型社会为目标与价值而存在。英格（Milton Yinger）认为宗教世界观常常是共有意义的基础，即使是在现代世俗化的社会中也不例外。同样有影响的学者，例如韦伯和特纳（Victor Turner），观察到宗教价值和组织是文化更新和社会变迁的源泉。那些因为社会变化而产生的宗教动员运动的现代事例，也包括印度的甘地（Gandhi）和美国的马丁·路德·金（Martin Luther King）在争取社会自由方面的努力。

心理学家参与到宗教对社会影响的争论中。现代心理学家之父弗洛伊德（Sigmund Freud）率先发起了对流行于欧洲的犹太教和基督教宗教和仪式的尖锐的批判。他认为宗教信仰的作用就是迷信，并将信徒的宗教行为视为是大脑有问题的表现。他解释幻觉是来自于幼年时代那些不能解决的情感矛盾，并预示宗教将会，也一定会在人类进步的过程中被抛弃。正如他在《幻觉的未来》一书中表达的那样，宗教是"人类普遍的幻想症"，他继续说道，"如果承认这种观点的正确性，就应该远离宗教。远离宗教是人类成长过程中所不可避免的，我们发现自己正处在发展中的这一关头。"[9]

著名的美国哲学家和宗教心理学家詹姆士（William James）（他和弗洛伊德同时代写作）对宗教在个人生活和对社会意义的作用给予了迥然不同的分析。在其经典著作《宗教经验的多样性》一书中，他证明了与宗教经验相关的积极的心理特征。

（1）"一种新的热情，作为礼物赋予人生"。詹姆士（James）注意到，在某些宗教人士中，这种活力表现在对简单生活的激赏。另外，它激发人们做出非凡的奉献和英雄主义的行为。

（2）"一种安全的保证和平静的心态"。这些情绪能够提高个人的适应力并加强自我价值与自我信心。

（3）"此外，在与他人的关系方面，是充满慈爱与热情"[10]。詹姆士（James）观察到宗教的体验为纯粹的利他主义行为和思想提供了基础。

E. 宗教研究——公众对象征意义话语的需求

通常，宗教研究这个词的用法很普通，就是用来形容那些对多种不同宗教传统的研究。例如，在欧洲和北美的很多大学都给其早先专门研究基督教神学的研究机构，增设包括佛教或伊斯兰教研究的课题。我们看到这样一种扩展的结果常常会出现机构名称的变化，如神学系改为宗教系。

不过很多学者仍然将宗教研究这个词用于对宗教和宗教性特别视角的研究。里科（Paul Ricoeur）定义宗教研究是一种"公众对象征意义话语的需求"，[11] 在这个具体的语境中，宗教研究是通过多学科和跨文化的视角来考察探讨代表超验的象征符号。

学者们采取一定的方式来看待人类宗教传统，而宗教传统往往是以历史为条件的符号系统。这些不同的传统被认为是人类对超越追求的多元表达方式。贝拉（Robert Bellah）认为他对宗教研究的方法是"象征实用主义",宗教研究是描述"象征符号发生影响的方式——在定义世界、建立社会组织、沟通有意识的意义和无意识的意义等方面——清楚地了解(这些)符号构成的现实世界是如何超越个人和团体的。可以说象征符号将人类生活固定在一个至高无上的现实中"。[12]

学术研究在宗教研究中受到现代批评方法的影响,转向考察宗教在文化的构成和传播中的角色。因为宗教观念、神圣的象征、仪式表现和组织形式等嵌入于特定的文化中,故比较研究和多学科的方法就显得不可缺少。考古学、文化历史、社会学、政治学、社会理论、认知心理学、语言学,每一种学科都提供了对宗教研究的有价值的方式。在另一种分析思考中,哲学家和神学家研究圣经和属于等方面自己与其他文化的宗教象征符号。这些学者中的一些人站在他们研究的宗教世界观的"内部",而另外对宗教传统的研究方法则是作为"外面人"。利用来自内部的和作为外面人的观察,宗教研究可以获得对特定宗教传统思想表达和概念意含一个更完善的理解。

天主教和基督新教致力于宗教研究。例如,典型的研究工作是关于圣经传统的象征系统。运用历史分析的方法,这些学者重新检视了上帝的形象和超越的观念,这些出现天主教、正统教义和改革的基督教思想等历史发展脉络。像宗教研究领域中其他的研究者一样,神学家要批判性和建设性地面对传递意义和价值中的神圣符号。他们学术研究的目的既不是为天主教信仰辩护,也不是传播基督新教。如神学家威龄(Frank Whaling)观察到的那样,从事宗教研究的神学家们发现,"在全球背景下来思考并领悟超越是很急迫的事情,那是一种人类对自然了解的超越,人类对人性了解的超越,以及人类对超越实体了解的超越。"[13]

二、清理用于宗教学术研究的词汇

正如我们上述所表明的那样,学者运用很多不同的方法来理解宗教。在研究中，我们越来越深刻地感受到，用于宗教研究的词汇是不统一的。不同的词语被不同的作者使用，有时候同样的一个词语被解释为不同的意思。这里我们呈现给大家的是我们在本书中使用的词汇"暂时的定义"，相信不是每一个宗教学者都会同意我们的使用方法。但是这些内容并不意味着与其他学者的争论，只是提供一些知识的澄清来帮助中国的读者理解宗教。我们将特别针对四个词：宗教、宗教性、信仰和神圣来进行讨论。

宗教 这个词比较典型地指信仰的制度形式，如伊斯兰教、基督教。宗教制度，如我们上面讨论的那样，它通常有明确的成员、专门的领导群体、权力结构、经典、正式的教义、道德原则以及仪式活动。

更宽泛些地讲，每一种宗教包括一个信仰的传统或者世界观，以及一套宗教活动方式让成员遵循，以追寻精神的觉悟、皈依和慰藉。

有关宗教的争论表现在这个词是否充分地囊括了东方文明的历史传统，如道教、儒家学说、印度教、佛教。作为人类学家，魏乐博（Robert Weller）观察到宗教一词常常带有西方的含义，是"信仰一个至高无上的神、有秩序的崇拜和道德原则"，加上神圣与世俗的。[14]道教学者施舟仁（Kristofer Schipper）注意到宗教这个词"或许用于伊斯兰教或天主教是正确的，但是当将这个词用在中国民间宗教和其更复杂的表达方式，……会产生出误解"。[15]哲学家白诗朗（John Berthrong）坚持认为"不能简单地用由西方制度性方式定义的宗教来解说儒家信仰的发展脉络。[16]有鉴于此，现在很多学者倾向于使用包容性更强的词，如以历史性的精神传统来讨论东方和西方的信仰资源。

宗教性（*religiousness*） 这是一个比较特别的词。在第一章中已经提到，在当代宗教研究中，"宗教性"用于表达人类建构意义的能力，因为使生活具有意义的种种努力存在于人生经验的最深层。由此我们可以理解，宗教性典型地代表了人类建构一个令人满意的生活方式之努力，这种方式以宽阔的襟怀来包容现实与焦虑，并超越日常意识的尘世。

宗教性回应了终极或有限性等人类经验的问题。这些重要的问题包括：人类生命的起源以及目标是什么？个人的存在是否有目的或价值？是否有值得为之生或为之死的价值存在？根据这种对现实存在深刻的理解，透过道德行为和其他的生活实践，宗教性也就包含着规范人的生活之力量。

一些社会科学家使用 religiosity 来描述同样的现象。但是在一般的英语使用上，religiosity 带有很强的负面含义。它意味着宗教活动的强制性，或极端的，甚至离经叛道的宗教观。有鉴于此，现在的学术界更倾向于使用中性的词 religiousness 来表述宗教性。

在宗教与宗教性之间有相当密切的联系。人类意识经常性地受到社会环境的限制，比如数世纪来，我们称作宗教性的对终极意义的追求常常会在有组织的宗教团体背景中被发现。宗教的这些制度形式在发展过程中，不断影响并支持着宗教观。没有这些社会背景所提供的秩序和持续性，个人宗教意识就难以存续下去。所以宗教和宗教性与人类经验密切联系在一起。

但是经过不断的时光洗炼，某些原本被民众共同认可的形式会由于缺乏效力，其组织体系显得僵硬，越来越远离启发宗教省悟的初衷。当这种情形发生时，宗教组织的某些成员会敏感地察觉到宗教变成了他们宗教性的障碍。

在今天的世界，很多人继续采用某种特定宗教或宗教传统的仪式和信仰作为他们自己宗教性的真实表现。但是还有另外一些人用其他的方式来表现其宗教性。有些人会汲取某些宗教传统的象征符号或实践；其他人则从某正规宗教传统之外选择象征意义，以表现其个人的宗教性，如自然、艺术或科学。

信仰　在英语里常见用信仰（*faith*）这个词表示那些特定的宗教传统。例如，我们会说天主教信仰、佛教信仰、犹太教信仰。在一些宗教的讨论中，有信仰的意思是就像对待真理那样毫不怀疑地接受某一信仰，而人们也发现某些核心的宗教教义是无法被理性证明的方式所认定。在这个意义上，信仰接近于宗教信仰。

在西方认知心理学和宗教心理学的学术领域中，信仰这个词已经被用于更特别的方式。在这种用法中，信仰意指正在持续的理解过程，通过这样的过程个人面对并解决人类生存的终极和有限性问题，如我们在第一章所讨论的内容。

宗教心理学家詹姆士·浮勒（James Fowler）是使用信仰这个词进行宗教研究的重要学者。对于詹姆士·浮勒来说，信仰是一个整体的、核心的变化过程：（a）给予个人生活以凝聚力和方向；（b）在共同的责任和忠诚中连接彼此；（c）将个人的承诺与社群的忠诚置于一个大的意义结构中；同时（d）通过运用其与生命中终极性的关系，让人们能够面对人类生命有限的状况。[17]

更为实际的是，信仰的这层意思指向正在进行的认知与情感发展的过程。由此，一个人寻找那些大于个人的存在，并投入其信任；努力确认价值以支撑个人生命的延续；力争去理解个人在天地间的位置；并试图与意义的更广阔的背景沟通起来。

认识到宗教信仰会被不准确的或甚至被破坏性的动机所左右，特雷斯（David Tracy）描述了纯正信仰的标志："当它是可以相信的，宗教信仰显示了所有现实世界基本奥秘的理解。奥秘是我们自己、历史、自然的、和宇宙的奥秘，奥秘高于所有的终极事实"。[18]

神圣 学者和宗教信仰者都努力地说明宗教信仰的神秘核心，在现实世界要远远地超出了人类的能力。在早期天主教仪式中，拉丁语 *deus* 用于指这种至高无上的神，在英文中这个词还是"神"的意思。由于 20 世纪早期宗教的学术性研究发展，奥托（Rudolf Otto）使用"神圣的"（*numinous*，来自于希腊语 *numen*）指神圣的经历——一个神秘的力量，令人向往又令人恐惧。早期的宗教社会学家涂尔干（Emile Durkheim）谈到了"神圣"的范畴。

詹姆士（William James）使用了"神的"（divine）这个词说明了"基本的事实"。primal 并不是原始的或不开化的意思，而是作为最根本的事实存在。这个事实（是否指定是 numinous，或 holy，或 sacred，或 divine）是取决于所有宗教的基础。所以，詹姆士将宗教定义为："个人的感觉、行为和经验……只要他们认为自己与他们视作神圣的东西有关。"[19]

当今有很多学者使用"神圣"（sacred）来称这种神秘的力量。在一篇全面跨文化的田野研究评论中，人类学家拉勃波（Roy Rappaport）发现了五种共性因素被用于描述神圣的或神灵的宗教经验。人们对现实世界最直接的反应是：

> 实际地存在——这个事实不只是一种目标或概念。
> 有活力——这个事实可以视为生机勃勃的状态、有能量，像气。
> 是强有力的——这个事实被理解为活跃的和有效力的。
> 但是非物质的——这个事实与感觉资料没有关联，无法供经验性的调查，不能通过东拉西扯的推理过程得到满意地了解。
> 它是开放的并建立各种人际关系——这个事实是通过爱、参与及个人化的过程形成。[20]

不管如何指定这种宗教经验的神秘来源，信仰传统最终发现：神圣的或神灵的事实无法被确定。来自犹太教传统的犹太教学者固执地认为耶和华的声誉太神圣了，以致于无法称呼出来或记录下来。于是在很多犹太教作品中，G*D 和 YHWH 这四个辅音字母似乎用于替代称呼耶和华。基督教的世界——天主教、东正教和基督新教——一直保持着一种语义忌讳的传统，警告人们不要提到有关上帝的任何事情，否则都会因缺少神秘的力量而无效。道家经典《道德经》，一语道破这种神圣之妙：道可道，非常道。

注释

[1] *The Concise Columbia Encyclopedia*, p. 712.

[2] Denise Carmody, "Women and Religion: Where Mystery Comes to Center Stage" in *The Study of Women*, p. 263.

[3] William James, *The Varieties of Religious Experience*, pp. 66—67.

[4] Wilfred Cantwell Smith 对理解 "生活的信仰" 有很突出的贡献；参见 *The Meaning and End of Religion* and *Faith and Belief*.

[5] Donald Swensen, *Society, Spirituality, and the Sacred: A Social Scientific Introduction*, pp. 50—57；对东西方宗教较敏锐、全面的介绍，请参见 Huston Smith, *The World's Religions*.

[6] Clifford Geertz, *Available Light*, p. 170.

[7] Clifford Geertz, *The Interpretation of Cultures*, p. 90.

[8] Karl Marx and Friedrich Engles, *On Religion*, p. 41.

[9] Sigmund Freud, *The Future of An Illusion*, p. 43.

[10] William James, *The Varieties of Religious Experience*, pp. 528—529.

[11] Paul Ricoeur, *Figuring The Sacred*, p. 14.

[12] 有关贝拉 "象征现实主义" 的讨论和其对宗教研究的贡献，请看 Richard Madsen et al., *Meaning and Modernity: Religion, Polity and Self*; the quotation is from p. xi.

[13] Frank Whaling, "Theological Approaches" in *Approaches to the Study of Religion*, p. 261.

[14] Robert Weller, "Worship, Teachings, and State Power in China and Taiwan" in *Realms of Freedom in Modern China*, p. 287.

[15] Kristofer Schipper, *The Taoist Body*, p. 3.

[16] John Berthrong, *All Under Heaven*, p. 197.

[17] James Fowler, *Faithful Change*, p. 56.

[18] David Tracy，*Plurality and Ambiguity*，p. 107.

[19] William James，*The Varieties of Religious Experience*，p. 36.

[20] Roy Rappoport 对于神圣的讨论清参考 *Ritual and Religion in the Making of Humanity*；on p. 397 他列举了神圣"普遍性经验"的因素。

第四章　中国民间宗教

> 中国宗教研究正在经历着深刻的转变……学者们不
> 再将宗教作为一个孤立的现象来研究，而是把宗教作为
> 社会与文化整体的一部分来探讨。[1]

当今很多从事宗教研究的学者在调整其研究的视角，从完全研究正式制度性的宗教组织和经典文献转向探讨普通民众生活中的信仰与活动。这种宗教社会学在当代的转变，为推动对中国文化中宗教的全新理解起到了推动作用。

现在学者们越来越谨慎地使用宗教（*religion*）这个抽象的词来描述中国的信仰传统。宗教这个词最初介绍到中国是在 1890年，实际上是将一个西方的概念移植到中国来诠释中国宗教的经验。英文中宗教一词的意思是：在神圣和世俗间尖锐的两元对立，正式的和排他的群体成员资格，专门训练的神职人员在不同团体中担任中心角色，在信仰和活动方面强调正统。正是以这些西方宗教形式为参照，很多早期的观察家坚持认为中国没有宗教。

不仅早期西方学者抱着怀疑态度来看待中国文化的宗教部分。在19 世纪末中西文化冲突、知识界一片混乱的情况下，很多中国学者张开双臂接受了欧洲启蒙运动的理性主义。由于不情愿承认中国文化中存在被当时西方知识分子所批判的那些信仰传统，胡适宣称"中国是个没有宗教的国家，中国人是个不迷信宗教的民族。这是近年来几个学者的结论"（胡适："名教"，《胡适文存三集》，卷一）。[2]

这种观点代表着胡适所处时代中国知识分子的整体态度，而且至今仍然在那些受到西方学术训练的中国学者中普遍存在。中国和西方的其他学者，严格地区分普通民众生活中多元性"怀疑论"的信仰与儒家、佛教、道教的"大传统"。

但是"文化大革命"以后，中国大陆学者们开始了新的文化研究，其关注点更加注意到普通中国老百姓的世界观和价值体系。他们的目标已经进入到那些塑造了绝大多数中国人生命的文化资源。在最近的研究中，令人惊喜的正面论调开始替代那些传统的将民间仪式与信仰仅仅当作迷信来看待的观点。殴大年（Daniel Overmyer）是一位国际著名的学者，他一直致力于对中国文化的学术研究。他赞赏中国大陆学者的重要贡献，总结道："我们在这里所看到的不仅是学术的新方向，而且是一个伟大的、有悠久历史的文化终于开始认识并接受其大多数人的宗教传统的表达方式。"[3]

当今宗教学者高度欣赏中国民间传统的精神价值。在学术讨论中，这种共有的信仰和仪式传统被称为中国民间宗教，"作为普通社会生活一部分，仪式由普通百姓在家庭和地方社区中进行，而信仰和价值与仪式联系在一起。"[4]

一、中国宗教的特点："天人合一"

1962 年，社会学家杨庆堃出版了《中国社会的宗教》一书，被宗教社会学界公认为研究中国宗教的经典之作。在前言中，他说："在欧洲、印度和中国这世界三大文明体系中，唯有中国宗教在社会中的地位非常模糊。由于事实上存有各种矛盾的因素，宗教在中国社会的位置始终是一个争讼不休的话题。"杨氏认识到"在中国漫长的历史中，没有强大的，特别是有组织的宗教"。他写作该书的初衷就是想搞清楚其中的原因。

　　杨氏从提出一个宽泛的定义开始其研究："从一个宽泛的视角，宗教会被看成是一个连续统一体，是从近似于终极性、有强烈情感特质的无神论信仰，到终极价值完全由超自然实体所象征和崇拜与由组织模式来支撑的有神信仰。"[5] 在这样定义的基础上，他提出了散开性宗教这个概念，来表明传统中国乡村流行的仪式活动与信仰同典型西方高度组织化的"制度性"宗教存在的差异。[6] 尽管学者为英文词"散开性"（*diffused*）是否足以概括中国社会的这种宗教传统功能而争辩，但杨氏对中国宗教的社会学研究无疑具有开拓性，所作出的贡献是毋庸置疑的。

　　从杨氏的视角来看，中国的佛教和道教能够被理解为制度性宗教，因为它们都有自己基本的概念及其组织。这些宗教发展出自己的经卷和特别的仪式来表现共同的关怀与价值。但是按照杨氏的判断，既不是佛教、也不是道教决定了中国社会的走向。中国历史没有出现如天主教/基督教世界观那样塑造了欧洲社会和政治结构的情形。相反，中国社会是由不可知论的儒家传统透过士绅阶层来构造的。

　　尽管人们普遍认为儒学是少数知识分子的世界观，但是中国宗教的整体如杨氏所言是遵循着经典的、或本土的传统。在杨氏看来，古代中国早期的世界观融进中国民间社会各个层面的日常生活中，民众的宗教感完全和日常生活的社会制度合而为一。共同的宗教观念和活动充满整个社会，意味着"社会环境作为一个整体具有神圣的氛围"而存在。[7] 于是，这种散开的宗教不需要独立的制度作为基础，如明确的神职人员或单独的权力结构，那就是其宗教功能通过中国社会的世俗结构而发生作用，家族制度和帝国大规模的社会政治网络。

　　在《中国社会的宗教》一书中，杨氏全面论述了中国宗教如何成功地维持着中国文明的伦理与道德秩序的长久存续。他意识到知识分子有着区别宗教的"精英"形式与"民间"形式的倾向，常常对信仰与仪式的民间表达方式带有偏见。为了消除这样的不良影响，杨氏强调，在中国历史长河中"精英文化与乡民文化之间从来都不存在楚河汉界，它们一向是互为表里、相互依存"。[8]

杨氏明确地论述了中国本土宗教的核心："信仰天和命，保留占卜，接纳阴阳五行理论，强调祖先崇拜。"[9] 在他的判断中，古典的宗教世界观在周朝时（公元前 1122—前 221）已经得到充分的发展，大大早于佛教传入和道教作为一个完全宗教的出现。到了 11 世纪，"这些仪式活动已经与佛教的宿缘和三世轮回观念、以及道教不同等级神明的教义混合在一起，从那时起就构成了中国民间宗教体系。"[10]

中国古代宗教传统的研究者意识到这一伟大传统的丰富与错综复杂性。在本章我们将对这一古代传统的世界观和信仰进行概述，包括用一些例证来说明它在当代中国乡村仍然存在并相当活跃。在第九章和第十章，我们将讨论中国古代信仰观念如何在现代深圳这个全球化城市的复兴。

二、中国民间信仰在乡村社区的发展

改革开放以后，中国政府采取了一系列有关宗教信仰和活动的新政策。逐渐放宽的官方限制始于 1982 年。1990 年，江泽民提出要有一个"更宽松的宗教组织管理"。较为宽容的态度适用于被中国法律认可的五大宗教——道教、佛教、伊斯兰教、天主教和基督教。尽管政府对法定认可的制度性宗教态度变得更温和，但普通民众的民间习俗信仰和活动还是没有摆脱封建迷信的标签，严格说来，没有合法地位或者合法的保护。

尽管知识分子和官方仍然忽视普通民众信仰和仪式活动的价值，但中国古代宗教传统在当代中国社会扮演着非常重要的角色。事实上，民间宗教活动获得了不同寻常的复兴，特别是它不仅仅只限于农村社区。在中国 13 亿人口中，大约 75% 生活在乡村，农村的发展仍然是今日中国非常重要的变化指标。

在这部分，我们将从在中国民间宗教活动中扮演重要角色的传统文化资源开始，探讨在经济改革时期中国民间信仰的复苏。

中国传统宗教活动包括对祖先和神明的崇拜、丧葬仪式、为地方神明诞日举行的庙会、不同形式的占卜、风水、驱邪、安魂以及其他的仪式。这些活动是普通民众在他们自己家中和村庄内进行的，构成了中国历史上宗教的主流。现在，在数个世纪中受冷落后，中国各地成千上万的庙宇重新修复或重新修建起来，数以万计的民众开始参加到公共仪式活动中，这些活动每年都有举行。简短地说，越来越多的事例表明，民间信仰活动在神州大地散布开来。

中国民间宗教的特征

在现代反宗教偶像崇拜观念普及之前，中国到处都有宗教存在的痕迹：每个家庭里有佛龛，地方和社区有庙宇。全国各地都一样，地方的庙宇往往是当地最漂亮的建筑，而且是一方的骄傲。寺庙常常都是由地方社区或者团体修建的，在农村各种会是由全体村民或者当地的团体创立的。"公共财产的管理，如建筑、土地、家具、收入等，是严格地遵循平等的原则。庙宇不仅用于祭拜供奉神明，同时也开放给所有的神和人。社区是一个共同的家园，大家举行各种不定期和正式的聚会。老年人到庙里讨论村子内部的事情，祖母们每天到庙里点上香烛代表全家祭神。音乐会、还有拳会、读书会、棋社、进香团、中医会、风筝会和文化会等，所有这些社团都选择庙当作其总部，当然这里也是他们供奉祖师爷的地方。"[11]

中国散开性宗教的发展引起中西方宗教研究学者的广泛关注。各种地方民间宗教活动的调查显示，在中国的乡村，除了一些年长的男性或女性任庙祝之外，社区一般不会聘请全职的宗教专职人员。只有在需要的时候，才会雇请灵媒或道士；只有在必要的时候，才会准备举行仪式所需的材料和祭品。

中国民间宗教生活的重要方面表现为与超自然相关的各种活

动。人们对生命的感悟在仪式和其他活动中得到抒发，而人们对所熟悉的问题——命运、缘分和报应等，也在日常生活中不断地得到更深刻的感受。但是这些并非与宗教制度结合在一起，而是借助民间的某些巫、筮、命相者等专门人员使民众的宗教信仰更多地保留在散开宗教的状态中。

三、今日乡村宗教

民间宗教在中国大陆的农村非常有活力地发展着。尽管在"文化大革命"的十年间（1966—1976年）很多庙宇和神像遭到了破坏，但是民众对地方神明的祭祀活动却日益蓬勃起来。从20世纪70年代后期以来，庙会越来越火，传统宗教也不断发展。寺庙重建、在仪式上使用的香烛和纸钱竟然成为大的生意，到处可以见得到民众熟悉的相面、占卜者。最近出现的这些庙宇重建和有组织的庙会与进香活动完全没有政府方面的财政支持，基本上是在地方的农民和普通百姓的支持下进行的。

按照年节习俗，村民一道参加重要的社区仪式，如中国的农历年和正月十五，或者当地神明的诞日。往往会是全家人齐出动，以叩头、鞠躬、摆供品、焚香燃烛等等方式来祈祷地方的神明。

在乡村社会，寺庙扮演了重要的角色，它既是贸易的中心，同时也是乡亲们彼此嗑家常、发牢骚寻求帮助的地方。地方寺庙也是供奉重要神明之处，人们相信大殿内的菩萨具有无边的法力。在中国传统宗教信仰中，很多受到供奉的神明是被神化了的有贡献的地方人物，人们相信这些神化了的人物具有特别的能力来保佑地方并满足人们的愿望。地方神明的灵验表现在祛除病痛和造福一方等方面。

地方的灵媒和萨满也能为当地民众与灵验的神明沟通，主要是提供道德方面的劝谕并实施治疗病痛的仪式，解梦和算命等也是民间信仰的一部分。在中国北方，祖先和地方神在单独的庙或祠堂中供奉着，在中国南方，和祖先崇拜有关的祠堂也逐渐恢复起来。

四、中国人的世界观：阴阳调和

每一个宗教传统，不论是弥散于整个文化还是发展成一种清晰的制度，不外乎为人们提供一个世界观。这种生活景观展示在植根于民众的对现实世界全面想象的信仰中，并通过仪式来表现这些信仰的实践。

斯马特（Ninian Smart）将宗教世界观定义为"通过象征符号和行为的信仰来调动人类感觉和愿望"的一套系统[12]。人类学家格尔茨注意到人的世界观是"事物全部事实的现状，是其自然的、自我的和社会的概念"。[13]

殴大年认为世界观是支撑中国文化中普遍存在的宗教性的基础，"这个世界本身是一个充满神灵和奥秘的神圣之处，同时……人类的重要使命是使这些神灵配合并使这一切在社会有效力。"[14] 在中国古代世界观中，西方宗教中那种神圣与世俗泾渭分明的区别从没有发生过。欧氏详细阐述了中国民间宗教这一明显的特征。

> 这个世界是一个充满活力的体系，一切存在都与大自然的规律密切相关。这些规律包括冷、黑暗等阴的力量，以及热、光明等阳的力量，与金、木、水、火、土"五行"结合在一起。这些力量构成"气"。自然存在与规律之间的互动产生了万事万物。[15]

在这个世界观里，"气"是充沛的力量，是物质的和超物质的、通过现实存在而有规律的脉动，它使所有的生命生气勃勃。阴和阳互动不是相互对抗（有人也许会比附西方的世界观），而是使"气"的力量在相辅相成中达到一种平衡。中国古代世界观的这些核心因素在日常生活中得到了强化，并作为所有中国信仰的根基而存在。

五、中国民间宗教的共同信仰

命运　如同其他的文明一样，中国人也早就注重于人类命运问题的探讨。天命观念原是先秦以来神学的核心，认为命运是一种道德报应的观点充斥着最早的周代文献，有些内容后来编入儒家经典中。《尚书》告诫说："作善，降之百祥；作不善，降之百殃。"（阴骘，指上天赋予每个人的"隐藏的性格本原"，后来用于指人为了改善自己的命运所积累的秘密功德。）《诗经·大雅》中认为统治者应该实现上天的道德期望："命之不易，无遏尔躬，宜昭义问，有虞殷自天。"

天命观念即是先秦以来中国宗教神学之核心，经过佛教、道教之丰富，便愈发地完整而富有弹性，故而始终被中国人所接受。不仅知识上层对天命不排斥，民间百姓更是以此作为解释生命之重要法宝。常言道：死生有命，富贵在天。在对"命"的认同中包含了中国人达到与宇宙和谐之诉求，即把个人的生命与宇宙时间相配合来解释所遭遇的一切。在民间信仰中，"命"是生来就决定了的，出生的年月日、时辰等因素与天干地支相配，预兆了其生命之历程。当然，信命不意味着宿命论，人生不会因此而消极，因为伴随"命"的还有"运"，正所谓："命由我作，福由己求。"我们可知中国人对良辰吉日的爱好以及对凶与不宜时日的避讳都是这种理念的表现。比如人们在可能的条件下，根据病人在家中的地位而采取相应的救治措施，有时还要去寺庙里烧香拜佛、磕头叩首，以此将罪愆揽到自己身上，祈求神仙帮助。最值得关注的一点是，在中国人的"天命观"中，核心的部分不是消极地信命与宿命，而是积极地寻找和命运挑战的方法，故"我命在我不在天"也是一般民众的信条。

缘分 缘分是一种不可解释的命运、巧合、机会或力量，在中国人的日常生活中扮演着重要的角色。杨国枢曾有专文探讨"缘及其在现代生活中的作用"。在日常生活中，缘和人的各种机遇有着千丝万缕的联系，比如说不论是幸福还是不幸的婚姻都被认为是前世缘分的结果。缘的观念始于何时已经渺不可考，但明显地是与佛教在民间的流传有关。大乘佛教"因缘"说，强调了事物不是鼓励自在的存在，也不会孤立自在的存在和运动。佛教的"因缘果报"之说与"三世因果流转"是缘的主要思想源头。

缘分是中国社会的一个重要信念，用以理解宇宙万物之关系，表示某些事情的产生绝非仅仅是偶然巧合，事物之关系的产生与消失，乃由一些先于个人而存在的强大力量所支配，非个人能力所能改变。这些外在势力可能是超自然的力量，也可能是个人所未能明白或控制的自然或社会规律。缘分的概念，固然有其消极的一面，使人"顺天应命"，但也有其积极的一面，使人先尽人事而后听天命。缘分观念是被广泛接受的文化传统，植根于日常生活的经验中，对某种命运巧合的认可会对某人生命带来不可思议的影响。

善恶报应 中国宗教中一个深植的传统，即是相信自然或神的报应。《尚书》中有"作善，降之百祥；作不善，降之百殃"。中国人相信报应是善有善报，恶有恶报。正如《易经》上说："积善之家，必有余庆，积不善之家，必有余殃"（《易经》卷一）。

对这种带有宿命论色彩的无定论思想，中国早期的宗教思想家并没有给予适当的解答。这不但事实上难以服人，而且将因此使人们不再做去恶从善的努力。直到佛教传入中国，其"业"报以及轮回的观念，说明果报不但及于今生，并且穿过生命之链

（chain of lives）成为前世今生以及来生共有的因果。佛教的业报最初假定是对普通个人而言，并非以家族为基础。从宋代以降，普遍都接受神明报应是在家族身上，并且穿过生命之链，可以世代地接受报应。由于没有人直率地否认报应力量在现实人生中的作用，报应作为一种民间信仰对人们把握道德命运和上天赋予的命运有着无可替代的督导功能。

六、中国民间宗教实践

世界观促使信仰产生，有关世界与人类生命的信仰所产生的各种实践，是表述个人信仰的实际行为。风水、进香和民俗医疗是中国民间宗教三种很有特点的实践。

风水 杨美惠（Mayfair Yang）写道，"风水"，字面上是"风和水"，是一种古代的艺术或技术，用于改变人类生物的和精神的生命，是通过对自己居住的阳宅与埋葬祖先的阴宅的恰当安排来发现风水与土地中'原生气'的流动相协调与相通"。[16]千百年来，风水活动直接影响着人们对"阴宅""阳宅"地理的选择。对这种信仰活动当代的应用常与"环境计划"和"种植与资源管理"等联系起来。[17]

风水的核心是一种世界观，认为生机勃勃的气之运动是以整个宇宙为舞台的。人体内部同样的"气"也透过自然环境运动，并为自然界提供能量。"在对宇宙整体的看法中，人体就是微观的地球，血脉就是相互交错的河流小溪。"[18]

对代表宇宙能量的活力运动——"气"的信仰产生了实际的效果："人们将个人的房子或村庄建在斜坡或山丘上"，"两面或三面被山脉和山环绕"，还有"山坡上的树林"和"一弯小溪"。风水信仰使人们相信"气"透过自然界进行运动，"在实际生活中风水保护人们免遭洪水和雷雨的袭击，提供物质资源建筑房屋，而水则供人饮用和清洁。"[19]

风水信仰的实际作用不仅是关注自然环境，"像中国这样人口如此密集的地方，传统社会没有法律保护个人的权利，于是就需要有一种方式来促使每个家庭保护其环境，以免彼此伤害。"[20]从而我们可以了解到，作为中国人世界观的特征，风水信仰与社会和谐密切相关。

朝圣（进香）　如果说对风水的信仰和实践是中华文化所独有的，那么朝圣则是人类文明的一种非常普遍的现象。沙特阿拉伯的麦加（Mecca）是穆斯林心目中最敬仰的圣地，每天穆斯林都朝这个方向拜五次。伊斯兰教经书《可兰经》要求每个虔诚的信徒在他的一生中应该至少参拜一次。这种朝圣——在阿拉伯语中被称作"麦加朝圣"或"努力"——每年穆斯林年历中的第十二月，这里都吸引着成百上千的宗教朝圣者。

恒河对印度人来说是一条神圣的河流。每年都有数以万计的人到恒河上的贝拿勒斯城（Benares）来沐浴神圣的河水。耶路撒冷城（Jerusalem）在几百年间成为犹太教徒、伊斯兰教穆斯林、天主教徒和基督徒的圣地。上海附近有两个宗教朝圣之处对中国人仍然有很大的吸引力：一个是位于浙江舟山普陀山的佛教圣地，每年有成千上万的进香客，其中既有虔诚的佛教徒也有信仰民间宗教的人；一个是位于佘山的天主教圣地。

位于北京西北四十公里处的妙峰山是著名的道教进香朝圣地，清楚地表现了中国文化与宗教之间血脉相连的关系。通过考察地方村庄进香团体筹划过程以及到这个著名的庙宇进香朝圣的全部活动，我们能够证实在相互交错的社会影响力下，典型的中国民间宗教信仰所起到的作用。

妙峰山的道教女神碧霞之君以其驱除病魔的能力而远近闻名，来参拜她的朝圣者也与日俱增。朝圣的团体称为"香会"，人们带着香和纸钱到庙宇中去许愿。正如世界上其他地方的朝圣行动一样，到达庙宇的旅途是充满艰辛的，但这正好增加了朝圣行动的神秘性。这里，韩书瑞（Naquin）描述了进香朝圣的行程："从北京到达妙峰山山脚下的旅程选择一天中最好的时间。从出发开始，一整天艰难攀登，始终是走在狭窄的岩石小径上，第二天绝大部分人都会双腿酸痛以至步履艰难。"[21]但是困难只是让进香朝圣的活动更具有神秘性。进香朝圣艰难旅途中的危险和困难，以及无法享用家中可口饭菜和舒服的环境是对进香者虔诚心的考验。也许，人们相信遭遇到所有的这些麻烦都会有助于他们积累功德，让神明保佑他们。

在北方，通常是由村子里的"花会"来组织到妙峰山的进香朝圣活动。最初花会是作为民间娱乐团体发展起来的，成群结队的歌手和乐手经常在宗教节日里表演音乐。这些团体是村庄的骄傲，并成为当地文化的象征。这些花会，正如韩书瑞所说，在庙宇中"演奏音乐用于敬神"。[22]特别是花会还筹集钱款，用于购买进香旅途中的食物或其他必需品，以及发放给朝圣者随身携带的帽子和袋子。在朝圣过程中，香会要求所有的成员行为端正，不许饮酒，不在路上丢弃垃圾，男女之间要保持距离。

其他村庄相同的组织——具有文化和宗教取向的团体，会在进香朝圣的路途上放置灯笼并定期修缮。其他团体会将茶棚从北京一直摆到朝圣的地方。韩书瑞（Naquin）对此评价道："从18世纪的路灯和免费茶棚上，我们可以看出为进香朝圣者所提供的系列服务开始成为妙峰山进香的一个明显特征，这些内容使在佛教徒和儒家信徒中间普遍流行的积德行善观念与这些组织具体的善行实践紧密地连在一起。"[23]

这些组织在充满危险和困难的进香朝圣途中起到了各种不同的作用。"作为长途远行的组织者和向导，努力地让人们了解进香与朝圣的意义，并最大可能地使进香朝圣变得不那样艰难；作为表演者，他们用音乐、色彩、兴奋的气氛和充满激情的表演来鼓舞人心，使原本令人精疲力竭的行程洋溢着欢快的情绪。"[24]

进香朝圣者的数量和活动在清王朝结束以后急剧减少，"文化大革命"时期更是几乎绝迹,最近几年才又复苏并蓬勃发展起来了。在所有这些活动中,我们可以看出中国农村的文化和宗教生活是如何在诸如进香朝圣这个简单的形式中与传统连结起来。

民俗医疗:蚕姑奶奶　2000年夏,社会学家范丽珠参与了对华北庙会文化的研究项目。一个偶然的机会她结识了吴老太太,一个以蚕姑奶奶化身治病闻名的老年妇女。蚕姑奶奶(吴老太太)所做的事情为我们提供了当代中国民间宗教性的一个非常具体的事例。

吴老太太生活在河北保定的一个村子里,这里离北京大约200里地的样子。她在这里出生、长大,并在这里结婚,有两个儿子,三个女儿。在她五十多岁的时候其丈夫就去世了。她没有信奉任何宗教,用她自己的话说,"我太穷了没有办法信教。"

1977年,在她60岁的时候得了严重的腿疾。她去看当地的医生,吃了很多的药都不灵。就在她忍受病痛折磨时,她连续做了一串奇怪的梦:她被好几个人围着,听到人们说她是蚕姑奶奶的化身,蚕姑奶奶是当地非常有名的女神。这个梦让吴老太太非常的苦恼,特别是这个梦在以后的两个月中经常出现。吴老太太跟自己的哥哥说起这些梦,哥哥非常生气,并警告她,千万不要动任何不恰当的心思。吴老太太本人不识字,也不知道哪里来的力量让她迫使哥哥在一张红色的纸上写下"全神落座"。后来,这张有着"全神落座"的纸就挂在她房间那个小小的蚕姑奶奶佛龛上,供人们祭拜。

起初,吴老太太还是怀疑自己是否能够胜任蚕姑奶奶。她没有接受过任何医疗的训练,对于帮助人治病完全没有经验。当她不断地拒绝梦中神的"启示"时,她的腿疼日益加剧。最后她接受了作为蚕姑奶奶化身的角色,于是她的腿疾便神奇地痊愈了。

这时候,当地一个医生给吴老太太推荐了一个胳膊痛的病人,吴老太太不知道自己是否有能力帮助这位妇女,她只是帮助病人按摩。正当她为病人按摩胳膊时，感觉到一股从没有过的力量从她的手传到病人的胳膊上。不过，她仍然很怀疑，"为何我有这样的力量？为何我的手知道如何治疗病人？"

经过一段时间后，吴老太太接受了自己作为蚕姑奶奶的化身为人治病的角色。随着她能治病的名声一传十、十传百，人们从不同的地方来找她看病或者让她解决难题。

蚕姑奶奶信仰的民间传统　在保定地区，对蚕姑奶奶的信仰是一个古老的传统。据说，一千年前蚕姑奶奶是邻村的一个女孩儿，由于积德行善，后来就成为女神，在当地保护人们并治病救人。

蚕姑奶奶的存在告诉我们古代中国蚕茧养殖与蚕丝生产的重要性。这个女神一直是这一重要经济行业的特别保护神，后来她的保护功能延伸到治病，包括身体上和心理上的。蚕姑奶奶的诞日在每年正月十五后二十天。数百年间人们为蚕姑奶奶庆祝生日的庙宇，却在 20 世纪受到了多次毁灭性的破坏，最近的是发生在抗日战争期间和文化大革命中。吴老太太受到神的召唤发生在七十年代的后期，我们可以将之视作一种民间信仰恢复的表现。

吴老太太作为蚕姑奶奶化身的身份显示了传统中国宗教性的本质特征。民间宗教传统在对民众产生影响的过程中，其特点是不需要专门训练的神职人员或被公认的层级权力。在她个人的那部分，吴老太太经历了直接的个人形式的"神召"。她不是被高级神职指定的，她没有得到过正式的医疗训练，她没有让自己的家庭成员来继承这种社会功能。她的角色暗示了中国宗教性的另一个特征：满足个人的需求和直接接触神圣的力量，远离制度性的操控。

吴老太太意识到自己与蚕姑奶奶成为一体会有各种不同的非议出现。在自己腿痛时去看中医，她也经常建议其他人同时接受医院的治疗。那些向她寻求帮助的人，所遭受的更多的是心理上或精神上的困扰。在诊断中，吴老太太常常通过谈话的内容来了解病人与其亲属、邻居的关系。吴老太太敏锐地认识到将生者与死者分隔又连在一起的无处不在的分界线。她运用所熟悉的与文化相关的习惯表述方式，比如谈到死去的家庭成员变成鬼时，督促病人与逝去的家人保持好的关系，因为即便是死人也对生者的心灵保留着相当的影响力。

直到近年，西方的心理学才开始将该学科与精神治疗区分开。现代治疗术的介入并没有利用鬼魂的观念。但是在二十一世纪的中国乡村，没有那些高雅时髦的心理服务，代替它们的是用传统的方式来缓解心理的压力。[25]

七、民间宗教的跨文化特征

中国民间宗教的世界观是很独特的，其中所崇拜的偶像和仪式受到了中国文化复杂丰富的象征符号之影响。但是我们在此可以发现由于民间宗教与多元文化的交汇而具有的不同特征。

典型的是民间宗教把世界看作一个有机的整体，并不存在将神圣与世俗区隔开来的界限。神圣与世俗的明显区别是：宗教意识承认神圣无处不在，同时努力地接近神圣的力量。另一方面，制度性宗教坚持神圣与世俗领域要彼此分界清楚，制度性宗教常常强调必须通过专门神职人员的修炼才能接近神圣，神职人员就是那些在教会中有权威的卫道者。

民间宗教的第二个跨文化特征是关于归属性（nature）。在民间宗教意识中，文化和信仰是一体的。每个人根据世界观、村庄的信仰和活动而生活，是人们生活在此世最简单的理由。不需要宗教的皈依，对个人也没有特别的要求。现代制度性宗教是作为自愿组织而存在，当某个人决定接受一种信仰时，首先要经过一定的入教仪式。

民间宗教跨文化的另一个重要方面体现在"地方性"上。正如我们上面已经看到的中国民间宗教的事例中，宗教的活动是按照地方实际情况来行事的。仪式常常是围绕着地方神和地方保护神进行的，事实上，很多的宗教仪式是在家庭举行的。进香朝圣是地方性特征的另一个重要表现，灵验是与某个特殊的地方——一个特别的庙或山或地方相关的。

这种地域的重要性对民间宗教其他两个显著特性产生了很大的影响。当宗教活动以某一个地方为中心时，会导致神明队伍的扩大。每一个地方都有各种灵验的神明受到民众的崇拜和赞美，既包括神也有其他有功于当地的人格神。西方制度性宗教——犹太教、基督教和伊斯兰教是注重唯一真神的宗教信仰，而民间宗教的信仰则保留着浓厚的地方色彩和明显的多元性。

在不同的文化中，民间宗教赋予地方社区显著地位的，是因为需要大量的非神职的宗教活动领袖。每个社区都有很多宗教活动的场所，民间百姓需要组织活动和举行仪式，而这使得民间宗教更是迥异于宗教生活的制度形式，制度形式要求受过专门训练的全职神职人员来组织普通信众。

但是，尽管中国民间宗教以这些跨文化、跨地域的同质性来否定各种对其不够严谨的评价，中国悠久的历史和非同寻常的复杂性，使得任何一种关于中国文化宗教性方面的结论都值得商榷。由于中国宗教信仰和活动是如此彻底地渗透到文化中间，那么宗教性的形式也就难以与典型的西方模式相吻合。是的，中国民间宗教和人类普遍的宗教性一样有着两个主要的特征（在本书的前面已经讨论过）：意义建构（见第一章）和超越（第二章）。在第九章和第十章我们会继续关注中国民间宗教问题，探讨它在深圳这样现代化的城市中的表现方式。

注释

[1] Catherine Bell, "Religion and Chinese Culture: Toward an Assessment of 'Popular Religion,'" *History of Religions*, pp. 35—36.

[2] Quoted in the introduction to C. K. Yang's *Religion in Chinese Society*, *p.* 5.

[3] Daniel Overmyer, "From 'Feudal Superstition' to 'Popular Beliefs': New Directions in Mainland Chinese Studies of Chinese Popular Religion," *Cahiers d' Extreme—Asie*, ♯12 (2001), p. 125.

[4] Ibid., p. 104, note 2.

[5] C. K. Yang, *Religion in Chinese Society*, p. 26.

[6] Ibid., p. 294.

[7] Ibid., p. 298.

[8] Ibid., p. 40.

[9] Ibid., p. 225.

[10] Daniel Overmyer, *Religions Of China*, p. 51

[11] Kristofer Shipper, *The Taoist Body*, pp. 20—22.

[12] Ninian Smart, *Worldviews: Crosscultural Explorations of Human Beliefs*, p. 55.

[13] Clifford Geertz, *The Interpretation of Cultures*, p. 126.

[14] Overmyer, *Religions of China*, p. 13.

[15] Overmyer, *Religions of China*, p. 12.

[16] Mayfair Mei—Hui Yang, "Spatial Struggles: Postcolonial Complex, State Disenchantment, and Popular Reappropriation of Space in Rural Southeast China," *Journal of Asian Studies*, 63, (2004), p. 731.

[17] E. N. Anderson, "Flowering Apricot: Environmental Practice, Folk Religion, and Daoism," in *Daoism and Ecology*, p. 157.

[18] Stephen Field, "In Search of Dragons: The Folk Ecology of Fengshui," in *Daoism and Ecology*, p. 186.

[19] Field, "In Search of Dragons," p. 186.

[20] Field, "In Search of Dragons," p. 187.

[21] Susan Naquin, *Peking: Temples and City Life*, 1400—1900, p. 529.

[22] Naquin, *Peking: Temples and City Life*, p. 528.

[23] Naquin, *Peking: Temples and City Life*, p. 533.

[24] Naquin, *Peking: Temples and City Life*, p. 539.

［25］关于神媒角色的详细讨论请参考范丽珠的 "The Cult of the Silk-worm Mother as a Core of Local Community Religion in a North China Village, *China Quarterly*，174（2003）；359—372.

第二部分　宗教性与现代性

第二部分　宗教性与现代性

第五章　重新评价世俗化与世俗性

本章将讨论世俗化理论在西方产生的历史背景。当代部分主要探讨现代化的社会内在力量和世俗性的文化态度之关系。最后则讨论"世俗化"用于解释中国宗教所存在的问题。

从历史的观点来看，东方文化的信仰传统和西方宗教传统的社会作用有很大的差异。正是人们认识到中西方宗教传统的不同，才使得一些学者开始谨慎地使用源于西方的宗教词汇与类别来描述中国宗教的状况。在这一点上，世俗化理论为我们提供了一个很好的例证。

在西方知识分子中，世俗化模式作为一个重要的解释性框架出现在一百多年前。至今围绕世俗化理论仍然争讼不止，既有赞同的也有反对的。世俗化理论模式假设，现代化社会的发展要伴随着宗教消亡的必然结果。不同的观察者对世俗化现象给予不同的关注，这个词逐渐地指涉历史的发展过程，而宗教世界观必将在现代社会中逐渐地失去其原有的无所不在的文化影响力。

众所周知，世俗化的过程——产生于科学知识和技术发明突飞猛进的时代，科学与技术正是起到了现代工业化燃料的作用——在西方已经持续了几个世纪。这一历史过程被理解为，在个人层面表现为正式教会活动的参与减少了，宗教认同日渐丧失和宗教感的衰弱。

世俗化的争论继续在西方宗教思想家和社会科学家中蔓延。不断扩大的经验研究和学科分析产生了更细微的理论解释，而某些论断则限制在更小范围。但是，在东方和西方知识分子的意识中，世俗化模式仍然决定着中国社会现代化讨论的走向。

作为一个概念性的模式，世俗化理论不是孤立存在的，其本身是关于现代化问题更广泛讨论的一部分，或者是现代文明发展的一部分。因此理解世俗化模式和评价其某些论断，我们必须从澄清现代化和现代性的因素开始。

一、现代化和现代性

现代化和现代性这两个词都关注现代生活，但是它们还是有很大差异。现代化指的是生活和工作结构中的变化，原来以农业经济为基础的社会变得越来越依赖工业生产。社会学家特别有兴趣来描述这些结构性的变化，并以追寻其产生的原因与结果为志业。

现代性指出了伴随着前所未有的社会变迁在文化和个人意识领域出现的转变。哲学家和社会科学家、历史学家、文化人类学家、文化心理学家都参与到对尚在持续的文化变迁的讨论中。

在真实生活中，结构性变化的内在力量被确定为现代化的因素，文化发展被确定为现代性的因素，二者在本质上是相关联的。现代化和现代性为普通的现象提供了两种视角。但是当这两个词一起用于某一共同的议题时，它们所描述的不是完全一样的事物。

哲学家查尔斯·泰勒（Charles Taylor）帮助我们澄清现代化与现代性之间的区别。[1]对他来说，现代化所描述的是社会过程的一个阶段。这个阶段的特征表现为从封建社会向民族国家的制度形式转变的社会运动。查尔斯·泰勒将这一结果归纳为源于那些有重要影响的历史事件，因为出现于 17—19 世纪的这些事件使欧洲发生了翻天覆地的变化。显然，现代化和现代性的概念完全与西方的历史与文化血肉相关。

对于查尔斯·泰勒来说，现代性是一个文化现象。现代性所标志出的思想和理想已经显露于现代化的社会发展过程中，并赋予大多数生活在现代社会的人以特别的思考与感觉。查尔斯·泰勒认为经由现代性而产生的是对个人、自然、社会和道德的理解较宽泛的一套体系，而这样的体系现在已被全世界大多数地方广泛地接受。他辩解到，现代意识的这些因素已经在全球化世界的多元社会架构中产生影响，并成为其中的重要部分。所以，查尔斯·泰勒注意到西方现代性的这些思想和理想与经济组织的某些形式、政治治理有着历史性的关联，但是他警告人们不要把历史的联系当成必要的和不可或缺的。

随着东方和西方大量学者的出现，查尔斯·泰勒相信有多元现代性，即历史和文化不同途径的多样性与现代社会发展相伴随。由于变化与社会和经济生活的新模式共同影响着不同的社会，其中不同的社会在"接受异文化"时，其反应是大相异趣的。当代大量的事例显示，多样的文化体系能够存续于工业经济体系中，同时支持在公民中发展现代意识。

下面的图表将有助于区分社会学概念"现代化"和文化概念"现代性"[2]

表二　与"现代化"相伴随的社会发展过程

工业化

以经济为基础的社会与工厂生产的产品和商品统一分配销售的关系日益密切的过程。

城市化

大量的人口从农村迁移到新发展起来的城市寻找工作机会，逐渐把以家庭为基础的传统社会控制模式打破了，出现对城市服务新的需要。

参与政治生活

政治团体推动各种形式的公民参与，作为较个人形式的市民治理（继承于君主政体和土地所有的贵族制）被非个人化的科层制所代替。

社会中结构分殊

社会活动的多种空间——经济的、政府的、科学的、教育的、宗教的、媒体的、艺术的都是相互关联的，而每一种社会结构都扮演其特殊角色，显示其特殊功能。

表三　与现代性相关的文化思想和道德理想

科学作为真理之源和进步的基础

作为被广泛接受的信仰，科学方法提供通向真理最可信的途径，而新技术的使用给人类福祉带来最大的希望。

工具理性

合理的计算原则对于达到某一确定结果是最有效的途径。投入—产出比率变成对成功与否最通用的计量方法。结果是，经济领域获得超过社会/政治生活及政策的影响力。

个人主义

坚信人有选择的自由，基于严肃的个人信念，跨越政治和道德的范畴，这些权力应该受到政治和法律的保护。

普遍的平等

作为一种工具，国家的概念是为个人服务的，是要为所有的利益提供平等的服务。原则上，所有公民有进入政治体系的机会，以便能够致力于改善社会现状。

二、世俗化

以对现代化和现代性的理解为背景，我们可以回到世俗化理论的讨论中。美国社会学家贝尔格的定义为我们提供了一个好的出发点："我们所谓的世俗化，意指这样一种过程，通过这种过程，社会和文化的一些部分摆脱了宗教制度和宗教象征的控制。"[3]

涂尔干（Emile Durkheim）是古典社会学家中最有影响的思想家之一，确定了功能性分殊在西方是向现代社会组织发展的内在动力。关于功能性分殊，如我们在图表二所示，一些社会组织自治领域脱离了早先关系较为密切的整体而出现。

在前现代的欧洲，天主教是社会功能的核心。基督教象征符号和宗教活动常常会起到稳定变化不居的政治忠诚关系的作用。天主教教会通过组织和个人，提供大量的社会服务，学校、医院、对需要者提供帮助，艺术扶持，交战双方的媾和等。这些文化和社会经纬交织在一起构成了中世纪基督教王国的社会结构。

在欧洲，功能性分殊对天主教（后来发展到对基督新教）产生了强烈的冲击，宗教的政治影响力逐渐地弱化了。新的政府治理形式不再需要寻求教会的认可，其作为主要的社会服务提供者的作用也大大地降低了，因为这时富有的个人和公民组织承担了越来越多对教育、艺术、及其他社区需要的责任。宗教的改革运动也动摇了宗教的文化主导地位，现代社会不再是天主教会一统天下的局面，教会有关道德的训诫不断地被质疑，甚至到了被人不屑一顾的地步。

正是欧洲的历史为社会学名词世俗化提供了文化背景。在过去五百多年的欧洲历史发展进程中，如贝尔格的定义所说的："通过这种过程，（欧洲的）社会和文化的一部分摆脱了（天主教和基督新教的）宗教制度和宗教象征的控制。"

但是在当代很多关于宗教的讨论中，世俗化这个词已经具有更宽泛的意义。不再单纯强调 20 世纪西方社会历史重要的发展动力，而是变成一种关于宗教在现代社会角色的普遍理论。言简意赅地讲，这个理论断定现代社会发展和宗教制度式微间有种必然的联系；它预示了随着现代意识的拓展，宗教信仰不可避免消亡的命运。

世俗化的假设　在学者间不断增长的共识表明，世俗化还不足以成为一种理论，只可作为一种对来自于经验事实的综合解释。更确切地说，世俗化只是一种假设，作为尚未确定的命题，可以引导人们进行更深入的经验性研究。

社会学家卡萨诺瓦（Jose Casanova）的研究有助于澄清世俗化假设。在他富有影响的著作《现代社会的公共宗教》中，他首次确认了世俗化讨论的三个核心观点。他坚信，"我们只有将这三者在分析时区别开来，""我们才能完全地弄清楚现代历史事实的复杂性。"[4]

第一个命题是世俗化在社会中产生了功能性分殊化。功能性分殊化是指社会活动的不同领域——经济的、政府的、科学的、教育的、媒体的、艺术的，渐渐地与宗教的领域分离取得自主性的过程。

第二个命题是世俗化引起了宗教的私人化。私人化是这样的过程，通过"宗教领域"被当作多方面的专门化活动，不断从公共生活中隐退，而更多地集中于私人的关怀——个人价值和个体的道德行为；家庭的稳定；对生活满意程度的主观感受。

第三个命题是世俗化导致宗教的消亡。当宗教的公共角色丧失和社会影响减弱时，宗教制度将失去其信徒，宗教信仰和活动对个体的影响力将降低。

表四[5]　世俗化假设的中心命题

通常人们理解的"世俗化"包括三个不同的命题：

世俗化在社会中作为功能性分殊

通过社会活动不同范围的变化过程——使经济的、政府的、科学的、教育的、媒体的、艺术的——功能脱离宗教领域，具有独立性。

世俗化作为宗教的私人化

"宗教领域"成为多方面的和专门的活动，不断从公共生活中隐退，而更多地集中于私人事务的关怀——个人价值和个体的道德行为；家庭的稳定；对生活满意程度的主观感受。

世俗化与宗教的消亡

当宗教的公共角色丧失和社会影响减弱，宗教制度将失去其信徒，宗教信仰和活动对个体的影响力将降低。

卡萨诺瓦（Jose Casanova）随后继续检讨目前的研究，来决定这些命题是否已经被确认。

有关功能性分殊问题，已经获得研究结果的普遍支持。宗教制度在现代社会被边缘化和专门化的预言在多方面的研究中被证明。多数民族国家通过各种不同领域的活动和影响而运作，每个领域都是独立的。而宗教制度常常要在这样大的范围内为确定自己的地位而斗争。这种斗争在某些单一宗教制度扮演主导性文化角色的社会中显得更为剧烈。在一个明确的排他性宗教世界观和信仰下，一些民族国家试图发展功能分殊的社会。比如，近日伊斯兰教在伊朗、沙特阿拉伯以及其他中东国家所扮演的角色。

关于宗教私人化的问题，研究结果显示是各种各样的。在西欧，教会已经受到极大的冲击，其影响力逐渐降到私人领域。在很多其他的地区，如，南美、中东和一些亚洲国家以及美国，现在不断争论的动力来自于——宗教团体在公共角色方面有增加的趋势。

但是现有的研究并没有对宗教不可避免要消亡的命题给予证实。原先预言的宗教认同和宗教信仰、宗教活动退出历史舞台的情形并没有出现。事实上，如卡萨诺瓦（Jose Casanova）所报告的那样：

> 从全球化的观点看，1950 年以来，在世界大部分地方，绝大多数宗教传统都经历了影响力增长或仍然保持的情况，这是事实。尽管全世界到处是工业化、城市化、教育以及其他方面的迅猛发展，在高度工业化的社会，如日本、美国等，宗教的活力依然广泛存在。

事实上，正如一些社会分析家所指出的那样，世俗化更常见的是在公共生活中宗教权力影响力的式微，而不是宗教信仰和活动的彻底隐退。

在宗教和现代社会的关系方面，我们看到对世俗化的理解是更复杂而不是过于简单。在不同的民族国家结构中，并没有任何事实显示作为社会制度的宗教死亡的普遍模式，也没有证据表明宗教性在个人生活中的消失。我们所见到不断增强的趋势是宗教制度不再只"固定于"其本土社会，不再拥有排斥其他社会组织的特别保护和特权。

三、世俗性

我们在前面的章节中，从社会发展方面讨论了现代化，从文化的角度讨论了现代性。在世俗化和世俗性间作一个相似的区分将是有价值的：世俗化指向社会进步；世俗性指出文化的视角。卡萨诺瓦的研究澄清了与世俗化相伴随的普遍社会动力。为了弄清楚世俗化的文化动因，我们将引用社会哲学家查尔斯·泰勒的著作，特别是他 1999 年在 Gifford 的演讲《生活在世俗时代》。[6]

在查尔斯·泰勒的思想和理想中，作为现代意识的中心是：自主的自我是个人自由的道德基础；科学方法和工具理性是人类最确定的向导；普遍的平等是政治生活的目标。这些思想很快在世界上广泛传播，其在社会上产生的影响力并非只是否定宗教信仰。因为每一种思想都有其自己的特征，从而对公众产生强烈的吸引力，于是在思想传播的过程中，人类受益颇多。

在西方，很多人喜欢现代性的观点和理想，认同自己是宗教的，并将自己的生活理解为与超验的上帝有关。但是现代性的这些思想同时也发展出一种文化立场，也许更是一种信仰的态度，它来自世俗性。在其核心部分，世俗化并非一定要跟宗教信仰和宗教制度势不两立，但是，世俗化的观点不需要以信仰上帝作为其世界观的基础。对于在现代社会生活的很多人来说，科学足以证明对自然的理解，没有必要有个创世的上帝。在个体间，社会秩序清楚地显露出以工具性契约为基础的特征，不需要上帝作为人类社群超越的基础。人类的仁慈足以成为道德标准的源泉，神秘的规则和上帝审判显得没有任何价值。于是，作为一种结果，多数传统神学信仰被摧毁了。

在查尔斯·泰勒的分析中，这种当代世俗化的世界观，包括几个重要的原则：解魅的世界观；个人满足的人道主义；独立的自我；宗教成为个人的关怀。下面的图表提供了关于这些原则的简单描述。在第二部分的章节中，我们将详细地讨论世俗化世界观的特征。

于是，世俗性是表述现代性思想和理想的一种方式。但是绝大部分世俗性的影响，或世俗文化，并不是信仰的绝对丧失，而是如何感觉在信仰中产生了一个巨大变化。今天，宗教信仰常常与怀疑相伴。宗教的信仰是作为个人觉悟而不是公共生活方式的核心本质。由于怀疑来自信徒群体内部和外部，于是，这把对上帝的信仰置于一个被挑战的位置。

表五[7]　当代世俗化世界观

世界的解魅

不需要神秘的意义或"超凡的"力量来解释或影响这个世界；原则上，宇宙的万事万物能够充分地通过科学对自然内部活动的研究来理解。

"排他的"或个人满足的人道主义

生命的终极目标——人自我的实现——能够通过社区现有的公共资源来得到满足。政治的合法性和道德秩序 可靠地以人类意愿为基础；不需要超越的方式或深刻的信仰原则。

自我的概念和"缓冲的"自我（"buffered" self）

人类行为以自我为基础的新观点，是指面对个人不能控制的力量，力争受到较小的伤害。个人行为相对于外在权力或命运的影响较少受到冲击，利用工具理性的资源，自我能够实现对来自欲望、热情、情感的内在骚动进行驾驭。

宗教作为个人的选择，而不是共同的文化资源

较早期的信仰观点，认同世俗的与作为神的上帝。早期的信仰方式，不再能够为现代西方社会提供公共文化基础。宗教信仰和活动的参与作为一种选择，但是只是在多种生活观念中的一种可能。

四、中国经验中的世俗化与世俗性

社会发展和文化理想在西方已经被冠以现代化和现代性，并成为世界范围的现象。当欧洲作为一种发展模式成为客观事实，人们也认识到现代性显然不仅限于西方。在世界范围内现代化的过程逐渐成为一种合理性的价值，但是现代性有不同的形式，这与接受现代化时所处的文化、历史背景以及当时的环境有关。所以，探讨中国的现代化和现代性在中国文化中的扩展，不仅是可能的，而且是非常有价值的。但是，用世俗化来解说中国的发展就显得有些复杂了。

世俗化确切地是指在西方社会出现的"政教分离"的历史性的社会发展过程。在西欧（以及受西欧文化影响的加拿大、美国和澳大利亚），制度性宗教在国家生活中失去了其早先特权地位，天主教和基督新教不再以国教的形式出现，于是教会失去了举足轻重的地位。在公共生活中，教会领袖只是很多其他社会力量之一，这种教会——国家关系的制度性内在力量，是西方社会的特别经验。

一些分析家认为，儒家学派的兴起并在中国成为一尊是世俗化的例证。他们指出孔子坚持"现世"的取向是本质上的世俗化。但是孔子时代的历史背景和社会发展状况迥异于 17 和 18 世纪的欧洲。在这种情况下，最好是描述早期中国历史的内部变化，而不要使用颇受历史条件限制的词世俗化。

即便在当代中国，使用世俗化来描述宗教发展也会造成误解。始于 20 世纪 70 年代末期的改革开放政策在中国社会开始了前所未有的经济与社会的现代化时代。但是，受到市场资本主义动力刺激和支撑快速产生的工业化，并没有简单地进入世俗化假设所预言的社会结构。在制度性宗教依旧发挥作用的政治控制的结构下，分析中国宗教的发展就显得非常复杂。在目前情况下，很难讲世俗化的内部变化与中国的现代化没有关系。但同样的，使用西方模式来研究中国宗教，也为时过早，我们必须认识到各种社会因素造成中国的宗教经验与众不同的状况。

人们有理由对世俗化在中国现代化过程中的影响持怀疑态度，不过，现代性所具有的内在动力也许会在当代中国的文化经验中找到相对应的部分。正如上面所表述的那样，现代意识出现在重大经济变化的状况下，并伴随着社会生活复杂化的增强而产生影响。现代性在解魅的心理学和文化经验中得到了表现。在第六章中，我们将探讨现代性与解魅的关系。

注释

[1] 查尔斯·泰勒对现代性的全面阐述，请参考 *Sources of the Self*；for his expanded discussion of modernity and modernization see "Two Theories of Modernity," *Public Culture* 11 (1) 1999, pp. 153—74.

[2] 本章表一、表二的内容基本上源自泰勒对现代性的分析，请参考 Ruth Abbey, *Charles Taylor* and Nicholas Smith, *Charles Taylor: Meaning, Morals and Modernity*.

[3] Peter Berger, *The Sacred Canopy*, p. 107.

[4] Jose Casanova, *Public Religions in the Modern World*, p. 20.

[5] 有关卡萨诺瓦世俗化理论讨论，请参考 *Public Religions in the Modern World*.

[6] Charles Taylor, *Living in a Secular Age* (forthcoming).

[7] 请参考 Ruth Abbey's discussion in *Charles Taylor*, Chapter Five "Sources of Secularity", pp. 195—212.

第六章　现代性与解魅

　　本章将对比现代性文化在西方的渐进发展与在中国
突然降临的差异。这种朝着现代意识方向的转变在中国
和西方文化中都各自产生了解魅现象。

　　如在上一章中我们所讨论的，现代化证明了一个多方面的社
会发展：生产的历史性变化（工业化）、金融交易（资本主义）和
人口密集（城市化）改变了人们的传统生活和工作方式。在另一
方面，现代性这个词描述了一种文化的视角，并受到现代化社会
内在变化的制约。在意识层面，这一种变化引导人们去理解在新
的生活方式中的世界。我们将在此探讨现代性现象，这里有两个
目的：更好地理解在欧洲基督教的传统角色作为现代化出现的内
部动因；理解 20 世纪初期中国大多数知识分子对宗教的态度。

　　作为一种文化态度，现代性发端于欧洲。英国伦理哲学家伯
纳德·威廉斯（Bernard Williams）察觉到现代世界是"一个由希
腊传统所操纵的欧洲创造"。[1] 如果说欧洲为现代性的开始提供了
社会结构，那么当代全球化的历程意味着今天每一个国家都要面
对融入现代化的挑战与机遇。我们将首先观察现代性在欧洲的出
现，特别是它对宗教的冲击，然后我们将探讨中国文化有关现代
性的不同西方国家的经验。

一、现代性趋势

我们可以设想现代性作为"一个长时间涌现的潮流，历时几个世纪"。[2]它标志着新的社会和文化力量的逐渐出现，确立了西方现代性的文化。这个长时间涌现的潮流是由很多浪潮构成，每一波浪潮都为现代化发展蓄积能量有所贡献，到了17—19世纪，当现代化潮流具有了摧枯拉朽之势，乃推动了欧洲和北美的变迁。

在西方现代性所代表的不是一个单一的事件，而是发展的结果，是发生在科学、政治、经济、文化等领域一系列世界性变化的内在动因。对中国来说，现代性的文化经验是迥异的。现代文化是在鸦片战争中伴随着西方列强的坚船利炮进入中国的，不是逐渐产生的，而是如同突然来临的海啸席卷堤岸那样对中国文化产生了巨大冲击。

在欧洲，现代性大潮的第一波由哥白尼革命（Copernican revolution）掀起，他提出行星是围绕太阳而不是地球运行的。在16世纪早期由哥白尼提出的太阳中心说，一个世纪后由伽利略更明确地指出了哥白尼学说是正确的，这个发现在人类如何理解自身在宇宙中的位置方面，引起了一场深刻的改变。

表六　现代性潮流在西方——三次浪潮

1600 年 .... 1700 年 .... 1800 .... 1900 年

1. 科学革命（伽利略到牛顿；达尔文到爱因斯坦）
理解并掌控自然世界的理性和能力的信心增加

2. 哲学和人文主义的启蒙运动
理解并掌控人类社会的理性和能力的信心增加

3. 法国和美国革命
对人权、自由、平等和民主新的兴趣

随后人类的一系列发现摧毁了前现代自然世界作为一个神圣宇宙的形象。把世界作为神圣力量存在的早期认识被宇宙的机械性形象所取代。在现代人眼里，世界只不过是被物理学和化学规律控制的庞大机体。对物理世界最基本元素的全面解释，比如万有引力和光谱，使牛顿产生了一种前所未有的信念，即所有自然现象会很快被人类所了解和揭示。如物理学家艾伦·莱特曼（Alan Lightman）所说的，"牛顿撼动了以往认为有些知识领域是人类头脑无法进入的观念，这一观念在西方文化中几百年间一直是根深蒂固的"。[3]

二、现代性潮流的延续

现代性大潮的第二波是以启蒙运动而闻名的知识分子的转变。整个 18 世纪，欧洲的知识分子围绕着人类社会的基本原则进行广泛的争论。君主应该有什么样的权力来统治国家和民族？宗教领袖，如主教或教皇通过什么样的权力来行使公共权威？人的道德是否只存在于宗教的真理中？没有宗教的指导，人类的理性能否发现令人置信的有关善恶的原则？启蒙运动的特征是使人类对通过理性去理解和架构社会的能力增强了信心。在新的自信鼓励下，很多知识分子断定，不需要将上帝的旨意作为道德意识和社会稳定的基础。

科学革命和启蒙运动知识分子观点的一个主要的遗产，是为了思考地理解限制人类能力的定义范围。给予寻找真理以优先于宗教的关键性理由，渐渐地理性更严格地限于"工具理性"，知识分子活动的作用是作为一种策略，为了达到一个特别的结果而算计一个最有效的方式。[4]其他通向了解世界的方式，比如欣赏，或同感，或情感，或意识想象力，被降至于次要地位。

现代性在西方的第三波来自美国革命（1776）和法国革命

（1789）的政治影响力，这些事件挑战了欧洲文明。人们对公民平等充满了热情，于是平等观念传播得异常之迅速，并取代了贵族和僧侣等精英集团的特殊地位。长期作为前现代欧洲标志的国王和宗教领袖等传统权威，现在让位于政治参与和社会权力的新模式。人们呼吸着自由的空气，作为公民兼宗教信徒的西方思想家肯定并支持人权的各项内容，认为人权对人类意义重大。因为这些权力被理解为植根于人的天性，而不是国王的命令或国家的决定。

1750 年到 1850 年的工业革命通过呈现由现代性所推动的社会进步，改变了英国。在技术方面革命带来了惊人的发明创造，大大增强了人类发明的信心并鼓励人们对未来无限的进步充满期待。工厂出现在城市中心，生产着由技术创新带来的产品。1789 年蒸汽机的使用引发了影响广泛的城市化运动，人们离开乡村的农场到这些工厂寻求就业机会。在过去几个世纪中，文化始终是以乡村为根本的，突然间来自城市化的需要和机会改变了传统的生活方式。

三、现代性和宗教

相互重迭、相互依赖的社会变迁造成了制度性宗教在欧洲文化中失去其传统特权地位的结果。几个世纪以来，教会一直扮演着为人们提供理解宇宙存在和人类命运基本世界观的角色。早期的现代科学家如伽利略和牛顿，都是宗教信徒，但是他们新的科学发明挑战并冲击了占支配地位的前现代的观点。

中世纪欧洲的教会同样支持君权神授的教义，作为对君主认可的回报，宗教权威在道德和宗教事务中具有相同的作用。于是，政教合一有助于强化单一宗教信仰，并使惩罚异教徒有了正当的理由。当欧洲社会逐渐地经历了现代化的内部变化，基督新教和天主教仍然是大多数欧洲人的宗教。但是很多原来教会的基本活动逐渐地被政府所接管，如教育、医疗，甚至新生儿出生登记、结婚和死亡等事务。被历史学家称为基督教国家内长时期由教会所把持的绝对状况，现在开始发生变化。如宗教学者布鲁斯·林肯（Bruce Lincoln）评价道：

> （这些变化）伴随着……社会契约理论的出现，人们认识到国家构成的合法性来自于人民，而与上帝无关。渐次地早期的现代国家脱离了对教会意识形态的依附，并在经济财政方面加强了世俗权力，对社会的影响力越来越大。教育、道德原则和监督、社会救助、记录保存，契约保障等等，这些事务以前完全在教会的手中控制着，而现在转移到政府公部门的控制下。[5]

于是，与现代性相印证的社会和文化发展逐渐摧毁了盛行欧洲几个世纪的世界观。越来越多的社会服务属于国家，知识分子的追求受到科学方法的主导。渐渐地宗教组织淡出了实验室、市场、工厂和公共政策等领域，宗教信仰和活动日益退到个人信仰的私人领地。

四、现代性的价值

在很多当代分析家的讨论中，现代性仍然是有歧义的一个命题，于是出现了众说纷纭的现象。现代性产生了进步，表现在人的自由和政治参与、医学研究和公共卫生、公共交通和运输方面。然而这些进步，却不断地被同时出现在现代生活中的国际冲突、种族悲剧和经济危机所抵消。很多国家的民众接受了现代文化观念，毫不犹豫地改变了世代相传的祖先传统。还有很多人观察到在世界范围内西方文化霸权作为一种影响力，导致社会一致性的降低，并威胁到其他非西方文明的文化传统的存续。

哲学家特雷斯（David Tracy）向我们提出现代性的价值和缺陷：

> 现代性的成就，在科学和技术、政治民主和文化多元化方面、在以人权对抗邪恶、通过持续发展之途达到技术救助贫困方面不应该受到否认，而是要保持。[6]

但是，他提醒我们，这些成就也伴随了其他的社会现象，问题更加严重。结果：

> 如康德所言，启蒙运动将我们从压制我们的传统羁绊中解放出来，同时告诫我们必须敢于独立思考。但是，正如启蒙运动的逻辑论证法所展示的那样，理性陷入一种困境，使得那些被当作真理和自由行动的东西落入狭隘的模式，也就是变成纯粹的自发行动……理性退到了形式的和基要主义的理性[7]。

五、神圣世界的终结

现代性的进步表现在多方面，特别是在科学、哲学方面，渐次地这些进步侵蚀了长期以来人们所依恋的神圣世界。在一个神圣的世界观中，宇宙是充满活力的，如精灵占据了山川河流；天神介入人间事务。而日蚀或者毁灭性洪水等天灾被视为神发怒的表现，一个天生双目失明的孩子意味着其父母在道德行为上的缺陷。这个神圣世界的表现为"万事万物和一切经历都充满了神秘的意义"。[8]

犹太教和基督教在《圣经》"创世纪"中的诺亚（Noah）和洪水的故事中，为这个神圣世界找到了一个无可质疑的例子。看到人们生活在邪恶中，创世主决定用洪水来摧毁所有的生命。"大地已在天主面前败坏，到处充满了强暴。"（《创世纪》6：11）正直的诺亚请求神宽恕一些人和动物。于是，诺亚和他的家人建造了一艘完美的大船，每一种动物带上两只。在毁灭性的洪水来到时，方舟上的人和物全部幸免于难。诺亚和他的后人重返家园，带着确保人类存活的那些动物们。劫后余生的人们要清理大灾难后的家园，神决定以后不再这样严厉地惩罚人类了。作为这一承诺的标志，神在天上设置了彩虹。雷雨之后彩虹出现，提醒人类和神之间曾经结下的神圣盟约。

> 这是我在我与你们以及同你们在一起的一切生物之间立约的永远标记：我把虹霓放在云间，作为我与大地之间立约的标记。几时我兴云遮盖大地，云中要出现虹霓，那时我便想起我与你们以及各种属血肉的生物之间所立的盟约（《创世纪》9：12）。

在多少个世纪中，犹太教和基督教信徒在雨后虹霓中找到慰藉。这道五彩斑斓的弧光在惊天动地的雷雨后出现，是神的显示和力量的展现。当牛顿证明出因为光线折射而出现全色光谱现象后，虹霓就失去了原有的其神圣意义。现在虹霓只不过是一个简单的自然现象，是根据物理原理产生的光活动。虹霓留下了一个美丽的景象，但是现在它已经没有任何特别的宗教意含了。

一个神圣的世界观展示了哲学家里科所称的"信仰的实感性"。在这里，世界是没有任何瑕疵的真实存在，神的影响力充斥于日常生活，信仰意义和个人价值受到尊敬是很自然的事情。里科使用初期阶段的纯真（first naivete）[9]这个词来描述人类意识支持这样一个充满神圣的世界观的时期。遗憾的是，这个早期的共识在现代性的冲击下没有幸存下来。

六、现代性：解魅的时代

由于现代性，原来宇宙充满的神明和人类意愿被非人性力量驱动的机械性世界所取代。于是，在意识上的这种变化产生了一种无处不在的文化心态，一种绝对理性，被社会学家韦伯公开地描述为解魅。

世界与神圣间神奇的和谐消失了。虹霓曾经是造物者仁慈的标志，现在只不过是一个简单的自然现象。科学能够证明彗星就是彗星，不是来自神的信号。自然界似乎能够根据物理和化学固定的宇宙规律运行；似乎没有理由能证明是神圣的造物主保证了宇宙有序的存在，于是各种充满深刻寓意情节的故事逐渐被科学研究冷酷的超然所取代。

在这几个世纪期间，有影响的政治变化出现在人们的视线中，并经由热情的知识分子的论争而得以强化。哲学家和其他学者认为，人类社会不是根据一些基本的自然布局结构而形成的，社会是作为契约的一种形式存在着，成员间的互动是以获得共同认可的利益与需要的交换为基础。政治统治者不再是以君权神授的方式掌握政权，而是取决于民众的意愿。与此同时，民主则需要通过哲学的认证来确定其价值。

最近这些年出现的另一个变化是自主的自我价值获得推崇，这是现代性文化的关键因素。如查尔斯·泰勒所言："在五百年前的神圣世界中，围绕心灵的边界在本质上具有渗透性。"[10]人们完全融入于他们的社区，是其家庭、部落、或封建王朝的成员，较少地作为个人而存在。在感觉变化过程中，现代性的核心部分是人们意识到什么是自己的个人趣味与志向。个人觉悟被查尔斯·泰勒称为"一个缓冲的自我"，较少地受到外力的伤害，而伤害往往来自那个神灵与魔鬼施展魅力的世界[11]。很显然，这种现代自我认识到在拥有个人选择自由的同还要承担起包括危险在内的责任。

解魅同时触及到宗教世界。启蒙运动思想以不太明显的自然神论取代了圣经宗教的慈爱造物主。对上帝的信仰依然存在，但是这个神远离日常生活，在一个超越的领域中产生作用。天主教和基督新教的神学家，受到科学进步的暗示，似乎要以宗教信仰为代价，在信仰和理性间建起一道防火墙。出于理智，他们放弃了科学的领域、自然世界和公共领域。他们宣称，宗教信仰仍然在某些能够掌控的领域，如个人救赎和精神慰藉等方面发挥作用。

现在，宗教安全地从自然世界和科学进步中分离出来，不再需要对其信仰提供理性的和哲学的合理性的解释。一些为宗教信仰辩护的人甚至返回到三世纪神学家特图尔良（Tertullian）的古老断言："我相信它，因为它是荒谬的。"

这样，基督教信仰遁入其自己建构的少数人的社区。如果它不能与科学竞争，至少它还有自己统御的权力。宗教不断地成为私人内心的事情以及厌世者的天堂。在社会上，和以前的教会作为公共领域的时期相比较，个人虔诚更加突出。

由于世界清除了神秘的魔力，而人类也因之失去了原来作为人类生活有机整体一部分的心灵意义，于是解魅成为这个时代主导性的氛围。

七、现代性和解魅在中国

现代化——社会进步产生了先进的技术、运输和交通——和现代性——以这个新时期在意识方面的变化为特征——在西方文化中逐渐出现。这些发展充分激荡起人类的乐观主义和自信心。当然这些都与中国近代历史上的情况无关。

如余英时所观察到的，"我们所接受的（现代化）是西方花了两个世纪的时间吸收并消化的东西，它进入中国只不过是短短的三十或四十年。"[12] 1840 年的鸦片战争，迫使中国开始不得不面对西方由现代化带来的坚船利炮的优势，突然间不仅香港，上海、天津和其他沿海城市被辟为通商口岸，西方列强也将抢占的租借地变为其势力范围。

这种用暴力向中国人民展示现代化西方威力的方式，无异于一种痛苦的宣告：中国必须进入现代世界。现代化对中国的第二个冲击发生在 1895 年，甲午战争中国败给了日本，用余英时的话说，中国人开始屈辱地意识到，"中国在世界上被边缘化了。"[13]

20 世纪初年，中国迅速地朝着现代化的方向发展，迫切地要接受现代化的各种制度，以便脱离儒家传统和前现代官僚体制的统治。于是，在 1911 年，中国的最后一个封建王朝——清王朝寿终正寝。科举考试早在 6 年前已经废除，取而代之的是欧洲模式的新式学校。比如北京大学建立于 1898 年，上海的复旦大学成立于 1905 年。

1919 年的《凡尔赛和约》，规定把德国在山东半岛的全部权益转让给日本，这对正在向现代化方向探索的中国无异于是一个重大的打击。五四运动的爆发就是对这一令人屈辱的决定表示不满的强烈反应，并要求中国政府和知识分子接纳现代化，拥抱现代化的象征"赛先生（民主）和德先生（科学）"。

这种急切的对现代化的追求表现为广泛地接受科学的思想，同时彻底否定中国传统民间信仰和仪式的价值。胡适、梁启超、冯友兰及很多其他的知识分子，坚称现代中国是一个没有宗教的国度。受到后启蒙运动欧洲和美国主导的理性主义哲学的影响，这些学者普遍认为宗教是现代性的主要障碍。

对现代化的热情始于 20 世纪初的头十年，但是后来不断出现的各种事件却无情地打断了中国人在现代化方面的持续努力。20 世纪 30 年代日本的入侵彻底打乱了中国人的正常生活，特别是在东北和东南沿海。30 年代持续到 40 年代的内战也使得现代化的进程成为不可能。

1949 年——进入政治神话时代　多灾多难的半个世纪使中国经历了摆脱自己文化传统的解魅过程——内忧外患频仍，阻挠了现代化的进行——直到 1949 年 10 月，毛泽东主席在天安门广场庄严地宣告"中国人民从此站起来了"，于是开始了重新进入政治神话的时代。

正如"现代化"和"现代性"这两个词在中国有些微妙的不同（在中国是突然出现，不同于西方是逐渐展开的），在中国神圣化的经历与西方的经验是迥异的。共产主义和"中国特色的马克思主义"时代进入了一个强烈的民族自豪感的阶段和努力建设现代化的时期。中国知识分子提出终结宗教，而这样的诉求在 20 世纪初期已经提出（目标是佛教、天主教和基督教，连同道教），最终接受了马克思主义的无神论，一种来自西方的现代化方式，从而得到了精神信仰的归宿。为了更好地了解二十五年间的政治神话，我们需要回溯社会学家贝尔格在四十年前所发展出来的以下概念。

马克思主义的神圣帷幕　贝尔格认为在很多社会，宗教扮演着"神圣帷幕"的角色。[14]神圣帷幕是笼罩社会的华盖，它将民众聚集于同一顶棚下，并以对所有事实的一种包罗万象的解释来覆盖他们。

一个神圣的帷幕可以保护其成员免遭外来的袭击，就像雨伞一样为人们挡住雷雨。作为权威性的意识形态，神圣帷幕同样阻挠人们的独立思考。显然在其保护覆盖下，帷幕有时会阻挡受其覆盖者的视野。形象地说，当某人居于华盖的保护下，他是无法看到天空的任何变化或呼吸到新鲜空气的。

对于贝尔格来说，神圣帷幕具有终极意义的专有权，它是"城内唯一的帐篷"。这种共有的意识给社会带来很多的好处，但是所付出的代价也同样很大，所有生活其间的人在保护范围内必须接受全部的既定思想。权威来自于神圣，因为它通过神授权力或者意识形态的需要而运作。

神圣的帷幕强化了神秘的世界。通过一个防卫性极强并充满仪式性活动的神圣化世界，神圣帷幕成为具有权威性的结构。当神圣帷幕破碎后，原来生活在其中的所有人既兴奋，又要承受迷失方向的困惑。此时公共的认知受到限制，个人失去了慰藉之源，但是得到了前所未有的自由机会去探索新的思想和选择的模式。

中国与西方当代社会学家认为，中国文化在1949年陷入了自己的神圣帷幕。马克思主义和毛泽东思想如中世纪的天主教那样为人们提供了一个包罗万象的有关现实解释的观念。除了一个明确的无神论和世俗性的方向，它的权威是被"神圣化的"——包揽了对所有现实世界的解释。借助社会原罪的解说（可以比较天主教对"罪"的理解）和消灭阶级的理想（一个现世的"救赎"），马克思主义的神圣帷幕表现得与宗教极为相像。

毛泽东式的马克思主义，向全中国人民提供一个新的世界观和道德原则以及政治的神圣秩序。共产主义理想社会向人们昭示了一个历史中的神圣彼岸，这一神圣彼岸与现世之间的紧张要求每一个人的献身。从社会功能的意义上说，历史情境中神圣彼岸的观念一方面使人们认识到社会生活中不可避免的不义、痛苦、艰辛、不平等现象是可以接受的，或是必须接受的，另一方面回答了现世人生的意义问题。毛泽东作为具有神圣魅力人格的领袖，被当作国家和人民的大救星。他的"红宝书"被当作经典来珍藏，他的画像成为新中国的偶像。

在中国历史上这个时期的理想主义者希望彻底根除所有的宗教，佛教寺院、道教宫观，以及基督新教和天主教的教堂几乎都被夷为平地。相比之下，儒家学说从来没有完全否认宗教的存在，或提出彻底铲除宗教的动议，而是以相当的理性宽容儒家教化以外的神秘信仰。

解魅：梦想破灭 20世纪70年代中期文化大革命结束，很快邓小平提出了改革开放政策,整个中国文化经历了一场深刻的解魅时期。很多人开始感到了理想破灭,曾经以极大热情投入到革命中的年轻人更是陷入了绝望中,他们所经历的是一种深刻的失落感——文化和精神价值的失落,被称之为信仰危机。

那么,当民众开始思考自我的时候,政治性的"神圣帷幕"也就面对着人性"世俗化"的挑战。就像当年尼采大声地宣称"上帝死了",中国民众突然觉醒,原来他们崇拜的不是神而是人,"我们痛苦地发现:原来自己所崇拜的并不是'洞察一切'的神,而是一个人,也会犯错误。轰!在我们心中耸立了二十年的、由无限信仰之砖筑起的精神圆柱顷刻崩塌!"[15]但是,革命的宗教和政治的"神圣帷幕"却无法经得起现实生活的诘难,因为非理性的狂热是绝不能长久地持续下去的。一代青年生命历程中曾经的对政党意识形态和领袖个人魅力的绝对服从与盲目崇拜展示出,政治化的"神圣帷幕"是何等的盖天盖地,具有何等的控制力。然而最有意义的是,人的自我意识在艰难环境下和心灵的伤痛中仍然在不顾一切地觉醒。因为他们觉悟到"旧的宗教像雪崩一样溃散了",在为泛政治化的神圣信仰唱挽歌的时候,他们正经受着的可怕的精神崩溃和精神折磨与失去信仰的痛苦和彷徨。

对物质的追求,在毛泽东时代被当作资本主义的尾巴受到打击,而在改革开放后变成了生活中有价值的目标。突然间,赚钱变成越来越可以接受的东西了。对物质利益的追求和消费主义一道与这种解魅相伴随而出现,"一个精神空虚的民族发现了一个目标,在这里不需要精神的介入。"[16]

正如现代化和现代性在中国有不同的意义一样,中国人经历的解魅也完全迥异于西方。在欧洲解魅是与基督教王国神圣帷幕的崩溃相伴随,宗教不再像以往那样具有权威,所以西方的解魅与世俗化是孪生的。在世俗化的西方文化下,宗教的地位大大降低,教会逐渐成为社会上多元化价值体系中的一种。

在中国,解魅出现的情境则大大不同。中国民众并非没有受到宗教神圣秩序的影响。在七十年代末期和八十年代初期，社会普遍的失望情绪是对文革时期政治挂帅的一种反应。伴随对"文革"政治信仰的破灭和政治神圣帷幕倒塌的是一种深刻的失落感——文化和精神价值的失落。

20世纪80年代初期"文化热"席卷整个中国。中国民众渴望了解：我们的国家到底是怎么了？伟大的文化真的落伍了吗？对儒家文化传统和对马克思主义的失望开启了普遍而又广泛的再检讨。

1980年第5期的《中国青年》刊登了女青年潘晓的一封信，"人生的路啊，怎么越走越窄……"，她在信中表示自己曾经是"对人生充满了美好的憧憬和幻想"，然而目睹了各种现实后，她的理想幻灭，她的心不再火热，渐渐冷了，甚至死了。在茫然、绝望之中，她感叹人生的路"怎么越走越窄"。潘晓的信一石激起千重浪，"几张纸片"真的"搅动了生活"，"影响了社会"，七个月里，《中国青年》编辑部收到了57000多件信稿，共编发了111位读者的111份稿件，约十七八万字。

在20世纪80年代末期，电视纪录篇《河殇》从中国文化中汲取核心象征——黄河与长城，提出同样的问题。在该片中将"黄色"作为中华民族和母亲河的象征，以"蓝色"代表开放和广阔的海洋以及蓝眼睛的西方人。长城的形象不再是光荣地抵御外敌入侵的保护，而是作为自我封闭的藩篱，"如果长城会说话，它一定会老老实实地告诉华夏子孙们，它是由历史的命运所铸造的一座巨大的悲剧纪念碑"。

伴随着这个解魅时代的中国，既有迷惘，还有一种兴奋。在比较开放的哲学讨论和艺术观念更新中，中国文化开始重新有了活力。这个时期，中国民众对宗教的兴趣突然间如雨后春笋般出现。佛教和道教的寺院重新开放，基督新教和天主教教堂重修，宗教学校开始招收学生、训练神职人员，很多中国人转向从中国传统民间宗教中获得精神慰藉。得益于改革开放在政治方面对人们精神世界控制的松动，大多数人有机会回到生命的原点，反省人生。事实上，很多人就是从自己把握命运开始进行个体生命意义探寻之旅的，因为只有自己才能解放自己。而经济上的开放，其意义和影响绝不仅仅限于经济的范畴，它对于推动中国社会精神生活世界的多元化有着不可没之功。

宗教在 21 世纪中国的角色还不是很确定，第九章和第十章将探讨在现代都市中，民众对精神意义的寻求。

注释

[1] Bernard Williams, *Shame and Necessity*, p. 3.

[2] Michael Gallagher, *Clashing Symbols*, p. 6

[3] Alan Lightman, "Einstein and Newton: Genius Compared," *Scientific American*, September, 2004, p. 109.

[4] 查尔斯·泰勒将工具理性描述为"我们用于计算最经济方式的一种理性，在成本效益比率中，利益最大化是成功的标准。"见 *Ethics of Authenticity*, p. 5.

[5] Bruce Lincoln, "Conflict" in *Critical Terms for Religious Studies*, p. 56.

[6] David Tracy, *Plurality and Ambiguity*, p. 23.

[7] Tracy, *Plurality and Ambiguity*, p. 31.

[8] Michael Pollan, *The Botany of Desire*, p. 34.

[9] Ricoeur, *The Symbolism of Evil*, p. 351. *naïveté* 意为简单和淳朴，出现在发展的初级阶段。里科使用这个词来描述前现代时期，很多人所经历的世界充满了奇迹和各种征兆。

[10] This statement, taken from Taylor's yet-unpublished 1999 Guifford Lecture, is quoted by Ruth Abbey in *Charles Taylor*, p. 204.

[11] Abbey, *Charles Taylor*, p. 203. 泰勒使用"缓冲区（buffer）"或"障壁（barrier）"的形象来暗示现代个人意识的某些含糊的特点：现代自我更多地避开外在的要求——不管是来自神权或是来自社群的义务；现代人将自己理解为更加独立的，因为个性就是以自主的个人选择为基础而不是共同的文化责任。结果现代人更倾向于将自我孤立起来。区别于自然世界并在人群中与众不同，每一个个体本质上是单独存在的。以这种现代的理解，

关系（relationships）不再是人类意识和幸福的基本母体，而相对于个人决定和行动是次要的事情。

[12] Yu Ying－shih, "The Radicalization of China in The 20th Century," *Daedalus*, 122, ＃ 2, (1993). p. 133.

[13] Yu, "The Radicalization of China," p. 135.

[14] 贝尔格对神圣帷幕的讨论，请参考他的著作 *The Sacred Canopy*.

[15] 夏中義：《中国青年》，1980 年第 11 期。

[16] Ci Jiwei, *Dialectic of The Chinese Revolution*, p. 11.

第七章　宗教在当代世界的境遇

本章将追溯在西方社会从前现代到晚现代这样长期的变迁中，天主教和基督新教角色的变化。对宗教的前景提出两个重要的出路，这是晚现代世界中有待探索的问题。

启蒙运动充满信心地预言宗教很快会消亡，这样的预言已经被证明是不正确的。具有历史传统的制度性宗教和以民间宗教为特征的对意义的追求始终没有死亡，反而在整个世界范围内兴盛起来。尽管如此，宗教的角色在晚现代社会已经有了非常巨大的变化。

首先，现在很多宗教信徒更多地意识到在宗教历史中有着不少含糊不清之处。宗教传统常常等同于慈善、公正、同情心等值得尊重的美德，宗教历史充满了丰富的内容。透过历史的考察和跨文化的背景了解，发现制度性宗教已经拥有了一定的政治影响力，大量证据表明在历史上制度性宗教曾经对那些异教徒毫不宽容，大肆挞伐，甚至暴力镇压。如特雷西（David Tracy）所观察到的那样：

　　不管是过去还是现在，事实证明，任何宗教一旦拥有权力定会使宗教运动像其他世俗事务一样，变得堕落。有关宗教狂热真实的记忆和历史留下的记载，以及宗教对所有文化产生的邪恶的影响，都是让人难以忘记的。[1]

是否有勇气承认、理解或否认制度性宗教的这一邪恶特性，对有信仰的人和宗教学者始终是一个挑战。

第二，社会宗教传统在晚现代——不管是佛教抑或印度教、天主教或基督新教、犹太教或伊斯兰教——必须在这个多元化信仰和价值的世界里找到一个自己的位置。由于在自己的文化中失去了特权地位，这些制度性宗教不得不开始面对一个不熟悉的处境。每个宗教都要在全球公共场合上与其他宗教站在一起，相互对视，接受自己只不过是社会公共组织中的一员的事实而已。

宗教团体对上述两种来自晚现代社会的挑战有不同的回应，因此未来宗教机构的角色会取决于其回应的方式。这里我们讨论当欧洲向晚现代文化转变后，宗教是如何改变自己的社会角色。

一、基督教世界和现代性

在公元纪年开始初期，耶稣的追随者不过是少数人的群体，他们不但没有权力，还经常受到迫害。公元 4 世纪，罗马帝国君士坦丁大帝皈依了天主教，使得天主教获得官方宗教的地位。由于天主教教会和欧洲的政治统治者之间密切的（通常是势不两立的）关系，历史学家用基督教王国来称呼这种文化和政治的状态。

从法兰克王查理大帝（Charlemagne，公元 800 年）到拿破仑（Napoleon 1800 年）是基督教王国最兴盛的时期。在整个欧洲，天主教和公元 1500 年以后的基督新教享有特权地位。在这一千年间，宗教信仰和欧洲的文化深深地融为一体。除了某些个别的例外（例如，在欧洲有数量不大的犹太教徒，中世纪在欧洲的边缘地区西班牙穆斯林有所发展[2]），教会的世界观和宗教活动主导了整个欧洲大陆。

基督教王国和欧洲的道德取向　在漫长的基督教统驭时期，教会的信仰和活动支配了整个欧洲的道德基础。出现在十二和十三世纪的最早的大学，是由天主教学者构成的，多数是神职人员。这种新的掌控知识的机构——特别是在意大利有博洛雅（Bologna）大学、法国有巴黎（Paris）大学、英国有剑桥（Oxford）大学，开始系统地学习法律，将其作为教会组织的主要原则和社会秩序合法性的基础。现代法学原理就发源于中古欧洲的大学。

今天社会历史学家从宗教信仰中来追溯"人权"的西方传统，人权观念在天主教文化中深受珍爱。这些早期的学者将有效的人类法则当作由造物主建立的自然法则的一种证据。自然法则的两个特征被证明：自然法则的常识是人类理性的产物，而非简单的宗教信仰问题；自然法则的需求具有一种独立于任何世俗统治者权威的特性。几个世纪以后，这些早期的观点支持了所有人类拥有基本的言论自由和责任的认知，并有助于人们对"造物主赐予的不可剥夺的权利"[3]原则的理解。当欧洲和北美的民族国家后来设计他们的法律体系时，很多原则就直接来源于宗教，同时，欧美法律体系中仍然保留了来自于基督新教和天主教传统的人权保护的道德取向。

基督教王国时期的文化为教会成员提供了一个普遍接受的世界观。然而此时基督教文化对于犹太教徒和穆斯林们，则就不那么富于同情心了。基督教徒普遍谴责犹太人造成耶稣的死亡，于是犹太教徒在基督教国家虽然时常也能够被接纳，但是却难以避免遭到迫害的厄运。在1492年，正当哥伦布远航跨越大西洋希望发现新大陆时，西班牙的天主教统治者从他们的家园放逐了犹太教徒和穆斯林们。[4]

基督教王国的终结　基督教王国构成了中世纪欧洲的神圣帷幕。哲学家查尔斯·泰勒称这种文化形式造就了欧洲的文化：

基督教王国的事业是力图将信仰与文化形式和社会模式联姻。在这个过程中它创造了某些非凡的东西……尽管基督教曾经在历史中有过辉煌的一页，但它最后注定是要死亡的。[5]

查尔斯·泰勒认为教会所支持的真正价值是所有人类的尊严和平等，个人追随宗教信仰的自我良知的权利等。只有在结束基督教凌驾于政权之上、享有特权的基督教王国时代终结以后，它才会被人们真正地认识到。只有当基督教允许其信仰价值接受世俗权力的批评时，教会所提供的社会关怀才会成为可能。当代文化已经出现了，查尔斯·泰勒坚信，"基督教王朝的保护层在何处被撕破，那里唯一正确的哲学就不再独霸天下了。"晚现代社会要求价值的多元化，这样"公共空间可以始终为竞争的终极观念提供平台"。[6]

在第六章，我们讨论了现代性的潮流如何冲击了欧洲文化，摧毁了基督教王国的基础。19世纪，新的民族国家开始承担原来教会把持的社会责任。教会数百年来第一次离开了对社会的绝对控制，不再对政治事务指手画脚了。对西方基督教教会来说，包括天主教和基督新教——从基督教王国时期具有特权的地位转变为现在单纯地提供终极价值的"无权无势"角色，这个过程一定是痛苦的。直到教会逐渐发现新的公共角色，找到新的定位才不得不适应这一切的变化。教会不再是终极真理的权威性来源，制度性宗教正在寻找其位置，以便在公共开放的众多文化中拥有较强的道德影响力。

二、宗教的新出路

在晚现代世界的整体中，两方面的发展为宗教提供了新的出路。此时，晚现代意识对此没有作任何预期的设想。宗教作为一种文化重新进入到大规模的对生命意义和价值的文化对话中：首先是如何理解人类的理性不断扩展；其次，是如何认识神秘世界重新觉醒的观念。

对理性扩展的理解 由于 18—19 世纪科学革命的势头渐盛，知识分子越来越热衷于探寻科学思维的力量。科学方法以精确的测量方法开始主导人类对事物的观察，同时人们渐渐地树立起对科学的信心，似乎只有科学才具有为人类生活的改善提供更大帮助的能力。于是，虽然人类理性有十分丰富的资源，但只有工具理性最终获得普遍的重视。理性方式在对世界自然规律的量化分析方面显示出优势，特别是为科学发明在应用技术方面的使用，让人们获得了前所未有的增加财富的机会。于是理性的科学方法大有排斥其他方法之势。那些质性的认识方式——比如艺术的、诗歌的或宗教的，几乎被当作和现代世界没有关系的东西，渐渐地失去曾经有过的对人类的影响力。在这种全新的知识气候条件下，科学与经济领域独领风骚，而宗教则黯淡地处于不断式微的状况。

人类的理性经过不断地磨砺，在各个方面都已经产生了非凡的成就，并在改善人类生活状况方面仍在不懈地努力。医疗技术的进步和药物的发明，大大地延长了人类的寿命，生产、交通和通讯方面也获得了前所未有的进步。然而，由于理性范围过于狭窄，它在满足人类需求的努力中，却无形中丢掉了其他有价值的资源。由于想象力和情感，鉴赏力和感知力，完全不符合作为科学知识的严格要求，结果人们越来越偏注于量化的方法，人类理性也就失去了容纳百川的胸怀。

恢复实践理性 在晚现代阶段，哲学家和其他知识分子正在回到亚里士多德（Aristotle）实践理性的认识上。正如玛莎·努斯鲍姆（Martha Nussbaum）所提醒的，亚里士多德认识到理性不仅用于寻求普遍原理，并依从一定的知识（科学领域，被亚里士多德称作知识的 *episteme*）。[7] 理性也常常用于制造东西，这种知识亚里士多德称作技术 *techne*（technology）。理性还用于我们生活中的日常事务，这种知识就是实践理性的范围（*phronesis*）。

实践理性较少地受普遍原则的影响，更多地考虑特别情境的需要。在这种情况下，人们怀疑理性没有遵循普遍原则，只是在此时或此地特别的情况下，产生出某种特别的应对之策。事实上在每一个道德判断的背后，都离不开个性化的考虑与具体状况相关的具体行动。毫无疑问普遍的原则和习惯会帮助我们来做决定，但是当我们想确定"这里或现在"该怎样做时，则不能保证从普遍原则中获得一个恰当的解决办法。

实践理性有取决于一种即时的特征，在某些特别的状况下需要当机立断地决定。注意到在特别的情境下会有某些具体的情况发生或出现危险的状况，一个人必须创造性地选择下一步该如何做。亚里士多德以在大河上航行的船长为例，船长必须掌握他要航行的那条河的基本情况：河水有多深，河水流动的情况，同样地也要对船本身特别地熟悉，如船的大小、宽度和行驶的能力等。但是面临具体的情况时，如天有不测风云，任何一场突如其来的雷雨都会导致河水流向的变化，而以往航行中积累的所有知识和经验，都使船长能够在危急的时候当机立断，做出解决眼前困难的决定。

实践理性就处于道德思考和宗教伦理的中心。实用性的智慧作为良知的核心部分，使得道德理性既依赖于规范和原则，同样也依赖于生活经验，一个良好的道德判断来自于修养良好的情感和值得信赖的想象力。当人们对实践理性给予越来越多的赞赏时，作为回应当代道德生活问题的资源，出现了柳暗花明又一村的情形，宗教寻到一条新的出路。

情感功能的恢复 理性在实践层面上得以展示其功能，必须依仗来自情感和想象力的支持。为了做出聪明的决定，一个人必须"尽可能完全地、充分地并具体地想象目标客体所有相关特征，全面掌握住他们，以便将我们带进某种特定的情景中。这样才有可能形成直觉和感情、计划和想象等"。[8]于是，通过这样的方式，理性的拓展有可能引导一个人朝着智慧与道德责任行为方向上做出选择。

在过去的四分之一世纪，在对理性不断认识的过程中，学术界（哲学、心理学、伦理学和脑研究）越来越明显地意识到情感的价值，并重新确认情感能为人类生活提供重要的认知信息。[9]玛莎·努斯鲍姆指出，这一发展是"在实践上论证了情感的复归"。[10]现在学者们已经普遍认识到情感与简单的生物感觉或荷尔蒙的变化相去甚远，情感逐渐适应了人类对其环境和"对世界理解的具体化方式"。[11]在一个比较聪明的决断过程中，我们从情感方面感觉到的信息"不仅不是非理性的标志，而且具有相当丰富完全的理性"。[12]

玛莎·努斯鲍姆提醒人们，亚里士多德充分意识到情感"不总是正确的，需要经过教化并将其引导到与人类良好生活正确观念的和谐互动之中。但是，教化并非像激发道德行为的东西那样具有本质性，而是对真实和价值的认知"。[13]

亚里士多德对情感的认同和当代对情感价值重新确认之间经历了两千年的时光。在这期间，哲学家从柏拉图到康德都轻视情感的存在，认为情感对任何认知的内容和可靠的信息却没有任何意义。这里再次引用努斯鲍姆的话：

> 柏拉图否认情感和欲望，将之作为堕落的表征，坚信正确的实际判断只能通过激发理智的"自我依靠"来实现，尽量地远离情感和欲望的影响。[14]

对情感的负面评价在富有盛名的哲学家康德那里仍然在继续，"对于康德来说，强烈的感情等同于确定无疑的自私和以满足自我为目的的东西。"[15]

罗伯特·昂格尔（Roberto Unger）认为情感是人类生活中必要的角色，并针对情感提出了最有力的辩护。"理性给予我们关于世界的知识，但是它不能告诉我们怎样想和怎样行事的最终事实。"这就是说，理性可以分析并理清充斥于我们心智的信息，但是堆积信息本身不能为道德选择提供一个必须接受的基础。而且，理性"不能为我们追求最合理的目标提供所需要的持续保证的品质"。[16]在人类事务中，动机和承诺来自于其他途径。

从这种关于情感作用的文化复归中，我们能够认识到忠诚与虔敬的美德是宗教生活的核心，绝非毫无意义的附属。当愤懑的情感受到很好的节制时，会激活人们对道德和宗教的期望，以便寻求公正。哀婉悲痛的宗教仪式，会使强烈的悲伤感得到升华，有助于医治因为失去至亲造成的心灵创伤，这些情感在追求最高精神价值中支撑着人类。对情感价值的重新承认，允许宗教的情感，包括惊异与敬畏、恐惧与感激，重回到晚现代的时代背景下。这里我们看到晚现代文化中为宗教敞开的另一扇门。

陶冶道德想象力 实践理性要依靠具体表现为情感的理解力和动机，同样也离不开来自于丰富经验的想象力。里科将这种难以捕捉的内在资源解释为，"一种受规则支配的创新形式……想象力被视为给予人类经验以特别形式的能力，或作为重新描述事实存在的能力。"[17]

想象力和情感一样，蒙受了一个不恰当的坏名声。由于西方文化中的传统智慧在某些情况下受到宗教信仰的支持，于是就出现各种偏见，认为想象力扭曲了事实，捏造了不真实的东西并祈求荒诞和危险的偶像来保佑。努斯鲍姆概括了这种普遍的文化偏见：

> 想象力常被认为是自我主义和过于自我纵容，过于关注特别状况以及与个人的关系。个人完全可以（被认为可以）全靠责任作动机，根本不需要发挥想象力。所以，这种想象力的发散性，好听一点说是奢侈，难听地讲就是危险。[18]

在过去的三十年，哲学家、心理学家和宗教学者已经开始认识到想象力如情感一样，在帮助我们认识价值的意义方面有很大的贡献。里科描述了在道德思考方面想象力的作用：

> 我们从未停止探讨用新的方式来评估行动和品性。我们在一个想象力的大实验室进行的思想试验，同样是在善与恶的范围内进行探索。[19]

努斯鲍姆论证通过开发道德能力来陶冶人性，因为道德能力根植于成熟的情感和经验丰富的想象力。她从早期讲故事开始追溯了道德想象力的发展过程：孩子在听儿歌中被启发了与生俱来的好奇心——"神秘的感觉混合了好奇心和敬畏心。"[20]努斯鲍姆继续道，"丰富而专注的好奇天性受到故事的激励，由此明确了他人具有相互不同的特质和值得尊重之处。"[21]对他人的痛苦情同身受的感觉和怜悯心等道德的情感作为最基本的宗教感，受到想象力的激发。这种内在的东西为人类提供了同情他人的观念以及产生了对他人的道德行为。

道德哲学家斯庞（William Spohn）追溯了想象力是如何被宗教经典以道德和宗教塑造出来的。例如，《圣经》中以触动人心的宽容饶恕他人的故事和神话，向读者的想象力灌输了那些无法拒绝的价值。在斯庞的判断中，"普遍认为，经卷的主要道德影响是作用于想象力……（这些故事）通过产生感情应合，以不同凡响的方式成为将来可能出现的行动的情景。"[22]宗教经典中的故事并非意味着道德原则的说明，没有非此不可的概念和鲜明的情感取向，而是暗示人们怎样选择恰当的生活方式。如斯庞所观察到的，"（圣经故事中）的形象没有直接说明怎样做，但是它们以自己的理性形式来鼓励某些特定的行为方式。"[23]宗教文本用于"想象力培养"方面，充满了有说服力和魅力的形象。[24]

情感的复归和道德想象力的再发现，为宗教在晚现代世界打开了一扇门。在人类历史的这一时期，我们从对人类知识有限性、理性的理解，转向承认启发并驱使人类生活的内在资源的广泛存在。有关人类的知识日益成熟、精致，结果，为宗教和里科所预言的"第二阶段的纯真"（second naivete）的到来敞开了大门。

三、向宗教再次开放：回到神秘

科学革命的降临和紧随其后的现代性浪潮，使曾经神圣的世界失去了光彩。以前充满神圣征兆和由彗星、虹霓来显现的宇宙，让位给"自然界"——按照物理学规律旋转的一堆毫无生气的原理。这样的世界不需要上帝，也没有任何空间留给宗教。神秘曾经赋予人好奇的灵感，现在变成了问题的对象。用里科的话说，神圣的世界让位给 desert of criticism*。

在 desert of criticism，自然世界和精神世界被毫不留情地拆散。现在彗星就只是一个呆板的东西在天空中移动，长期的干旱也和上天的发怒没有干系。desert of criticism 给宗教造成巨大的灾难。用里科的话说，

> 无论怎样看，某些东西就是丢失了，信仰的实感性无法挽回地失去了。但是如果我们不再按照初期信仰，生活在大量的神圣象征符号中，我们现代人能够透过批评（ciriticism）达到第二阶段纯真的目标。[25]

第二阶段的纯真（*A Second Naivete*）　　今天来自不同文化的人们——普通百姓连同诗人和科学家，正在找回世界上的神秘感觉。现在我们居住的星球更像个机器，在按照严格的牛顿物理学

---

* desert of criticism 是与宗教发展密切相关的重要现象，但是只有在西方的文化背景下才能理解，很难找到合适的中文，故搁置未翻译。

定律运转。反映在个人生活事务上，人们发现了意义和目的的迹象，各种非随意的机会越来越显出复杂性。这种当代（对神秘的）赞赏不同于前现代意识中的神秘魅力。在被里科称为"第一阶段的纯真"的任何自然的事情会带有灵性方面的信息。比如，天上出现的彗星或河水泛滥都具有道德意义，杯中茶叶的形状及方向同样可以预示着人的命运。对于绝大多数生活在晚现代社会的人来说，这种神秘的情形已经一去不复返了。今天人们所经历的已不同于前科学时代对宇宙的敬畏，而是后科学时代对我们充满奥秘的世界加以重新思考。

重返神圣伴随着对好奇的重新认识。在第一章我们讨论了好奇是超验的标志。历史学家拜纳姆（Caroline Bynum）这样描述好奇的经验："我们感到好奇的是，我们不能在任何意义上具体化、毁灭或包含我们心灵的范畴，我们好奇于神秘的事物以及似是而非的隽语。"[26]

科学方法的成就连同对科学本身有限性的认识，使得后现代意识已经重新找回好奇心。对自然世界更完善成熟的科学认识——不可能出现在前现代时期——在我们这个残破的星球上催生好奇，并和非常巨大的神秘相互联结。

西方开始复归对自然的好奇，最早出现在 1962 年的环境保护论者卡森（Rachel Carson）的那本非常有影响的著作，《沉默的春天》。卡森揭露有毒杀虫剂和其他污染物给自来水供应带来彻底的破坏，造成野生动物和植物物种的毁灭。她证据确凿的描述令读者大为震惊，开始意识到地球所遭到的破坏。她分析了土壤活力、土地肥料中所施农药中包含的化学成分和生物有机物间错综复杂的平衡关系，这样的思考取代了传统的"土壤"概念。突然间，地球被重新想象了，不再是取之不尽，用之不竭的了，而是一个易于受损害的肌体，它的存续有赖于人类的理解和行动。

此后气象学家和宇宙学家描述了一个资源被过度攫取、令人充满忧虑的世界。我们怎样全面了解这个包含着上百万星系和上亿星星的世界？巨大的资源过度攫取意味着什么？为什么这里有如此多的存在？也许最深切的好奇是，为什么会有世界万物的存在？

今天科学记载了宇宙间所有存在的令人惊奇的内在联系。流淌在人体血管中的血液含有和卫星、行星一样的铁，人体骨骼中的钙和在海洋中发现的物质一样。生物科学家泰勒·沃尔克（Tyler Volk）撰写了"全球性的新陈代谢"一文，它是通过光合作用中氧气和二氧化碳的交换，将行星调整为单独呼吸的有机体系。[27]其他科学家观察到诸多不同寻常的化学的巧合，使人在地球上的生存成为可能：温度的持久性，丰富的水，大气层的氧气水平保持在20％，这些恰恰符合生命延续的要求。到底是什么使得这些"巧合满足我们的需要"？欣赏和好奇或许是人类最好的反应。

美丽的神秘 美丽如好奇一样，是神秘的起点。当我们惊奇于周围美丽的事物时，会问：为何而美丽？评论家斯卡瑞（Elaine Scarey）论道："美丽欢迎我们，要吸引我们的注意。"她还说，"美丽的东西出现在世界上的每个角落，唤醒了人们的悟性。"[28]

美丽拓展了我们的注意力："如马蒂斯（Matisse）展示的那样，美丽的东西总是带着来自他方的问候。"[29]斯卡瑞补充说，"在我们发现某些东西异常美丽的时候，我们便立刻感到完全地为之倾倒了。"[30]我们为之失魂落魄，"所有以前用于保护、防备、提高自我（或威望）的门禁，现在竟然全都开放给它了。"[31]

可怕的脆弱、过度的消耗资源、神秘性的内在联系，这些我们共同面对的问题，都使人类对重新拥有好奇心充满了期待，因为唯有好奇心的拥有才会使我们再次尊重世界的神秘。[32]

四、宗教信仰和晚现代社会

在晚现代社会，经典传统的神圣经卷，例如希伯来圣经和佛经，作为来自宗教世界的文学受到关注并广为人们阅读。现代性的到来，使很多年轻人失去了欣赏这种简单宗教信仰的"第一阶段的纯真"。

那些进入解魅阶段的地方，被里科称为 desert of criticism。现在，经过了几个世纪的解魅，里科认识到，"第二阶段的纯真（second naivete）"的出现，是唤醒超越人类理解力神秘象征的标志。今天很多善于思考的人们开始以自创宗教信仰的方式来适应晚现代世界。

关于 desert of criticism，里科指出，在西方思想史中的无秩序时期，很多人被迫放弃前现代宗教的信仰和活动。在这个 desert of criticism 期间，核心人物是弗洛伊德、马克思和尼采。他们积极的贡献在于揭开了宗教行为的虚伪面纱：对惩罚的恐惧、孩子般地祈求保佑、逃避个人责任。

弗洛伊德将宗教理解为一种幻觉，是"对生活苦难的一种补偿"。[33]马克思对宗教经典的定义是"人民的鸦片烟"。在他看来，宗教无异于镇静剂，吞下去可以缓解由于社会不公正所带来的痛苦症状，但他没有探究更深层的原因。德国哲学家尼采批评基督教，因为它倾向于将信徒变成婴儿，或更糟糕地变成奴隶。

从里科的判断来看，尼采所言"上帝之死"，指的是前现代宗教意识的死亡。从中可以体会出宗教的趋势——所有的宗教，不论是基督教、佛教或伊斯兰教——保佑人们远离无法逃避的恐惧和悲剧等痛苦的人类生活。

desert of criticism 成为纯化的时期，信徒努力地改变超越"怯懦地恐惧神的惩罚与感念神的恩宠护佑"[34]的状况。神的死亡被当作对神的惩罚来庆祝，因为神要求人做到的是无独立性的服从和怨恨。在里科看来，宗教的未来需要"信仰从暗处走出来，（寻找）一个神，面对生活的危难不是保护我而是屈服我，这样人才配得上称作人"。[35]这样的宗教信仰是"一个本质上悲剧性的信仰，超出了所有信念和保护的范围"。[36]

晚现代的挑战针对所有的宗教信徒。里科判断，人类此时要重新设想如何对待权威，对于立法者和监察者不要一味地卑微地服从，因此服从不是毫无个人主见的屈从，而是"一种对于其他人和环境合乎情理的和必要的依赖，这种依赖可以是服从和接受"。[37]它对很多人的挑战就是要寻找到某种生活方式，在这种生活方式下"依赖和服从都与谴责、禁止和罪罚无关"[38]。

这种晚现代的宗教信仰提供了"一种慰藉的形式，不需要借助外在的补偿（如神的保障和奖励），也不需要任何形式的复仇（要服从或引起怨恨的神）"[39]。

在晚现代世界，宗教有很多不同的方面。今天很多的信徒不去管现代性旋风般的变化，仍然处于"第一阶段的纯真（first na-ivete）"的神秘世界里。很多当代人停留于 Desert of criticism 中，认为宗教意识的任何表达方式都是非科学的和幻觉的。但是，多数晚现代人经历了"第二阶段的纯真"，我们共同居住的星球和对宇宙资源的挥霍惊醒了人们的好奇感。好奇的情感有时候就存在于怎样表达一种宗教崇敬，从而起到一个通向神圣的起点和宗教通道的作用。

注释

[1] David Tracy, *Plurality and Ambiguity*, p. 85.

[2] Maria Rosa Menocal 在她的书中 in her book *Ornament of the World：How Muslims，Jews and Christians Created a Culture of Tolerance in Medieval Spain*，讨论了西班牙宗教的多样性。

[3] 这段话来自于美国独立宣言，The Declaration of Independence of the United States, initially published in 1776.

[4] Menocal, *Ornament of the World*, p. 260.

[5] Charles Taylor, *A Catholic Modernity*, p. 17.

[6] Taylor, *A Catholic Modernity*, p. 18.

[7] 为了更好地理解亚里士多德关于知识的论述，请参考 Martha Nussbaum, "The Discernment of Perception：An Aristotelian Conception of Private and

Public Rationality" in *Love's Knowledge*, pp. 54—105 and her essay "Non—Scientific Deliberation" in *The Fragility of Goodness*, pp. 290—317.

[8] Nussbaum, *Love's Knowledge*, p. 74.

[9] 这些学者包括哲学家 Robert Solomon, *The Passions: The Myth and Nature of Human Emotions*, 心理学家 James Averill, *Anger and Aggression: An Essay on Emotion*, 教育家 Carol Gilligan, *In A Different Voice: Psychological Theory and Women's Development* and 哲学家 Roberto Unger, *Passion: An Essay on Personality*.

[10] Nussbaum, *Love's Knowledge*, p. 42, note 76.

[11] Nussbaum, *Therapy of Desire*, p. 369.

[12] Nussbaum, *Love's Knowledge*, p. 100. Nussbaum 补充道："因为情感在其结构中具有认知趋向，故很自然地将其看做我们伦理媒介的理性部分、思考活动的回应、以及成就不可或缺的要素。"(p. 40)

[13] Nussbaum, *Therapy of Desire*, p. 96.

[14] Nussbaum, *Love's Knowledge*, p. 76.

[15] Nussbaum, *Love's Knowledge*, p. 76.

[16] Unger, Passion: *An Essay on Personality*, p. 101.

[17] Paul Ricoeur, *Figuring The Sacred*, p. 95.

[18] Nussbaum, *Love's Knowledge*, p. 76.

[19] Ricoeur, *Oneself as Another*, p. 164.

[20] Nussbaum, *Love's Knowledge*, p. 89; see also her essay "Literature and the Moral Imagination" in *Love's Knowledge*, pp. 148—67.

[21] Nussbaum, *Love's Knowledge*, p. 90.

[22] William Spohn, "Jesus and Christian Ethics," *Theological Studies*, 56 (1995), p. 104.

[23] Spohn, "Jesus and Christian Ethics," p. 104.

[24] Spohn, "Jesus and Christian Ethics," p. 105.

[25] Ricoeur, *The Symbolism of Evil*, p. 351. 里科将历史理解为（特别是西方历史）一通过三个阶段的进化：在第一阶段纯真（first *naïveté*），人们简单地认为世界上在自然秩序和道德秩序之间没有任何区别。到了 "the desert of criticism" 时期，在科学革命之火的燃烧下，欧洲的很多人丢掉了对世界简单的看法，开始把世界当作物理现象的集合，没有

任何神秘，更不需要精神的价值。下面的讨论将进入到里科对第二阶段纯真
（"second *naïveté.*"）出现的解释。

[26] Caroline Bynum, *Metamorphosis and Identity*, p. 52.

[27] See Tyler Volk, *Gaia's Body: Toward a Physiology of Earth*.

[28] Scarey, *On Beauty and Being Just*, p. 81.

[29] Scarey, *On Beauty and Being Just* p. 47.

[30] Scarey, *On Beauty and Being Just* p. 111.

[31] Scarey, *On Beauty and Being Just* p. 113.

[32] 关于这些问题的神学讨论，请参考 Sally McFague, *Super,
Natural Christians*. Also see Mary Evelyn Tucker and John Berthrong,
eds., *Confucianism and Ecology: The Interrelation of Heaven, Earth,
and Humans.* 其中历史学家 Lynn White 最早评论了基督教对全世界依
然普遍存在的环境污染和对自然攫取方面的作用，请参考他的著名文
章，"The Historical Roots of our Ecological Crisis," *Science*, 155
(March, 1967), pp. 1203－1207.

[33] Ricoeur, *The Symbolism of Evil*, p. 458.

[34] Ricoeur, *The Symbolism of Evil*, p. 460.

[35] Ricoeur, *The Symbolism of Evil*, p. 455.

[36] Ricoeur, *The Symbolism of Evil*, p. 460.

[37] Ricoeur, *The Symbolism of Evil*, p. 448.

[38] Ricoeur, *The Symbolism of Evil*, p. 449.

[39] Ricoeur, *The Symbolism of Evil*, p. 467.

第八章 晚现代宗教性的特征

本章探讨作为晚现代意识一部分的宗教敏感性的变化，并讨论当今支持宗教参与的不同动机。

第一章提到的贝拉（Robert Bellah）将宗教定义为："一套既存的关于终极条件的象征符号形式与行动。"[1]他接着证明道，纵观人类存在的广阔领域，在象征形式发展过程中有过几个关键性的阶段。他注意到，他所描述的人类有关宗教意识的发展，并非追寻宗教制度的历史变化。他还提醒人们，他理解的进化模式是一层层递进的思考，而不是所有宗教现象的简单经验纪录。本章用这一模式作为基本情况的背景，以帮助我们理解塑造当今宗教意识的文化变化。

在文章中，贝拉强调，历史智慧传统的重要性出现在文明的轴心时代，大约是公元前 600 年到公元 800 年。[2]佛教、基督教和伊斯兰教的起源——连同印度教、犹太教和中国宗教传统的重要发展，都可以在这几个世纪的历史中追溯到。这一时期在世界很多地区出现的先进文明中，人们不约而同地寻找终极唯一的力量或存在，以涵盖所有现实世界中的生命境遇问题。这种唯一超越的力量被作为普遍道德原则之源泉，每个个体对此都要承担责任。对不完美生活的不满和对日常生活的宽容，使人们始终不懈地寻找生存的理想王国，以"另一个世界"来象征理想王国。在经典文本里，在知识分子的讨论中以及正统的表达方式中，都能看得到这种新的、包罗万象的世界观。

在西方社会，对宗教的理解在很大程度上受到宗教制度的影响。而宗教制度就是被贝拉在宗教发展纲要中所确认的历史智慧传统：犹太教、天主教、基督新教、伊斯兰教。一个普遍的现象是西方的这些传统信仰系统常常彼此猜忌怀疑，相互攻击，西方历史上充满了这些宗教传统之间不间断的社会歧视和残酷的战争。但是现在来自于这些宗教的很多宗教领袖和普通信众，都渴望着抛弃这种充满痛苦的相互敌对的传统。例如，当代宗教学者欣然地认识到，在伊斯兰教、犹太教、天主教和基督新教中，共有的资源和相互影响是历史长河中富有价值的一部分。

伊斯兰教和犹太教、天主教和基督新教等都各自发展出很多特别的象征符号和仪式活动。这些传统中基本上都呈现出三个特征，这些特征分别被贝拉确认为传统宗教信仰系统的一部分：

1. 终极的真实性：寻找一个唯一的原则，这个原则可以解释万事万物。

2. 普世性：信仰只有一个基本真理、或关于所有事情的一套真理。

3. "拒世性"：完美秩序和理想的传统观念，导致人们对在现实世界中不完美的日常生活秩序产生出不满足感。

这些历史传统都伴随着信众对得救充满信心的期待，或对超越尘世存在的完全救赎的领悟。传统的宗教观念凭借对人性不完整和罪的神学解释，得以表现出其意义。这些典型宗教传统的精神资源在当今世界仍然保持影响力，作为成千上万信徒信仰和慰藉的来源。

一、晚现代意识中的宗教

贝拉的宗教意识模式超越了轴心时代，他以宗教模式的差异来区分现代社会早期以及其他时期。这些历史性的变化已经极大地影响到今日人类对宗教意识探究和表达的方式。例如，在当代世界，很多热衷于宗教的人认识到宗教话语是最基本的象征符号，它存在于古典文献中尽人皆知的形象中，包含在宗教仪式的艺术和形式中。越来越多的宗教意识的经验和表达方式不再限于传统宗教制度的范围。

在贝拉研究的基础上，迈克·巴恩斯（Michael Barnes）探讨了当代宗教意识的内在动力。巴恩斯是如此描述晚现代宗教的：

> 无论如何，有一种宗教性是彻底现代的，它使用科学的世界观语言，具有关注当代社会问题的兴趣和世俗取向，提倡有责任心的自主性、个人以坦然地面对新观念和变化的方式生活。这种晚现代的宗教性从未完全取代旧有的宗教形式，在吸取传统遗产的同时，会对传统宗教继续产生影响。[3]

在高度复杂与相互依赖的当今世界社会中，这种新的宗教意识正在人群中流行开来。在这样的环境中，普通民众经历了日益增加的跨文化间交往和面临来自全球多元性的挑战。伴随着对个人自主的广泛认可，当代宗教意识坚决反对任何令所有人都遵循一种信仰方式的企图。我们看到，传统宗教绝对真理的教义在现代社会越来越行不通，不得不接受更多的讨论和争论。

这里我们将探讨晚现代宗教性的几种特征：

1. 对人类经验的终极信仰更深刻的体悟；
2. 不断增加对所有知识有限性的认识；
3. 对日常生活中信仰重要性的高度赞赏；
4. 对宗教多元化和价值多样性的真正开放。

对人类经验的终极信仰更深刻的体悟 在晚现代宗教意识中，神秘的事物比信仰更引人注目。民众宗教的体悟主要不是以某一神学教义为基础，替代教义信仰的形式是，信众精神信仰直接表达了关于人类生活和人类所有存在方式、所有困惑的更大关心。当然，正统的神学概念仍然受到普遍尊重，与此同时却难以避免受到民众的质疑和批评。因为个人的生活经验和批评性的思考在评价宗教所表达的内容过程中，变得更加重要。

晚现代的宗教性受到存在于我们经验世界中心的神秘现象的可信性的影响。神秘性存在作为一种天赐而出现在现实生活中，带着创造、承受、和谐与复元的力量。这种力量由于有人们的亲身参与并全力地投入，从而超越了狭隘的个人利益。尽管神圣的存在是难以捉摸的，但却给人以真实的感受。其真实性挑战了概念性定义，这种情形似乎难以通过不着边际的理性语言给予令人满意的表述。

晚现代宗教性吸收了多种精神资源的营养，世界所有的智慧传统都可以成为信仰感悟的支持系统。比如通过使用神话、诗歌、雕像和动作等象征语言，使这些多元化的传统得以拓展，并深化了人类与神圣真实性的关系。

不断增加对所有知识有限性的认识 在晚现代社会，人们能够接近多元化的知识和真理资源。科学和科学方法极大地拓展了人类知识的界限，通过定义我们知道，眼下所有通行的科学理解都是暂时性的并允许大家来不断地修正。哲学和人类、宗教信仰和政治意识形态都声称将为人们提供最本质性的知识，以便理解"事情是怎样的"和"事情应该是怎样的"。不可否认现在对这些解释的认识有所提高，但同时，还是留下大量的东西没有解释。越来越多的人认识到知识是来自社会性的建构，"理解"需要熟悉相关的特定情境，而"真实"只能从特别的视角或立场来表述。

在当代世界，很多拥有宗教信仰的人认识到宗教的表达方式必然是有限的。如历史性宗教传统的神圣经卷只反映了其出现时的文化背景。神学作为宗教经典和各种戒律形式，反映了宗教对信徒的生活及更大范围社会的关系规制，故而现代人接近宗教就必然会涉及到对这些宗教象征符号的解释和再解释。近日的神学家和普通的信徒认识到传统宗教的经卷并非意在提供真实的信息或历史的记载，其对人类社会的馈赠是关于生活意义的观察和体悟。很多传统宗教的象征符号具有永恒的价值，但是如果要在当代社会保持对民众信仰的影响力，这些象征符号需要经过一番改造、精炼与更新。

在神学家中，这种意识显示在日益增加的谨慎中。伴随着对宗教信仰传统形式的认识，人们逐渐发现：传统宗教包罗万象，而且概念过于丰富、过于清楚、过于确定无疑。在晚现代神学著作中，传统宗教思想的学说被重新探讨并重新建构，开始承认在很多情况下任何有关人类生存终极方面的解释都不过是片面的，并且有时间限制的。神学家保尔·莱克兰（Paul Lakeland）就以谨慎的方式表达了自己对晚现代宗教性神学的意见，他注意到基督教世界观是"关于一般性的一种看法，但不是普世性的看法"。[4]

对日常生活中信仰重要性的日益赞赏 在传统轴心时代出现的宗教传统受到超越此世追求完美热情的影响。但是在晚现代宗教性中，这种对"彼世"的关注受到挑战。

当今很多人形式上献身于宗教信仰，其他人也正在寻找"此世"的信仰归宿。我们发现，人既会对纯粹的美，同时也会对这个世界不那么完美的暧昧产生深深的感应。快节奏的生活方式和全球文化的电子环境造成很多人的精神空虚。他们渴望与自然世界有更深层的联系，与家庭和朋友保持更真挚的情意。于是他们迫切地要在其所拥有的价值和来自工作环境的日常要求间进行调适，寻找平衡的可能。

一个此世的信仰承认日常生活的价值充满了喜悦和责任感，日常生活作为神圣空间和召唤奉献的存在之处。这里，爱、工作、公民参与在日常生活中相互作用；还是这里，生活的遭遇和痛苦要求人类做出回应。通过不断的理解和反思，晚现代的宗教意识找到参与世界的方式，即唤起简单的快乐，因为简单的快乐充满了纯真的喜悦；大胆面对复杂的事物，因为复杂的事物承载了我们时代的价值内容。

莫楚（Daimund O'Murchu）留心到晚现代宗教性的"此世"观，以此来重新关注神学著作的价值。他建议，神学的探讨"不再始于上帝而是从下层开始，从寻找与追求人类体验出发向外行动，以便拥抱生命以及现实世界中更宽阔的地平线"。有了这样新的焦点，他继续论述到，"勾勒信仰的图景而非宗教的传统，成为神学家的工作目标。"[5]

对宗教多元化和价值多样性的真正开放　宗教多元化和价值多样性定义了当代文化的特征。传统宗教要求对唯一神学正统的绝对忠诚，而把宗教多元化当作要克服的问题，把多神信仰作为要消除的现象。故而唯一神学宗教绝少与其他宗教发生联络，甚至禁止信徒与其他宗教信仰有任何瓜葛，唯恐正统信仰的纯洁性受到威胁。如此的正统宗教定位造成了一种在不同宗教团体间竞争和相互猜忌的氛围，而此种氛围足以令这些团体为了某种共识而联合起来的任何努力付诸东流。

晚现代宗教的敏感性常常将多元化视为一种应变策略。世界多样性的宗教传统连同其核心的道德信仰与价值承担，为人们提供了康复与希望的方式。晚现代宗教性承认人类面对的问题对于任何单个的组织来说，都过于复杂而难以解决。因此，宗教人士必须寻找跨文化传统的合作途径，超越形式上的宗教，为在全球范围内做出解决问题所需要的回应和承担责任寻找共有的基础。在这里，内在信仰的合作并非以神学的一致为目标，而目的在于道德的稳定，联合起来以特别有效的途径来回应世界的需要。

第三章所提到的世界宗教议会，为这种寻找全球道德回应提供了一个有价值的例子。1993 年 8 月在美国芝加哥召开的世界宗教议会第二次大会上，由德国基督教神学家孔汉思（Hans Kung）起草的《走向全球伦理宣言》被来自全世界几乎所有现存宗教的

6500 个代表批准通过了，显示了发自宗教界的共同呼声。早在
1983 年，由 40 位前任政府首脑组成的"相互促进委员会"成立。
这一非宗教性国际组织也对通过改善人类道德水准来解决全球性
问题方面给予了密切关注。《走向全球伦理宣言》发表后的 1995
年，由德国前总理勃兰特（Willy Brandt）领导的"全球政治管理
委员会"发表了《全球是邻居》的报告，倡议以"全球性公民伦
理"作为不同国家和文化之间合作解决全球性问题的基础。同年，
由联合国前秘书长德奎利亚尔领导的"世界文化与发展委员会"，
呼吁建立一种由共同的伦理价值和原则所组成的"全球伦理"。
1996 年，"相互促进委员会"通过了"寻求全球伦理标准"的报告
书，呼吁制定一套"全球伦理标准"，以应对 21 世纪人类所面临
的全球性问题。1997 年这个委员会又通过了一个"世界人类责任
宣言"，旨在确立一种推动人类进步和保证人类追求完善的全球普
适的价值标准。现在全球伦理基金会的成立，是对这个世界面临
很多挑战进行多方合作性回应的支持。

　　全球化的努力将不同信仰的人和没有宗教信仰的人联结在一
起，这种合作的成功要求宗教信徒有一种新的立场。当有信仰的
人接近不同宗教传统或那些没有宗教信仰的人时，一种有意识的
转变成为必然。在这样的背景下，莱克兰建议，信徒必须认识到
其所珍爱的宗教信仰是站在其"背后"并非在"前面"。在他背后
推动、支持、支撑他个人投身于为社会变迁而协力完成的艰巨任
务，而不是在其"前面"作为一种关卡，迫使人们接纳其宗教观
念。在晚现代意识中，宗教信仰是"出自我们所操作一切的背
景"，而不是"为了历史的蓝图，或世界改革的程式"。[6]

二、今日多种宗教的动机

　　宗教心理学的研究为我们提供了另一个关于当代宗教意识的

视角。学者们确认了三种原因，尝试去理解导致当今人们参与宗教活动的动机。

工具性的宗教动机　在很大程度上是功利主义的。这里一个人寻找宗教的认同或教会会员身份，有助于他达到目的。例如，成为一个有很高声望的教堂的会员，会提高家庭的社会地位。或者宗教活动似乎提供了一个神奇的安全庇护，保护信徒免于家庭问题的困扰。一个宗教团体强化了传统的观点和道德价值，通常会为个人变化和社会变迁提供帮助。于是一些人参加这样的团体，以便为他们选择的价值和生活方式获取支持。在这些例子中，宗教性的介入会与直接的个人利益有关，而不是跟神圣事物在转变中邂逅。

内在的宗教动机　包含着个人对某种宗教传统所投入的深刻感受。具有内在信仰的人们寻找与神圣事实（不管是称作上帝、或在其他信仰传统中，都具有较高的真实性）的个人关系，并在这种关系中获得力量与支持。他们将其宗教信仰看作是生存的指南，是世界观的主要决定因素。某种宗教传统的价值和道德规范已经实际地影响着他们的决定和行为，推动着信徒朝着个人和社会变迁的方向发展。而克服个人中心的努力作为信仰的目标得到普遍接受。既使对信仰的执着绝非简单易行，信徒们仍会保证自己对利他主义行为和道德正义的宗教理想具有责任。心理学上的收益——希望、慰藉、目标感、喜悦作为信仰的天赐受到欢迎，但这些并不是宗教信仰和活动的最初目的。

内在信仰的价值较能够适应当代世界多数信徒的感受，这些信徒信仰传统宗教，如佛教、犹太教、天主教和基督新教以及伊斯兰教。值得称赞的是，坚定的信仰和个人牺牲的行为构成了内在信仰的特征，个人与社会都从这种全身心的宗教信仰中得到恩惠。但是评论家注意到，这种内在信仰的投入会导致对某一种固定宗教正统形式的支持，从而出现对其他信仰传统给与不尊重的评价的可能。

当代研究者们报告了在晚现代宗教性中扮演重要角色的一套不同动机。宗教心理学家丹尼尔·巴特森（Daniel Batson）和他的同事将这一观察方式称作探索取向。[7]人们对精神层面的寻觅是因为意识到宗教的觉悟是一个正在进行的过程。简单结论的质疑意在对复杂的问题提出讨论，一旦人们对新宗教思想保持开放的态度，就有可能愿意重新检视正统信仰。暂时性和怀疑精神结伴地出现在现代人精神追求的旅途中，结果，他们对传统宗教的很多观点表现出一种健康的怀疑主义。

尽管如此，很多具有探索取向的人认为自己在某种宗教传统中是一个忠诚的参与者。但是其忠诚是开放的而不是有局限的，即对自身信仰传统所接受的宗教观念表示赞许，同时承认其他智慧传统的象征资源具有同样的价值。当今的一些信徒倾向于承认自己具有多元忠诚，比如认为自己是儒家基督徒或天主教的佛教徒。

涉及到精神性，探索取向对二分法提出挑战。二分法一直是传统宗教理解的一部分。特别是在西方，内在信仰将精神生活用反义词来定义：精神发展被理解为一个克服身体欲望的过程；超自然领域被认为是与日常生存的自然世界截然不同的；精神性被解释为神圣领域的实践，用以保证抵御来自世俗生活的混乱和诱惑。

有着探索取向的人们表现了一个较无种族界限的宗教意识。神圣的事物、个人的发展和社会的同情心被认为在本质上是相互联系的，其精神层面的觉悟根植于个人和社群的经验，而绝非受到传统权威的影响。他们的精神实践更多地关注于在变迁方面（变迁既是个人的同时也是社会的）而不是关注禁欲和克己。

有着探索取向的人们寻找保持价值沟通的机制，不是仅仅传递或维护某一道德原则。他们渴望参与真诚的对话，对话的内容包括，我们生活中的价值是什么，我们在何处可以感受到这些价值，以及我们怎样在生活的真正境遇中表达我们的价值。

　　在各种不同的晚现代社会中，社会科学研究的例证继续报告了制度性宗教信徒的流失状况。但是，其他的社会现象令贝拉足以坚持世俗化理论不是当代制度性宗教式微的最佳表述。他建议宗教的个人化——人必须找到自己终极答案的意识，为了塑造我们生活的价值，个人要承担应有的责任。这些在晚现代宗教性中扮演了主导的角色。对于这些精神性的探讨，宗教制度不是最终的归宿，相反，既有的宗教角色为持续的个人意义寻求提供了一个适合的环境。[8]

注释

　　[1] Robert Bellah, *Beyond Belief*, p. 21.

　　[2] 不同学者提供各种不同的历史时期来定义轴心时期（axial age）。该名词引入现代讨论要归功于卡尔·贾斯珀。他认为在人类意识中，公元前800年开启了历经千年的变迁。贝拉在自己的文章中，并没有为他称作"历史宗教"的出现给出一个确定的时间，关于轴心时期的重要性，请参见James D. Whitehead and Evelyn Eaton Whitehead, "From Consciousness to Conscience: Reflections on the Axial Age," *Fudan Journal* (No. 3, 2001) pp. 132—138 (Chinese Language).

　　[3] Michael Barnes, *In the Presence of Mystery: The Story of Human Religiousness*, p. 309.

　　[4] Paul Lakeland, *Postmodernity: Christian Identity in a Fragmented Age*, p. 91.

　　[5] Daimund O' Murchu, *Quantum Theology*, p. 21.

　　[6] Lakeland, *Postmodernity*, p. 102.

　　[7] In *Religion and the Individual*, Daniel Batson, Patricia Schoenrade and Larry Ventis 在宗教动机的不同功能方面提供了理论的背景和经验发现，请参见第 155—364 页。

　　[8] Robert Bellah, *Beyond Belief*, p. 44.

第三部分　宗教·中国与未来

第九章　作为道德资本的中国宗教传统

　　　　本章将探讨至今仍然普遍流行的中国民间信仰的理想和形态。这一关注点得到了对经济特区——深圳的经验研究的支持。

　　深圳，一个与香港只间隔一小时车程的城市，在不久以前还是一个沉睡的渔家村落。1979 年，作为中国改革开放政策的组成部分，邓小平宣布深圳及其周边大范围地区成立经济特区。在 20 世纪 80 年代的第一波向深圳移民的浪潮中，大量技术含量低的劳动者和复员军人是当时最主要的劳力资源，满足了工厂生产和城市建设的需要。到了 20 世纪 90 年代，随着移民深圳第二次浪潮的来临，国内的很多中产阶级都参与到了这个城市的发展中来，或成为管理者，或开始了自己的创业。由于这里引进国外投资可以享受宽松的税收政策，于是深圳逐渐地建成一个拥有千万人口的大型都市。在这千万人口中，有好几百万都是在深圳临时居住的，就是人们常说的"漂族"。他们从事各行各业的工作，但是他们没有深圳户口，其法律权利和各种社会保障是这个大都市要解决的问题。

　　深圳具有很多特点，在中国的城市中是独一无二的。如非本地出生的居民占 90％以上，当前流动居民的平均年龄小于 30 岁。这里的居民在生活中所承受的社会和心理压力，与中国内陆目前仍然盛行的主流生活方式相比，有着引人注目的差异。深圳变化的速度之快，甚至超过了中国东部沿海地区其他发展迅速的现代化大型都市。

但是，这样的经济自由特区并非今日中国的典型代表，不过它可以描绘出中国未来发展的景象。全球化的推动力在这里表现的如此突出，因而，深圳理所当然地成为考察社会变迁对人们的宗教意识造成影响的理想场所。

一、蛇口风波

1988年1月，在中国的改革开放十周年的时候，在深圳的蛇口发生了震惊全国的"蛇口风波"。两位官方认可的大学政治思想工作辅导员李燕杰、曲啸在蛇口工业区与青年座谈，他们曾在国内许多所大学成功地轮回演讲，在蛇口也是照旧以抒情的方式为官方伦理辩护。然而，没料到在场的一位青年这样说："你们到这里来宣传，肯定没有市场！独资、合资企业里的工人没有人会听你们的。我们就是为了自己赚钱，什么理想、信念，为祖国做贡献，没有那回事！报纸上的宣传有几句真话?"[2] 这样，政治思想工作辅导员不但没有机会将"神圣的人生观"以习惯的方式向蛇口青年灌输，反而陷入一场与深圳青年难辨是非的争辩中。政治思想工作辅导员感到在场青年的诘难是对他们献身"主义"的不尊重，甚至感到很委屈，但是却没有意识到蛇口青年并非难为他们，而是由于蛇口工业区按照市场经济秩序运作，为人们提供了一个相对宽松的精神空间。有位青年大胆地为到深圳"淘金"辩护："淘金者有什么不好？美国西部就是靠淘金者、投机者的活动发展起来的。"[3]

"蛇口风波"通过媒体的有关报道很快就被传开了，生活在这个经济特区的人们面临着一次新的挑战。在深圳这样的沿海开放城市出现的自由气氛，为人们提供了工作的机会，这些机会却使得人们从全面供给、全面控制的"单位"[4]中摆脱了出来。个人职业选择的自由度很快超出了经济的范围，随着选择范围的不断拓宽，个人的责任感逐渐地被唤醒了。在何处生活，选择怎样的生活方式，遵从怎样的价值观，现在的人们必须面对这样的问题并作出决定。在这些新移民当中，有人不再拘泥于过去传统中所惯有的价值观念，不再局限于"单位"的体制之中，个人责任的尝试将会唤起追求更多的个人自由的欲望。深圳青年可以没有顾虑地发表自己对人生和伦理相当个人化的观点，不仅将民间对意识形态的挑战明朗化，更表达了人们在实现自我的同时确立属于自己的人生价值观。也就是说，当深圳的人开始在为自己的前途而奋斗和"淘金"的时候，他们也开始了对个体生命的探索。

从 1998 年夏天开始，社会学家范丽珠在深圳经济特区展开了为期 18 个月的田野调查，目的是考察在中国的现代化过程中，个人和社会对这些变化所做出的响应。[5]这些访谈对象中既有男性也有女性，他们都是在过去的十多年中到深圳的。他们或是高级白领，或是私营企业主，总而言之，都已经普遍融入到这个城市之中，成为中产阶级的一部分。

在对深圳进行研究的过程中，不难发现某些普通词语开始频繁地出现在访谈对象的谈话中。为了解释在这个充满挑战的新环境中所付出的努力和取得的成功，被访者频繁地使用某些词语来强调这些深深地根植在中国传统当中的宗教是如何给他们人生以方向的经验。由此我们发现，中国的民间信仰和实践的精神遗产已融合在民众宗教信仰当中，将作为一种道德资本在当代中国继续发挥作用。

二、中国的道德资本

朱迪斯·柏林（Judith Berling）在对 17 世纪的一本小说——《三教开迷归正演义》（The Romance of The Three Teachings）——进

行研究时使用了"道德资本"一词。该小说描述了明朝时期人们在经济利益和道德良知之间感受到的双重压力。明朝是一个社会急剧变迁的时期，在南京附近所呈现的是"充满竞争的城市环境"，这种情形所揭示的社会问题酷似今天的深圳。

该小说要揭示的是：美好的人生就是道德资本不断积累的结果，个人的功德是可以通过诚实而富有同情心的行为来积累的，就像钱可以攒起来一样。这些自然累积的功德成为精神遗产，为子孙后代传承下去。如果一个人在自己的一生中浪费了这些精神财富，他便无法面对自己的孩子，因为结果是没有任何遗产留给他们。在典型的中国传统中，这本小说所强调的"道德资本（功德积累的价值）是一项留给子孙的极为重要的遗产，就如同土地和金钱一般。事实上，对财产长期成功的管理也是依赖于道德资本的，这二者是不可分离的"。[6]

朱迪斯·柏林断定："作为对道德资本的管理，宗教还包括了承担以下责任：学会把握人情世故和协调人际关系，而不是将道德关系完全消耗殆尽。"所以，她主张，"我们认为这是基于宗教的工作伦理，和西方加尔文教的伦理是没有什么不同的。"[7]

正如朱迪斯·柏林对中国历史上的道德资本所分析的那样，非常有影响力的道德哲学家阿利斯泰尔·麦克泰洛（Alisdair MacIntyre）已经验证了个人的美德是如何为一个社会经济的良好地运行做出贡献的。"美德是资本的一种形式，它是以传统的道德资本的形式附着在每个个体身上的，在任何一种可以再生产的资本当中都是找不到的。"[8]

宗教和文化，常常被描述成与道德完善和精神圆满的传统有关。而这种传统往往以集体积累的形式表现出来，既可以作为一份宝贵的遗产而受到珍惜和收藏，又可以作为一种资本为将来做投资。当一种文化或宗教的资源被恣意浪费的时候，文化的认同感将受到破坏，甚至有面临破产的危险。

三、西方社会的从社会资本到道德资本

近年来，社会科学家罗伯特·帕特南（Robert Putnam）和弗朗西斯·福山（Francis Fukuyama）的研究使得"社会资本"这个概念被广泛地用来描述社会赖以发展繁荣的人力资源了。福山将社会资本定义为"社会力凝聚或厚植社会资本方式，……它主要地表现为信任"。[9]对于帕特南而言，社会资本是指一种关联性，这样的关联性让人们感受到彼此的存在，并产生与之相关的信任。社会资本足以促进团体成员合作的非正式价值或规范发挥作用，比如信任是使组织运作顺畅的润滑剂。

> 社会资本的核心含义在于社会网络是具有价值的……就像物质的资本与物质对象有关，人力资本与人的属性有关，社会资本依赖于人们之间的相互联系——社会网络、互惠规范（norms of recipocity）、信任等。而由此产生的社会资本的存量，往往具有自我增强性和可积累性。[10]

随着将"信任"定义为一种社会资本，以上两位作者都指出，社会资本除了让社会变得更加祥和以外，还有更重要的意义，那就是生产更多的资源。社会资本暗含着一个社会通过社会资源方面的投资获得更大益处的能力。如果得不到合乎伦理的回应，那么这个社会也将陷入信任危机；如果一次又一次的信任危机累积起来就有可能整个社会的信任消耗殆尽的话，甚至会带来道德崩溃的危险。

如果社会资本描述的是在某一特定社会普遍存在的人类资源，那么，问题就产生了：这些资源发端于何处？福山认为，这些有价值的资源是来自于"某些前现代文化传统。"[11]他后来进一步发展了这一见解：在社会资本中处于核心地位的信任，"起源于……如宗教、传统伦理等现象。"[12]

"可信性"通常被定义为个人的美德或道德，还可以被理解为社会凝聚力的表现。许诺并兑现承诺和社会制度具有可靠性等，作为整个社会的共识，是社会凝聚力的核心部分。这种公有的信心可以被看作是一种资源，从而产生其他的资本；这种信心既可以不断积累，又可以投资于未来。如果一个社会对他们的道德资本只是一味地使用而不进行补给的话，它同样有被消耗殆尽的时候。

因而在西方社会，现在常常被描述为"后基督教社会"，国家政策和社会规范依赖于一种公共的气质，这种气质扎根于基督教的想象力当中，它不再强调社会成员对社会积极的效忠。这里存在的危机是，一个现实社会的存在是超越任何道德意义的，这和过去是一样的，它所带来的道德资本并不具有积极补充的作用。同样的道理，在后基督教徒时期的西方社会和后马克思主义的中国，政府时常倡导人们要有奉献个人和公共利益的理想。福山对这种现象所带来的可怕的后果做出了评论："社会资本一旦被消耗怠尽，它就可能需要花费几个世纪来修补，如果这种修补仍然可行的话。"[13]

四、道德资本在深圳的运用

"道德资本"这个概念明确地将当代社会行为和所承继的传统宗教价值联系在一起。我们在深圳的研究就揭示了这些精神的资源——道德资本——这样的精神资源与中国当代的中产阶级市民生活相关，他们在这个城市中应对着由于急速的现代化而带来的各种经济的和社会的变化。在讨论他们面对"新世界"所带来的种种挑战时，访谈对象富有创造性地运用了中国民间信仰中的宗教比喻和道德词汇。

对命运的疑惑 周先生在安徽的农村长大。在他成长过程中，民间信仰是受到批判的，所有的宗教仪式都被禁止了。大学毕业后，他在家乡做了一名中学教师，并计划结婚成家。不幸的是，他的未婚妻接受了一个有钱人的追求而抛弃了他。周先生感到了极大的羞辱和绝望，他离开了家乡。在经历了一路上种种挫折之后，他来到了深圳，最初只找到了一份薪酬非常低的工作。3年之后，他有了经验并积累了足够的本钱，开始做印刷的小本生意，如印制银行、邮政专用的信封、存单、收据本之类的东西。在深圳经济快速增长的大环境下，他的业务发展的非常顺利。周先生惊异地发现自己忽然富裕了起来，有足够的经济实力买了新房子，并购置了一辆私家车。

周先生回忆了那段贫困和奋斗的岁月。在那段时间里，他似乎没有因为彷徨和生计无着而被生活目的或意义这样的终极问题而困扰。反倒是在摆脱生活窘境后，他开始反思自己的成功：为什么他的财运这么好，而另一些人同样付出了艰辛的努力，却仍然要为可怜的一点奖金而奋斗？他记得之前，他还嘲笑过信仰道教的父母，而现在，周先生第一次感受到对个人命运问题的困惑是那么迫切地需要一个解说。这个以前想都不敢想到的好运是否意味着将来会有更多的幸运？是不是在他的心里还有对生命更深刻的渴望？在不知道如何将好的命运保持下去的情况下，他开始把自己的注意力转移到了附近的一座佛教寺庙上。他曾一次性地为该庙捐了一大笔钱，同时鼓励自己的妻子参加各种宗教仪式活动，想着这样做或许能够帮助他们维持好的命运。在他生气或感到疲惫的时候，他自己也会驱车来这个庙休息，寻求内心的宁静。

和其他文化中的人们一样，中国人长期以来在个人的命运方面都表现出双重性：一方面认为命是上天安排好了的，另外一方面又认为命是可以被控制并加以改变的。也就是说人的命运既是确定的，又是不确定的。中国词汇中的"命运"就囊括了这种二元性。"命"是指上苍注定的（天命），是命运中相对确定的部分——父母的遗传、在历史上特定的时间和地点等等相关内容。[14]"运"则是指环境和机遇，它在人生命中的出现具有某种灵活性，为人们提供改变命运的可能。[15]

在中国的前儒教时代，正如包筠雅（Cynthia Brokaw）说的那样，"'命'可能是指一个人出生时接受的最初的、先定的运数"。但是即便是在早期，命也隐约地包含两个互相矛盾的观念，既指"预先安排好的，不可改变的命"，又指"通过个人的道德努力所赢得的成功或失败"。孔子和孟子强调"人有为善本身而行善的责任"，自此以后，个人命运的道德尺度逐渐显得重要了起来。[16]

《中庸》将"俟命"的道德倾向与不计后果的冒险行为加以区别："故君子居易以俟命，小人行险以徼幸。"（《中庸》，第十四章四）。孟子同样相信一个人的命运必须要等待。但是他补充了积极地"立命"的含义，人除了关注和接受既定的命运之外，还要履行自己的命运。孟子将这些对命运的挑战过分自信的响应看作是命运更高级的组成部分，例如夭折或长寿："夭寿不二，修身以俟之，所以立命也。"（《孟子》尽心上· 第一章）但是，孟子还是意识到了许多方式会导致人们丧失自己的最大利益。他告诫那些热衷于改变自己命运的人，"莫非命也，顺受其正。是故知命者不立于岩墙之下。"（《孟子》尽心上·第二章）

到了明朝，人们对命运所带来的紧张状态和命运在个人生命轨迹中的影响给予了特别的关注。《了凡四训》的作者袁了凡（袁黄）是明朝人。他幼年时，有一位孔先生为他算命，判定他"县府考学院考名次，并某年补廪，某年出贡，某年当卒，寿五十三岁，无子"。（见《有福读书堂丛刻续编》第17册，第1页。）袁黄前几次考试的名次和年份，完全符合孔氏当初的预言。他就因此而相信命运的安排是不可改变的，心情也因此而沮丧。后来他在栖霞山遇到云谷禅师，云谷禅师告诉他天下只有庸庸碌碌的人才被运数所限定，最好和最坏的人都不受这个定数所限制。"一切福田，不离心造，皆可以人力挽回。"他将一本功过格交给袁黄，"照此奉行，不特富贵功名可得，即希贤希圣，尽在是矣。"袁黄拿到这本书后，就在神前发心许愿。行三千功之后，就通过举人考试；又许立三千功，得到了儿子。袁黄有了这两次经验后开始相信，只要努力行善，就可以改变命运。他原来命中无子，因为行善，就有了儿子。于是再立愿行一万善，以求得进士。为此，袁黄做了很多善事，并一一把它们记录了下来，希望将这些善举积累起来，以达到改变他的命运的目的。这种"功德的积累"既可以影响个人的命运，又可以积累道德资本。就像我们从下面将要讨论的关于报应（moral reciprocity）观念也将看到，功德的积累能够成为对下一代的福报。[17]

　　在当代的深圳，随着经济的快速增长和就业方式的多样化，人们常常会说"把握自己的命运"，而不再依赖于国家的"铁饭碗"，也不再把自己的将来寄希望于体制内的"单位"。在这里，命运一定程度上是掌握在自己的手里的。

　　给大家再举一个发生在深圳的例子。记者彼得·赫斯勒（Peter Hessler）报道了一名年轻女性的经历，这名女性曾经在师范学院里是他的学生。他在那里供职一直到 20 世纪 90 年代末。他所教的那些学生在毕业之后都各自在他们的家乡找到了教书的职位，搭上了"铁饭碗"的末班车。而就在那个年代，这位女性却选择了来到深圳寻求发展。在谈起当初的选择时，她说："（留在家乡）那样做可能会过上非常舒服的生活，但是，我觉得如果太舒服了，就会像死了一样。"[18]在深圳，她有很多的机遇，她期待能够抓住和掌握自己的命运。

　　缘分　王女士"文革"前出生在天津，在她长大成人的环境中没有受任何宗教信仰和活动的影响。她至今还可以回忆起她的祖母——一位虔诚的佛教信徒，试图将她的信仰和祈祷仪式隐藏起来，瞒住周围邻居中的监视者们警惕的眼睛。从大学的经济系毕业后，王女士在天津找到了一份很有前途的工作，后来为了一份更具挑战性的工作她又去了海南。

后来，她获得了一个事业发展的机会，需要去英国学习一段时间。她在动身去伦敦的途中遭到了歹徒的抢劫。她身上的所有东西——护照、现金、奖学金证书全部丢了。在遭遇了这次不幸之后，王女士来到深圳，希望从她男朋友那里寻找安慰。他也刚来到这个城市，但是他没有去见她，并且拒绝为她提供任何帮助。

在感到深深的绝望以后，她决定留在深圳，最后在一家公司找到了会计师的工作。随着业务的提高，她屡获晋升，很快成为高层管理人员，有一份相当不错的薪水收入。现在，她四十出头，对自己的工作状况非常满意，在经济方面也没有后顾之忧。王女士反思她在深圳的生活。她回忆了那一系列痛苦的遭遇，也正是这些事情是促成她来到深圳的"缘分"，使她在这里获得了良好的发展机会。她反思，也许这些让人费神的选择比单一的选择多，也许在她的生命中有一种隐藏的逻辑，对人生的思考在不经意间引导着她行为的方式和生命的轨迹。如果真是这样的话，面对复杂的人生，她怎样才能很好地把握不同的机遇？这种对人生的思考使王女士更多地参加了民间信仰活动。她经常去附近的庙宇和佛教圣地参拜，并且操持组织每年一次的象征慈悲和怜悯的地方性放生活动。

在深圳所做的访谈中，第二个反复出现的话题是关于"缘分"的经历。"缘分"表现在一些偶然的事件或表面上的巧合。这个词语在当代中国人的生活中是很常见的，和英语中"good luck"的含义大致上是一样的。今天的中国人喜欢这样描述令他们感到愉快的事情。例如，在超市偶然遇到了一个多年未见的好朋友，这就是"缘分"。当然这个词语同样用来描述那些发生的不幸遭遇，相当于英语当中的"an unlucky break"。

在深圳，王女士试图去理解自己的生命之旅。她现在富足的经济状况看上去是和目前的生存环境有关，而这个环境对她而言是源于某些事先无法预料的缘分，因而所领悟到的逻辑就带有某些神秘性。在接受采访的时候，她细细回忆了过去那些让她痛苦的事情——失败的恋爱经历，在出国求学途中遇到的被盗打击。但是，现在她意识到这些不愉快的经历——她的坏缘分竟然是她今天的好运气做了铺垫。和周先生一样，王女士用了一个传统文化韵味极深的词语来描述她现代生活的经历就是"缘分"。

在这个反思的过程中，王女士对"缘分"的解释是经过变化的。她说，现在这个传统的词语不再仅仅指简单的巧合或每天偶然发生的事情。"缘分"这个传统文化中的词语实际上包含着极为丰富的意义，在某种程度上可以说暗含了人的生活轨迹。对王女士而言，"缘分"不再是来自传统文化的陈词滥调，而是充满了生命意义，在现实生活中仍然鲜活的字眼。

"缘分"的概念在中国文化的道德资本中是非常流行的，与佛教的"因缘或业"有异曲同工之妙。在正统的佛教信仰中，宇宙万物都是有深刻的道德涵义的，个人的生命历程是由其行为的善或恶决定的。在这样的世界观中，没有什么是偶然发生的，善恶皆有因缘。虔诚的信徒都对此虔诚信仰，以求坦然地面对一切的发生。作为偶然发生的事件而导致的现象——比如一个人推迟结婚日期或者公司例会意外缺席，而那天刚好发生了灾难性的火灾——事实上任何结果都与那个人过去的道德表现有关系，因此是道德资本决定了他的命运。

杨国枢和何大卫（David Ho）已经讨论了这种传统信仰在心理学上的价值。通过"外部归因"和关于缘分的消极结果的归因，让个人理解其与某事或某物的关系。人们认识到缘是一种外在的、前定的、有非世人所能预见和控制的力量，是超越个人的控制范围的。团体有可能"建立和睦的关系，减少冲突，促进社会的和谐"。[19]同样地，个人不能坐以待缘，必须主动探求。重要的是中国人相信缘分不是固定的，要依靠人为的力量来争取，使缘分的观念有助于加强或扩展社会关系。

报应[20]　　沈女士出生在山东省的一个军人家庭，家里父母对宗教的态度基本上是反对的。由于深圳建设的需要，1992 年她和前夫来到深圳，在深圳的新机场担任管理人员。

来到深圳之后，她和丈夫离婚了。沈女士开始陷入与深圳的一位资深官员的恋情，对方承诺找个机会先离婚，然后才能和沈女士结婚。然而一切并不顺利，他们的婚事一拖再拖。在这种境遇下，她非常失落，开始祈求（只是随意，而没有任何目的）各种各样的神灵，希望给饱受感情折磨的自己带来一丝的安慰。沈女士承认，儿时的家庭氛围和后来所接受的教育，都让她觉得这些祈祷仅仅是迷信，但是她不顾一切地继续拼命祈祷。在这一困惑迷惘阶段，沈女士离开了飞机场的管理岗位，开始经营一家广告公司。在这里她全身心地投入，只是想方设法地赚钱，为了获取最大利益，她曾经无所不用其极。

几个月以后，一个朋友邀请她去听佛教大师净空法师的讲座。这位净空法师游历海内外，对生命有着直指人心的认识。大师的讲座对沈女士的触动很大，让她了解到命里的一切是一个定数，所以根本就不需要使用非正当的手段来达到某种目的。"人生的一切都是因果关系，任何果都与前因有关。"多少天来这句话在她的脑海中反复出现，最后使得她开始怀疑自己所获得的一切。她开始检讨自己的商业活动，决定停止所有的欺诈行为，诚实经营。这样的一种认知改变了她为人和做事的方式，在做生意时的理念跟原来截然不同了。用她自己的话说，最主要的是"现在不贪心了"。"以前总是想着怎样把人家的钱赚来，现在不这么想了，而是怎样做好，让人家满意。看问题的方式，实际上就是一念。"然而，她发现诚实经营的结果更好过以往的贪心无度，因此她在现实生活中得到的某些觉悟，已经远远超出了商业活动的范围。

"报应"是在深圳的访谈中出现频率很高的另一个词汇。在道德的领域里，"报应"的观念是植根在中国的传统文化之中的，这种观念中的任何一个人的行为，不论好与坏，都会得到相应的报偿。在《功过格》（The Ledgers of Merit and Demerit）一书中，包筠雅（Cynthia Brokaw）将"报应"的重要性总结为：

> 在善恶体系的宗教哲学核心中，存在着对超自然报应的信仰。这种信仰从中国有文字记载的历史开始，就一直是，而且经常是中国宗教的基本信仰。……

包筠雅将这种信仰定义为：

> 相信某些力量——既包括诸如上帝、神灵这样的超自然力，也包括宇宙间无意识的的反应——势必以一种合理的方式赏罚人的行为：它对某些"善"行予以褒奖，如宗教的牺牲、官方义举或个人的善行；也包括对恶行的惩罚。[21]

报应的核心信仰就像"缘分"一样，认为万物都是有道德的。好的行为具有持久的功效，个人的佳德善行将会贡献于世界的改善。这一信条也可以促使人们愿意参与一些行善的实践，从而构成中国社会做善事的传统。

包筠雅追溯了中国历史上报应信仰的演化过程。在早期有对这种道德报应的判断，比如《尚书》："作善，降之百祥；作不善，降之百殃。"所有这些都假设"上天或诸神是存在的，他们关注着人的活动并且精力充沛地实行惩罚或奖赏"。[22]

到了汉朝发展出有关报应的新解释：

> 报应不再必须依靠道德清醒、行动公正的上天或诸神，而是通过宇宙"气"的运动自动地、真实地反映人的行动。这种复杂的弥漫的"气"组成了万物。[23]

东汉是报应说发展的第三阶段，包筠雅描述了当时追求成仙的黄老学派的活动"为长生不老而践履各种善行：养育孤儿、修桥补路等等"。[24]

最后，随着佛教在汉代进入中国，这种信仰更加流行。报应的观念加入了因果或感应的法则，使得善有善报、恶有恶报的思想在人们的意识当中更加强化了。在中世纪早期，"中国主要的信仰派别儒家、神仙崇拜和佛教，都基本相信某种方式的宇宙感应。"[25]

对于中国人而言，道德修行暗含着某种报偿，常常是超越个人私事的。《易经》开宗明义地阐述了这样的原则："积善之家必有余庆；积不善之家必有余殃。"包筠雅（Brokaw）列举了袁黄的例子。袁黄是明朝时期出生于浙江的一位学者官员，他认为那些通过了科举考试获得功名的人之所以会成功，是因为得益于其祖上的积德行善。于是，他和妻子将他们各自的功德都记录在一个共有的账本上。[26]因而，功德积累不仅仅会对个人的未来生活造成影响，这种影响还会波及到他的家庭乃至整个社会。这些努力形成的功德积累构成了未来的精神资源和道德资本。

杨联生证明了"善书"在20世纪的中国仍然继续流行着。"善书"包含了大量的对"报应"观念的解说。[27]在深圳调查的报告中，"报应"的反复出现进一步证明了杨氏的发现。事实上，包筠雅对明朝"报应"观念所具功能的考察，对理解当代深圳的信仰问题也同样有助益。例如，她发现，"在一个快速发展、价值观和信仰变动不居的时代里"，"善书"作为道德规范的来源，是极有价值的。[28]"报应"观念在明朝时期对中国人生活所形成的挑战，与当代深圳的状况是极为相似的："假如相信人能够创造自己的道德和物质命运，就能给个人以前所未有的力量和自由的话，报应观念也会使人增强对人对事的责任感。"[29]

中国人关于命运、缘分和报应的观念是紧密相关的。缘分无论大小都会影响到个人的命运。但是，对于某些机遇的认识会成为人们在人生中积极争取的动机。另外，信仰在宇宙间的核心部分道德同缘分和报应的概念连在一起。功德善行不仅仅是要在功过格中记录下来，而且更与人们日常生活的各种机遇相关。

道德资本的概念与关系和报应有连带关系。在《礼物的流动》一书中，人类学家阎云翔将关系视为"社会的矩阵，人们从中学做一个社会的人"。他明确地探究"关系"、"人情"在中国文化的"道德经济"方面所扮演的角色。[30]

杨美惠（Mayfair Yang）在对中国市场经济新条件下"关系"的研究和分析中，提出了同样的建议，认为可以将中国传统文化中的资源进行转化以适应当代中国社会的需要。她主张，关系的深层的文化本能也许能够在资本获得和积累的压力中起到平衡作用。"当关系适应于资本主义，金钱就失去了它的独立性。因为金钱的实现必须通过符号性资本作为媒介，而关系则只能通过慷慨的行为才能获得。"[31]杨氏对"关系"作为一种象征性资本持乐观态度，因为这些关系是深深地存在于传统文化中，人们彼此慷慨和互惠，关系可以继续支撑中国社会的良性互动、甚至鼓励人们面对来自资本主义在金钱方面的普遍压力。

深圳经济发展的机会和政治方面的宽松气氛，为中国新一代人提供了寻找意义和生活目标的可能。在当代的社会状况下，现代中国人回到了传统寻找精神补救的内容，来自于传统道德资本的信仰和实践足以帮助他们来适应其所处的现代生活环境和各种挑战。

注释

[1] 本章中的某些内容发表在 "Fate and Fortune: Popular Religion and Moral Capital in Shenzhen, *Journal for Chinese Religions*（2004），pp. 83—100.

[2] 马立诚：《蛇口风波》，中国新闻出版社，1989 年版。

[3] 马立诚：《蛇口风波》，中国新闻出版社，1989 年版。

[4] 在过去的半个世纪中，"单位"在中国人的生活中十分重要。这种

制度支配着包括职业、教育、医疗保障等社会生活的诸多方面，严格地限制着人们的选择。例如，个人结婚需要单位开介绍信，经过单位许可。2003年10月出台的《新婚姻法》取消了这项要求，"单位"制度对中国人个人生活的影响逐渐减弱，可见一斑。

[5] 研究中具体细节的记录和最初的发现，可参见范丽珠著：《当代中国人宗教信仰的变迁：深圳民间宗教信徒的田野研究》，台北：韦伯文化，2005。

[6] Judith Berling, "Religion and Popular Culture: The Management of Moral Capital in The Romance of the Three Teachings" in *Popular Culture in Later Imperial China*, p. 208.

[7] Berling, "Religion and Popular Culture," p. 218.

[8] Quoted in John Gunnemann, "Capital Ideas" in *Religion and Values in Social Life* (Fall 1998), p. 3.

[9] Francis Fukayama, Trust: *The Social Virtues and the Creation of Prosperity*, p. 3.

[10] Robert Putnam, *Bowling Alone*, p. 5.

[11] Fukuyama, *Trust*, p. 11.

[12] Fukuyama, *Trust*, p. 325.

[13] Fukuyama, *Trust*, p. 324.

[14] 对命较详细的讨论请参见 Christopher Lupke, ed., *The Magnitude of Ming: Command, Allotment and Fate in Chinese Culture*.

[15] 唐君毅对命运此方面的评价，请参见他的文章 "The Heavenly Ordinance (T'ien-ming) in Pre-Ch'in China," in *Philosophy East and West*, (April 1962), p. 31.

20 Ibid.

[16] Cynthia Brokaw, *The Ledgers of Merit and Demerit*, p. 53.

[17] Brokaw discusses Yuan Huang in Chapter Two of *The Ledgers of Merit and Demerit*.

[18] Peter Hessler, "Boomtown Girl: Finding a New Life in the Golden City," *The New Yorker*, (May 28, 2001) p. 119.

[19] K. S. Yang and David Ho, "The Role of Yuan in Chinese Social Life: A Conceptual and Empirical Analysis" in *Asian Contributions to Psy-*

chology，p. 270.

[20] 包筠雅（Cynthia Brokaw）以及其他一些学者更喜欢将"报应"翻译成"moral retribution"。尽管包筠雅有时候也用"reciprocity"，（参见 The Ledgers of Merit and Demerit，p. 28）。"retribution"这个词本身带有某些贬义，"retribution"的功能主要是惩罚，而不是奖励。在我们看来，"reciprocity"则能够更好地表达奖励和惩罚的区别。

[21] Brokaw, *The Ledgers of Merit and Demerit*，p. 28.

[22] Brokaw, *The Ledgers of Merit and Demerit*，p. 29.

[23] Brokaw, *The Ledgers of Merit and Demerit*，p. 29.

[24] Brokaw, *The Ledgers of Merit and Demerit*，p. 30.

[25] Brokaw, *The Ledgers of Merit and Demerit*，p. 31.

[26] Brokaw, *The Ledgers of Merit and Demerit*，p. 87.

[27] Yang Liansheng, *"Zhongguo Wenhua Bao，Bao，Bao De Visi."* Lecture given in honor of Qian Mu，Qian Binsi Xuexhu Wenhua Jiangzuo，published by Chinese University press，1987.

[28] Brokaw, *The Ledgers of Merit and Demerit*，p. 3.

[29] Brokaw, *The Ledgers of Merit and Demerit*，p. 119.

[30] Yan Yunxiang, *The Flow of Gifts：Reciprocity and Social Networks in a Chinese Village*，p. 222.

[31] Mayfair Yang, "The Resilience of Guanxi and its New Deployments：A Critique of Some New Guanxi Scholarship," *China Quarterly*，(June，2002)，p. 475.

第十章　接受与调适中国宗教传统

> 本章将展现的是，在深圳这个当代中国大都市，民间信仰活动仍然充满活力；在比较中揭示中国人宗教性新的表现形式与传统实践的相同与相异处。

星期六的深圳，在这个毗邻香港的繁华都市，中午时分，一个非常大的斋餐馆里汇聚了各种各样的食客。有的是全家聚餐，有的是出来逛街要填饱肚子的人。餐厅内高朋满座，大堂外还有不少候位的人。

这个斋餐馆和普通餐馆相比的确有着独特之处。大堂外面的走廊里布置了一个很大的布告栏，旁边还有一排书架，使那些等位的人可以浏览布告栏中有关素食的知识和佛教的道德文章，而不会感到无聊。书架上的书基本上是佛教知识的书籍，在这些书籍中人们可以找到一系列修行和积累功德方面的内容：在当今日益复杂的生活中如何保持内心的平静；如何在和朋友交往、生意往来中保持诚信，如何理解婚姻和家庭中出现的问题，改善身体和感情状况的方式，等等。布告栏引人注目的内容还包括海内外高僧大德的演讲以及居士们研讨会的通知。当在餐桌前就座后，那些年轻的服务生会引导顾客到摆放自助食品的中央部位，那里有大量冷热的素食供人选择。

餐厅中，人们不仅有规则地选取食物，品尝食物，同时还有人离开餐桌经过厨房到餐厅的后面去察看。原来，这个餐厅特别开辟了一个厅专供讲座使用。这个厅的门是关闭的，当有人走过来，一个老年妇女会把门打开，请人进去。里面已经有人席地而坐。这个厅的前方是一个小的佛龛，房间里没有多余的家具陈设，所以来人都是要坐在地板上。

这个讲座大约有三四个小时，五位穿着佛教僧衣的年轻法师主持这一系列的仪式，如在佛像前焚香行礼，大声地诵经。餐厅的顾客来来往往，一些人加入到法师主持的仪式中，多数人只是坐在里面静静地看着。

这时，一个中年的法师走进来，房间里的人和年轻的法师很尊敬地向他致意。很快这个厅里就挤满了人，还有一些人因为无法进入而失望地离开了。这位法师开始讲话，拥挤的人群立刻肃静下来。演讲结束，众人散去，法师离开，房间重新恢复了餐厅的功能。

大家可能疑虑餐馆里为什么会有这样的活动？宗教的仪式为何以这种形式举行？一个普通的餐厅——深圳正常的经济活动的一部分，不是一个正式的宗教场所，这里却在举行佛教的仪式，显然和尚们在这种场合扮演了重要的角色。不过和尚们不是发起人，发起人是几位自认是佛教徒的人。这个活动的组织者杨先生是餐厅的经理。杨先生把在这个餐厅里的经营活动——提供素食和道德修行的系列图书、不断通报当地宗教活动信息以及一些参与仪式的机会等，作为其个人信仰实践的重要内容。

深圳作为中国大陆毗邻香港的都市，现代化的力量与人们寻求精神意义的活动交互影响。市民中的中产阶级有选择地从中国本土文化传统中吸取营养，支持其个人的精神追求。不过在这种新的宗教环境下，传统因素也经过一番调整以适应于新的生活状况。于是，在迅速发展的城市环境中，精神意义的寻觅更多也体现为强调个人选择的特征。

一、深圳的精神寻觅

在深圳这个大都市，根据中华人民共和国法律而被官方认可的五大宗教——道教、佛教、伊斯兰教、基督新教和天主教都有其活动的场所。准确的信徒数字很难掌握，虽然像很多其他地方一样，信徒数量不断增加。但是，通过在深圳的田野调查也发现，人们对中国现代化的观察普遍关注经济发展的部分，没有注意到民众对精神方面的需要。而事实上，在深圳这个现代化程度较高并且十分世俗化的城市中，宣称自己信仰某一宗教的人日渐增多，其中自认为信佛的人又占很大的比例。这些信徒非常坦率地表明自己的宗教信仰和对佛教信仰的认识与执着程度，以及对宗教的热忱等，这样的发现远远地超出了学者们通过文献研究和目前中国大陆有关宗教政策探索所得出的一些刻板印象。

范丽珠在深圳的研究主要探讨人们精神世界的变化。由于深圳是个年轻的城市，其所接触的这些信徒的年龄基本上是 20—50 岁之间，没有年纪很大的人。有个非常有趣的状况是多数人坦言在来深圳之前根本没有任何信仰宗教的背景。多数经历过"文化大革命"的人，他们对传统信仰和实践的接纳完全作为个人精神觉悟的一部分。

面对有关意义和人生目标的新问题，这些市民并没有完全转向制度性宗教来寻求帮助，而是在丰富的传统中国文化中寻找个人的解释。尽管在过去的一百多年间中国传统文化受到来自基督教传教士、西方文化影响的中国知识分子、马克思主义政治哲学的各种挑战，但这一精神传统仍然对民众有广泛的影响。

这种共同的宗教传统在中国大陆乡村所保持的活力已经被当代中外学者田野研究所证实。[2]我们在深圳研究中的发现显示，中国民众共同的信仰传统继续给中国民众提供精神资源，而民间信仰中所提供的多元化价值体系在中国社会迈向现代化进程中起到了重要的作用。

但是当很多城市人满怀热情地来拥抱中国传统文化时，这些信仰与实践的经验表明他们并非简单地重复了中国乡村的模式。在深圳，我们看到人们既保持了传统文化，同时又有多方面的调适。所谓保持的方面包括（a）精神关怀的实践；（b）开放的，或如欧大年所描述的"非教派的"态度[3]；（c）自由地从多种精神资源中获得支持；（d）从多元文化中选择信仰；（e）社区支持和信仰结构的新模式；（f）在精神信仰和实践的个人选择方面增强自主意识。

二、宗教在深圳的持续性

精神关怀的实践性 这是传统中国信仰的特点。深圳受访对象的信仰和实践都从日常生活出发并关注生活中遇到的实际问题，如健康和求医，获得好运气，搞好人际关系等等。例如，在电台作节目主持的石女士，坚持每天清晨起床以后，在她书房里端放的观音菩萨像前燃上一柱香，听着佛教音乐（南无阿弥陀佛）默默地打坐。她每天都会在观音菩萨像前供奉水果，随后将供过神的水果分送给家庭出现问题或身体不适的朋友。她认为供过观音的水果已经带有某种"灵"气，会帮助生活中遇到问题的人。她的工作非常忙碌，但是她仍然坚持，她觉得"每天早晨这样打坐一会儿，整天心情都好"。她已经坚持三年了。虽然她会偶尔地到弘法寺去烧香，但是她没有愿望皈依，因为她已经有了自己的菩萨了，最关键地是要在生活中自己去"悟"。

我们看到，人们在生命历程的点滴之中寻找获得意义的机会，基本上是相当个体化的。只是这种个体化的意义体系与传统的神秘信仰有着血源的关系，同时又充分地在社会化的过程中体现出来。所以，个体"宗教性"的意义也就不仅仅限于个体间的行动，而是包含在整个社会建构意义体系的过程之中。

信仰实践从多元文化传统中汲取营养 不知情者一定会为石女士混合的宗教信仰感到奇怪，她家的佛龛既有道教的神像，也有佛教的神像，同时她还有一些独特的个性化信仰。这种创造性地将不同信仰来源的神像摆在一起的做法，可以视为现代意识的一种反映，它注重于自我相关的事物和个人选择。但是我们这里看到的是，开放和选择同时与深层的文化传统产生了共鸣。

历史上中国人的宗教性吸收了多元的文化资源。中国三大文化传统——儒家、道教、佛教的所谓"三教合一"是普遍流行的多元化信仰的核心部分，也是民间宗教实践的重要内容。这种极具开放性的特征，也反映了中国人共同信仰传统的倾向。

数百年来，中国民众的公共仪式活动始终和较为正式的传统儒家、道教、佛教和平共处。正如我们在第四章所提到的，中国民间宗教在发展中不需要创造自己与众不同的仪式和经典，也不需要全职的专门神职人员。传统上，中国人从"三大"传统儒家、道教、佛教那里吸收信仰和仪式，加以调整以便适应民间的需要。迄今为止，根本的世界观始终保持在共同的信仰传统中。

关于佛教的作用，是有目共睹的，佛教对中国人精神世界的影响还表现在它的信仰元素大量地与民众日常生活混合在一起，从而淡化了其制度性的成分。汉化佛教的文化遗产在漫长的中国历史上，始终是民众信仰活动的重要资源。但是，深圳访谈对象在寻找精神滋养的信仰和实践中，并非是明显的或绝对的"佛教"信徒。

例如，多数访谈对象和成千上万的深圳市民一样参加观音诞日的活动。虽然有些人认为自己是佛教徒，但是我们在这里看到的佛教既不与官方认可的正统教义有关，也不是在寺庙和尚监督下的训诫修行。这是数百年来中国民间通行的佛教信仰表达形式，现今编织进中国文化的经纬，成为其重要的部分。

所以多数深圳访谈对象对宗教信仰的理解和实践虽然是历史性的，与佛教有着千丝万缕的联系，但是多数人并不承认自己已经是佛教徒了。很少有人对通过某种正规仪式正式地"皈依"佛门有兴趣，也并不经常到庙里参加仪式并供养师傅，给香油钱。事实上，不少人像石女士那样，很清楚地表明自己不是佛教徒。

下面我们提到的张女士认为自己是个佛教居士，不过，这样的称呼与西方宗教信仰的绝对性还是截然不同的。

地方领袖的主导性　正如欧大年所提示的那样，中国民间的宗教传统，"是由日常生活来决定的，关注于实效和有求必应的效果……尽管有些和尚和道士会做一定的参与，但是这一传统的重要部分表现为老百姓自我领导和组织并延续下去。"[4]在中国的乡村，可能除了一些年长的男性或女性庙祝之外，社区不会聘请全职的宗教专职人员。只有在需要的时候，才会雇请灵媒或道士；只有在必要的时候，才会准备仪式的材料和祭品。由于仪式活动是人们日常生活中自然和永久的一部分，所以那些在村子里比较德高望重和有影响力的人，很自然地会在村里的仪式中担任重要的角色。

在深圳，我们发现民间领袖继续扮演着重要角色，并决定了这种非正式聚会和大型活动的特色。在中国的宗教制度中没有一个统一规定，要信徒捐献占收入的多大比例，而一切均以"随缘"为笼统标准。也就是说要按照自己的实际经济能力及心力来供养寺院和出家人。即便是信徒自己组织的各种民间宗教活动，同样也无法避免一些必要的开销，而所有的花费自然是要由参与者共同承担，因而俗众在活动中的作用就显得很重要了。有不少的宗教活动并非由寺院的法师出面组织，而是由信徒中的热心者张罗的，法师出现只是为扮演仪式主持人的角色而已。而在深圳市内的两个素菜餐馆反而更像佛教信徒的活动中心，每年都有多次的放生活动，其目的是为了提倡佛教的慈悲精神，爱护生物，爱护环境。放生活动由于受到信徒的支持而成为这些中心普遍举行的活动。

放生活动的信息通过电子邮件、电话通知或口口相传，不过很多人并不一定熟识活动的组织发起人。人们把从市场上买来的小鸟和乌龟装进笼子，把鱼类放到有水的箱子，一起运到安排好的放生地点，一般都是在河边或海边。他们还会事前邀请两三位附近寺庙的法师或从其他地方来的法师主持仪式，为放生的动物诵经。很明显的是，这些普通的民众是这样集体活动的策划者和主人。

在深圳，这些民间的领袖与乡村传统中的领袖不同。这些领袖基本上具有愿意作为活动召集人的个性和号召力，同时也在经济方面有一定的能力，可称之成功的新移民。比如张女士承担了大量活动的组织工作。她将此作为个人修行的部分，同时还十分主动地邀请其他寺庙的高僧到深圳，与对佛教有兴趣的人非正式地聚会。一位很成功的商人经常在家中招待远处来的法师，于是他的宅邸也就成为居士们的聚会之处了。

在这样的都市环境中，职业宗教人员不是这种松散的信徒网络的核心，相反他们只是被邀请来的客人。那些参加聚会的信众通常会给师傅们一些红包，作为对出家人的供养。从表面上看，这些活动以佛教内容为主，但是多数民众不会接受只能对某一种宗教具有绝对忠诚信仰的观念，相反他们会对不同的宗教和派别都有兴趣，比如说道教、儒家，甚有人会对文化基督教表现出热情。

传统信仰在城市现代化环境中经过改造调适后，仍然保持对中国民众的影响力，从中主要讨论让我们有机会发现深圳人的信仰活动与传统信仰的某些相异之处。这里我们将讨论其中三个比较明显的不同方面。

三、宗教在深圳的适应性

较宽泛的信仰选择范围 在深圳，一些人的宗教信仰活动就是简单地参与祭拜活动。但是大多数的访谈对象表示，是通过阅读宗教经典（道教故事、佛教经文、《论语》和《孟子》等）以及善书和宗教评论等书籍来寻求深层次的理解。在图书馆和书店里，有关宗教和相关的书相当丰富，图书在某种程度上成了人们充盈精神、得到人生启迪的重要法门。有的人甚至是读了南怀瑾有关佛教的书而感兴趣并接近佛教的。也有人是受了柯云路的书的影响，特别是柯的《大气功师》曾经风行一时。结果，深圳各种各样的途径使人们接触到滋养精神、培育信仰的内容，于是个人选择的就有了实现的可能。

　　越来越发达的大众媒体在宗教信仰复兴的过程中扮演了重要的角色。书店出售的图书为人们提供了生活方式的各种选择和道德指南。正当政府方面再三强调重新回到共产主义理想和价值之际，来自于台湾、香港地区和北美有关佛教和基督教的电视节目和网上的资讯也不断地传输过来。面对这如此众多的可能和选择，深圳人需要、也渴望为自己寻找到适合其状况和品位的精神营养之源。

　　新的共同体模式——斋餐馆的作用　深圳，一个中国版图上的新城市，是新的移民城市。固然我们可以从来自不同地方的人那里听到不同的乡音，感受到千差万别的生活习俗；人们可以保留乡音，保存生活中很细微的习惯，但是，聚集到这里的人基本上是将过去的荣辱留给过去，一切从头开始。也许这就是深圳对年轻一代的诱人之处。当人们享受了能够将过去的种种留给过去的自由时，也就远离了原先熟悉的精神支持网络。尽管在深圳人们可以抛弃过往的种种，寻找"东窗不亮西窗亮，黑了南窗有北窗"的机会，在轻松得没有人知道自己底细的同时，其实也面临着另外的问题，那就是没有朋友。当可以十分直接地将自己的诉求与现实利益结合在一起的时候，同时也就要将与利益无关的温情忍痛割舍，现实中选择机会多的另一面，则是要承受来自于工作与生活不稳定的危机与焦躁。故而，通过个人选择而参与的松散的社会网络，使精神信仰的寻觅者们在新的意识层面上相互鼓励并强化了逐渐显露的精神认同。

　　深圳将人们从五湖四海吸引到这里，这种多元而异质的人群影响到公共的宗教传统。多数访谈对象在某种程度上不喜欢受任何制度性宗教的限制，而是倾向于通过共同体的方式来进行精神修炼。但是，在这种新的都市环境中，中国宗教性的共同实践将用不同的方式来组织。

很多访谈对象与信仰同契者经常地聚集在一起。这些聚会作为一种松散联系的网络，作用比正式会员制的团体还要大。斋餐馆常常扮演着聚会场所的角色，除了我们前面对那个规模较大餐馆的描述外，还有其他几家斋餐馆也是信徒们经常的聚会之处。

在市中心高楼林立处，有一个临街的小斋餐馆和普通餐馆一样，人们随便走进去吃饭。其中不同的是，这个餐馆在明显的位置上有一个小的佛龛。靠墙边是一排书架，上面摆着各种佛教的结缘品，有书籍、录音带、录像带和照片等等。还有一个小的布告版经常有放生活动或者法师来访聚会以及环保活动需要志愿者等消息。

这个餐馆并非由宗教团体开办或有外面的投资。经理是一个没有任何宗教背景，也没有皈依佛门的年轻人。他表示之所以非常投入地来经营斋餐馆，完全是为了个人的修行。一些人来此聚会，一边品尝斋餐，一边分享阅读佛教书籍和修炼的体会。有时餐馆经理会邀请当地的法师或外地来访的高僧大德来此讲经说法。人们在讨论中常常会提到日常生活中的经历，中国传统文化的主题也会提到比如"悟"、"缘"以及"命运"和很多更加丰富的内容，比如报应、因果、轮回等。他们对这些问题的历史发展或正统的理解并无兴趣，而更多地分享对现实生活的体会和感触。他们有时候会邀请一些对中国宗教毫无认识的人一道用餐，以便创造缘分让更多的人感受人生觉悟带来的喜悦。

这种聚会的动机来自于人们对相互支持与鼓励的需求。在日常生活磨砺和宗教实践中，人们内心对超验的向往来自于作为团体活动重要部分的友情和仪式，他们通过人群中广泛的道德修养和觉悟来达到改变世界的目的。显然，中国现代社会道德的建立与维持如果单单依靠民间通过神秘信仰的努力是不够的。但这至少反映出普通人在面对这样巨大的社会转型时，其社会良心没有因物质的丰富而丧失，反而因物欲的过于强烈而产生对精神满足的渴望。在和深圳人接触过程中，常会听到这样的字眼：开悟、做善事、积功德、消业、报应等等。而在各种神秘信仰中都不乏对道德、价值以及人生原则的解说，显然民间信仰对人的影响远远超过了以往的政治伦理。尽管在某种程度上宗教被看作是个人的选择，但同时道德渐成了个人的而不是社会或公众的事。不过在这里暗含着一个条件，即人们在日常生活中包括宗教行为在内的言行举动要符合公共规范。同时，人们对正义、公平、善良等的期望，不仅诉诸于法律和行政的帮助，也在超自然信仰中得到某种合理化的解释。虽然我们可以将当代社会神秘主义信仰的发展视为私人生活的一部分，或由私人生活的角度来考察，但是，这些完全属于个体的宗教信仰选择其实在很大程度上影响着人们的公共生活，使民间宗教信仰在社会中的存在显得更加重要。当代中国人宗教信仰的变迁，其意义也就不仅仅是神秘主义信仰本身，人们对善的共识往往是在超自然的信仰体系中得到保证，比如，涉及善与恶这样简单、平常的道德价值判断。当个体生命的意义得到关注的时候，这会直接或间接地帮助人们重新确立对社会的信心，从而使道德因素的重要性得到了重新发现。

通过信仰和修行来提高个体的觉悟 在这些自主选择的活动中，我们证实了在个人和群体关系中新动力的存在并决定着通向现代意识变迁的特征。过去在中国乡村，全家以至于全村人生活在共同信仰的环境中，共同拥有的价值作为个人经验的保护体。这样，群体要为其成员提供并保证意义系统。在这样的文化当中，似乎不需要也没有机会来体会精神选择的意识觉醒。

"让一部分人先富起来"的经济策略使在深圳生活的人们在精神方面得到了一块"自由地"，"打破铁饭碗"的意义不仅是民众可以吃饱饭，还可以赢得私人的空间和广阔的社会活动空间。因为个人在经济上、人格上的独立，个性、个人尊严的充分体现逐渐成为社会的先决条件，而不再以国家为先决条件，这样又促进了人们意识到自己的个体特殊利益。早在十几年前深圳人就率先提出"时间就是金钱"。经济上的富足，与其说使人们得到了拥有金钱的快感，倒不如说在某个时候因为通过对金钱的占有而开始有了自主感。自主感是现代工业社会的典型个人特征，这种感觉对于我们关注的这个时代的中国人相当重要。因为唯有能够自主的人，才有可能在精神诉求上表现出真实的一面。"我的信仰跟任何人都没有关系"。

在深圳，如同在典型的中国乡村一样，很多人并不参加制度性宗教团体或者绝对信仰一个教派。但是这里的人们自有理由保有如此多元化的信仰，一些人认为官方认可的宗教团体变得越来越世俗化。尽管深圳社会也流行着各种各样的神秘方式，来自不同寺院的和尚和喇嘛也时常出入，不过人们还是把信仰当作很严肃的事，而且绝对不情愿受他人的左右。

在深圳这样一个新移民占人口绝大多数的地方，自然不会有由于地缘所组成的邻里的和宗教信仰上的公庙祭祀组织与活动。而个人有关超验的经验和对神秘信仰的寻觅都成为无法叙说的个人事件，个人的信仰被彻底"私人化"。我们找访谈对象，希望清楚地了解其新的道德信仰和仪式活动，何以代表其个人的抉择。这样的选择决定是个性化的，因为不受任何来自家庭和村庄的社会压力的制约，其宗教信仰选择的个性化也因为没有政府的控制或政治正统的胁迫。

个人选择是以选择的标准为基础的，这个标准可以用于反映人的觉悟。深圳中产阶级中意识的基本变化证明，既使现在有很多人热切地拥抱中国传统文化的因素，但是他们的信仰和实践经验则绝不是传统的，相反，他们将传统信仰和活动作为一种资源，用于建构一个对自己生命个性化、有意义的解释。深圳人到底选择信仰什么，以"灵验"作为独特标准的中国实用主义为基础——"什么灵验"——他们选择象征方式和信仰实践，以便在治疗、健康和心灵平静方面获得有求必应的效果。在这个最为世俗的都市里，他们选择信仰，意识到任何形式的个人信仰都会有机会发展，当然也可以不相信。在这些选择中，中国共有的精神信仰传统的活力得到重新肯定，并成为中国未来的资源。

注释

［1］本章部分内容发表在 "The Spiritual Search in Shenzhen: Adopting and Adapting China's Common Spiritual Heritage," *Nova Religio*, 9, ♯2 (2005): published by the University of California Press.

［2］See, for example, Robert P. Weller, *Unities and Diversities in Chinese Religion* and Kenneth Dean, "Local Community Religion in Contemporary Southeast China," China Quarterly, 174 (2003): 338—358.

［3］Daniel Overmyer, "God's, Saints, Shamans, and Processions: Comparative Religion from the Bottom Up," *Criterion: Journal of the University of Chicago Divinity School*, 34 (2002): 7.

［4］Overmyer, "God's, Saints, Shamans, and Processions," p. 4.

第十一章 公民社会、宗教与共善

本章将介绍晚现代文化话语中两个很重要的概念："公民社会"和"共善。"对这些概念的讨论提出了当今制度性宗教能够为社会做出独特贡献的可能性。

多元化是晚现代文化的本质特征，知识分子不再受哪一种宗教或哲学单独的主导，换言之，笼罩一切的神圣帷幕不再存在。在这样新的环境下，制度性宗教努力地寻找切实可行的方式来见证人类的价值并提供社会的需要。卡萨诺瓦（Jose Casanova）描述了这种挑战如同"宗教的重新定位，从前现代公共性的形式到公民社会的公共空间"。[1] 比如，天主教和基督新教都失去了其在欧洲基督教王朝时期曾经有的特权地位，现在必须通过努力才能再进入公共领域。在卡萨诺瓦（Casanova）看来，这就要求宗教的转变，发展出" 一套从政府取向到社会取向的制度"。[2]

这是 21 世纪制度性宗教的挑战：宗教以何种形式参与到现代社会的公共生活中，并为社会大众做出贡献。为了帮助大家理解宗教面对的这一挑战，有必要提到哲学家哈贝马斯（Jurgen Habermas)[3] 称为公共领域的讨论。哈贝马斯的观点引起学者、评论家广泛的关注，由此而对公共空间有了更深刻的理解。公共领域是现代民主价值多元化的产物。作为公开讨论的场所，公共领域维持着"一种生活形式，在其间权威对公共规范负有责任，而公共规范则以公民中普遍的、公开的和理性的讨论为基础"。[4] 这些规范不是由政府所赐予，也不是任何一个有特权的宗教机构来决定的。相反，规范出自公众的讨论，并在公开争论中越辨越清楚。

其他西方社会理论家以公民社会（civil society）来认定这种自由的公共话语。在当代生活中，很多不同类型的社会组织都不在政府或经济组织的有效控制下，比如在西方，私立教育机构、公共媒体和自由出版机构是公民社会的一部分。公民社会包括将有相同爱好的人结合起来的志愿组织。例如，医生协会、律师协会或教师协会。还有非正式组织，以成员募款来支持文化生活——博物馆、艺术展、音乐演出。因为某些特别的问题或事情，比如家有严重病患孩子的家长、试图战胜某些不良癖好、新移民问题等，人们经常性地聚集在一起互相帮助。社会学家赵文词（Richard Madsen）将公民社会定义为"一种生活的领域，这里传统忠诚的实现不再具有意义，人们更在乎彼此间需要的相互满足"。[5]

在一个多元化的民主社会，任何个人或团体都可以自由地参与到这个公共"自由域。"在很多国家，宗教制度在公民社会中找到了位置。尽管宗教的声音只是公共对话中的一种，其独特的作用在于提出意义和道德的问题，但这些问题往往被社会其他方面所忽略的。卡萨诺瓦描述了宗教的这种特别贡献："通过进入公共领域，影响某些问题的公共讨论，宗教迫使现代社会在日益官僚化的社会结构中有机会反映公共和社群的意见。"[6]

一、公民社会：有关意义对话的舞台

什么是公民社会？公民社会或公共领域是指在政府与私部门间的中间部分。公民社会是社会生活的领域，既不是由官僚体系来认可，也非经济市场的生产需要。社会分析家本杰明·巴伯（Benjamin Barber）注意到，公民社会"不是我们投票的地方，也不是我们买卖交易的场所"，而是"我们与邻里交谈的地方，为社区学校计划一个慈善义演，讨论我们的教会……能够收留无家可归的人……"[7]巴伯在其描述中归纳到："公民社会因此是公共的，不带半点强迫的，志愿的而非任何人私有的。"

公民社会，正如社会伦理学家阿伦·沃尔夫（Alan Wolfe）观察到的那样，"带我们进入到与其他人的联系中，在这样的途径中我们不得不承认我们对于他人的依赖。"[8]很多各种各样的群体在公民社会中非常活跃：邻里协会采取行动确保社区运动场安全地为孩子们使用；志愿者在社区医院为艾滋病患者提供帮助；年轻人义务地召集一起修复娱乐中心。

公民社会成就了什么？在多元化的现代社会，没有任何一个宗教传统成为社会规范的监护者或担保者，相反，市民自我必须对道德义务有责任感。公民社会是一种具有媒介作用的空间，现代社会的成员有能力认识并描述其共有的价值。在这里，市民们打造他们的道德，包括认识到去欣赏不同道德观的意义，培养当代相互妥协让步所需的能力技巧。

公民社会的一个独具的特征是民众不再局限于旧有的"我的"道德遗产或"我的"宗教传统，而是愿意和那些带有不同价值观和不同文化遗产的人接触。阿伦·沃尔夫（Alan Wolfe）对公民社会有如下的评论："社会实践使我们能够移情他人，尽管是陌生人或晚生后辈。"[9]

沃尔夫注意到，公民社会的讨论"并非通过更自由的市场逻辑来运作，而是按照早于资本主义的旧的道德逻辑"。[10]因此，在这样的聚会中，价值的问题并不是根据市场的经济标准自动解决的。这里需要价值和意义的另外创造者。友谊的价值是什么？社会团结的价值是什么？"相互拥有的"感觉是如何在公民参与的多元化中被熔炼出来？这些价值的判断不是根据金钱方面的逻辑所决定的，而更明显的是一个社团必须决定并维护的道德价值的问题。

赵文词（Richard Madsen）强调在公民社会中社区所蕴含的力量："扩展公民社会的道德范围是很关键的，公民社会组织不仅只是利益群体，更是具有社区属性。"[11] 通过更大范围的对话（对话常常是市民参与的一部分），一个原本始于对个人利益狭隘关注的团体会发展进入社区，更多地关注支撑共同福祉的较深层次的价值。沃尔夫（Wolfe）补充道，在公民社会中我们将自己的时间和精力献给公共的项目，因为这些中介机构"给予人们真正的希望，共同的行动产生出的结果是值得为此而努力的"。[12]

二、共善：关注意义的对话

共同的行动支持一个共同的福祉——共善。在西方社会理论中，这个词明显带有传统色彩，与公民社会的现代概念有关。在天主教漫长的哲学传统中，共善被看作善治的目标和责任。在共善这个概念的核心部分，有着对人类生活的利益或福祉的理解，不管私人的或个人的。从这个角度看，人类社会的基本福利——如政治自由、普遍教育、有保障的医疗，这些并没有被恰当地理解为"个人的权力"。尽管理论上这些福利应该由社会来提供，但不可能个人性地获得或私人化地保有。这些是公共福利——"我们应该作为公共物品来掌握，愿意共同来实现。"[13]

在中世纪早期哲学家讨论之始，天主教社会思想已经确认追求公共福利是人类社会所有正当形式中的基本事业，人类的尊严和社会的发展都有赖于这个目标的实现。今天继续这一讨论，天主教教会已经将共善（共同福利）定义为"社会生存状况的整体，取决于男人和女人们能够完全地和方便地获得其福祉"。[14] 天主教的道德传统也以公民社会的参与性与公共福利相关，从而得到发挥作用的机会。

在基督教王国时期的欧洲，公共福利常常被认为是占主导地位的宗教世界观、价值和规范的体现。晚现代社会的多元化已经扩大了公共福利的内容，于是公共福利也就包括了范围更广泛的需要和更深远的价值。

对公共福利的批评　公共福利作为社会目标的共同认识挑战了个人主义，这在今日西方社会依然是很普遍的现象。很多世俗批评家坚持认为现代社会太多元化，以至于像共善这样的概念很难具有任何意义。今天的社会生活已经碎片化，各种不同的群体表现出不同的价值，使得在相同社会里生活的市民拥有迥异的文化和道德信仰。评论家们对此很担忧，因为在这种普遍的多元化背景下，只有通过政府的强制才能够令某一项公共福利计划得以实施。

其他评论家认为社会的工具性倾向仍然主导着西方社会理论。这种观点认为，人类社会需要"安全和繁荣，而不需要干扰个人和他们的自由与权力"。[15] 在这种世界观之下，没有天然的团结，团结成为公共福利（共善）的基础。而事实上，社会由各种利益集团构成，有时候为了个人安全和财富不断增长的目的，社会会被迫使做出让步。

对公共福利概念的批评同样来自于一些保守的基督徒。受到政府腐败和公共道德败坏等现实的困扰，基督教思想家"越来越不相信法律、政治、政策和公共领域会轻易受到道德变化的影响"。在这些信徒中，"强调个人皈依占据优先地位，甚至优先于社会变迁的需要。"对这一类宗教信徒来说，"在基督教社区外的基督教价值完全地不可思议"，而"相对于基督教伦理来说，公民道德是要消除的一种妄想"。[16]

其他基督教思想家也参与到相关的争论中。神学家罗宾·洛维（Robin Lovin）坚持认为真正的道德"会在基督教社区中得到了解，基督教社区要求的是一个市民社区的参与，纵使虚伪、自我利益和没有道德，都呈现在那里"。罗宾·洛维与很多当代基督徒的信念一样，认为天主教和基督新教一样在上帝的概念下，

"当我们怀着信心走进社会时，要比在一个与世隔绝的环境紧闭自我，更能够全面真实地享受我们的生命。"[17]

共善，人权和宗教 人权的现代概念开启了对共善（公共福利）的更广泛的理解。人权的概念确切地说是现代性的一种发展。人权宣言（The Declaration on Human Rights）是由联合国在1948年颁布的，从此开始了对所有人类基本权力的更广阔的理解。"人权目录是人类历史上第一个获得普遍共识的有关道德范畴的内容。"[18]

人权的概念已经伴随着现代性的进步获得了进展。在19世纪的进程中，现代国家确认了公民的某些经济权力，比如私有财产权以及买卖商品的权力。这些被评价为"人类发展必须的物质条件"[19]。"文化权力"基本上是群体的认同和自我决定，它出现在20世纪的讨论中。21世纪面临着道德自由的问题，也就是说，每一个个体有权力来形成或遵循个人的良知。[20]

普遍人权的概念平衡了启蒙运动以来将人类社会简单地理解为一种契约性安排的观念。正如哲学家玛丽·米奇利（Mary Midgley）所注意到的那样，启蒙运动理想本身具有积极的影响，特别是在克服旧有的"君权神授"观念方面。[21]但当启蒙思想走到了极端，社会契约理论则暗示社会只有通过个人间契约的方式才能被整合在一起，契约的构成——最终地——是追求个人的自我利益。在这个角度下的道德，也被看作是个人间自由契约的结果，并且唯一可依赖的就是自由契约。在这样的社会，不再强迫个人要承担起对他人的责任，特别是任何人都没有必要对他人和不在自己国家的社会契约内的人承担责任。

对普遍人权的认识重新建构了超越个人自我利益和社会公共道德的理想。正如哲学家观察到的那样，"只有在他人能够做到利人利己的情况下，我们每个人才可以完满我们的自我善行……"[22]

天主教、基督新教为共善（公共福利）提供了文化背景，通过一个逐渐的过程缓慢地承认了普遍人权的概念。许多历史事实帮助我们认识到这种迟缓的过程。中世纪哲学的处境在于"过错者没有权力"，致使很多宗教领袖坚持那些不是天主教徒的人也不能与教会所尊崇的信仰相左。后来，在法国大革命中，暴力和反教权主义成为对个人化政治权利的诉求，并进一步威胁到教会。这里再次显示，人权似乎与宗教价值和宗教机构在当时享有的特权有冲突。正如社会学家约翰·科尔曼（John Coleman）所评价的那样，在相当长的历史时期内，基督教教会较好地"照顾人的需要"而不关心人权问题。[23]

共善（公共福利）是一个美好的共同追求。在晚现代民主国家，自由市民必须在各种集会和协会的场合探讨自己的价值问题，以便创造共同的道德观，为整个社区提供发展的最大可能。这里宗教会找到在晚现代参与到公共世界的出路。每一个宗教传统都承载了丰富的道德信仰遗产，特别是对公正和同情、个人的忠诚与相互的责任等基本价值方面很重视。通过将这些价值和信仰带入公共领域，不是作为宗派的要求而是作为思想和理想，宗教机构会在公民社会得到受人敬重的地位。

三、宗教、公民社会和共善

如果制度性宗教假定要在晚现代社会扮演公共角色，那么需要何种变化？赵文词对台湾的佛教和道教团体的研究为我们提供了一些思路。

赵文词调查了台湾宗教性的几种走向，认为宗教性反映了现代化内在动力。自从1980年中期以来，台湾经历了急剧的经济发展和文化变迁。1987年解严以后，出现了"台湾公民社会的春天"[24]。1999年灾难性的地震在台湾发生后，慈济功德会动员了10万名志愿者来帮助营救、清理和重建工作。法鼓山的圣严法师经常出现在电视上，鼓励台湾民众"不要把灾难当作对以前罪恶的恶报，而是作为一个契机，为了下一代让台湾更安全、更美好。"[25]我们看到宗教在实践中出现的变化，个人从内在的修炼转向更广泛的社会关怀，宗教思考将对个人奖罚的关注转为对社会良机的认识。

第二个例子是，在由慈济功德会建立的医学院中，解剖尸体的课程是训练学生所必需的，但解剖人的尸体在传统佛教中是严格禁止的。然而，这种现代医疗的程序在这所佛教支持的学院里常规地进行着。但是，这样的教学实践毕竟是在佛教的环境下进行，"学生在教室中开始解剖尸体之前，他们为死者的灵魂祈祷。在教室的墙上，张贴着他们将要解剖尸体的生前传记，学生们写文章表示其对捐献身体者的敬意。"[26]这样，在面对人类死亡"普遍"神秘的情境下，现代医学实践邂逅了传统的佛教信仰。

赵文词在他尚未发表的文章中提出了一些乐观的判断：

> 佛教和道教具有适应现代性，同时让现代社会人性化的能力。这是因为全球化有助于促使宗教的某种复兴，而这种复兴又会促进不同文明间的对话，而不是文明间的冲突。[27]

但是赵文词认识到由不断更新的制度性宗教所倡导的不同文明间的对话，并非是件可靠的事情。很多因素都在不同程度地制约着宗教复兴和文化间的对话。到目前为止，赵文词对于文明间对话作用还是深抱希望："我们看来对正面结果的期待是有赖于带来好运气的方式，如果用佛教的话说，是缘分（fate），而用基督教的观点说，那是上帝的恩宠。"

四、公民社会、非营利组织和宗教

在公民社会新的社会空间，制度性宗教和非营利组织已经获得一定的进展，都有可能对公共福利（共善）做出贡献。非营利组织的期待是有赖于带来好运气的方式是出现在晚现代社会一个明显的社会现象，在很多国家都以不同的表现来回应人们在医疗、教育、环境保护以及其他领域方面的需要。一些非营利组织与宗教团体有直接的联系，如作为佛教团体的慈济功德会，不断地为台湾地区和世界其他地方提供公益方面的服务。[28]总部设在南京的爱德基金会（Amity Foundation）是一个有基督教背景的民间团体，多年间在中国各地做了大量的扶贫工作来回应社会的需要。[29]还有北方进德是天主教的社会服务团体，它是近年在石家庄成立的一个非营利组织。

在中国，非政府组织同时也被认定是非营利组织。随着这类组织在中国的发展，人们会发现它们在一些方面与西方的同类组织相异。在对亚洲非营利组织的初步研究中，魏乐博（Robert Weller）指出，亚洲国家的公民社会组织常常是"以家族和村落的传统社区组织为基础的"[30]，和西方非营利组织比较，它们较少是志愿的，而更多地与家庭相关联。亚洲的非营利组织都类似地与政府关系密切，而非营利组织在西方则经常采取与政府不相同的态度。魏乐博列举了在越南准非营利组织的例子。那里"退伍军人协会和老年妇女佛教信徒组织"是"松散的组织而且是非常地方性的团体"，它们"提供了动员地方社会关系的具体网络"。[31]

认识到东方和西方存在的差异，我们希望了解宗教价值是否会在将来推动非营利组织在中国发展方面起到一定的作用。比如一些非营利组织，如慈济功德会和北方进德就结合了佛教或天主教传统的道德价值。在第十章和第九章，我们注意到中国共有的信仰传统在当代中国人意识中仍然具有相当的活力。学者们也发现积德行善的观念和做法仍然牢牢地保存在中国民间宗教传统中，这将会有助于非营利性组织的发展具有"中国特色"。

　　近年来，一些在中国国内召开的或国际会议已经在探讨非营利组织在中国未来发展的可能性。以宗教为基础的非营利组织扮演的角色还不很明朗。但是非营利组织的市民方向和有弹性的结构会成为一种重要的背景，制度性宗教将会在中国为共善（公共福利）做出贡献。

注释

[1] Jose Casanova, *Public Religions in the Modern World*, p. 222.

[2] Casanova, *Public Religions in the Modern World*, p. 220；他评价只是作为制度性宗教，较好地回应了启蒙运动的批评，会为"现代公共领域的重新焕发活力做出贡献"。p. 233.

[3] 请参见 Jurgen Habermas, *Structural Transformation of the Public Sphere*.

[4] Richard Madsen, "The Public Sphere, Civil Society and Moral Community," *Modern China*, 19, ♯1 (April, 1993), p. 186.

[5] Madsen, "The Public Sphere, Civil Society and Moral Community," p. 186.

[6] Casanova, *Public Religions in the Modern World*, p. 228.

[7] Quoted in A. J. Dionne, "Faith, Politics, and the Common Good," *Religion and Values in Public Life*, 6, ♯2 (1998) p. 2.

[8] Alan Wolfe, *Whose Keeper? Social Science and Moral Obligation*, p. 18.

[9] Wolfe, *Whose Keeper?* p. 104.

[10] Quoted in Dionne, "Faith, Politics, and the Common Good," p. 2.

[11] Madsen, "The Public Sphere, Civil Society and Moral Community," p. 192.

[12] Dionne, "Faith, Politics, and the Common Good," p. 2.

[13] John Coleman, "Pluralism and the Retrieval of a Catholic Sense of the Common Good," Commonweal Spring 2000 Conference, p. 10; for discussion of Asian concepts of the common good, see Theodore De Bary, *No-*

bility and Civility: *Asian Ideals of Leadership and the Common Good*.

［14］Coleman, "Pluralism and the Retrieval of a Catholic Sense of the Common Good," p. 8.

［15］Coleman, "Pluralism and the Retrieval of a Catholic Sense of the Common Good," p. 4.

［16］Robin Lovin, "Civil Rights, Civil Society, and Christian Realism," *Religion and Values in Public Life*, 6, ♯2, (1998), p. 6.

［17］Lovin, "Civil Rights, Civil Society, and Christian Realism," p. 6.

［18］John Haughey, "Responsibility for Human Rights," *Theological Studies*, 63 (2002), p. 755.

［19］Haughey, "Responsibility for Human Rights," p. 765.

［20］See Alan Wolfe, "The Final Freedom," *New York Times Magazine* (March 18, 2001), p. 48.

［21］See Mary Midgley, *The Myths We Live By*, p. 8.

［22］Alasdair MacIntyre, *Dependent Rational Animals*, p. 107.

［23］Haughey, "Responsibility for Human Rights," p. 783.

［24］Madsen, "Religious Renaissance and Taiwan's Transition to Democracy," p. 8.

［25］Madsen, "Religious Renaissance and Taiwan's Transition to Democracy," p. 7.

［26］Madsen, "Religious Renaissance and Taiwan's Transition to Democracy," p. 36.

［27］Madsen, "Religious Renaissance and Taiwan's Transition to Democracy." p. 59.

［28］See Julia Huang, "Global Engagement and Transnational Practice: A Case Study of the Buddhist Compassionate-Relief Foundation in Taiwan", 见范丽珠主编:《全球化下的社会变迁与非政府组织》,上海人民出版社,2003 年版。

［29］See Katrina Fiedler's essay, "We Change Society, Society Changes Us-The Example of the Amity Foundation." 见范丽珠主编:《全球化下的社会变迁与非政府组织》,上海人民出版社,2003 年版。

［30］Robert Weller, "Civil Institutions and the State" in *Civil Life*,

Globalization, and Political Change in Asia: Organizing Between Family and State, p. 4.

[31] Weller, "Civil Institutions and the State," pp. 7 and 17.

第十二章 中国和宗教的未来

本章将讨论发生在当今中国对宗教的重新评价以及宗教对文化持续的影响，特别是在提供道德方面的贡献等问题。本章以对宗教和人类发展理想的思考来结束。

"宗教确实没有消亡"[1]。前国家经济改革委员会副主任潘岳，在重新评价社会主义制度下中国宗教的作用时提出了这样的看法。他认为世俗化理论所预言的现代性会带来宗教的死亡已被事实证明是错误的。他指出缺乏信仰对中国的危害，认为"宗教鸦片论"使中国付出了沉重的代价。现在，在 21 世纪的开端，人们重新认识到宗教是文化中的永恒因素。如潘氏所表明的那样，宗教现象对中国的挑战在于如何确认宗教的正面价值和确信宗教在中国的存在并能够为社会主义社会的建设做出贡献。

潘氏以提出宗教的三个积极方面来表明宗教会对社会和谐做出可能的贡献。人不仅是物质存在，也是精神存在；不仅是理性存在，也是情感存在。压力与困惑，幸福与快乐，都是心灵对现实的主观反映。很多人对人生中的种种不幸与压抑，需要通过宗教的途径来求得慰藉。他告诫人们，宗教的这一倾向不应该再简单地视为幻想，而是作为对民众和社会的一种纯粹帮助。宗教的第二种贡献与它的道德功能有关。潘氏向中国读者提到宗教曾在理想主义普遍失落，功利主义到处泛滥的时期，成为一种保持信念道德的精神生活方式。如在 16 世纪，当西方工业文明发展过快而导致物欲横流时，正是新教伦理支撑并恢复了西方道德文明。[2]随着社会突然地向市场经济变迁，并伴随着对消费主义和个人财富积累的大力推崇，今天的中国领导人敏感地意识到宗教价值的某些功能。宗教的第三种贡献是其文化的功能。在许多以宗教为文化传统的国家中，抽去宗教就等于没有文化。例如，基督教塑造了欧洲与美洲文明，在那里，文学艺术、绘画雕塑、音乐戏剧、伦理哲学等领域，有许多东西均以基督教为表现形式。中国文化也是如此，宗教文化是中国传统文化的一部分，而中国传统文化又是中国社会主义先进文化的一部分，先进文化指导我们以德治国，以德治国是为了重建我们的道德信仰体系。

潘氏在这篇文章中开诚布公地发表了他的看法，宗教"属于信仰范畴"，并且"探讨意义世界"。[3]这样的认识表明，中国高层对宗教的看法有一个重要变化，不再简单地把宗教看作是本质上的迷信。这种新的观点承认了学术领域对宗教研究的价值，学者也越来越多地将宗教信仰理解为，它是植根于人类的本能，运用语言和其他象征来寻求意义的。

欧大年（Daniel Overmyer）新近发表了一篇对 1994 年以来中国大陆学者宗教研究的书评。欧大年发现在学者中出现新的和更开放的宗教研究视角。例如，他注意到，在《中国民间信仰》一书的前言称赞宗教信仰具有"团结民众的力量，鼓舞其勇气并修养其道德价值"。[4]前言的作者陶阳观察到宗教"仍有它存在的社会基础。下令禁止是不明智的，就如同妄图消灭宗教一样，是决然行不通的"。[5]作为马克思主义的信仰者，陶阳和该书作者乌丙安都认同宗教迟早会成为不必要的东西，以后会"自然消亡"[6]。但是，他们认为在这个时候到来之前，中国政府应该承认宗教能够给社会带来某些益处。

在对今日中国宗教的分析中，潘岳解释了在中国领导人中出现的对宗教新的宽容态度。他注意到，中国共产党已经从初期的"革命是主要任务的"革命阶段转向新的时期，目标是建设一个安定团结的社会。现在，认识到宗教的"主要的目的是作为稳定社会的基础"，[7]所以政党应该不把宗教作为敌人，而作为建设中国小康社会的支持力量。

一、宗教的目的是什么？

在晚现代世界，虽然已经否定了宗教"消亡"的命运，然而宗教在社会上扮演的角色仍然受到质疑。那么，宗教现象的存在是否能够对世界文明有所贡献？宗教又如何表现其贡献？

社会学家卡萨诺瓦（Jose Casanova）观察到："当世俗化的意识形态呈现出式微或失去势力时，宗教作为一个规范的力量又回到公共舞台。"[8]但是，当社会努力地适应全球化的动力时，宗教无疑会面临着在其本文化中失去原有的特殊社会身份的历史记忆和文化象征的危险。哲学家里科认识到文化的倦怠所造成的后果，"我们个人和共同的世界仍然停留在发展不充分和贫困的状态，因为我们不再拥有共同的象征语言来表达在我们生活中超越的不完全和各种意向。"[9]里科相信宗教作为终极目标"有助于我们完善生存的状态"，[10]它在发掘"一个共同的文化象征"而讨论最深刻价值的同时，推动文化的发展。

中国社会科学院世界宗教研究所所长卓新平，强调宗教传统和一种文化道德生活之间的密切关系，"作为人类文化传统的源泉，道德植根于世界的各种各样的宗教中，并通过宗教表现出来。"[11]根据他的判断，宗教不是附加在文化生活上的现象，"宗教和其道德资源是人类文化和精神传统的重要组成部分。"[12]卓氏在此所论之道德不完全是某个宗教中规范和戒律的内容，而是包含了更深的道德意向来引导人们在世界上生活。

二、定位：后现代世界我们的出路

后现代性的一个特征就是"以往生活经验中最基本的坐标性

内容崩溃了，这种崩溃包括时间、空间和秩序"[13]。更直接地讲，在这深刻的变迁时代，很多人彷徨无定。哥白尼学说的革命（Copernican revolution）使人类不再享有宇宙中心的优越感；达尔文的进化论理论把人类从原来在自然世界的特殊地位上拽下来了；永远进步的现代性神话的幻灭，逐渐蚕食了人类对未来的希望。世界范围出现的关于道德价值的问题，不论是对个人还是社会整体来说都是相当混乱的。晚现代世界几乎没有了可靠的人生路标。

哲学家南乐山（Robert Neville）谈论到人类对普遍的和稳定的人类天性已经失去了信心。"晚现代关于人类共性的观点是我们必须关注人的本性。任何对人类本性的定义都一定会带有我们自己阶级和社会身份的成见。"[14]但是，南乐山坚持认为"如果没有我们完全可以依赖的人性"，会有"一些与之近似的规范，决定我们责任义务内容的一个定位方向"。[15]

与早期过于自信的西方分析不同，南乐山提出一个更中国化的路径。他建议不要忘记"我们要熟悉世界的情况，我们能够通过恰当的行为和坚持均衡以及保存道德中的和谐来展现人性的方向"。[16]以这个视角看，道德自我发展在寻求个人良知普遍标准的过程中，较少需要通过内在的东西，而更多地要通过朝着外在世界以及大量迅速变迁的环境。

对南乐山来说，定位方向是我们自己如何与多样化的环境保持和谐关系的问题，即我们与亲友间的关系网，我们与自然世界相关的周围事物，我们的人道和宗教目的的终极状况。

南乐山提出："确定方向指的是，在这些途径中我们让自己与生存的某些部分，或者生存的范围相适应。而生存方式具有其特有的性质和规律。"他补充道："定位意味着情感上的态度，以及理解与反映的习惯……"[17]因此，对万事万物的一个恰当的定位包括惊异与尊敬的情感；我们对相互彼此的定位包括感激与慷慨豁达的反应。

对南乐山来说，"平衡"对"现实生活中的不同方向起到协调的作用，它有助于我们领悟并回应永远变动不居的各种各样的存在，因为这些存在常常很难天衣无缝地相互配合"。[18]

宗教提供信仰和活动，帮助人们确立基本的人生方向——面对他人，面向世界，面向其终极处境。它通过创造永恒的象征、经典故事和仪式，作为生活的指南，帮助人们和社群找到恰当的道路，这就是宗教传统在现代社会存在的作用。

在晚现代世界确定我们的方向　彷徨的形象既有文学的意含（如在一个陌生的城市，初来乍到的人会走错路，甚至会迷路），又有隐喻性的指向（个人困惑于生活中太多的选择和可能性，不晓得该"走哪条路"）。"确定方向"隐喻的吸引人之处是兼有地理上的概念：一个是我们提供的地域，一个不是我们自己创造的环境，它决定何处适合我们以及我们如何处理的机会。这个隐喻提示我们：地图、观星仪和地球定位系统及其他飞行仪器的价值。

西方文化的经典，比如早期希腊故事奥德赛（Odyssey）和关于《圣经》的书籍，包括了充满危险的海上探险和自由旅行，他们的故事描述了失去方向的危险和新发现的安慰。这些经典还描述了一个需要不断重新调适的人世，一个帮助人在繁复的变迁中保持协调的世界。

宗教强调在时空中，在同时面对稳定与变化之际的方向问题。中世纪天主教的世界观创造了一个神圣的天堂在"上"，地狱在"下"的宇宙论。诗人布朗宁（Robert Browning，1812－1889）写道："上帝在他的天堂，世界万物均无恙！"来表述这种足以慰藉的精神定位。穆斯林每日为自己确定方向（兼顾地理和心灵上的），当他们在每天例行的祈祷中鞠躬时朝向麦加（Mecca）。在中国的传统中，风水提供了一种实践，将物理上的方向定位与人类直接的和终极的状况联结在一起。

宗教传统同样及时地提供方向。根据圣经七天创世的记载，犹太教徒将每礼拜六作为安息日（Sabbath）举行仪式，那是每个星期休息的日子。基督新教和天主教徒继续这种仪式取向，但是将仪式的时间改为礼拜日，即主日。穆斯林将礼拜五作为他们一周内的圣日。宗教活动构成了充斥于日历，即便不列在日历上，也总是人们实际生活方式的重要表达。

宗教通过发展仪式来支持精神方面的定位。哀悼和悲伤的礼仪给因为失去亲人而出现的混乱状况带来新的秩序。节奏缓慢的葬礼仪式通过规模不大但是很有意义的方式，逐渐消除了因为哀伤出现的混乱与彷徨。在天主教传统中，安魂仪式为人们提供了认识失败和罪过以及寻求宽恕、安慰的机会。每个宗教传统都有特别的仪式，如感谢上天所赐之福的秋天收获时节的宴席，新年时的庙会以及生日和婚礼。诸如此类的庆典塑造了人们的意识。引导参与者向往着生活世界的美好与善良，宴乐仪式滋养着感激报恩的心情和慷慨豁达的胸襟。

在晚现代世界，很多仪式已经不具备提供方向的功能，天堂与地狱的宇宙观现在看来有些奇怪了，购物商场、运动场馆和电影院占据了以前用于休息的时间。显然，对于人类来说，寻找生活方向还是在继续。

道德取向 最新的关于伦理的讨论开始接受人类"确定（在这个世界的）自我方向"的概念。神学家施韦克（William Schweiker）观察到："在道德认识方面，我们并非简单地发现或领悟有关此世的任何道德上的教训，而是希望在这个世界安顿我们自己。"[19]道德生活不是一个发现描述道德详图以便给人们提供遵循步骤的问题，当代道德要求我们判断，该站在何种立场以及在哪个位置上转向进行更快速的决定。斯庞把这个隐喻解释为："生活的宗教通过与有秩序的客观环境的联系来帮助自我调理；通过在此世的存续参与来为自己安身立命；通过形成意向来认识世界以便激励个人。"[20]

传统基督教的定位是朝着"上面的天堂"的，如今已经被面向"外面的地平线……"的认识所代替。查尔斯·泰勒认为人类已经具有一种能力去判断某些东西比其他的东西更有价值。查尔斯·泰勒称这种"卓越的判断"是一种从直觉而产生的洞察力，并得到成熟感情和生活经历的支持。一些好人值得我们的尊重，因为我们相信他们具有的内在价值。比如，对某人与生俱来之品性的赏识，或对一个受伤者给予同情的表达，我们所感受的这些价值是"对个人的召唤或要求"。[21]

人类认识基本价值的能力是道德判断的实践。这些判断，依次创造了"道德框架或界限"，并"在道德空间安顿人们的心灵"。[22]查尔斯·泰勒提醒我们有很多此类的道德框架。比如，马克思主义和女性主义作为道德方向，对当今人们的生活选择具有一定的影响。类似的还有当前的道德悲观主义者，他们认为人类在全球化时代的迷失，是因为全球化将世界引入了新的"黑暗时代"，基本上是以一种负面的概念作为决定和行为的道德标准。

当社会处于相对平稳的时期时，道德的界限是相似的和有规律的，这样人们几乎很难注意到价值取向对自己选择的影响。但是，剧烈的社会变革会导致人们方向的迷失，而这种经历迫使人们质疑现存的道德框架。在人们常常感觉到威胁存在的同时，也使可靠性选择的出现有了可能的机会。在变化多端的时期，我们不能不对价值做出选择，因为价值塑造着我们的生活。要做到这一点，就要恢复我们在道德世界的平衡稳定。

在我们的世界里，为自己定位是一个意义创造的实践。如在第一章所讨论的那样，当人们向"终极状况"（宇宙及其目的）的问题和有限的问题敞开心扉时，创造意义就成为明白无误的宗教的了：我生命的目的是什么？人们为什么样的价值而活着？世界上是否有值得为之献身的价值？很多当代民众从哲学或科学、自然或艺术中获取营养，进而探讨这些终极意义的问题。但是，有事实证据表明，对于越来越多的人们来说，在世界范围内制度性宗教的信仰传统，如佛教、天主教、基督新教和伊斯兰教，提供了社会认同和道德取向的基础。

三、宗教与人的发展

对宗教角色在晚现代世界的更深层次观察，表现在对人类发展理想的思考。跨越不同的文化，这一理想代表了"更多"的超越：超越个人有限性和社会分化的界限，对所有一切进入到更全面生存之愿望。当这样的理想被广泛地接受，人类释放自我的有效方式仍然是保持今日的竞争。

在西方文化中，亚里士多德是最早比较详细地讨论这一理想的思想家之一。他写道：社会最佳的状况是每个人都能够感受到生活的完满（eudaimonia 希腊文）。带有现代西方思想的个人主义倾向，希腊语 eudaimonia 或"茁壮成长"常常被解释为"个人幸福"。亚里士多德个人利己主义的见解受到今日强烈的挑战。例如，哲学家玛莎·努斯鲍姆（Martha Nussbaum）描述了亚里士多德关于个人发展理想的大背景："最佳的人类生活是那种对外于自我的人和物也要怀有丰富的感情包括友情、家庭、财产和财富等等。"[23] 人类不可能独自地发展，只有在信任和友谊、相互帮助和宽容的关系中，人类生活才能日益完满。

道德哲学家阿拉斯代尔·麦金太尔（Alasdair MacIntyre）让我们注意人类社会的相互联系，这些联系展现在家庭、邻里和社会生活这些基本的关系中："如果没有对社会关系中所有成员的善，任何单独的善都难以达成。"[24] 他又说："在我们最无能为力的时候，通过与人为善而获得安慰，使得做善事成为成就我们个人、完满人生的方式……"[25]

里科强调，在一个较为哲学的框架中，这一共同的方面将人的发展成长定义为"在合法的公共团体中，与他人在一起并为了他人得到好的生活"。[26] 最乐观的看法是，人们不仅和他人一起活着，而且还要为他人而活。但是，没有适当公正制度的支持，这些最美好的愿景很可能难以成功。

从当代社会全球化的观念看，亚里士多德关于个人发展的社会观念似乎显出某些危险的偏狭性。在他的想像中，蓬勃的市民生活并不包括女性和儿童，也排斥那些在希腊文化之外的奴仆和"野蛮人"。在希腊，这种观念的狭隘在一定程度上已经受到了亚里士多德同时代的斯多葛学派（Stoic）哲学家的纠正。斯多葛学派极力主张"世界公民"的理想，其目的是使人类超越希腊城邦的地理限制，认识到政治国家不能够在孤立中，也不能够在暴力的相互对抗中发展起来。正如今天很多人发现的那样，人类真正的发展是继承了传统的全球化意识。

在现代世界的发展　近年来，个人发展的理想受到了相当多的批评。其中的批评包括：由于发展的目标呈现多元化趋势，故而理想本身逐渐变得没有意义。另外，人类发展的一个重要内容包括参与为所有人争取公正的活动，比如反对动乱，寻求和平的生活。

一个更有影响的批评来自于 20 世纪出现的各种恐怖事件。战争、恐怖主义、有计划的种族灭绝和屠杀，难道这些历史事实还不足以使任何人类发展的主张变得苍白无力吗？再者，弗洛伊德证明了受到幻想和自欺行为困扰的人类意识的范围。那么，到底什么是人类要永不气馁地追求理想的出发点呢？英国心理学家亚当·菲利浦（Adam Phillips）概括了现代人以各种不同的方式摆脱幻想。他说，在今日世界"我们并非在寻求进步和自觉全部"。那些曾经塑造了启蒙运动的目标，现在好像不在人类关心的范围之内了。相反，很多当代人处理事情的时候更加世俗化，"我们在寻找好的方式来承受由于我们不完善的结果。悲剧就发生在我们因自己的无能而被摧毁时；喜剧则使我们能够获得乐趣"。[27]

痛苦：宗教和发展　关于痛苦的普遍经验常常成为讨论宗教对现代文化贡献的最后关注点。从肤浅的观点来看，人类发展的理想会令人满意地摆脱痛苦。为了获得一个完满的生活和真正的发展，似乎应该这样避免痛苦，而苦难和发展看起来并不是绝对矛盾的。一个老于世故的看法是，承认人类真正的发展不是避免痛苦，而是努力发现将痛苦的经历转变为有意义的实体的途径。于是，宗教就获得了机会，将它的智慧和仪式带给社会。

宗教为人们提供了慈善服务并在一定程度上支持人们对公正的追求。世界各地都有由宗教机构办的医院和救济院，无论穷国还是富国的宗教机构都资助支持了孤儿院和诊所。在支持对公正的追求方面，宗教团体常常会责难强势的文化，敦促检讨和改革社会制度。通过这种双重的关注，包括同情与正义，宗教组织面对人类的痛苦给予两种回应。

现在，人们已经感到没有必要只是由宗教对人类的痛苦大声地说"不"了。虽然在很多地方，人们已经把痛苦当作命运简单地加以接受，认为它是无法避免的。但是今天，人们对各种痛苦有了更多的认知，比如由于饮用受污染的水和缺乏营养造成的疾病是可以预防的。在 21 世纪，每年数百万的人死于营养不良或痢疾，而这些疾病完全可以通过预防而减少对人类生命的威胁。人类社会中有太多的痛苦，宗教能够加入到说"不"的声音中。

在这方面，犹太教有着丰富的表达哀悼的传统。在非常悲伤的时候，圣经人物约伯（Job）祈祷到，"我厌烦我的性命，必由着自己述说我的哀情。因心里苦恼，我要说话。对神说，不要定我有罪，要指示我，你为何与我争辩"。（约伯 10：1）在祷告中做痛苦的回答，就如同艺术或戏剧中悲剧的代表作那样，以承受痛苦的方式来安慰那些忍受痛苦的人。他们的痛苦会被演绎到一个生活故事中，告诉人们即便面对不幸和死亡，一朵生命之花也同样会盛开。

本书前面的章节，我们追溯了苏格拉底和孟子关于超越的暗示。他们的智慧有彻底的人间性，同时又接近宗教的核心部分，承认那些为之生并为之死的价值。对于这些中国的圣贤来说，人的发展绝不排除痛苦。晚现代宗教性的"此世"精神，将帮助人们在此生实际的生存的发展。但是宗教意识保持开放，用查尔斯·泰勒的话说，就是：

我们在不幸和死亡中得到的见识不仅仅是消极的。目睹完满和生命被残酷地摧毁，同时也是对某些超越生活之存在的证实。[28]

注释

[1] 潘岳：《马克思主义宗教观必须与时俱进》http：//newmind40. com/01_10/pyue. htm *China Study Journal*，18，# 2 (2002)，p. 7.

[2] Pan, "The Marxist View of Religion," p. 8.

[3] Pan, "The Marxist View of Religion," p. 5. 在文章中，潘岳提到了正统马克思主义对宗教的理解，"宗教幻想的本质来源于现实生活中的很多问题，在很长一段时间里，既使是科学也无法解释，无知不能给人们提供所有的满足感"。在这样的理解条件下，宗教具有其功能。无神论和科学无法克服民众对死亡的恐惧，宗教却能够做到。潘氏又说："无神论是对共产党员理论纯洁性的要求，而不是对公众的要求。"

[4] Overmyer, "From 'Feudal Superstition' to 'Popular Beliefs,'" p. 114.

[5] Quoted in Overmyer, "From 'Feudal Superstition' to 'Popular Beliefs,'" p. 115.

[6] Quoted in Overmyer, "From 'Feudal Superstition' to 'Popular Beliefs,'" p. 116.

[7] Pan, "The Marxist View of Religion," p. 8.

[8] Casanova, *Public Religions in the Modern World*, p. 227.

[9] Paul Ricoeur, *Figuring the Sacred*, p. 15.

[10] Ricoeur, *Figuring the Sacred*, p. 14.

[11] Xinping Zhuo, "Religion and Morality in Contemporary China," *China Study Journal*, 15, (1999), p. 5.

[12] Zhuo, "Religion and Morality in Contemporary China," p. 9.

[13] Paul Lakeland, *Postmodernity：Christian Identity in a Fragmen-*

ted Age, p. 2.

[14] Robert Neville, *Religion in Late Modernity*, p. 2.

[15] Neville, *Religion in Late Modernity*, p. 44.

[16] Neville, *Religion in Late Modernity*, p. 40.

[17] Neville, *Religion in Late Modernity*, p. 180.

[18] Neville, *Religion in Late Modernity*, p. 180.

[19] William Schweiker, "Understanding Moral Meaning" in Lisa Sowle Cahill and James F. Childress, eds. , *Christian Ethics*: *Problems and Prospects*, p. 87.

[20] William Spohn and Thomas Byrnes, "Knowledge of Self and Knowledge of God: A Reconstructed Empiricist Interpretation," in Lisa Sowle Cahill and James F. Childress, eds. , *Christian Ethics*: *Problems and Prospects*, p. 124.

[21] Ruth Abbey 关于泰勒道德观点的讨论，请参考 *Charles Taylor*, p. 26.

[22] Abbey, *Charles Taylor*, pp. 33—34.

[23] Martha Nussbaum, *The Therapy of Desire*, p. 42.

[24] Alasdair MacIntyre, *Dependent Rational Animals*, p. 107.

[25] MacIntyre, *Dependent Rational Animals* , p. 108. MacIntyre argues here that "communal flourishing will include those least capable of independent rational reasoning, the very young and the very old, the sick, the injured, and otherwise disabled..."

[26] Paul Ricoeur, *Oneself as Another*, p. 172.

[27] Adam Phillips, *Terrors and Experts*, p. 95.

[28] Charles Taylor, *A Catholic Modernity*? p. 20.

参考文献

（一）中文参考资料

1. 《孟子》

2. 《庄子》

3. 《道德经》

4. 胡适："名教"，《胡适文存三集》，卷一

5. 《诗经·大雅》

6. 李沛良：《中国文化的宿命主义于能动取向》，乔健、潘乃谷编：《中国人的观念与行为》，天津人民出版社，1995 版。

7. 杨国枢：《缘及其在现代生活中的作用》，《传统文化与现代生活研讨会论文集》，中国文化复兴委员会，1982 年。

8. 《易经》卷一

9. 《书经》《汤诰》

10. 《中庸》

11. 《有福读书堂丛刻续编》第 17 册，第 1 页。

12. 夏中义：《中国青年》，1980 年第 11 期。

13. 马立诚：《蛇口风波》，中国新闻出版社，1989 年版。

14. 范丽珠：《当代中国人宗教信仰的变迁：深圳民间宗教信徒的田野研究》，台北：韦伯文化出版社，2005 年版。

15. 乌丙安：《中国民间信仰》，上海人民出版社，1996 年版。

16. 范丽珠主编：《全球化下的社会变迁与非政府组织》，上海人民出版社，2003 年版。

17. 潘　岳：《马克思主义宗教观必须与时俱进》http：//new-mind40.com/01_10/pyue.htm

(二) **BIBLIOGRAPHY**

Abbey, Ruth. *Charles Taylor*. Princeton: Princeton University Press, 2000.

Anderson, E. N. , "Flowering Apricot: Environmental Practice, Folk Religion, and Daoism. " In *Daoism and Ecology: Ways Within a Cosmic Landscape*, edited by N. J. Girardot, James Miller and Liu Xiaogan, 157—83. Cambridge: Harvard University Press, 2001.

Averill, James. *Anger and Aggression: An Essay on Emotion*. New York: Springer Verlag, 1982.

Barnes, Michael Horace. *In The Presence of Mystery: An Introduction to the Story of Human Religiousness*. Mystic, Conn. : Twenty-Third Publications, 2003.

Batson, Daniel, Patricia Schoenrade, and Larry Ventis. *Religion and the Individual: A Social Psychological Perspective*. New York: Oxford University Press, 1993.

Bell, Catherine, "Religion and Chinese Culture: Toward an Assessment of 'Popular Religion,'" *History of Religions* 29. 1 (1989): 35—57.

Bellah, Robert. *Beyond Belief: Essays on Religion in a Post-Traditional World*. New York: Harper & Row, 1970.

_____ . *The Broken Covenant*. New York: Seabury, 1975.

Berling, Judith. "Religion and Popular Culture: The Management of Moral Capital in *The Romance of the Three Teachings.*" In *Popular Culture in Late Imperial China*, edited by David Johnson, Andrew Nathan, and Evelyn Tawski, 188—218. Berkeley: University of California Press, 1985.

Berger, Peter, ed. *The Desecularization of the World: Resurgent Religions and World Politics*. Grand Rapids, Mich: Eerdmans, 1999.

_____ . *The Sacred Canopy: Elements of a Sociological Theory of Religion*. New York: Doubleday, 1969.

Berthrong, John. *All Under Heaven: Transforming Paradigms in Confucian-Christian Dialogue*. Albany: State University of New York Press, 1994.

Brokaw, Cynthia. *The Ledgers of Merit and Demerit*. Princeton: Princeton University Press, 1991.

Brown, Peter. *Body and Society: Men, women, and Sexuol Reuni Cation in Early Christianity*. New York: Columbia University Press, 1988.

Bynum, Caroline. *Metamorphosis and Identity*. Cambridge: MIT

Press, Zone Books, 2001.

Buruma, Ian. *Bad Elements: Chinese Rebels from Los Angeles to Beijing*. New York: Random House, 2001.

Carmody, Denise. "Women and Religion: Where Mystery Comes to Center Stage. " In *The Study of Women: Enlarging Perspectives of Social Reality*, edited by Eloise C. Snyder, 262—95. New York: Harper and Row, 1979.

Carson, Rachel. *Silent Spring*. Boston: Houghton Mifflin, 1962.

Casanova, Jose. *Public Religions in the Modern World*. Chicago: University of Chicago Press, 1994.

Ci, Jiwei. *Dialectic of the Chinese Revolution: From Utopianism to Hedonism*. Stanford: Stanford University Press, 1994.

Coleman, John. "Pluralism and the Retrieval of a Catholic Sense of the Common Good. " Paper presented at the Commonweal Spring 2000 Colloquium. This text is available at www. catholicinpublicsquare. org (3/31/2004) .

Concise Columbia Encyclopedia. Edited by Judith S. Levey and Agnes Greenhill. New York: Columbia University Press, 1983.

Connolly, Peter, ed. *Approaches to the Study of Religion*. London: Cassel, 1999.

Cotter, Holland. "The Jade of China, Alive with Meaning Yet Glossily Elusive." *The New York Times*, August 6, 2004, 31.

De Bary, Theodore. *Nobility and Civility: Asian Ideals of Leadership and the Common Good*. Cambridge: Harvard University Press, 2004.

De Bary, William, ed. *Sources of Indian Tradition*. New York: Columbia University Press, 1958.

Dean, Kenneth. "Local Community Religion in Contemporary Southeast China," *China Quarterly* 174 (2003): 338—58.

Dionne, A. J., "Faith, Politics, and the Common Good," *Religion and Values in Public Life* 6.2 (Spring, 1998): 2—3. (A Harvard Divinity School publication.)

Ellwood, Robert. *Introducing Religion from Inside and Outside*. 3rd Edition. Englewood Cliffs, N.J.: Prentice Hall, 1993.

Fan, Lizhu. "The Cult of the Silkworm Mother as a Core of Local Community Religion in a North China Village," *China Quarterly* 174 (2003): 359—372.

————. *Dang dai zhongguoren zongjiao xinyang de bianqian-*

Shenzhen minjianzongjiao xintu de tianye yanjiu.
Taipei: Weber Culture Press, 2005.

_____. "Popular Religion in Contemporary China. " *Social Compass* 50. 4 (2003): 449—57.

_____. "A Study of Modern Chinese Religious Beliefs-The Case of Shenzhen Economic Zone. " Occasional Paper #12. The Centre for the Study of Religion and Chinese Society, Chinese University of Hong Kong, 2003.

_____, ed. *Quanqiu hua xiade shehui bianqian yu fei zhengfu zuzhi* (*NGO*) . Shanghai: Shanghai Peoples' Press, 2003.

_____, Evelyn Eaton Whitehead, and James D. Whitehead. "Adopting and Adapting China' s Common Religious Heritage," *Nova Religio* 9. 2 (2005): 50—61.

_____, James D. Whitehead, and Evelyn Eaton Whitehead. "Fate and Fortune: Popular Religion and Moral Capital in Shenzhen," *Journal of Chinese Religions*, 32 (2004): 83—100.

Fiedler, Katrina. "We Change Society, Society Changes Us-The Example of the Amity Foundation. " In *Quanqiu hua xiade shehui bianqian yu fei zhengfu zuzhi* (*NGO*), edited by Lizhu Fan, 382 — 97. Shanghai: Shanghai Peoples' Press, 2003.

Field, Stephen. "In Search of Dragons: The Folk Ecology of *Fengshui.*" In *Daoism and Ecology: Ways Within a Cosmic Landscape*, edited by N. J. Girardot, James Miller and Liu Xiaogan, 185 — 200. Cambridge: Harvard University Press, 2001.

Fowler, James. *Faithful Change: The Personal and Public Challenges of Postmodern Life.* Nashville: Abingdon Press, 1996.

_____. *Stages of Faith: The Psychology of Human Development and the Quest for Meaning.* New York: Harper and Row, 1981.

Freud, Sigmund. *The Future of an Illusion.* Trans. W. D. Robson-Scott. New York: Doubleday, 1957.

Fukuyama, Francis. *Trust: The Social Virtues and the Creation of Prosperity.* New York: Free Press, 1995.

Gallagher, Michael. *Clashing Symbols: An Introduction to Faith and Culture.* New York: Paulist Press, 1998.

Geertz, Clifford, *Available Light: Anthropological Reflections on Philosophical Topics.* Princeton: Princeton University Press, 2000.

_____. *The Interpretation of Cultures.* New York: Basic

BIBLIOGRAPHY

Books, 1973.

Gilligan, Carol. *In a Different Voice: Psychological Theory and Women's Development*. 2nd edition. Cambridge: Harvard University Press, 1992.

Greeley, *Andrew. Religion as Poetry*. New Brunswick: Transaction Publishers, 1995.

Gunnemann, John. "Capital Ideas," *Religion and Values in Public Life* 7. 1 (Fall, 1998): 3—4. (A Harvard University Divinity School publication.)

Habermas, Jurgen. *Structural Transformation of the Public Sphere*. Cambridge: MIT Press, 1989.

Haughey, John. "Responsibility for Human Rights," *Theological Studies* 63 (2002): 764—85.

Heaney, Seamus. *The Redress of Poetry*. New York; Farrar, Strauss & Giroux, 1995.

Hessler, Peter. "Boomtown Girl: Finding a New Life in the Golden City," *The New Yorker*, May 28, 2001, 109—19.

Hick, John. *An Interpretation of Religion: Human Responses to the Transcendent*. 2nd Edition. New Haven: Yale University Press, 2004.

Huang, Julia. "Global Engagement and Transnational Practice: A Case Study of the Buddhist Compassionate Relief Foundation in Taiwan. " In *Quanqiu hua xiade shehui bianqian yu fei zhengfu zuzhi*, edited by Lizhu Fan, 496－515. Shanghai: Shanghai Peoples' Press, 2003.

James, William. *The Varieties of Religious Experience*. New York: Modern Library, 1999.

Lakeland, Paul. *Postmodernity: Christian Identity in a Fragmented Age*. Minneapolis: Augsburg Fortress, 1997.

Legge, James. *The Works of Mencius*. New York: Dover, 1970.

Li Peiliang. "Shehui kexue yu bentu guannian: li yiyuanwei lie. " In *Shehui ji xingwei kexue yanjiu de zhongguo hua, yan tao hu*, edited by Yang Guoshu, 361－380. Taipei: Academia Sinica, 1982.

————. "Zhongguo wenhua de suming zhuyi yu nengdong quxiang. " In *Zhongguoren de guannian yu xingwei*, edited by Qian Jian, 240－52. Tianjin: Tianjin Peoples' Press, 1995.

Lightman, Alan. "Einstein and Newton: Genius Compared," *Scientific American*, September, 2004, 108－110.

Lincoln, Bruce. "Conflict. " In *Critical Terms for Religious*

Studies, edited by Mark Taylor, 55—69. Chicago: University of Chicago Press, 1998.

Lovin, Robin. "Civil Rights, Civil Society, and Christian Realism," *Religion and Values in Public Life* 6. 2 (Spring, 1998): 6—7. (A Harvard University Divinity School publication.)

Lupke, Christopher, ed. *The Magnitude of Ming: Command, Allotment and Fate in Chinese Culture*. Honolulu: University of Hawaii Press, 2004.

MacIntyre, Alasdair. *After Virtue*. Notre Dame, Ind: University of Notre Dame Press, 1981.

————. *Dependent Rational Animals: Why Human Beings Need the Virtues*. Chicago: Open Court, 1999.

Madsen, Richard. "The Public Sphere, Civil Society and Moral Community," *Modern China* 19 (1993): 183—98.

————. "Religious Renaissance and Taiwan's Transition to Democracy. " Paper for Globalization and Chinese Popular Culture Conference, Shanghai, September 16 — 18, 2003.

————, William Sullivan, Ann Swidler, and Steven Tipton, eds. *Meaning and Modernity: Religion, Polity and Self*. Berkeley: University of California Press, 2002.

Marx, Karl, and Friedrich Engles. *Marx and Engles on Religion*. New York: Schocken Books, 1964.

McFague, Sally. *Super, Natural Christians*. Minneapolis: Fortress Press, 1997.

Menocal, Maria Rosa. *Ornament of the World: How Muslims, Jews and Christians Created a Culture of Tolerance in Medieval Spain*. New York: Little Brown, 2002.

Midgley, Mary. *The Myths We Live By*. London: Routledge, 2004.

Naquin, Susan. Peking: *Temples and City Life, 1400 — 1900*. Berkeley: University of California Press, 2000.

Neville, Robert. *Religion in Late Modernity*. New York: State University of New York Press, 2002.

Ning, Chen. "The Concept of Fate in Mencius," *Philosophy East & West* 47. 4 (1997): 495—520.

————. "The Genesis of the Concept of Blind Fate in Ancient China," *Journal of Chinese Religions* 25 (1997): 141—167.

Nussbaum, Martha. *The Fragility of Goodness*. Cambridge: Cambridge University Press, 1986.

_____ . *Love's Knowledge*. New York: Oxford University Press, 1990.

_____ . *Therapy of Desire*. Princeton: Princeton University Press, 1994.

O'Murchu, Daimund. *Quantum Theology: Spiritual Implications of the New Physics*. New York: Crossroad Books, 1997.

Overmyer, Daniel. "Chinese Religions-The State of the Field, Part II," *Journal of Asian Studies* 54 (1995): 314— 395.

_____ . "From 'Feudal Superstition' to 'Popular Religion': New Directions in Mainland Chinese Studies of Chinese Popular Religion," *Cahiers d' Extrême-Asie* 12 (2001): 103—126

_____ . "Gods, Saints, Shamans, and Processions: Comparative Religion from the Bottom Up," *Criterion*, Autumn, 2002, 2—9, 34. (A University of Chicago Divinity School publication.)

_____ . *Religions of China*. New York: Harper & Row, 1986.

Pan, Yue. "Marxist View of Religion Must Keep Up with the Times," *China Study Journal* 18. 2 (2002): 5—18.

Phillips, Adam. *Terrors and Experts*. Cambridge: Harvard University Press, 1995.

Pollan, Michael. *The Botany of Desire*. New York: Random House, 2002.

Putnam, Robert. *Bowling Alone: The Collapse and Revival of American Community*. New York: Simon & Schuster, 2000.

Rahner, Karl. "Christian Humanism." Vol. IX. *Theological Investigations*. New York: Seabury Press, 1976.

Rappoport, Roy. *Ritual and Religion in the Making of Humanity*. Cambridge: Cambridge University Press, 1999.

Ricoeur, Paul. *Conflict of Interpretations*. Chicago: Northwestern University Press, 1974.

————. *Essays in Biblical Interpretation*. Philadelphia: Fortress Press, 1980.

————. *Figuring the Sacred*. Minneapolis: Augsburg-Fortress Press, 1995.

————. *Freud and Philosophy*. New Haven: Yale University Press, 1970.

_____. *Oneself as Another*. Chicago: University of Chicago Press, 1992.

_____. *The Symbolism of Evil*. Boston: Beacon Press, 1967.

Scarey, Elaine. *On Beauty and Being Just*. Princeton: Princeton University Press, 1999.

Schipper, Kristofer. *The Taoist Body*. Trans. Karen Duval. Berkeley: University of California Press, 1993.

Schreiter, Robert. *The New Catholicity*. New York: Orbis Press, 1997.

Schwartz, Benjamin. "The Age of Transcendence," *Daedalus* 104. 2 (1975): 1—7.

_____. "Transcendence in Ancient China," *Daedalus* 104. 2 (1975): 57—68.

_____. *The World of Thought in Ancient China*. Cambridge: Harvard University Press, 1986.

Schweiker, William. "Understanding Moral Meanings: On Philosophical Hermeneutics and Theological Ethics. " In *Christian Ethics: Problems and Prospects*, edited by Lisa Sowle Cahill and James F. Childress, 76 — 92. Cleveland: Pilgrim Press, 1996.

Smart, Ninian. *Worldviews: Crosscultural Explorations of Human Beliefs*. New York: Scribner, 1983.

Smith, Nicholas. *Charles Taylor: Meaning, Morals and Modernity*. Cambridge: Polity Press, 2002.

Smith, Wilfred Cantwell. *Faith and Belief*. Princeton: Princeton University Press, 1979.

————. *The Meaning and End of Religion*. New York: Macmillan, 1963.

Solomon, Robert. *The Passions: The Myth and Nature of Human Emotions*. New York: Doubleday, 1983.

Spohn, William. "Jesus and Christian Ethics," *Theological Studies* 56 (1995): 92—107.

————, and Thomas Byrnes. "Knowledge of Self and Knowledge of God: A Reconstructed Empiricist Interpretation." In *Christian Ethics: Problems and Prospects*, edited by Lisa Sowle Cahill and James F. Childress, 119—33. Cleveland: Pilgrim Press, 1996.

Su, Xiaokong, and Luxiang Wang. *Deathsong of the River*. Translated by Richard Bodman and Pin Wan. Ithaca: Cornell University Press, 1991.

Swensen, Donald. *Society, Spirituality, and the Sacred: A So-*

cial Scientific Introduction. Orchard Park, N. Y.: Broadview Press, 1999.

T'ang, Chun-I, "The Heavenly Ordinance (*T'ien-ming*) in Pre-Ch'in China," *Philosophy East and West* 12. 1 (1962): 29—49.

Taylor, Charles. *A Catholic Modernity?* James Heft, ed. Oxford: Oxford University Press, 1999.

————. *The Ethics of Authenticity*. Cambridge: Harvard University Press, 1992.

————. "Living in a Secular Age. " The 1999 Gifford Lectures (forthcoming) .

————. *Sources of the Self*: *The Making of the Modern Identity*. Cambridge: Cambridge University Press, 1989.

————. "Two Theories of Modernity," *Public Culture* 11. 1 (1999): 153—74.

Tracy, David. *The Analogical Imagination*. New York: Crossroad, 1981.

————. *Plurality and Ambiguity*. New York: Harper & Row, 1987.

Tucker, Mary Evelyn, and John Berthrong, eds. *Confucianism* and Ecology: The Interrelation of Heaven, Earth, and Humans. Cambridge: Harvard University Press, 1998.

Unger, Roberto. Passion: An Essay on Personality. New York: Free Press, 1984.

Volk, Tyler. Gaia's Body: Toward a Physiology of Earth. New York: Copernicus, 1997.

Weller, Robert. "Civil Institutions and the State." In Civil Life, Globalization, and Political Change in Asia: Organizing Between Family and State, edited by Robert Weller, 1—25. London: Routledge, 2005.

————. Unities and Diversities in Chinese Religion. Seattle: University of Washingtan Press, 1987.

————. "Worship, Teachings, and State Power in China and Taiwan." In Realms of Freedom in Modern China. edited by Palo Alto, CA: Stanford University Press, 2004.

Whaling, Frank. "Theological Approaches." In Approaches to the study of Religion, edited by Peter Connolly 226—274. London: Cassell, 1999.

White, Lynn. "The Historical Roots of Our Ecological Crisis." Science 155 (1967): 1203—07.

Whitehead, James D., and Evelyn Eaton Whitehead. "From Consciousness to Conscience: Reflections on the Axial Age," *Fudan Journal* (*Social Science*) 3 (2001): 132 —38.

Williams, Bernard. *Shame and Necessity*. Berkeley: University of California Press, 1993.

Wolfe, Alan. "The Final Freedom." *The New York Times Magazine*, March 18, 2001, 40—8.

————. *Whose Keeper? Social Science and Moral Obligation*. Berkeley: University of California Press, 1989.

Yan, Yunxiang. *The Flow of Gifts: Reciprocity and Social Networks in a Chinese Village*. Stanford: Stanford University Press, 1996.

Yang, C. K. *Religion in Chinese Society*. Berkeley: University of California Press, 1962.

Yang, K. S., and David Y. F. Ho. "The Role of *Yuan* in Chinese Social Life: A Conceptual and Empirical Analysis." In *Asian Contributions to Psychology*, edited by Anand C. Paranjpe, David Y. F. Ho and Robert W. Rieber, 262—81. New York: Praeger, 1988.

Yang, Liansheng. *Zhongguo wenhua bao, bao, bao de yisi*. Beijing: Chinese University Press, 1987.

Yang, Mayfair Mei-Hui. *Gifts, Favors and Banquets: The Art of Social Relationships in China*. Ithaca: Cornell University Press, 1994.

————. "Spatial Struggles: Postcolonial Complex, State Disenchantment, and Popular Reappropriation of Space in Rural Southeast China," *Journal of Asian Studies* 63. 1 (2004): 719—55.

————. "The Resilience of *Guanxi* and Its New Deployments: A Critique of Some New *Guanxi* Scholarship. *China Quarterly* 170 (2002): 459—76.

Yoshinori, Takeuchi, ed. *Buddhist Spirituality*. New York: Crossroad, 1995.

Yu, Ying-shih. "The Radicalization of China in the 20th Century," *Daedalus* 122 (1993): 125—50.

Zhuo, Xinping. "Religion and Morality in Contemporary China." *China Study Journal* 15 (1999): 5—10.

后　记

　　这部书开始于 5 年前的一个学术机缘，1999 年旧金山大学利玛窦中西文化历史研究所（Ricci Institute for Chinese-Western Cultural History at the University of San Francisco）酝酿提出了一个跨学科与跨文化的研究计划："涵养精神：今日中国的社会变迁与精神发展"（Nourishing the Spirit：Social Change and Spiritual Development in China Today），三位作者都参加了研讨。期间，利玛窦中西文化历史研究所主任吴小新博士非常认真地建议，三位作者能否在这个题目下进行跨文化的合作研究。坦白地讲，当时我们三个人都对合作的可能性持怀疑的态度，因为毕竟以前没有任何合作的基础，更何况三个人有不同的专业方向（社会学、社会心理学、宗教历史）。

　　也许真的应了中国人所笃信的缘分能给人生带来意外的结果。记得 2001 年秋天，James D. Whitehead 与 Evelyn Eaton Whitehead 到复旦大学讲学。他们二位抵沪不久，还带着旅途的疲惫就到我在上海的新居小坐，似乎没有太多的寒暄，我们彼此就一致认定，可以开始这一跨文化、跨学科研究方式的宗教对话。于是，我们的合作研究就这样开始了。三个人无论是在上海还是在旧金山，一起进行研讨的时间几乎是雷打不动的，每一次研讨都有令人兴奋不已的心得，不仅从知识层面上越来越认定这种对话与讨论的价值和意义，同时还彼此启发从而激荡出很多新的想法。于是，就在我们一起合作发表了两篇学术论文以后，我们再次将研究的心得汇入了这部书稿中。跨文化对话使我们意识到，因为人类彼此缺乏理解，在宗教问题上无端地制造出了那么多不应该的隔阂。在日益全球化的时代，我们有可能通过对宗教——人类基本的精神追求上，寻求一个互相理解、宽容的共有价值，在这方面，长期被忽视的中国传统文化无疑将会有新的作为。在本书中，与其他宗教讨论一个最大不同就在于我们更多地关注人类共性部分，更把中国人的精神价值摆在一个相当重要的位置。

读者在这本书中所看到的内容历经了几个寒暑的认真工作，就在完成本书的时候，我们都很激动，为这个初步的成果感到兴奋，更期待着给读者奉献新的研究成果。

在本书的研究过程中得到了各方面的支持与帮助，这里要感谢路斯基金会（Luce Foundation）、亚洲基督教高等教育联合董事会（United Board for Christian Higher Education in Asia）的支持，感谢旧金山大学利玛窦中西文化历史研究所支持并为研究的进行提供一些可能的帮助，感谢复旦大学社会发展与公共政策学院的支持。特别感谢利玛窦中西文化历史研究所吴小新博士对我们研究成果毫不动摇的信心和不变的友情。感谢复旦大学社会学系研究生邢婷婷的帮助，她非常有耐心地帮助我校对中文稿。感谢时事出版社苏绣芳女士在编辑出版此书过程中付出的耐心和努力。

范丽珠
写于上海逸仙路文化花园寓所
2005 年 12 月 9 日

RELIGION IN THE LATE-MODERN WORLD

By Lizhu Fan, James D. Whitehead,
and Evelyn Eaton Whitehead

School of Theology & Ministry - Seattle University

for colleagues Mark Markuly
& Sharon Callahan

honoring shared commitments
to China ~

Evelyn Eaton Whitehead   Oct 5/2010
James D. Whitehead

Current Affairs Press

The authors gratefully acknowledge the financial support of:

The EDS-Stewart Chair of the Ricci Institute for Chinese-Western Cultural History at the University of San Francisco Center for the Pacific Rim

The Henry Luce Foundation

The United Board for Christian Higher Education in Asia

Center for the Study of Sociology, Shanghai Fudan University

TABLE OF CONTENTS

目　录

INTRODUCTION

Scholars find evidence of religious behavior everywhere there is evidence of the human species. Like language, religious behavior is distinctive of what it means to be human. Like language, religious awareness is part of the capacity for meaning-making, for making sense of the human experience of living in the world. Like language, the personal capacity for religiousness both shapes and is shaped by culture. Thus religion finds many forms of expression across the vast span of human history and diverse civilizations.

This book draws on the research perspectives of the academic study of religion, to examine the **contemporary experience of religion and religiousness**. It is intended as a resource textbook, to serve Chinese university students in advanced undergraduate courses and masters' level seminars focusing on religious studies. The book will also be of service to a wider audience of Chinese readers interested in understanding the role of religion in contemporary culture, East and West.

Several distinctive features make this book useful to the reader. First, each of the chapters is included here in both Chinese and English language text. Second, the book focuses on the current interaction between religiousness and culture rather than on the historical development of particular religious traditions. Third, the three authors represent a broad range of disciplines—sociology, philosophy, social psychology, history of religions—that are crucial in the scientific study of religion: their collaboration has produced an integrated inter-disciplinary text. Finally, this book brings a strong cross-cultural perspective. Dr. Lizhu Fan is native Chinese with advanced degrees in classic Chinese culture and in sociology of religion; her pioneering research on the contemporary forms of Chinese popular religion has received international recognition. Dr. James D. Whitehead and Dr. Evelyn Eaton Whitehead are natives of the United States, where their university teaching and prolific writing have focused on themes in Catholic and Protestant Christian tradition. Since 1998 the Whiteheads have traveled annually to China, offering university courses and lectures in Shanghai, Hangzhou, Nanjing, Beijing and Hong Kong.

Part One of this volume introduces several essential elements of religiousness: *meaning-making* or the need to make sense of life's deeper dimensions, and *transcendence* or the search for values that are worth living for—even worth dying for. This initial section includes an overview of the academic disciplines through which religion and religiousness are studied in the West, as well as those spiritual convictions that lie at the heart of the Chinese heritage of popular belief and practice.

The chapters in Part Two take up several interrelated themes of modern religious consciousness, beginning with a review of the previously influential but now widely questioned *secularization hypothesis* that had predicted the inevitable decline of religion in the face of modernization. Discussion then turns to the similarities and contrasts in the dynamics of modernization as experienced in China and in the West. Next the analysis moves to the place of religion and the shape of religiousness in late-modern cultures.

Part Three offers several perspectives on the future of religion in China. Chapters Nine and Ten examine the beliefs and practices of the Chinese traditional heritage, as potential resources in China's 21st century development. The two final chapters reflect on possible contributions of religion and religiousness in the emergence of the new China.

Over the past six years, the authors of this book have collaborated in the study of religiousness in the context of Chinese society 's rapid contemporary development. Working together in China and in the United States, they have experienced both the benefits and challenges of serious cross-cultural research. This ongoing collaboration has been initiated and encouraged throughout by Xiao-xin Wu, Director of the Ricci Institute for Chinese-Western Cultural History at the University of San Francisco Center for the Pacific Rim. The publication of this book is part of Ricci Institute's long-standing and continuing commitment to developing scholarly resources in support of intellectual dialogue and mutual understanding between China and the West.

PART ONE
MAKING MEANING

CHAPTER ONE:RELIGIOUSNESS AND MEANING-MAKING

This chapter examines religiousness as an expression of the human need and desire to make sense of life. The religious traditions of the world respond to ultimate questions that confront humanity: issues of human origins and destiny,experiences of suffering and death.

"Humans,by their very nature,desire to know. " This famous statement of the Greek philosopher Aristotle opens his book on metaphysics,written more than two millennia ago. Since that time western philosophers have lavished much attention on questions of how humans know:What is the difference between opinion and certain knowledge? Between science and wisdom? Much less attention has been given to the desire that spurs human curiosity,the foundation of knowledge and science. This chapter reflects on the deep longing and enduring desire that humans display to understand their world and fathom life's meaning and purpose.

Anthropologist Clifford Geertz has observed that "the drive to make sense out of experience,to give it form and order,is evidently as real and as pressing as the more familiar biological needs. "[1]Religion embodies a form of reflection and a way of acting that are rooted in this drive or capacity,especially as this desire addresses, in Geertz' words, "the inescapability of ignorance, pain and injustice."[2]

We exercise our capacity to make meaning both by recognizing patterns in the world and by creatively giving shape to the myriad details of our lives. We *discover* order in our world: the seasonal climate changes that move in their repeated cycle year after year represent an order that exists separately from us. And we also *impose* an order on our world: we devise a week of seven days and invent periodic festivals that put human imprint on the year. This combination of discovery and invention lies close to the core of the human capacity for meaning-making.

Philosopher Paul Ricoeur observes: "We invent in order to discover; we exert creative energy in making meanings so as to apprehend the character of our existence and our world."[3] Ethicist William Schweiker comments on Ricoeur's words: "Human beings make moral, religious, cultural, scientific, and poetic meanings in order to grasp the truth of their world and their lives."[4]

The "invention" that Ricoeur speaks of is not mere fantasy. He is pointing to the creative efforts in all fields of human endeavor— moral, cultural, scientific, religious—to make sense of our lives by devising patterns of purpose. Each of us exists in a social world that has already been arranged for us: the language and laws, the cultural ideals and moral norms that are part of the layers of meaning our predecessors have invented to "humanize" the world we all inhabit.

Sociologist Max Weber described this world that humans both discover and invent when he observed that a human "is an animal suspended in webs of significance he himself has spun."[5] The image of a spider's web is compelling: the web both forms the platform on which the spider lives and is a home it has spun out of its very substance. For many centuries humans accepted the existing social world as simply an objective fact or perhaps as a gift of the gods. Once humankind recognizes that we shape our social structures and even our moral ideals, then we bear responsibility for the moral, cultural and religious world we have crafted.

MAKING-MEANING: TELLING STORIES

How do humans make meaning as they seek to discover the purpose and direction of their lives? We do this by telling stories. In stories, we attempt to uncover the mysteries of suffering, death and destiny. The building blocks of these stories are symbols, with their special power to simultaneously reveal and conceal new meanings. Some of these stories endure, becoming the classic texts that typically form the core of a religious tradition such as Buddhism or Christianity.

The impulse to tell stories seems to be universal. We tell stories to our small children at bedtime. We listen to our grandparents recount experiences and adventures from their own youth. As we tell a story we organize many disparate aspects of our experience into a single plot; the many details of a lifetime—some remembered and many forgotten in the telling—are made into a narrative. The life of a person or community becomes a story.

Our interest in stories seems insatiable. We read biographies of famous people—political leaders, military heroes, holy sages and popular celebrities—to discover facts about their lives, but also perhaps to gain insight into ourselves. Stories help us all make sense of our lives. Reading the story of another's life often sheds light on the unfolding mystery of our own.

Nations also tell stories. The account of Mao Zedong's famous long march is a heroic story that still engages many readers. The story of the voyage of Christopher Columbus and his discovery of the "new world" is central to the story of the birth of the United States. Cultural stories like these function as "founding myths"—heroic official accounts of important times in a people's history.

LANGUAGE, MEANING-MAKING AND MYTHS

Early in the 20th century philosophers in the West developed a deeper appreciation of language as a central feature of humankind. Philosophers Ludwig Wittgenstein and Martin Heidegger, for example, devoted attention to the role of language in the human effort to make sense of life. Heidegger, in his typically cryptic fashion, declared that language is the house of being. Philosopher David Tracy sums up this new interest in language:

> Language is not an instrument that I can pick up and put down at will; it is always already there, surrounding and invading all I experience, understand, judge, decide and act upon. I belong to my language far more than it belongs to me. [6]

Whether conversing with friends or telling stories to our children or developing a philosophical theory, humans use a language that is "already there. " Each language has its particular history and special vocabulary of meaning. Each language is a product of a long cultural history; we speak in the language we learn as a child, with its particular reservoir of images and symbols. From this repertoire of nuance and emphasis we build the stories that help us understand, to some degree, the shape and movement of our lives. Thus there are no private stories; our language always reflects the culture in which we live and whose language we utter.

Story-telling entails the creation of what scholars call *myths*. Here myth does not mean a false story or a lie; instead myth points to the kind of story-telling through which humans try to fathom the "big questions" of life. Such myths are not simple historical accounts; they are works of the human imagination in our search for meaning. Philosopher Mary Midgley defines myths: "They are imaginative patterns, networks of powerful symbols that suggest particular ways of interpreting the world."[7] In the Greek language *myth* means plot—a story with a certain purpose and direction. Sociologist Robert Bellah reminds us, "myth does not attempt to describe reality; that is the job of science. Myth seeks rather to transfigure reality so that it provides moral and spiritual meaning to individuals and societies."[8]

The Greek dramatist Aeschylus wrote *Prometheus Bound*, a tragedy that is still performed today, twenty-five hundred years after its first production. In this mythic tale the author presents a story about the god Prometheus who brought the miracle of fire to humankind as a gift. The other gods, convinced that the dangerous power of fire should have remained the sole possession of the gods, decreed that Prometheus suffer an eternal penalty for his act.

This myth is not recording an historical event. Instead its author is using a story to explain the appearance among humans of an extraordinary power. At the literal level, the story is about the momentous cultural achievement of harnessing fire, with its enormous potential for improving human life. But in this dramatic telling we confront a special characteristic of myth: in this story *fire* has more than a literal meaning. The dramatist uses fire as a symbol. He draws on the multiple meanings of this image, to explore the ambiguous human capacity for reflective consciousness and moral insight. The mythic tale acknowledges both the achievement and the danger of rational consciousness, an ability so powerful that it seems to find its source in some transcendent realm.

In the Hebrew bible we find a story about the beginnings of the human race. This too is a myth, not because of its content but because of the intent of its authors—the story attempts, in Ricoeur's words, "to grasp the truth" of our human origins.

This myth, recorded in the Book of Genesis, describes an original garden where the first humans—Adam and Eve—live in harmony with a loving creator God. But this garden is also inhabited by a snake. The snake in this myth plays a symbolic role. This poisonous animal, a familiar danger in the lives of the desert Hebrew tribes, symbolizes evil. The story warns us that evil—this mysterious, destructive dynamic that can poison personal integrity and destroy human relationships—has been present in human experience from the beginning.

In these ancient myths of Greece and Israel we see the human imagination at play, struggling to make sense of some mysterious aspect of human life—whether the ambiguous power of reason in the human community or the puzzling presence of evil at the dawn of the human story. And we see how symbols serve as dynamic elements in these myths.

SYMBOLS AND THEIR SURPLUS OF MEANING

The power of symbols—such as the fire and the snake in the stories above—lies not only in a literal meaning but in the greater significance they carry. Fire means many things to us：protective warmth, illuminating light, painful destruction. In the western i-magination, the snake stands for hidden danger, malicious intent, and sudden death. Paul Ricoeur writes that symbols have "a surplus of meaning." Because of this evocative quality in symbols, we con-tinue to find new meaning in stories, myths and classics.

The Chinese sage Zhuangzi tells the engaging story of a butch-er extraordinarily adept at his trade. [9] He was able to carve the carcass of an ox so expertly that his knife's blade never needed to be sharpened. This dramatic tale, another example of myth, has an al-most comic-book appeal：the butcher is a larger-than-life figure with a magically-endowed blade. A small child hearing this fable is sim-ply charmed by the butcher's extraordinary power. The child grows older and reads the story again. This time a new detail catches the reader's attention：it has taken the butcher many years to become this adept. So the butcher's ability is more than magical；years of pa-tient practice have been required to develop his skill. It is not the text of the story that has changed, but the capacity of the reader to discern a larger meaning. As a result there is "more" to the story than before.

Later, as a mature adult re-reads the tale, another element in the story becomes prominent. Through experience over time, the butcher learned to identify the small gaps between the joints in the oxen bones. Moving through these unresisting spaces, the butcher's knife was never dulled. Through an imaginative leap, the reader recognizes new meaning here: perhaps in every challenge—whether with physical objects that seem solidly resistant or with a personal problem laden with conflicts—there may be a "space" where a skillful person might find a way through. Again, the text of the story has not changed, but its significance for the reader has expanded. The symbols in this story—as is the case in every enduring myth—reveal a surplus of meaning. This surplus, Ricoeur suggests, may be "virtually inexhaustible in depth. "[10]

SYMBOLS, MYTHS AND CLASSICS

Many of the stories we hear survive only one or two tellings. Others so fascinate us that we want to listen to them again and again. Yet others touch themes in human life with such force that they survive over many years and even centuries. Stories that endure in this way we call *classics*.

David Tracy defines classics as "simply those texts that helped found or form a particular culture. "[11] The symbols and ideals portrayed in such enduring stories become the substance of a culture or religion. The ancient epics *The Iliad* and *The Odyssey* remain the pride of Greek culture even today. Other classics—the Hebrew bible, the Qur'an of Islam, the sutras of Buddhism—continue to serve as foundations of great historic religions.

The stories we call classics have intriguing characteristics. First they are—simultaneously—both particular and universal. That is, each is written in a particular language in the particular historical context of a particular people. Yet the stories of a classic are so compelling that people of other cultures and different times embrace these texts, translating them into new languages that extend and expand their influence. New English translations of the Daoist classic *Dao De Jing*, for example, appear almost yearly in the United States.

Second, these classics have both a literal meaning and a surplus of meaning. The text of the story, which does not change, provides a stable basis. But when read in new contexts and new translations, the story often yields novel interpretations. New meanings rise up from ancient texts. As Paul Ricoeur writes, the myths and symbols of these classics have the potential to "disclose new possibilities (that) offer the reader an expanded view of the world and a deeper capacity for selfhood."[12]

For centuries religious texts have been widely understood to be records of historical fact. Only in recent decades have scholars reached consensus that many of these accounts are not attempts at history; they are efforts at meaning-making. These classics explore, examine, reflect on aspects of life that continue to resist simple resolution—the puzzle of suffering and death; the mystery of the gift of love; the challenge of discerning one's own destiny. As Clifford Geertz observes, "the view of man as a symbolizing, conceptualizing, meaning seeking animal ··· opens a whole new approach···to the analysis of religion."[13]

THE LIMIT SITUATIONS IN LIFE

The human struggle for meaning comes to special focus in the face of limits. Ricoeur refers to "those limit situations···including solitude, fault, suffering and death···where the misery and grandeur of human beings confront each other. "[14] Geertz points to the radical challenges posed for humanity by meaningless confusion and ethical paradox, where "chaos—a tumult of events which lack not just interpretation but interpretability—threatens to break in upon man at the limits of his analytic capacities, at the limits of his powers of endurance, and at the limits of his moral insight. "[15]

Human suffering provides a perennial limit case. Recognizing that suffering seems inevitable, humans struggle to show that suffering is not simply absurd. We desperately want to discover—or to create, if necessary—some explanation for our pain. The great religious traditions of the world attempt to confront human suffering; sometimes by alleviating the pain, often by pointing beyond the pain toward some deeper significance.

There is an instinct in human consciousness that finds moral meaning in suffering. Many cultures, for example, believe that suffering comes as punishment. In the New Testament embraced by both Catholic Christians and Protestant Christians, Jesus's friends show him a man born blind and ask whether this handicap was due to his parents' sin. Hindu and Buddhist understandings of *karma* trace present suffering to past moral actions. This interpretation is echoed in the popular Chinese belief in *bao ying*, a cosmic reciprocity that links current pain to previous evil behavior. But the puzzle of suffering endures. Religious or not, humanity struggles to make sense of suffering.

Death raises a second limit. Human experience confirms that death is a most natural event, since every living thing dies. Yet history records humanity's profound desire to skirt death, to forestall it, to somehow continue an embrace of life beyond personal perishing. Death stands as limit not only to survival but to comprehension: we cannot penetrate its mystery nor fathom its meaning. So the question remains: Why must we die? Is death inevitable? Does anything of "me" survive my dying?

Every culture attempts to assuage the mystery—and the fear—of dying. Most graphic examples come in the rites and rituals of burial which anthropologists suggest are the earliest evidence of humanity's religious behavior. Parents are buried with respect. The graves are marked, and mourners return regularly to these places to make symbolic gestures of gratitude and reconciliation. The lives of the survivors are disrupted, as time and money are devoted to required expressions of grief. Burial customs differ across cultures, but expressions of reverence for those who have died seem universal. And in many places this reverence includes awareness of the continuing presence and power of the dead in the lives of the living.

The term *religiousness* refers to these enduring efforts to make sense of life, especially in the face of these "limit situations." Sociologist Peter Berger observes that "the religious impulse, the quest for meaning that transcends the restricted space of empirical existence in this world, has been a perennial feature of humanity."[16] This religious capacity points to a characteristic of humans: our need to ask questions that we cannot answer. And for many people, asking these questions is itself a source of comfort and consolation. Reflecting on the human condition, even its inevitable suffering and death, enriches our humanness.

THE ULTIMATE CONDITIONS OF
OUR EXISTENCE

Sociologist Robert Bellah defines religion as "a set of symbolic forms and acts that relate man to the ultimate conditions of his existence. "[17] Three instances of these ultimate conditions are cosmic origins, the order of the universe, and personal destiny.

The religious capacity for meaning-making draws attention to origins. How do we account for the fact of existence? Is the universe merely a random event or is it part of a larger design? The cosmologist can explain much of the universe's evolution: original matter, unimaginably condensed, suddenly expanded in what is commonly called "the big bang. " These scientists take us back to the first nanosecond after this explosive beginning. Yet the human mind continues to inquire: what of the nanosecond *before* the beginning?

Many religious traditions, too, include accounts of origins, usually crafted as stories of creation. The Hebrew bible, in fact, includes *two* creation accounts—testifying to different religious imaginations at work confronting the mystery of human origins. These are not historical accounts since, by definition, no witnesses were available to record this inaugural event! These literary inventions are, as Ricoeur describes, efforts to "apprehend the character of our existence" and to "grasp the truth" of our lives.

A second ultimate question that attracts the religious impulse concerns a deep moral order in the world. We notice that physical matter and much of the biological world operate according to generally consistent laws. Are there similar, even if more hidden, laws of the moral order? Catholic Christian thinkers, along with others, have long sought to clarify such a "natural law. " Is there a universal code—"do not murder, do not lie, do not steal"—that is designed into our species? Chinese culture has long sensed that there exists a *dao* or natural/moral structure that runs through the world: a pattern of respect and yielding whose observance brings its own reward of harmony. Confucius himself remarked "if I could hear the *dao* in the morning I would be content to die that evening. " Mencius suggests the possibility of discerning, at certain privileged moments, the patterns and make-up of human moral character: " Just at first light, in the fresh air of dawn, one can recognize the human propensity for good and evil. " But he acknowledges the fragility of this insight: "The busyness of the day causes us to lose this realization. "

A third ultimate question concerns the mystery of human destiny. Is human life simply a random offshoot of evolution, no more than a flickering light soon extinguished? Or does each life have a more enduring purpose? Does the pattern of one's life come predestined, as fate? Or is the plot finally in our own hands? In either case, how is a person to respond? Is fate fixed or alterable? Does destiny imprison us or liberate the spirit? These are questions that religious traditions confront. Both Chinese convictions about *ming yun* and Christian beliefs in God's providence represent religious responses to the puzzle of human destiny.

RELIGIOUS RESPONSE—PERSONAL
AND CULTURAL

Religious personages, such as Buddha and Jesus, represent profound religious awareness. Their compelling experiences, both intense and unique, became the foundation of continuing spiritual traditions. When these religious geniuses spoke of their unique experiences, they used the language and imagery of their surrounding cultures. Buddha's experiences were recorded in the Indian languages of Pali and Sanscrit, as well as in the cultural imagery of lotus flowers and elephants. Jesus spoke in Aramaic, a dialect of Hebrew that carried with it all the imagery and vocabulary of the Torah, the scripture of the Jewish religion. His words were remembered in the Greek language of the New Testament, an idiom that brought with it its own cultural imagery and nuances.

All personal experience is communicated through cultural language. So it is with religious experience. A person's intense experience of *Tian* or Allah or God may feel utterly unique, but it finds expression only through the language of one's culture. As sociologist Andrew Greeley observes, "it is out of the inherited and acquired metaphors of our culture that we attempt to explain life. "[18] Robert Bellah adds, "religious awareness must be symbolized in order to be completed as experience. "[19]

In each generation the religious experience of individuals both draws on the idioms and imagery of their cultural heritage and—if the experience is forceful enough—adds to the fund of shared stories and common symbols. A culture's spiritual heritage is sometimes expressed in the distinct language of an institutional religion such as Islam or Christianity, sometimes expressed through a more diffused language of spiritual search and religious meaning that is part of the culture itself. China, as we shall see in Chapter Four, serves as a strong example of a spiritual heritage that is diffused throughout the culture.

CULTURAL CODES: LEARNING TO SPEAK A CULTURE'S LANGUAGE

Each culture includes distinctive symbols that convey the values and ideals that it cherishes. In the Chinese culture, for example, the dragon and the *dao* function as core symbols. Scholars who specialize in the semiotic study of culture focus on such core symbols. Robert Schreiter outlines the approach of the semiotic study of culture: "culture is studied as a communication structure and process. It focuses on signs (*semeia* in Greek) that carry messages along the pathways (codes) of culture. "[20]

Dragons and fishes. Codes are the interpretive frameworks that provide the nuanced meaning of a culture's central symbols. In western Christian cultures, a dragon has come to symbolize evil forces. Familiar portraits of St. George slaying the dragon remind the western viewer of the cultural code that gives this animal its special meaning: the dragon is like the evil snake in the biblical story of creation. But in the Chinese culture, the dragon functions as a sign of goodness and extraordinary strength. The dragon dance is a featured part of many cultural festivals. Guan Yin is pictured astride a powerful dragon as she moves through the world performing her works of mercy. The same symbolic animal assumes very different meanings when interpreted through the lens of different cultural codes.

A religious tradition may even deploy different meanings (code) for a single symbol. In the Catholic Christian celebration of Easter which commemorates the resurrection of Jesus, fire plays a prominent part. The ritual begins in the dark of night with the lighting of a fire; a large candle, lit from this flame, is carried into the church to bring illumination. But elsewhere, for both Catholic Christians and Protestant Christians, fire has a very different significance: the pain of hell is represented as an eternal fire, a symbol of punishment for sin.

The codes of a culture carry the implicit sense of a group's shared understanding of life. These codes, as part of the ethos of a particular culture, are widely—even if not always consciously—embraced by members of that group. Their meaning is so obvious that "it goes without saying." These coded images serve as the grammar of a culture; only as one becomes familiar with them is one able to truly understand the culture. In the Chinese culture, for example, the fish has come to symbolize abundance and well-being. This is because the Chinese characters for "fish" and "surplus" share the same sound—*yu*. Outsiders who are unfamiliar with this cultural code cannot appreciate the significance of including fish in the menu of a Chinese banquet.

Food as Symbol. At the height of Communism in China Mao Zedong, in a ceremony honoring the nation's workers, presented a representative of this group with a mango. The ordinary piece of fruit was meant to represent the government's gratitude for the workers' contribution to society. Soon the mango, used by Chairman Mao in this way, took on great symbolic significance. Quickly, wax replicas of the mango were mass produced and placed next to Mao's picture in every home in China. A new symbol had entered into China's cultural code, representing the Communist Party's nourishing care of the nation and its workers.

Food functions at an even deeper level in the Chinese cultural code. Chinese traditional medicine identifies most food items as either "hot" or "cold" and pays close attention to the balance of these dimensions of nourishment. This designation does not refer to the temperature at which the food is served or the level of spicy seasoning. Instead it highlights the essential interplay of *yin* and *yang*. In Chinese culture, harmony and health depend on more than securing sufficient calories; these benefits are influenced by balancing the *yin* and *yang* of various foods.

Jade Stone. Art critic Holland Cotter notes that appreciation of jade is much stronger in Chinese culture than in the West. "Jade registers slowly on the western eye. Its surfaces can look glassy or gummy. Its colors are imprecise, difficult to describe. " But this stone is seen according to a very different code in the Chinese culture. "Jade in China is a whole other story. There it is rich with moral and spiritual meaning; it's alive. Luminous and quick to warm to the touch···" Cotter continues, "Confuciusattributed human virtues to jade, among them integrity, purity, and fortitude. "[21]

Night and Dawn. The symbol of night, like that of jade, functions with different meanings in eastern and western classics. Western culture favors dichotomies: good/evil, spirit/flesh, and light/darkness. Thus night is coded with meanings of ignorance and risk. In the biblical Book of Genesis, for example, we find the hero Jacob beset by a dangerous adversary in the dark of night. Jacob wrestles with this unknown assailant until dawn, when he finally comes to recognize this combatant is his own mysterious God. In this ancient and intriguing story, night stands as a time of threat, a period of darkness when one can neither identify the danger nor avoid its assault.

Chinese culture, guided by deeply established convictions of the rhythm of *yin* and *yang*, emphasizes the regular interplay of day and night. Thus the Chinese imagination responds more positively to the symbolic meaning of the night. Mencius, for example, speaks of the "restorative night" (*ye qi*). [22] It is just at the breaking of the day, he suggests, that the thoughtful person may briefly glimpse the desires and aversions that make up human nature. What is glimpsed at this precious, quiet moment is easily lost as the distractions and concerns of the day demand our attention. In this cultural code, night is a time of rest and restoration.

Confronted by mysteries we cannot fully fathom—suffering and death, origins and destiny—every culture has crafted religious beliefs and practices that seek both to explain and to console. Since religious classics and rituals find expression only in the language and imagery of their surrounding environment, religion and culture enjoy a special and complex relationship. In the coming chapters we will further examine the place of religion in human life and in its relationship to culture.

NOTES

[1]Clifford Geertz, *The Interpretation of Cultures*, p. 140.

[2]Geertz, p. 108. Geertz describes the challenge of making sense as "a matter of affirming, or at least recognizing, the inescapability of ignorance, pain and injustice on the human plane while simultaneously denying that these irrationalities are characteristic of the world as a whole."

[3]Quoted in William Schweiker, "Understanding Moral Meanings: On Philosophical Hermeneutics and Theological Ethics" in *Christian Ethics: Problems and Prospects*, p. 78.

[4]Schweiker, "Understanding Moral Meanings," p. 79.

[5]Max Weber, quoted in Geertz's *The Interpretation of Cultures*, p. 5. Geertz adds here: "I take culture to be one of those webs, and the analysis of it to be therefore not an experimental science in search of laws but an interpretative one in search of meaning."

[6]David Tracy, *Plurality and Ambiguity*, pp. 49—50.

[7]Mary Midgley, *The Myths We Live By*, p. 1.

[8]Robert Bellah, *Broken Covenant*, p. 3.

[9]This well-known story appears in Book Three of the Inner Chapters of the Zhuangzi.

[10]Ricoeur, *Figuring the Sacred*, p. 5.

[11]Tracy, *Plurality and Ambiguity*, p. 12.

[12]Ricoeur,*Figuring the Sacred*,p. 8.

[13]Geertz,*The Interpretation of Cultures*,p. 140.

[14]Ricoeur,*Essays on Biblical Interpretation*,p. 86.

[15]Geertz,*The Interpretation of Cultures*,p. 100. Geertz names the human experiences of "bafflement,suffering,and a sense of intractable ethical paradox (as) radical challenges···with which any religion···which hopes to persist must attempt somehow to cope. "

[16]Peter Berger,*The Desecularization of the World*,p. 13.

[17]Robert Bellah,*Beyond Belief*,p. 21.

[18]Andrew Greeley,*Religion as Poetry*,p. 25.

[19]Quoted in Robert Ellwood,*Introducing Religion from Inside and Outside*,p. 8.

[20]Robert Schreiter,*The New Catholicity*,p. 30.

[21]Holland Cotter,"The Jade of China,Alive with Meaning Yet Glossily Elusive," p. 31.

[22]Mencius 6A 8 in James Legge,*The Works of Mencius*,p. 408.

CHAPTER TWO : RELIGION AND TRANSCENDENCE

The focus of this chapter is transcendence—the human desire to go beyond the ordinary and the mundane, to discover values that may be more important than life itself, to encounter reality at its deepest core.

Humans hunger for *more*, not only for more wealth and many possessions but for meaning and purpose—for more profound reasons for living. Throughout history and across cultures, despite the evidence of endless violence and frequent wars, humans yearn for a better world. This desire for *more*, for what is *not yet*, manifests the human capacity for *transcendence*—for "going beyond" the apparent limits of the ordinary and mundane.

Philosopher of religion John Hick has defined religion in terms of this desire for transcendence:

religion (or the particular religious tradition) centers upon an awareness and response to a reality that transcends ourselves and our world, whether the 'direction' of transcendence be beyond or within or both. [1]

Hick's definition includes four elements: awareness, response, reality, transcendence. Religion begins in *awareness*—an insight or realization or conscious conviction. This awareness elicits a *response*, often expressed in the beliefs, rituals and practices of the world's religious heritages. Religious traditions testify that this awareness is not a fantasy nor an illusion but a recognition of *reality*. A recognition, in fact, of the *transcendent* dimension of reality, a recognition that opens us to "more" than is available in our customary experience of ourselves and our world. Exploring the phenomenon of transcendence brings us to a richer appreciation of religiousness.

INTIMATIONS OF TRANSCENDENCE

In Greece, in the 5th century before the common era, Socrates functioned as an influential teacher, what we might call in contemporary terms a public intellectual. In stimulating discussions with the privileged young people of Athens, Socrates raised questions about the existing norms of their society and the deeper meaning of their lives. Civic authorities, disturbed by these potentially disruptive discussions, demanded that Socrates cease his work. Socrates refused to honor this demand and chose to continue his teaching. Subsequently he was called to trial to justify his refusal.

As Plato records in his classic book *The Apology*, Socrates explained to the judges that he was not able to honor their demand. A higher authority—the inner voice of his conscience—claimed his allegiance. Threatened with death if he did not desist from his work with the youths of Athens, Socrates reasserted his intention to follow his conscience. And for this decision he was condemned to death, forced to drink a poisoned draught. This episode marks an introduction into western moral awareness of the priority of personal conscience—even when this interior source stands in tension with social norms.

In his commitment to conscience, Socrates embraced a value that was for him more important than life itself. His choice exemplifies an awareness of transcendence. Socrates had identified not only values that constitute the good life—values worth living for. But in a profound moment of moral choice, he also embraced values worth dying for—a principle of integrity that went beyond or transcended the ordinary life goals of personal safety and security.

A half-century later the Chinese sage Mencius described a similar transcendent conviction. He wrote,

> I like life but there are things I like more than life;
> so I do not seek to hold onto life at any cost.
> I dislike death but there are things I dislike more than
> death; so there are some troubles I will not avoid. [2]

At first glance, life itself seems the greatest value to humans and death their greatest threat. But reflecting on these questions, many today can imagine situations in which we would be ready to "transcend" the legitimate demands of personal safety. There are values—our child's life, our family's reputation, the defense of our country, our personal honor or self-respect—for which we might be willing to put our life at risk. How are we to account for these values? From what source do they arise? These questions of transcendence are part of the discussion of religion and religiousness.

Neither Socrates nor Mencius was a member of an organized

religious tradition. Neither identified a transcendent God or a supernatural realm as source of their moral commitments. But each of them spoke about, and lived their lives in accord with, values that reflect the human capacity for transcendence.

OTHER-WORLDLY TRANSCENDENCE

Centuries before the time of Socrates and Mencius, a religious figure in India articulated a moral vision that transcended the world of suffering. In the 6th century before the common era Siddhartha Gautama, known to his followers as the Buddha, recognized that human life is surrounded by poverty, illness and death. If such suffering is the primary truth of human experience, what is the remedy? Buddha believed that humans could discover the cause of their suffering and, recognizing the source of their pain, they could rise above it. Humans were capable of living in such a way that they could transcend these universal dilemmas of human life.

In Buddhism the path to this goal is to recognize that humans create most of their own suffering. We do this by assuming, falsely, that each of us is a separate and independent being. If we could recognize the truth—that we are all part of a single cosmic consciousness or Self—we would be free of our frantic struggles and anxious competitions. In this state of freedom, physical afflictions, too, would be recognized as of no ultimate consequence.

Thus Buddha and his followers envisioned a realm of peace and enlightenment that exists beyond this world of suffering. Beyond the ordinary realm of *samsara* (the Sanscrit term for the everyday world of illusion and suffering) there exists a realm of *nirvana*. [3]

Once *nirvana* is attained, all suffering is recognized as ephemeral—like the flickering light of a candle, easy to extinguish. The resultant state was one of profound peace, illustrated repeatedly in artistic depictions of Buddha—"the Enlightened One"—in meditative postures of calm and contentment.

The religious tradition that developed from Buddha's insights devised spiritual strategies for attaining this state of peace and enlightenment. The first requirement was to cease involvement in the confusing and all-absorbing affairs of ordinary life. To seek enlightenment one should leave home and enter a monastery, where there would be fewer distractions to disturb the practice of meditation, whose ultimate fruit was enlightenment. In later centuries, when Buddhism entered Chinese culture, *chu jia* (leaving home) would become a technical term for this practical effort to transcend one's ordinary life.

Six centuries after Buddha, the followers of Jesus struggled with similar challenges. How should a person live, in order to fully embrace Jesus's message? What must one leave behind, in order to pursue a way of life that transcends sinfulness and death? Are there ideals and values that go beyond this earthly existence?

The first followers of Jesus lived in the Roman Empire, a culture that was hostile to their religious beliefs and practices. Facing death for their loyalty to these beliefs, these early followers of Jesus looked to a better life—one that would transcend their present experience of suffering and persecution. In their hope to be united with God forever, they envisioned heaven as a realm of respite and peace after death.

As with the religious heritage of Buddhism, the early traditions of Catholic Christianity developed moral disciplines and spiritual strategies to facilitate entrance into this heavenly realm. Practices of prayer and works of charity could facilitate the personal transformation that would merit eternal life. These transformations would purify the soul, in preparation for entrance into fullness of God's presence. For many believers, heaven was the "true home" and life on earth merely a necessary testing ground.

As with Buddhism, early Christian religion valued a transcendent world at the expense of ordinary experience of everyday life. In the biblical New Testament, the author of the First Letter of John wrote:

Do not love the world or the things in the world. The love of the Father is not in those who love the world···the world and its desires are passing away, but those who do the will of God live forever. (I John 2:15).

From such counsel arose the desire of many early followers of Jesus, like the Buddhist monks, to seek out distant deserts and establish secluded monasteries where the pursuit of the spiritual life could proceed unimpeded by worldly concerns. [4]

In these historic traditions, the lure of the transcendent ideal often led to a neglect of the needs of this world. While keenly aware of human suffering and social injustice, Buddhism and Christianity have sometimes been tempted to turn their attention away from the ordinary plight of human society rather than to challenge the causes of this distress. Thus religious insight into a transcendent world did not always fuel efforts to improve the circumstances of society's ordinary life.

THIS-WORLDLY TRANSCENDENCE

Buddhism and Christianity—both Protestant and Catholic—remain influential throughout the world today. Over the course of history, in each of these religious traditions new convictions developed about the nature of religious transcendence. These new beliefs would, in turn, make both religious traditions immensely more acceptable within Chinese culture.

In Buddhist tradition, an ideal of the bodhisattva emerged. The bodhisattva is a person well along the path of spiritual enlightenment. Yet, in an act of moral solidarity, this holy person delays crossing over into the transcendent peace of *nirvana*. Instead the bodhisattva chooses to remain in the suffering world, offering help to those in need—so that all living things might be saved. "All creatures are in pain···all that mass of pain and evil karma I take into my body. I take upon myself the burden of sorrow···for I am resolved to save them all. "[5]

Another development also shows an expansion of the meaning of transcendence in the Buddhist tradition. Near the beginning of the common era, a new Buddhist sutra told the story of the bodhisattva Vimalakirti. This holy man did not leave the world or enter a monastery in order to seek enlightenment. Instead he remained fully involved in the joys and concerns of the world, combining a life of holiness with the responsibilities of marriage and family. In doing so, Vimalakirti re-interpreted the Buddhist ideal of "leaving home" or *chu jia*. He insisted that this discipline of seeking enlightenment and turning away from superficial concerns could be performed "in one's heart. " Following this new ideal, a Buddhist could pursue holiness while living in this world: now transcendence and immanence embraced. This radical re-interpretation of Buddhist transcendence greatly expanded the importance of the virtue of compassion. The many charitable works of Buddhism today can be traced back to Vimalakirti's affirmation of this-worldly transcendence.

In the Christian tradition a similar re-interpretation of transcendence evolved. In his preaching ministry, Jesus announced that his mission was to seek the "reign" or "kingdom" of God. This ideal was a world transformed by justice and love, a world in which care for the poor and forgiveness of enemies would flourish. Since this differed so dramatically from the societies in which Jesus's followers actually lived, the ideal of God's kingdom was initially understood as a promise that pointed beyond worldly existence. Thus many early Christians assumed that the kingdom of God existed exclusively in heaven, to be enjoyed only after one's death. In addition, among the first generations of Christians there was a strong apocalyptic conviction—the belief that the world would come to an end in their lifetime. Thus it made sense to turn away from a world that is passing away, and wait expectantly for God's reign in heaven.

As the decades passed and Christianity spread beyond the earliest generations, Christian thinkers found new meaning in Jesus's teaching about the kingdom of God. Jesus was remembered as saying: "my kingdom is not of this world. " But in another context, he had said "the kingdom of God is among you. " When asked for signs of the kingdom's arrival, Jesus listed acts of compassion and healing in this world: "the blind see, the lame walk … the poor hear good news. "

Catholic and Protestant theologians began to speak of a dual promise of the reign of God—both "present" and "not yet." The transcendent ideal of justice and love is not meant to function simply as a reward to be experienced in the bliss of heaven; it is a challenge that encourages followers of Jesus to work for the transformation of their own societies today. God's reign in the world is "present" wherever people of good will work to respond to the needs of the world. At the same time, the kingdom of God is "not yet" since this religious ideal seems never to be fully realized in this world.

In the contemporany world, members of many religious traditions commit themselves to charitable works, intended to reduce suffering and bring healing to the world. Today the transcendent vision embraced by these religious traditions leads believers into a deeper appreciation of the complex issues of contemporary life and to a wholehearted commitment to contribute to their resolution. This is a religious transcendence that must be experienced in the midst of this world.

CHINA: THIS-WORLDLY TRANSCENDENCE

In the ancient cultures of Israel and India, religious founders charted ways of living that recognized values transcending this world and that brought these values to bear on actions of justice and compassion. They were imagining a better world.

In ancient China a quite different approach to transcendence was underway. Confucius saw the troubles and suffering that Buddha had seen and that Jesus would, centuries later, also recognize. Confucius likewise imagined a better way to live, a style of living that would transcend this present reality. He had recognized, in the words of the China scholar Benjamin Schwartz, "the yawning abyss between the ideal social order and the actual state of affairs. "[6] But for Confucius this transcendent ideal was *within history*; it had existed in the virtuous time of an earlier dynasty in China. As Chinese,Confucius did not imagine some other ideal world existing apart from the one reality of this life. Though he was committed to a better life,transcendence for him and his followers was to be pursued in the context of one's ordinary life responsibilities.

Perhaps the spiritual orientation that most exemplifies religious transcendence within the Chinese culture is the practice of ancestor veneration. Schwartz notes "the pervasiveness of what we call ancestor worship" in Chinese civilization; he reminds us that this is part of the "religious orientation" of this culture. [7] From the earliest times the Chinese have centered their spirituality in the family; it was here that the virtues of respect and loyalty were developed; it was in the family that personal cultivation began. While ancient Greek culture gave extensive attention to the public forum as the place where personal and civic virtue was cultivated, the Chinese gave their first attention to the family. For Confucius,it is

> in the family that humans learn those virtues which redeem the society,for the family is precisely the domain within which authority comes to be accepted and exercised not through reliance on physical coercion but through the binding power of religious moral sentiments based on kinship ties. [8]

The rituals of ancestor veneration point to a relationship within the family that transcends death itself. The focus of ancestor veneration in this culture is "not simply on the world of the departed as such but on a numinous 'biological' continuity through kinship flowing from the world of the ancestral spirits to the world of those yet to be born. " The "numinous···continuity" between oneself and one's ancestors transcends "the barrier of life and death. " A ritual veneration is directed to

> the spirits who continue to maintain an organic relationship with their living descendents. As members of a familial community *across the barrier of life and death* , they continue to play a familiar role in that community···[9]

Because its spiritual concerns are centered in this world—and despite the evidence of transcendence implied in ancestor veneration—Confucianism is most often described as an example of humanism.

TRANSCENDENCE AND HUMANISM

Another form of "this-worldly" transcendence, more contemporary and more typically western, appears in various humanistic efforts to improve the world. Philosopher Martha Nussbaum advocates a kind of transcendence that does not turn our attention away from this life, but fosters the impulse "to transcend our ordinary humanity. "[10] She calls this "a transcendence···of an internal and human sort. "[11]

Catholic philosopher Charles Taylor agrees that humanism turns our attention to "the affirmation of ordinary life," putting "the center of gravity of goodness in ordinary living, production, and the family. "[12] But Taylor objects to a style of humanism that

denies any values or beliefs beyond the immediate "here and now. "
He points to many contemporary people whose humanistic commitments are shaped by religious values—whether Muslim or Christian
or Buddhist. For these people, the human capacity for transcendence
resonates with the religious conviction that "the point of things isn't
exhausted by life. "[13] Taylor insists that there is an "insight that
we can find in suffering and death—not merely negation, the undo-
ing of fullness and life—but also a place to affirm something that
matters beyond life. "[14]

For the Nobel Prize winning poet Seamus Heaney, art and poetry also address the question of transcendence. Heaney writes of
"poetry's high potential, its function as an agent of possible transformation, of evolution towards that more radiant and generous life
which the imagination desires. "[15] Poetry, in Heaney's vision, sear-
ches for "a glimpsed alternative, a revelation of the potential that is
denied or constantly threatened by circumstances. "[16] Art and poetry seek to "see through" the ordinary and the mundane; they as-
pire to the "more" of human life that is so often neglected or ig-
nored.

Humanism and transcendence meet at the question of life's significance. Is the meaning of human life exhausted in each one's existence? If this is so, then suffering and death remain simply negation. Or might there be something "more"—values that give meaning to a human life, even in the face of suffering and death? Religious scholars like Karl Rahner, William Schweiker, and Charles
Taylor insist that one can be both a committed humanist and one
who believes in transcendent values.

TRANSCENDENCE: COMING TO THE HORIZON

The horizon is a familiar sight. Each morning we watch the sun rise above this line that separates earth and sky; each evening we trace the sun's disappearance as it falls below the horizon. The horizon marks the limit of our vision; it is as far as we can see. Yet it is a curious boundary. We notice a tree on the distant horizon. But as we walk toward the tree, the horizon moves away. Soon we realize that we can never actually reach the horizon. The horizon retreats, even as we approach.

The horizon separates us from what lies beyond our sight, as it links us to what may exist beyond our limited perspective. Visions of what lies beyond the horizon have fired the imaginations of sailors and poets, as well as scientists and religious thinkers.

These features of the horizon—so ordinary and so symbolic— make it an attractive metaphor for scholars of religion. Like the "limit situations" and "ultimate questions" we discussed in Chapter One, the horizon marks the boundary beyond which our rational grasp of certainty cannot proceed.

Paul Ricoeur has described the horizon as "the metaphor for what approaches without ever becoming a possessed object."[17] The horizon stands at the edge of our vision, reminding us of the many barriers beyond which our knowledge cannot go. This realization may engender frustration or, alternatively, respect. For some people, as Ricoeur observes, "it is the horizon that reflection does not comprehend, does not encompass, but can only salute as that which quietly presents itself from afar."

As a symbol, the horizon marks the place where our desire to fully comprehend our lives meets its boundary. It is here that our questions about suffering and love, about death and destiny find no answer. Why do just people suffer? Is death simply the annihilation of personal existence or might there be "more" to life? How does a person comprehend her own destiny—who she is, who she might become? These questions give way to no fully satisfying answer. Rather they remain alive, as invitations and irritants to "think again."

At the horizon of our knowledge lie these questions of meaning that continue to test our confident grasp of life's purpose. But the horizon is not only a place of questions, but also a place of emotions. Two in particular stand out.

Wonder and Longing. At the boundary of our knowledge we experience the curious emotion of wonder. Wonder has traditionally been understood as the beginning of philosophy; it may also stand at the starting point of religion. We are dazzled—as we often are in the face of dawn or the sunset—by the unexplained puzzle of our world. The starry universe and the vast ocean are so immense. In the face of these natural phenomena, we are acutely aware of our littleness, our insignificance. Yet we are not diminished by wonder; the sense is both poignant and pleasurable. As scholar Caroline Bynum remarks, "we wonder at what we cannot in any sense incorporate, consume, or encompass in our mental categories; we wonder at mystery, at paradox…"[18] Wonder is very much like awe and reverence. This emotion often accompanies a lively curiosity that, disciplined over many years, may lead to scientific discoveries. Wonder also generates the stories, myths and rituals that form the substance of religious living.

In the Greek tragedy *Antigone*, the heroine praises the marvel that is the human person: "Many are the wonders, but none is more wonderful than what is man···He has a way with everything···only against death can he call no means of escape." We marvel both at the workings of the human mind and at its limits. Wonder—at the gift of love, the miracle of a child's birth, the splendor of a work of art—evokes a particular kind of appreciation. Wonder reminds humans that though we may fail to "solve" all the aspects of our lives, we may still savor them.

A second emotion that arises at the boundary of the horizon is longing. Meeting the limits of rational understanding opens many people to a richer appreciation of life's mysteries. We long to overcome the distance that stubbornly separates us from others; we long for relief from suffering and injustice. We long for freedom or healing, states of the soul that we may not be able to accomplish on our own. Above all we long for "more"—more life, more love, more meaning. While wonder often leads to gratitude, longing elicits hope—a hope that impels us forward, expanding our horizons.

Crossing the Horizon. Emotions of wonder and longing motivate us to transcend limits. The explorers of 16th century Europe, driven by wonder, crossed the seas to discover what lay beyond. Astronauts today cross horizons in space once closed to humans, as they investigate distant places in our universe. With imagination and hope, humans continue to find ways to go beyond the limits of the horizon. Not only in ships and space vehicles, but in story and fantasy and religious rituals, human have attempted to transcend the barriers of their natural knowledge.

Some exercises of transcendence amount to little more than escapism; we create a fairy tale or a science fiction novel that will transport the reader, momentarily, across the borders of the ordinary world. But when the story is finished, the reader returns to the limits of daily life.

Other exercises of the imagination produce different results. Buddhist images of a world in which people refrain from violence toward all living things lead to practical actions of compassion, restraint and justice. Christian images of "the kingdom of God"—the hope of a human community that is more caring and more just—have engendered actions of forgiveness and charity that have changed people's lives. Artistic images and religious reflection in every culture have crossed the horizons of ordinary understanding, challenging—if only for a time—the customary boundaries that separate humans from one another and from their own best hopes.

AT THE HORIZON: DAWN

Each morning, dawn draws our eye to the horizon. Dawn is a daily occurrence. But, like the horizon, it has great symbolic suggestiveness. With the dawn we come out of darkness; once again we are given the gift of sight. Dawn marks the moment of enlightenment, but the light and the vision it provides come as gift more than as personal achievement. In many cultures, people associate the natural image of dawn with mental insight. In English one may say, "it dawned on me. " In Chinese, the word for dawn—*xiao*—also means knowledge.

Classics, both religious and cultural, have turned to this metaphor to express how insight arrives as gift, how new hopes and convictions cross the horizon to enter our world, enlarging and enriching it with their arrival.

At the end of Chapter One we recalled the biblical story of the night-time struggle of Jacob with an unknown assailant. The story begins with an ominous statement: " and Jacob was left alone " (Genesis 32). In the night an unrecognized force assaults Jacob and they began to wrestle. As the two struggled in the darkness, Jacob was injured in the thigh. Then the unknown wrestler said to Jacob, "let me go for the dawn is coming. " But Jacob replied, "I will not let you go unless you give me a blessing. " As he received the blessing, Jacob realized that the assailant was divine: "I have seen God face to face and yet my life is preserved. " And the story concludes: "the sun rose upon Jacob as he passed this place, limping because of his thigh. " This mysterious story, perhaps composed as early as the 9th century before the common era, contrasts the dangerous nighttime struggle with the dawn that brings enlightenment. It unites a painful memory of struggle and injury with the blessed memory of relief and insight.

In the Chinese classic attributed to Mencius the author turns to the metaphor of dawn to describe the fragile and fleeting quality of some privileged insights. "Sometimes just at that moment between night and day one can perceive the nature of man's propensity for goodness and evil. " This special enlightenment comes at that brief moment between the restful night and the distracting busyness of the day.

For the Chinese author as well as for the biblical writer, dawn is a symbol of revelation. Insight into the human condition comes at privileged moments as a gift. Martin Heidegger reminds us that the Greek word for truth is *aletheia* or "no longer hidden. " He further observes that truth is not something humans achieve by strenuous thinking; rather it is manifested to us. In art as in religious consciousness, insight and inspiration often come as gifts that uncover what had been hidden. In these transforming moments the truth, so frequently obscured by either the darkness of the night or the distractions of the day, is made manifest. At such rare and privileged times, humans may transcend the ordinary horizons of their knowledge and come to greater insight into human life and its meaning.

The capacity for transcendence, rooted in the deep human desire for a better life, lies close to the core of human religiousness. The emotions of wonder and longing lead humans beyond the boundaries of their customary understanding into mysterious depths that are the substance of religious living.

NOTES

[1]John Hick, *An Interpretation of Religion: Human Responses to the Transcendent*, p. 3.

[2]Mencius, 6A 10.

[3]For a contemporary discussion of the history and development of Buddhist beliefs and practices, see the essays in *Buddhist Spirituality*, edited by Takeuchi Yoshinori.

[4]In his important book *Body and Society*, historian Peter Brown traces these early developments that have shaped understandings of "other-worldly" transcendence in both Catholic Christianity and Protestant Christianity.

[5]William DeBary includes this quotation in his *Sources of Indian Tradition*, p. 161.

[6]Benjamin Schwartz, "Transcendence in Ancient China," p. 61.

[7]Benjamin Schwartz, *The World of Thought in Ancient China*, p. 20.

[8]Schwartz, "Transcendence in Ancient China," p. 70.

[9]Schwartz, *The World of Thought in Ancient China*, p. 21.

[10]Martha Nussbaum, *Love's Knowledge*, p. 378.

[11]Nussbaum, *Love's Knowledge* p. 379.

[12]Charles Taylor, "*A Catholic Modernity?*" p. 20.

[13]Taylor, "*A Catholic Modernity?*" p. 21.

[14]Taylor, "*A Catholic Modernity?*" p. 20.

[15]Seamus Heaney, *The Redress of Poetry*, p. 114.

[16]Heaney, *The Redress of Poetry*, p. 4.

[17]Paul Ricoeur, *Freud and Philosophy*, p. 526.

[18]Caroline Bynum, *Metamorphosis and Identity*, p. 52.

CHAPTER THREE: THE STUDY OF RELIGION IN THE WEST

This chapter discusses five approaches used by western scholars in the academic study of religion. Then several key terms are defined: religion, religiousness, faith, and the sacred.

APPROACHES TO THE ACADEMIC STUDY OF RELIGION TODAY

Today religion is a significant topic of study within the social sciences— sociology, psychology, anthropology, history, and political science—as well as among philosophers, theologians and proponents of critical theory. Scholars in each of these areas recognize that religion is a multifaceted phenomenon that cannot be fully understood by any one discipline alone.

Western approaches to the academic study of religion may be grouped under five main perspectives. In fact, these categories are not always distinct from one another, since particular scholars often pursue several approaches to understanding the complex reality of religion. And these five categories may not adequately represent the contributions of all important scholars in this field. But this outline

WESTERN APPROACHES TO THE ACADEMIC STUDY OF RELIGION

A. Religious Experience   **Personal Awareness of One's Relation to Ultimate Reality**

B. Religious Institutions   **Structures and Functions of Religious Groups**

C. Religious Traditions   **(Comparative) Study of the World's Wisdom Traditions**

D. Religion's Role in History   **Positive/Negative Impact of Religious Ideas and Groups**

E. Religious Studies   **Public Inquiry into Meaning of Symbolic Discourse**

Figure One

will provide a framework to begin the discussion.

We will start with a basic description. In the western academic tradition, religion is studied as

a system of thought, feeling, and action shared by a group that gives members an object of devotion; a code of ethics governing personal and social conduct; and a frame of reference relating individuals to their group and the universe. [1]

Even as religion touches people's lives at the level of their everyday needs and hopes, it concerns itself with what transcends the ordinary awareness of daily life. Religion acknowledges deeper dimensions of human experience, by affirming the reality of the sacred. As Denise Carmody remarks, religion recognizes "that ultimate dimension of human life, personal and social alike, where Mystery comes to center stage ."[2]

A. RELIGIOUS EXPERIENCE—PERSONAL AWARENESS OF ONE'S RELATION TO ULTIMATE REALITY

Academic perspectives in the West often explore religion as a human product—examining the stories, moral convictions, ritual actions, organized groups that are part of human religiousness. But, as scholars of religion remind us, and as religious persons themselves report, these products are not "the whole story. " In fact, these elements are the result rather than the source of religion. Religion is, at its essential core, a human response to a reality experienced as greater than humanity.

William James sought to express this greater reality:

It is as if there were in the human consciousness *a sense of reality*, *a feeling of objective presence*, *a perception* of what we might call "something there," more deep and more general than any of the special and particular "senses" by which current psychology supposes existent realities to be originally revealed. [3]

Religious consciousness recognizes that reality is richer than simply what is available to us in the immediate evidence of sense experience. There is a level of existence, of meaning, of significance that goes beyond or transcends what we ordinarily have access to. Religious awareness affirms that this level of reality is the true basis of the visible and tangible universe of our everyday experience.

Throughout history, humans have been aware of a dimension of reality that somehow transcends the ordinary quality of daily existence. This transcendent dimension has been recognized as profoundly significant—as both Source of all reality and Sustainer of life and its deepest values. And human communities have responded to this transcendent Source through conscious efforts to deepen their understanding (by developing narratives, doctrines, and theological systems that express their awareness of the transcendent realm) and to strengthen their connection (by devoted actions of prayer, worship, moral action, and compassionate service in the world) with this sacred Reality.

For people who embrace an awareness of this transcendent Reality, religion becomes something that is lived, not just doctrines that are believed or organizations that are joined. Living religion includes the cultivation of a relationship to *ultimate reality*. In the vocabulary of Catholic and Protestant Christianity, this is religious faith or spirituality—a personal response to the living reality of God. [4]

The western religious heritage—exemplified in Judaism, both Protestant and Catholic Christianity, and Islam—characteristically embraces a *dialogic* approach. These major western religions are frequently grouped together as "religions of the book," because each honors a classic text as the sacred word of God. For the Jews, the book is the Torah; for Protestant and Catholic Christians, the Bible; for Muslims, the Qur'an. And the connections go deeper: each honors the ancient near-eastern religious figure of Abraham as one of its spiritual founders. In addition, the Bible used by Catholics and Protestants incorporates large portions of the Hebrew Scriptures (identified as the Old Testament) along with the New Testament's focus on the life and message of Jesus; the Qur'an acknowledges the role of the Jewish prophet Moses and religious figure Jesus as part of the lineage that culminates in the Prophet Mohammad.

In western religious consciousness, the spiritual life involves a deepening personal relationship with a transcendent Source of all reality. This transcendent reality—Ultimate Mystery—is named Yahweh by Jews, God by Catholic and Protestant Christians, and Allah by Muslims. An intimate relationship between the person and the transcendent Source both 'is' and 'is not' similar to the interpersonal bonds of mutual love and support that link humans to one another. In the western approach to religious experience, recognition of human brokenness (or sin) plays a prominent role and the need for conversion receives a great emphasis.

The wisdom traditions of the East, such as Hinduism and Buddhism, as well as some mystical threads woven into the fabric of western religions, emphasize the *unitive* quality of religious experience. Rather than moving toward an intimate relationship with a transcendent (and yet personal) Other, these traditions foster recognition of the illusory distinctions of ordinary awareness. These distinctions—self/other, mind/body, good/bad—disguise the deeper unity of Reality. In these unitive traditions, religious experience dissolves the sense of one's separate self in an appreciation of true identity with the Self or Absolute.

While there is great diversity among the religious sensitivities of the east, some common elements can be identified. First, eastern traditions stress the sacred as both above the cosmos and yet mysteriously immanent in all things. In most eastern traditions, the goal of the spiritual search is to recognize one's non-identity—since self and cosmos are one. Eastern traditions are more interested in personal transformations and symbolic rituals than in revealed truth and theology. And, unlike Judaism, Christianity, and Islam, there is no one unique divine manifestation. The universal transcendent mystery is recognized in many personifications and manifest in a rich variety of ritual activities. The multiple gods of Hinduism and the innumerable deities in local Chinese temples exemplify this approach to religious experience. Finally, instead of personal sin, this approach stresses illusion and self-deception; in place of conversion, it emphasizes the surrender into the fullness of Reality. [5]

An analysis of religious experience is foundational for the academic study of religion. But the study of religion and religiousness must then expand to explore other dimensions of the complex human phenomenon. As anthropologist Clifford Geertz has observed, "experience no longer seems adequate to frame by itself our understanding of the passions and actions we want ··· to call religious. "

Instead, other aspects of humanity such as meaning, identity and power "must be deployed to catch the tonalities of devotion in our time. "[6]

B. RELIGIOUS INSTITUTIONS—EXAMINING THE STRUCTURES AND FUNCTIONS OF RELIGIOUS GROUPS AND ORGANIZATIONS

In modern western societies, particularly in Europe and North America, religions often function as organized social movements with established doctrines and moral codes. Sociology of religion focuses attention on these religious organizations, studying the religious groups themselves and their interaction with the societies they are part of. In western sociological theory, religion is commonly described as a social group with a shared world-view and a common ethos.

Social group. Religions operate as organized groups with identifiable membership and distinct leadership personnel. People join the group voluntarily, in the sense that members see themselves as making a personal decision to participate, even when cultural heritage and other social factors influence that decision. Typically, close relationships develop among members of a religious group, leading to a strong sense of community support and loyalty.

Shared worldview. Members share a comprehensive perspective on life, rooted in classic texts (understood as "sacred scripture") and foundational teachings of their religious heritage. Significant beliefs are held in common—convictions about personal destiny (as shaped by *karma* or influenced by *Tian* or guided by God's providence), the universe (as created by Yahweh or Allah), and human society (as guided by God's free command or by a "natural law" imbedded in creation). Core beliefs are often defined and monitored through a recognized authority structure of specially trained or ordained clergy, functioning within an explicit leadership system. This religious worldview functions as a lens, an interpretive framework through which other aspects of members' experience are understood and evaluated.

Common ethos or "way of life". Standards of personal and social behavior flow from the group's core beliefs. Shared values shape members' sense of *who we are* and *how we should act*. These moral sensitivities are expressed both in devotional activities of prayer and worship and in ethical behavior in everyday life. Religious groups develop rituals of personal prayer and communal worship, to strengthen believers' relationship with God or the sacred/transcendent dimensions of reality. And religious groups promote character formation and ongoing moral commitment, to guide believers in their actions of compassion, justice, reconciliation, and peace.

Sociologists have examined many aspects of the internal organization of religious groups. These investigations provide factual information about a religious group's membership: for example, the age range of group members and their socio-economic status; the ratio of men to women, of young people to older members. Their work also gives an analysis of important dynamics of the group's life: for example, the level of personal commitment among members, their initial reasons for joining the group, their reasons for continuing participation, how long members remain in the group and why those who leave stop participating in the religious group's activities.

Sociologists and other analysts also explore relationships between religious institutions and the larger societies in which they function. Their research findings indicate that religious groups play an ambiguous role in human societies. On the positive side, religious groups often contribute to the moral values, social stability, and the public welfare services of a society. On the negative side, religious groups are often sources of moral intolerance, ethnic conflict, and social discrimination.

A major focus in the sociology of religion has been the contested issues surrounding the *secularization hypothesis*—which states that religious institutions inevitably lose their social significance in the face of society's modernization. We will examine this ongoing debate on secularization in Chapter Five.

C. RELIGIOUS TRADITIONS—(COMPARATIVE) STUDY OF WORLD'S WISDOM TRADITIONS

For several decades, anthropologists and other social scientists have undertaken field studies to identify the beliefs and ritual practices of different ethnic groups and national cultures. These studies initially focus on behaviors, describing the activities and social exchanges of daily life and recording the interpretations that local people offer to explain what is happening. Many of these interpretations can be traced to an underlying religious worldview, a shared spiritual vision represented in the sacred stories and symbols that are honored within the group.

The influential definition developed by cultural anthropologist Clifford Geertz typifies this approach. In *Religion as a Cultural System*, Geertz describes religion as:

    (1) a system of symbols which acts to establish

    (2) powerful, pervasive, and long-lasting moods and motivations in people

    (3) by formulating conceptions of a general order of existence and

    (4) clothing these conceptions with such an aura of factuality that the moods and motivations seem uniquely realistic. [7]

Geertz's definition of religion has been widely adopted among contemporary social scientists for use in many cultural settings. In his own field work Geertz compares the contemporary practice of Islam in the village culture of Indonesia and in modern Morocco. Today the contemporary practice of the beliefs and rituals of China's rich cultural heritage is being studied extensively, as well. In the next chapter and again in Part Three, we will discuss the findings of research into the Chinese classic religious heritage and its expression in contemporary China.

    An understanding of any distinct religious tradition is also increased by comparative study. The field of comparative religion today provides a context for such fruitful dialogue among and about the human family's diverse expressions of belief and ritual practice.

    The comparative study of religion has emerged only recently as a legitimate focus of academic research. German scholar of Hinduism and mythology Max Muller was the first to call for such a "scientific study of religion. " In 1870, Muller argued that advances in the study of foreign languages and in the research disciplines of archeology and mythology made it possible to undertake a more critical and systematic study of the world's major religions. In the subsequent decades of the 19th century, departments for the scientific study of religion (as distinct from the traditional departments of Christian theology that had long been part of western universities) were established in the major centers of learning in Europe.

In the mid-20th century a second surge of interest in the comparative study of the world's religious traditions occurred. In the 1950s only three professorships in the academic study of religion existed in the United States; by the 1970s there were thirty established positions. Mircea Eliade joined the faculty of the University of Chicago in 1957; Wilfred Cantwell Smith moved to the Center for the Study of World Religions at Harvard University in 1964. With these faculty appointments, the comparative study of the world's religions achieved acceptance as a legitimate research endeavor in United States higher education.

In 1968, in his inaugural address as the first professor of religious studies in Great Britain, Ninian Smart called for a comparative study of religions that would include five areas: history of religions; phenomenology of religions (that is, a critical description of the practices and beliefs of these many traditions); sociology of religions (which would examine the relationship of these faith traditions with their surrounding cultures); philosophy of religion; and theology.

Today it is not only religious scholars who are interested in establishing links among the world's spiritual traditions. The Parliament of the World's Religions, an international meeting now held every five years, has become a gathering place for people from many countries and many religious backgrounds. These week-long conferences provide opportunities not only for intellectual exchange, but for experiences of fellowship and shared worship among people who represent a broad array of spiritual sensitivities.

The initial Parliament meeting, held in Chicago in 1893, was largely a Christian initiative. Its approach to interfaith dialogue was welcoming, but the underlying mood reflected a "fulfillment" theological perspective: the truth and worth of all other religious traditions find fulfillment in Christianity. By the time of the next Parliament gathering, held in 1993 as a one-hundred-year anniversary event, the mood of interfaith dialogue had changed dramatically. Gone were the underlying attitudes that placed Christianity in the role of primary or even exclusive model of genuine religion. These were replaced by commitments—on the part of religious leaders and ordinary believers from many of the world's religions—to work together to expand awareness of sacred transcendence, and to make the world a better place for all its inhabitants.

D. RELIGION'S ROLE IN HISTORY—THE POSITIVE AND NEGATIVE INFLUENCES OF RELIGIOUS INSTITUTIONS AND IDEAS IN CIVILIZATION

There is a long tradition of scholarship tracing the positive and problematic links between religion and society. One of the most influential theories of the negative influence of religion (particularly Christianity) was advanced by Karl Marx and Friedrich Engels. Marx saw religion as a form of "false consciousness" which has been used throughout history to keep men and women in bondage. Marxism understands the determinants of history to be located in economic factors; characteristically, then, religion functions in service of the dominant economic system. In their own period of history, Marx and Engels saw Christianity as offering false hopes to the masses of people suffering under the inequitable economic system of capitalism. "Religion is the general theory of that world (the world of capitalism)…its enthusiasm, its moral sanction…its universal ground for consolation and justification…it is the opium of the people. "[8]

Other social scientists have examined the positive effects of religion in the lives of people and cultures. Challenging the economic determinism of Marxism, German sociologist Max Weber emphasized the constructive role of religious ideals and values in shaping society. With other influential scholars—Victor Turner, for example—Weber sees religious values and organizations as sources of cultural renewal and social change. Modern examples of such religiously-motivated movements for social change would include the social liberation efforts of Gandhi in India and Martin Luther King in the United States.

Emile Durkheim, who stands with Weber as founder of the modern discipline of sociology of religion, stressed the role of religion as a source of common moral values in society. These values can unite believers into a single moral community, a community that often provides support for moral order and sometimes serves as agent of control. Many western scholars have stressed the contributions of religion to social stability. Talcott Parsons sees religious belief and behavior as supporting social cohesion, integrating church members into the goals and values of larger society. Milton Yinger has shown that a religious worldview is often a basis of shared meaning, even in modern secular societies.

Psychologists, too, debate the effects of religion. Sigmund Freud, the father of modern psychoanalysis, mounted a blistering critique of the religious themes and rituals of European Judaism and

Christianity of his own time. He judged religious beliefs to function as superstitions and saw religious behavior as resembling mental illness. He interpreted these illusions as arising from the unresolved emotional conflicts of early childhood and predicted that religion would—and must—be abandoned in the ongoing movement of human progress. Religion is, as he states in *The Future of an Illusion*, "the universal obsessional neurosis of humanity. " He continues, "If this view is right, it is to be supposed that a turning-away from religion is bound to occur with the fatal inevitability of a process of growth, and that we find ourselves at this very juncture in the middle of that phase of development. "[9]

William James, prominent American philosopher and psychologist of religion who was writing at the same time as Freud, offered a profoundly different analysis of the role of religion in personal life and its implications for society. In his classic work *The Varieties of Religious Experience*, James identifies positive psychological characteristics that are associated with religious experience:

(1) "a new zest which adds itself as a gift to life. " In some religious people, James remarks, this vitality is expressed in appreciation of the simple delights of living; in others it leads to acts of extraordinary commitment and heroism.

(2) "an assurance of safety and a temper of peace. " These moods expand personal resilience and strengthen self-worth and self-confidence.

(3) "and, in relation to others, a preponderance of loving affections. "[10] James sees religious experience serving as a foundation of attitudes and actions of genuine altruism.

E. RELIGIOUS STUDIES—PUBLIC INQUIRY INTO THE MEANING OF SYMBOLIC DISCOURSE

Sometimes the term *religious studies* is used in a very general sense, to describe any program that studies more than one single religious tradition. Many universities in Europe and North America, for example, have expanded the scope of earlier programs devoted to Protestant or catholic theology to include courses in Buddhism or Islam. Often this expansion leads to a name change from Department of Theology to Department of Religious Studies.

But many scholars reserve the term *religious studies* to a particular perspective on the study of religion and religiousness. Paul Ricoeur defines religious studies as a "public inquiry into the meaning of symbolic discourse. "[11] In this more precise meaning, religious studies signifies a multi-disciplinary and cross-cultural approach that examines symbols of transcendence.

Scholars who adopt this approach view humanity's religious traditions as historically conditioned symbol systems. These varied traditions are recognized as diverse expressions of the human quest for transcendence. Robert Bellah has identified his approach to religious studies as "symbolic realism," which traces "the way symbols operate—defining the world, constituting social groups, and bridging conscious and unconscious meanings—(and how these) symbolically constituted realities transcend individuals and groups. Thus they anchor human life in a transcendent reality. "[12]

In religious studies, scholarship is guided by modern critical methodology; its goal is to examine the role of religion in the formation and transmission of culture. Since religious concepts and sacred symbols and ritual expressions and organizational forms are so embedded in particular cultures, comparative research and multidisciplinary tools are essential. Archeology, cultural history, sociology, political science, social theory, cognitive psychology, linguistic studies—each of these disciplines bring tools useful to religious studies. In another kind of critical reflection, philosophers and theologians study the sacred texts and religious symbols of their own and other cultures. Some of these scholars stand "inside" the religious worldview they are studying, others approach the religious tradition as interested "outsiders. " Drawing on the observations of both insiders and outsiders, religious studies seeks a more comprehensive understanding of the intellectual claims and conceptual implications of particular religious traditions.

Catholic and Protestant Christian theologians engaged in religious studies, for example, characteristically work within the symbol system of the biblical tradition. Using the critical-historical method, these scholars re-examine the images of God and the concepts of transcendence that have emerge across the historical trajectory of the Orthodox, Catholic, and Reform Christian thought. Like other researchers in the field of religious studies, theologians pursue a critical and constructive understanding of the role of sacred symbols in transmitting meaning and values. The goal of their scholarship is neither the defense of Catholic belief nor the spread of Protestant religion. As theologian Frank Whaling observes, theologians engaged in religious studies recognize "the urgency of conceptualizing and apprehending transcendence in a global context—transcendence in the human awareness of nature, the human awareness of humans, and the human awareness of transcendent reality. "[13]

CLARIFYING THE VOCABULARY USED IN THE ACADEMIC STUDY OF RELIGION

As we have indicated above, scholars use many different approaches in their efforts to understand religion. As a result, the terminology used in religious studies is not always uniform. Often different words are used by different writers; sometimes the same word is used, but takes on a different meaning. Here we offer "working definitions" of terms that we will use throughout this book. Not every religious scholar will agree with all of our usages. But these statements are not meant to dispute other scholars, Our intent is to offer some basic clarifications to assist the Chinese reader. We will look especially at four terms: religion, religiousness, faith, and sacred.

Religion. This term characteristically refers to an institutional form of faith, such as Islam or Christianity. Religious institutions, as we saw in the discussion above, usually have identifiable membership, specialized leadership groups, authority structures, classic texts, formal doctrines, moral codes, and ritual practices.

In a broader sense, each religion includes both a spiritual tradition or *worldview* and a set of religious *practices* that members follow in pursuit of spiritual awareness, transformation and consolation. These religious practices usually include rituals of prayer and worship, codes of moral behavior, and acts of service and compassion.

Debate exists on whether the term *religion* is adequate to encompass the great historic traditions of eastern civilizations, such as

Daoism, Confucianism, Hinduism, Buddhism. As anthropologist Robert Weller observes, religion often carries with it western connotations of a "belief in a supreme power, ordered worship, and a code of ethics," plus sharp distinctions of sacred and secular. [14] Daoist scholar Kristofer Schipper notes that the use of the term religion "may be correct for Islam or Catholicism, but when this term is used for the Chinese popular religion and its highest expression, Daoism ··· it can only create misunderstandings. "[15] Philosopher John Berthrong insists that "one simply cannot use the term religion or religious as defined in a western institutional sense to encompass the Confucian spiritual trajectories. "[16] For this reason, many scholars today prefer to use the more inclusive term *historic wisdom traditions* to discuss the spiritual resources of both eastern and western cultures.

Religiousness. This more specialized term, mentioned already in Chapter One, is often used in contemporary studies to speak about the human capacity for meaning-making; in particular, the effort to make sense of life at the deepest level of experience. In this understanding, religiousness signifies the characteristically human effort to compose a satisfying life perspective, a perspective broad enough to embrace realities and concerns beyond the world of everyday awareness.

Religiousness responds to the *ultimate or limit* questions of human experience. These significant questions include: What is the origin and goal of human life? Does my own existence have purpose or significance? Are there values worth living for? Is there anything worth dying for? Religiousness embraces efforts to shape one's life according to this deeper understanding of reality, through moral behavior and other life practices.

Some social scientists use the term *religiosity* in this context. But in ordinary English usage, "religiosity" carries many negative connotations; it suggests compulsive preoccupation with religious activities or extreme, even deviant, religious sentiment. For that reason, current scholarship is moving toward the more neutral term *religiousness.*

There are links between religion and religiousness. Human consciousness is always and necessarily shaped by social contexts. And across centuries, the search for ultimate meaning that we call human religiousness has often taken place within the context of organized religious groups. These institutional forms of religion have been developed to shape and support religious awareness. Without the order and continuity these social settings provide, personal religious awareness is not easy to sustain. So religion and religiousness are closely linked in human experience.

But history shows that over time the communal patterns can harden into cumbersome organizations, more and more removed from the initial religious insight. When this happens, some members in these groups find that *religion* becomes a barrier to their *religiousness.*

Throughout the world today, many people continue to adopt the symbols and beliefs of a particular religion or spiritual tradition as authentic expression of their own religiousness. But many other people today express their religiousness in other ways. Some may draw symbols and practices from several spiritual traditions; others look outside all formal religious traditions to symbols from nature or art or science to express their personal religiousness.

Faith. Frequently in English the term *faith* designates a particular religious tradition; for example, we might speak of the Catholic faith, the Buddhist faith, the Jewish faith. In some religious discussions, *to have faith* means to confidently accept as true, certain core religious doctrines that cannot be proved by ordinary methods of rational verification (such as strictly logical analysis or scientific experiment). In this meaning, *faith* is close to *belief*.

In the academic fields of cognitive psychology and psychology of religion in the West , the term *faith* has come to be used in a more specialized way. In this usage, *faith* names the ongoing process of interpretation through which individuals face and resolve the ultimate or limit issues of human existence, such as those we considered in Chapter One.

The work of religious psychologist James Fowler has been important in the research tradition that uses the term *faith* in this way. In Fowler's understanding, faith is an integral, centering process that (a) gives coherence and direction to persons' lives, (b) links them in shared trusts and loyalties with others, (c) locates their personal commitments and communal loyalties within a larger frame of meaning, and (d) enables them to face the limit conditions of human life, by drawing on their relationship with what is Ultimate in life. [17]

More practically, this meaning of faith points to the ongoing processes of cognitive and emotional development, through which a person

    (a) searches for something larger than *self* in which to
        place one's trust;

    (b) tries to identify values to stake one's life on;

    (c) struggles to understand one's place in the universe; and

    (d) attempts to make contact with this larger context of
        meaning.

Acknowledging that religious faith can be guided by misinformed or even destructive motives, David Tracy describes the signs of an authentic faith: "When it is believable, religious faith manifests a sense of the radical mystery of all reality: the mystery we are to ourselves; the mystery of history, nature, and the cosmos; the mystery above all of Ultimate Reality. "[18]

Sacred. Both scholars and religious believers have struggled to describe the mysterious core of religious awareness, a Reality that lies beyond the human ability to name it. In early Catholic practice the Latin word *deus* was used to refer to this transcendent power; this word survives in the English language as "deity. " As the academic study of religion developed in the early 20th century, Rudolf Otto used the term *numinous* (from the Latin word *numen*) to designate the experience of the holy—a mysterious power that was at once fascinating and fearful. Emile Durkheim, an early sociologist of religion, spoke of the sacred domain.

William James adopted the term divine. For James, divine names the "primal reality"—primal not in the sense of primitive or uncivilized but as the most fundamental reality. This reality— whether named numinous or holy or sacred or divine—stands as the foundation of all religion. So James defines religion as "the feelings, acts, and experiences of individuals ··· so far as they apprehend themselves to stand in relation to whatever they may consider divine. "[19]

Many scholars today use the word *sacred* to designate this mysterious power. Anthropologist Roy Rappaport, in a comprehensive cross-cultural review of field studies, has found five common elements used to describe the religious experience of the sacred or divine. People report an immediate awareness of a reality that:

actually exists—this reality is not just an idea or concept.

has vitality—this reality is recognized as alive, as *energy*, as *qi*.

is powerful—this reality is understood as active and efficacious.

but is not material—this reality is not contacted through sense data; is not available to empirical investigation; cannot be known adequately through discursive reasoning.

and is open to and invites relationship—this reality can be personally encountered through love, participation, absorption. [20]

Despite the determination to name this mysterious source of religious experience, faith traditions acknowledge that, finally, the sacred or divine reality cannot be named. Rabbinical scholars in the Jewish tradition came to insist that Yahweh's name was too sacred to be pronounced or recorded—thus the term G * D or the four consonants of YHWH appear instead in many Jewish writings. Christianity—Catholic, Orthodox, and Protestant—has long sustained an *apophatic* ("beyond speech") tradition, which cautions that anything humans can say about God falls short of the divine Mystery. And the Daoist classic, the *Dao De Jing*, opens with the paradoxical assertion: "The Dao that can be spoken is not the Dao."

NOTES

[1] *The Concise Columbia Encyclopedia*, p. 712.

[2] Denise Carmody, "Women and Religion: Where Mystery Comes to Center Stage," p. 263.

[3] William James, *The Varieties of Religious Experience*, p. 66—67.

[4]Wilfred Cantwell Smith has made significant contributions to this understanding of "living faith" as distinct from religion and religious belief; see his discussions in *The Meaning and End of Religion* and *Faith and Belief*.

[5]Donald Swensen, *Society, Spirituality, and the Sacred: A Social Scientific Introduction*, pp. 50—57; for a sensitive and comprehensive introduction to both eastern and western religions, see Huston Smith, The *World's Religions*.

[6]Clifford Geertz, *Available Light*, p. 170.

[7]Clifford Geertz, *The Interpretation of Cultures*, p. 90.

[8]Karl Marx and Friedrich Engles, *On Religion*, p. 41.

[9]Sigmund Freud, *The Future of an Illusion*, p. 43.

[10]James, *The Varieties of Religious Experience*, pp. 528—529.

[11]Paul Ricoeur, *Figuring The Sacred*, p. 14.

[12]For a discussion of Bellah's "symbolic realism" and its continuing contribution to the study of religion, see Richard Madsen et al. , *Meaning and Modernity: Religion, Polity and Self*; the quotation is from p. xi.

[13] Frank Whaling, " Theological Approaches" in *Approaches to the Study of Religion*, p. 261.

[14]Robert Weller, "Worship, Teachings, and State Power in China and Taiwan," p. 287.

[15]Kristofer Schipper, *The Taoist Body*, p. 3.

[16]John Berthrong, *All Under Heaven*, p. 197.

[17]James Fowler, *Faithful Change*, p. 56.

[18]David Tracy, *Plurality and Ambiguity*, p. 107.

[19]James, *The Varieties of Religious Experience*, p. 36.

[20]Roy Rappoport's discussion of the sacred is found in *Ritual and Religion in the Making of Humanity*; on p. 397 he lists the elements of the "universal experience" of the divine.

CHAPTER FOUR: CHINESE POPULAR RELIGION

The study of Chinese religions is undergoing a fasci-
nating shift ⋯ (adopting) a focus which does not iso-
late religion for the sake of a false clarity but rather
explores religion as fully imbedded in society and cul-
ture. [1]

Today many scholars of religion are adjusting their focus from
a nearly exclusive study of formal religious organizations and classical texts to an exploration of the beliefs and practices in ordinary
people's lives. These contemporary approaches to the academic
study of religion have stimulated a fresh evaluation of the religious
dimensions of Chinese culture.

Scholars today are cautious about using the abstract term *re-*
ligion to describe China's spiritual heritage. The translated term
zong jiao that was first introduced in China only in the 1890s is
essentially a western concept grafted onto Chinese experience. In
both English and Chinese, the word carries connotations that are
foreign to Chinese sensibilities: a sharp dichotomy between sacred
and secular, formal and exclusive group membership, the central
role of a distinct group of professionally trained leaders, heightened concern for orthodoxy in belief and practice. Responding to

these western nuances, many early observers insisted that China had no religion.

It was not only western scholars who were slow to recognize the religious dimensions of Chinese culture. In the intellectual ferment that characterized the East-West cultural encounters of the late 19th century, many Chinese scholars embraced the rationalism of the European Enlightenment. Reluctant to have Chinese culture identified with practices that were being discredited by western intellectuals of the time, the influential Chinese scholar Hu Shi declared that "China is a country without religion and the Chinese are a people who are not bound by religious superstitions. "[2]

This view, representative of the broader intellectual climate of Hu Shi's time, continues to be expressed by some Chinese scholars who received their academic training in theWest. Other scholars— both in China and the West—distinguish sharply between the multiple "suspicious" beliefs adhered to by the masses and the "great traditions" of Confucianism, Buddhism, and Daoism.

But in the post-Mao period, researchers in mainland China began a new era of cultural studies, focusing more attention on the worldview and values of ordinary Chinese people. Their goal has been to assess the cultural resources that shape the lives of the vast majority of the Chinese population. In nearly all these studies, a surprisingly positive tone has replaced the more conventional view of local practices and beliefs as mere superstition. Daniel Overmyer is an internationally recognized scholar who has devoted his professional career to the study of Chinese culture. Praising the important contributions being made by mainland scholars today, Overmyer has concluded "What we see here is not only a new direction in scholarship, but also a great and historic culture finally trying to recognize and come to terms with the religious traditions of the great majority of its people. "[3]

Religious scholars today speak more appreciatively of the spiritual significance of China's local traditions. In academic discussion, this common heritage of belief and practice is often identified as *Chinese popular religion*: "the rituals carried out by ordinary people in families and local communities as part of their normal social activities, and the beliefs and values associated with those rituals. "[4]

THE DISTINCTIVENESS OF CHINESE RELIGION: "HEAVEN AND HUMANS ARE ONE. "

In 1962 sociologist C. K. Yang published *Religion in Chinese Society*, a book widely acclaimed as a world classic in sociology of religion. This work was the fruit of Yang's effort to understand the place of religion in Chinese culture. As he states in the introduction: "Among the three leading centers of civilization—Europe, India, and China—the place of religion in society is the least clearly recognized in the case of China. " Yang recognized that "there was no strong, centrally organized religion in most periods of Chinese history" and he wanted to understand why.

Yang began his study by offering a broad definition: "Religion may be viewed as a continuum ranging from nontheistic belief systems with an emotional intensity that borders upon ultimacy, to theistic belief systems with ultimate values fully symbolized in supernatural entities and supported by patterns of worship and organization. "[5] With this definition in mind, he introduced the term *dif-*

fused religion to show how ritual practices and beliefs in traditional Chinese villages differed from the highly organized "institutional" religions that characterize the West. [6] While scholars debate whether this English word *diffused* adequately describes how this religious heritage functions in Chinese society, Yang's analysis remains a primary source in the sociological analysis of religion in China.

From Yang's perspective, Chinese Buddhism and Daoism could be understood as institutional religions, since they each have their own basic concepts and their own recognizable organizations. These religions developed sacred texts and specific rituals that expressed universal concerns and values. But in Yang's judgment neither Buddhism nor Daoism shaped Chinese society to the extent that the Catholic/Christian worldview shaped the social and political structures of European society. Instead, Chinese society was shaped by the seemingly agnostic Confucian tradition through the influence of the scholarly official class.

But while Confucianism was the acknowledged worldview of the educated minority, the Chinese religious landscape was dominated by what Yang called the classical or indigenous tradition. In Yang's view, this original worldview of ancient China was thoroughly incorporated into the daily life of Chinese people at every level of society. Its spiritual sensitivities were so completely absorbed into the social institutions of everyday life that religion and culture were all but merged. This absorption of a shared religious vision and practice throughout society meant that "the social environment as a whole had a sacred atmosphere. "[7] Thus, this diffused religion needed no independent institutional base, such as an identifiable priesthood or a separate authority structure. Its religious functions were performed through the ordinary structures of Chinese society—the kinship system and the vast socio-political network of the imperial state.

In *Religion in Chinese Society* Yang gave a comprehensive account of the success of Chinese religion in sustaining the long-lasting ethical and political order of the Chinese civilization. He was aware of the tendency among intellectuals to distinguish elite forms of religion from folk religion, often with prejudice against the popular expressions of belief and practice. To counteract this approach, Yang emphasized that across Chinese history "the elite culture and the peasant culture were not two different things; they were versions of each other. "[8]

Yang identified the core of China's indigenous religion: "the belief in Heaven and fate, the condoning of divination, the close alliance with the theory of *Yin-yang* and the Five Elements, the emphasis on sacrifice and ancestor worship. "[9] In his judgment, this classic religious worldview reached full development as early as the Zhou dynasty (1122—221 bce), long before the foreign influence of Buddhism and the rise of Daoism as an explicit religious system. Overmyer comments that by the 11th century "these practices had been blended together with Buddhist ideas of *karma* and rebirth and Daoist teachings about many levels of gods to form the popular religious system common from then on. "[10]

Scholars of China's classic religious heritage are aware of the rich complexity of this vast tradition. In this chapter we will offer an overview of the worldview and beliefs of this classic tradition, including examples of its continuing vitality throughout rural China today.

CHINESE POPULAR RELIGION THRIVES
IN RURAL CHINA

Since the beginning of the Opening and Reform, the Chinese government has adopted a series of new policies regarding religious belief and practice. The gradual liberalization of official regulations began in 1982; in 1990 Jiang Zemin himself called for a "more tolerant management of religious organizations. "This more accommodating attitude now prevails in regard to the five religions officially recognized by Chinese law—Daoism, Buddhism, Islam, and both Catholic and Protestant Christianity. But even as the government has softened its view of these legally recognized institutional religions, the customary beliefs and practices of ordinary Chinese are often dismissed as feudal superstition (*fengjian mixin*) and—as such—have no legal status or legal protection.

While some officials and intellectuals continue to ignore or depreciate the beliefs and ritual practices of ordinary people, China's classic religious heritage plays a very significant role in contemporary Chinese society. In fact there has been an extraordinary renaissance of popular religious activity, especially but not exclusively in rural China. Since people living in rural areas account for seventy-five percent of China's 1. 2 billion inhabitants, rural developments continue to be indicators of changes affecting the new China.

In this section we will explore this resurgence of popular religion during this period of China's economic reforms. We will begin with a description of the classic elements that have long been part of Chinese local religious practice.

BASIC CHARACTERISTICS OF CHINESE
POPULAR RELIGION

"Before modern iconoclasm held sway, religion was in evidence everywhere in China: each house had its altar, each district and village its temple. They were numerous and easy to spot, for as a rule, the local temple was the most beautiful building, the pride of the area···(Temples) were always built by an association or a local community···In the countryside, they were erected by all the members of a village community or regional association. Management of the common property—buildings, land, furnishings, and revenue—was strictly egalitarian···(W)orship in a temple is not reserved exclusively for the saint or gods to whom it is dedicated. The *miao* is a place open to all beings, divine and human. A community as well as a communal house, it is a place for casual and formal meetings. The elders go there to discuss village affairs. Grandmothers, the family delegates in religious matters, go there every day with offerings of incense and to fill the lamps with oil. Music and theater associations, along with clubs for boxing, reading, chess, charity, pilgrimages, automatic writing, medical research, kite flying, and cultural associations of all kinds create their headquarters in the temple, and find there as well a place of worship for their particular patron saint. "[11]

China's classic religious practices include worship of ancestors and deities, funeral rituals, temple festivals of community renewal in honor of the birthdays of local patron gods, various forms of divination, geomancy, spirit-possession, exorcism of harmful forces, and other rituals. These activities, carried out by ordinary people in their homes and villages, have formed the mainstream of Chinese religion throughout history. And now, after decades of neglect, thousands of temples have been restored or rebuilt throughout China. Millions of Chinese people once again take active part in public ritual events, which become more frequent and more elaborate each year. There is, in short, increasing evidence that local religious practices are spreading all across China.

These developments in China's diffused religious tradition have attracted the attention of religious scholars, both in China and in the West. Different investigations of local communal religious activities show, for instance, that there are no full-time religious specialists in Chinese villages who are paid by the community for their work—except perhaps for old men or women serving as temple caretakers. Spirit-mediums and Daoist priests are hired when they are needed, and materials for rituals and offerings are provided as necessary.

Important aspects of Chinese popular religious life are activities related to the supernatural. These sensibilities are expressed in rituals and other practices which are especially attuned to questions of fortune, fate and chance (*ming yun*, *yuan fen*, *karma*). But these activities do not coalesce into religious institutions that are serviced by professional personnel. Instead they remain at the level of diffused religion.

RURAL RELIGION TODAY

Popular religion is alive and well developed in the rural areas of mainland China. Despite the violent destruction of temples and statues during the decade of the Cultural Revolution (1966—76), devotion to local deities continues to thrive. The increasing popularity of temple festivals and the growth of traditional religions in China have been significant phenomena since the late 1970s. Shrines are being rebuilt; the sale of incense sticks and paper money used in rituals is once again big business; local persons recognized as mediums representing the gods are to be found everywhere. Recent efforts of rebuilding temples and organizing local festival and religious pilgrimages have been accomplished almost entirely without government funding. These projects have relied solely on donations of cash and personal labor by local farmers and villagers.

Villagers participate together in communal rites on important annual ceremonies such as Chinese New Year and Lantern Festival, or on the birthdays of the gods. But they also go to village temples at other times, alone or with family members, to worship the local gods by prayerful bowing, proclaiming vows, making offerings of food and drink, and burning incense and spirit money.

The temple plays a key role in village society, as a market center and a place to air local grievances and search for answers. The local temple is also the site of significant deities, whose power resides in statues and other depictions. Many of the gods venerated in traditional Chinese religion are deified spirits of important local personages, believed to be particularly responsive to the prayers and petitions of local people. The power of local gods is manifested in both physical healing and in the general prosperity of the village.

Local mediums or shamans can also mediate the efficacious power of the gods to ordinary folk, offering moral advice and performing rites of health and healing. Specialists in dream interpretation and fortune telling also contribute their skills to local communal religion. In north China, ancestors and local gods are customarily venerated in shrines established in individual homes. In many communities in southeast China, the practice of ancestor veneration halls has been revived. Many of these communal shrines have been funded by overseas Chinese whose families originally lived in the village.

THE CHINESE WORLDVIEW: BALANCE OF *YIN AND YANG*

Every religious tradition, whether diffused throughout a culture or developed into a distinct institution, provides a worldview. This life perspective is manifest in both *beliefs* rooted in a comprehensive vision of reality and in *practices* which express these beliefs in activities.

Ninian Smart defines a religious worldview as a system of "belief which through symbol and actions mobilizes the feelings and will of human beings. "[12] Anthropologist Clifford Geertz notes that a people's worldview is "their picture of the way things in sheer actuality are, their concept of nature, the self, of society. "[13]

Daniel Overmyer offers this description of the worldview that underpins the classic religiousness that is common to Chinese culture: "The world itself is a sacred place of power and mystery, and···tohuman beings belongs the important task of cooperating with this power and making it operative in society. "[14] In the classic Chinese worldview the distinction between sacred and secular, so significant in western religious consciousness, has no place. Overmyer elaborates on this distinctive feature of Chinese popular religion:

The world is a living system in which everything is connected by shared rhythms and resonances···these rhythms are discussed as the cold, dark forces of *yin* and the hot, bright forces of *yang*; together with the five powers of metal, plant life, water, fire, and earth; these forces are modes of *qi*, "vital substance. "Their interaction produces all things. [15]

In this worldview, *qi* is the vital energy—material and more—that pulses through reality, animating all of life. The dynamic movements of *yin* and *yang* are not antagonistic (as one might expect in a western worldview) but complementary facets of this energy of *qi*. These core elements of China's classic worldview undergird all aspects of life and serve as the taproot of all Chinese spirituality.

COMMON BELIEFS OF CHINESE POPULAR RELIGION

Beliefs flow from worldviews. Seeing the world a certain way leads to particular beliefs about this world. Here we will consider three beliefs at the core of Chinese popular religion. These beliefs are the idiom or vocabulary through which the classic Chinese worldview is expressed in the lives of Chinese people.

Ming yun. Like other great civilizations, China has long been absorbed in the puzzling question of human fate. Is human life simply random? Or does each person have a particular fate? How do humans come to recognize their own destiny? Can one's destiny be changed, influenced by conscious choices made throughout life?

Early in Chinese history the notion of "heaven's mandate"

(*tian ming*) dominated the discussion of human destiny. *Ming* referred to forces outside a person's control that shaped the direction of a life. But Chinese thinkers were aware of other events—the circumstances of a specific time or particular place—that also influenced one's fate. From this dual awareness grew the sense that a person's destiny is both fixed and flexible.

The widely shared cultural understanding of *ming yun*—destiny as determined by *ming* and fate shaped by *yun* or chance events—has definitively shaped Chinese culture. This belief in fate as fixed and flexible underpins a wide variety of common practices, from the ancient practices of divination (established rules for interpreting the cracks in tortoise shells) to the still popular practice of visiting fortune tellers.

At different times in Chinese history the more fixed or fatalistic aspect of destiny has been strong; eras when extreme poverty or rigid government control seem to allow little freedom for choice or change. At other times—such as the present when economic opportunity and political freedom are emerging in China—the flexible aspects of fate come to predominate. But at all times the ever-changing and mysterious blend of *ming* and *yun*, fate fixed and flexible, is understood to be at play in shaping the individual's personal destiny.

Yuan fen. Chinese culture has for centuries recognized the importance of coincidences or chance events in determining the direction of a person's life. Due to personal illness, a person cancels a planned trip to another city; later that day the train on which the person was to travel is involved in a terrible accident, and many riders are killed. Is this simply luck? By chance we meet the person whom we later marry. Why and how do such coincidences occur? What governs these chance events which, from another perspective, appear to be more than chance?

The Chinese phrase *yuan fen* captures the conviction that some events may be more than coincidence. Some apparently random events seem to be mysteriously linked with one's destiny. The phrase *yuan fen* is so commonplace in contemporary Chinese speech that it has become, to a large extent, a cultural cliché. But even clichés are rooted in experience: the recognition that a fortunate coincidence has made a profound difference in one's life gives the phrase deeper significance.

Bao ying. A third belief that lies deep in Chinese culture is a conviction that the universe is ultimately moral. This is a longing that finds expression in many cultures: those who act virtuously should be rewarded by the events of their lives; evil persons should be punished.

In the Chinese culture the notion of *bao ying* expresses this belief. In the ancient text of the *shijing* we read: "On the doer of good, heaven sends down blessings, and on the doer of evil, he sends down calamities." This conviction, already at the heart of ancient Chinese culture and popular religion, was reinforced by the later introduction of the Buddhist understanding of *karma*. In this understanding, there are no coincidences: whatever one experiences— whether fortunate event or painful accident—comes as a result of one's previous moral behavior.

PRACTICES IN CHINESE POPULAR RELIGION

Worldviews give rise to beliefs; beliefs about the world and human life lead to practices—practical actions that express one's beliefs. Three distinctive practices are part of Chinese popular religion: *feng shui*, pilgrimage, and charismatic healing.

Feng shui. As Mayfair Yang writes, "*Feng shui*, literally 'wind and water,' is an ancient art or technology which tries to improve people's physical and spiritual life by aligning the buildings in which they live and the graves in which their ancestors are buried, to harmonize with and tap into the flow of the 'primordial energy,' or *qi*, of the earth. "[16] The practice of *feng shui* has directed the location and orientation of human dwellings and tombs in China for millennia. Contemporary explanations of this spiritual practice speak of it as "environmental planning" and "cultivation and resource management. "[17]

At the heart of this practice is the worldview that sees the vital energy of *qi* moving through the entire cosmos. The same *qi* that animates the human body moves through and gives energy to the natural environment. "In a holistic view of the cosmos, the human anatomy is a microcosm of the earth, and the blood veins of one correspond to the rivers and streams of the other. "[18]

Belief in the dynamic movement of cosmic energy leads to practical actions. "One should put one's house or village on a slight slope or rise" that is "surrounded on two or three sides by higher ridges and hills" with "a grove of trees upslope" and "a stream at hand. " The goal of *feng shui* is to ensure that *qi* or vital energy flows properly through the environment; "in practice it protects against floods and storms and provides materials for building and water for drinking and waste removal. "[19]

But this practice is concerned with more than the natural environment. "In a densely populated place like China, with no laws to protect the rights of individuals, a system was needed that motivated one family to maintain its environment in order not to adversely affect another's. "[20] As is characteristic of the Chinese worldview, *feng shui* is ultimately concerned with social harmony.

Pilgrimage. While the belief and practice of *feng shui* is distinctive of Chinese culture, the practice of pilgrimage is more universal. Mecca in Saudi Arabia is the holiest site for Muslims. So powerful is this location that Muslims throughout the world turn toward Mecca in prayer five times each day. The Qur'an, the sacred book of Islam, requires that every devout believer should visit this holy city at least once in a lifetime. Annually, in the twelfth month of the Muslim calendar, this pilgrimage—in Arabic, called *hajj* or "effort"—draws several hundred thousand religious visitors.

The river Ganges in India serves as a sacred river for Hindus. Each year many tens of thousands journey to the city of Benares on the banks of the Ganges, to bathe in its sacred waters. The city of Jerusalem has functioned for many centuries as a sacred site for Jews and Muslims, Catholics and Protestants. Near the city of Shanghai two pilgrimage sites remain influential among Chinese today. The low mountain at Sheshan just outside the city has become a pilgrimage destination for thousands of Catholic Christians who visit this shrine dedicated to Mary, the mother of Jesus. South of the city the Buddhist monastery and temples at Po Tu Shan continue to attract thousands of pilgrims, both devoted Buddhists and those of other faiths.

The Daoist temple at Miaofengshan, located forty kilometers northwest of Beijing, is a pilgrimage site that clearly illustrates the close connections between culture and religion in China. By examining the local village associations that plan and conduct pilgrimages to this famous temple, we can trace the interconnected social dynamics typical of Chinese popular religion.

The Daoist goddess associated with Miaofengshan is renowned for her healing powers. Groups of pilgrims,calling themselves "incense associations," visit the temple bringing incense and paper money along with their petitions. As with the practice of pilgrimage in other parts of the world,the journey to this particular temple is arduous. China scholar Susan Naquin describes the trek:"It took the better part of a day to reach the foothills from Peking; from there,a full day's hard climb lay ahead, up steep narrow rocky paths;much of another day was necessary for the knee-jarring return. "[21] But the difficulty only adds to its mystique. The hardships of pilgrimage—danger and difficulty in travel,being away from the familiar food and comforting routines of home—testify to the pilgrim's devotion. Perhaps these inconveniences will even help merit the favor of the gods.

It is often village "flower societies" or *hua hui* that today take on the tasks of organizing a pilgrimage to Miaofengshan. Originally,flower societies were local entertainment troupes, singers and musicians who often performed at religious festivals. These groups were the pride of the village as they contributed to its cultural identity. The flower societies came in time,as Naquin says,to "orchestrate the worship" at the temples. [22] Practically this entailed the collection of money needed to buy food and other supplies for the journey,and the distribution of hats and bags that the pilgrims would bring with them. During the pilgrimage members of these associations would monitor the good behavior of the people,encouraging them to avoid alcohol,not to litter the pilgrimage path, and to keep the women separate from the men.

Similar organizations in other villages—groups that were at the same time both cultural and religious in orientation—might decide to place and maintain lanterns along the pilgrimage route. Other groups would service the tea-stalls that lined the route from Peking to the pilgrimage site. Naquin comments, "We see in the road lanterns and free tea of the 18th century the beginning of an array of services for pilgrims that became a distinctive feature of Miaofeng shan···they were in keeping with the spirit of good works that characterized Buddhist and Confucian lay piety in general and these associations in particular. "[23]

These associations served a variety of functions contributing to a pilgrimage's success: "As travel agents and tour directors, they advertised and facilitated the pilgrimage; as performers they punctuated the exhausting route with sound, color, excitement, and action. "[24]

These pilgrimages were curtailed with the end of the Qing Dynasty (1911) and disbanded again during the Cultural Revolution. They have resumed in recent years and are now once again thriving. In these practices of pilgrimage we see the interplay of cultural and religious life that has characterized rural China throughout much of its history.

Charismatic Healing: Silk Worm Mother. In the summer of 2000 sociologist Lizhu Fan was involved in research on temple festivals in north China. By chance she met Mrs. Wu, an older woman reputed to be a spirit-medium or shamanistic healer. The story of Mrs. Wu's vocation offers a concrete example of popular religiousness in contemporary China.

Mrs. Wu lives in Zhiwuying village in the Baoding area of Hebei Province, about one hundred miles south of Beijing. This is her home village, where she was born, grew up, married, and raised a family of two sons and three daughters. At the time her husband died, in her own fiftieth year, Mrs. Wu did not practice any religion. In her own words, "I was too poor to believe in God. "

In 1977, at sixty years of age, Mrs. Wu began experiencing severe pain in her legs. The local doctor gave her medicine but the pain did not subside. During this difficult period she experienced a strange dream: several people appeared, telling her she was to serve them as an incarnation of the Silk Worm Mother, a goddess long revered in this area. Mrs. Wu was troubled by this dream, especially as it returned with some frequency over a period of two months. When Mrs. Wu shared this dream's content with her brother, he was upset and insisted that she should just ignore it. Herself illiterate, she finally prevailed on him to write on a large sheet of red paper the words "all the gods are here. " This paper she hung in her humble one-room house.

Mrs. Wu still doubted that she could serve as the medium for the Silk Worm Mother goddess. She had no training in healing and she completely lacked confidence in helping other people. And as she continued to resist the "calling" revealed in her dream, her leg pains continued. Finally, when she consented to play the role of spirit-medium, the leg pains disappeared.

At this time the local doctor sent one of his patients who was suffering pain in her arm to see Mrs. Wu. Mrs. Wu was unsure how she could help the woman, but began to simply massage the woman's arm. As she did so, Mrs. Wu reported, she felt power flowing through her own hands into the woman's arm. Still doubting her calling, she wondered, "How do I have such power? Why do my hands know how to treat patients?"

Over time Mrs. Wu allowed herself to take up the role of shamanistic healer. As her reputation spread, people came from surrounding villages to consult with her about their troubles.

The Local Tradition of Silk Worm Mother. In the area around Baoding the cult of Silk Worm Mother is an old tradition. It is believed that the original Silk Worm Mother was a human person who lived in this area thousands of years ago. After a highly virtuous life, she became a goddess who served as protector and healer of people in this locale.

The name Silk Worm Mother suggests the importance of silk cultivation and production in ancient China. This goddess was perhaps originally identified as special protector of this economically important crop. Later her protection was expanded to cover ailments, both physical and psychological. The birthday of Silk Worm Mother was celebrated at a temple festival on the 20th day of the first lunar month. The temple where this celebration had taken place for many centuries has been destroyed a number of times, most recently in the Sino-Japanese war and then during the Cultural Revolution. Mrs. Wu's calling in the late 1970s has led to another renewal of this local devotion.

Mrs. Wu's position as Silk Worm Mother shows many of the essential qualities of classical Chinese religiousness. Popular religious traditions characteristically function without the service of professionally trained clergy or the approval of official authorities. For her part, Mrs. Wu experienced her spiritual calling in a directly personal manner: she was not appointed by a religious official; she had no formal training in the healing arts; she did not inherit this social function through her family. Her role as shamanistic healer points to yet another characteristic of Chinese religiousness: the desire for personal and direct access to divine power, quite apart from institutional control.

Mrs. Wu is well aware of differences among the various complaints that are brought to her. She herself sought conventional medical treatment for her leg pains and she often recommends that others consult medical practitioners as well. But most of those who seek her help display distress of a more psychological and spiritual nature. In many of her treatment sessions, Mrs. Wu combines massage with conversation to explore the person's relationship with relatives and neighbors. Mrs. Wu was keenly aware of the permeable boundaries that both separate and link the living and the dead. Using the cultural idiom, she speaks of these deceased family members as ghosts. She urges patients to find ways to reconcile with these persons who are now gone, but who remain influential in the minds and hearts of the living.

Until only very recently, western psychological disciplines have distinguished themselves sharply from any efforts at spiritual counseling. And modern therapeutic interventions do not employ notions of ghosts or efforts to exorcise their presence. But in rural China at the beginning of the 21st century sophisticated psychological services are not yet available. In their stead more traditional approaches to the release from psychic distress continue to serve. [25]

CROSS-CULTURAL CHARACTERISTICS OF POPULAR RELIGION

This worldview of Chinese popular religion is distinctive, in that its images and practices are shaped by the elaborate codes of Chinese culture. But we can discern here several characteristics of popular religion across diverse cultures.

It is typical of popular religions to see the world as an organic whole, without boundaries separating sacred and secular. Oblivious of such divides, this religious consciousness recognizes the sacred everywhere and strives for direct access to this sacred power. Institutional religions, on the other hand, emphasize a clearly marked division between sacred and secular realms. In institutional religions access to the sacred must often be sought through the mediation of professional clergy who serve as authoritative guardians of the sanctuary.

A second cross-cultural characteristic of popular religion concerns the nature of belonging. In popular religious consciousness, culture and belief are one. Everyone lives according to the world-view, beliefs and practices of the village, simply by reason of living here. No religious conversion is envisioned; no explicit personal commitment is required. Modern institutional religions, however, usually function as voluntary organizations, with established rites of initiation marking a personal decision to embrace the requirements of their particular faith.

Another cross-cultural dimension of popular religion is the importance of the "local." As we have seen above in the examples of popular religion in China, religious activities are tailored to fit a particular place. Rituals often focus on local deities or patron saints strongly identified with *this* local area; many devotions, in fact, take place in the home. Pilgrimages offer another example of this localizing characteristic: sacred power is identified with specific venues—a particular temple or mountain or shrine.

This local focus influences two other distinctive features of popular religion. When religious devotion is centered in particular places, this leads to an expanded number of deities. Each locale celebrates its manifestations of sacred power, its list of gods and other intercessory figures. The institutional religions of the west—Judaism, Christianity, Islam—focus on a single deity that demands universal devotion; devotions in popular religion remain intensely local and so, extravagantly diverse.

Across cultures, popular religions also give prominence to local—and therefore lay—leaders. With many centers of devotion, local people are needed to initiate activities and organize rituals. This further distinguishes popular religion from institutional forms of religious life, which place great stress on the professional preparation of full-time clergy.

But even with these cross-cultural similarities, Chinese popular religion defies easy analysis. Its long history and remarkable complexity make any single statement about China's cultural religiousness subject to dispute. With its beliefs and practices so thoroughly diffused throughout the culture, this form of religiousness does not fit western categories. Yet Chinese popular religion shares two chief characteristics of human religiousness that are discussed earlier in this book: meaning-making (discussed in Chapter One) and transcendence (discussed in Chapter Two). In Chapters Nine and Ten we will continue our discussion of Chinese popular religion, looking there at its urban expression in the modern city of Shenzhen.

NOTES

[1]Catherine Bell, "Religion and Chinese Culture: Toward an Assessment of 'Popular Religion,'" pp. 35—36.

[2]Quoted by C. K. Yang, *Religion in Chinese Society*, p. 5.

[3]Daniel Overmyer, "From 'Feudal Superstition' to 'Popular Beliefs': New Directions in Mainland Chinese Studies of Chinese Popular Religion," p. 125.

[4]Overmyer, "From 'Feudal Superstition,'" p. 104, note 2.

[5]Yang,*Religion in Chinese Society*,p. 26.

[6]Yang,*Religion in Chinese Society*,p. 294.

[7]Yang,*Religion in Chinese Society*,p. 298.

[8]Yang,*Religion in Chinese Society*,p. 40.

[9]Yang,*Religion in Chinese Society* p. 225.

[10]Daniel Overmyer,*Religions of China*,p. 51.

[11]Kristofer Schipper,*The Taoist Body*,pp. 20—22.

[12]Ninian Smart,*Worldviews:Crosscultural Explorations of Human Beliefs*,p. 55.

[13]Clifford Geertz,*The Interpretation of Cultures*,p. 126.

[14]Overmyer,*Religions of China*,p. 13.

[15]Overmyer,*Religions of China*,p. 12.

[16]Mayfair Mei-Hui Yang,"Spatial Struggles:Postcolonial Complex, State Disenchantment,and Popular Reappropriation of Space in Rural Southeast China," p. 731.

[17]E. N. Anderson,"Flowering Apricot:Environmental Practice,Folk Religion,and Daoism," p. 157.

[18]Stephen Field,"In Search of Dragons:The Folk Ecology of *Fengshui*," p. 186.

[19]Field,"In Search of Dragons," p. 186.

[20]Field,"In Search of Dragons," p. 187.

[21]Susan Naquin, *Peking:Temples and City Life*,1400-1900,p. 529.

[22]Naquin,*Peking:Temples and City Life*,p. 528.

[23]Naquin,*Peking:Temples and City Life*,p. 533.

[24]Naquin,*Peking:Temples and City Life*,p. 539.

[25]For fuller discussion of the role of the charismatic healer,see Lizhu Fan,"The Cult of the Silk Worm Mother as a Core of Local Community Religion in a North China Village. "

PART TWO
RELIGION AND MODERNITY

CHAPTER FIVE: SECULARIZATION AND SECULARITY RE-EXAMINED

This chapter examines the historical background in the West which has given rise to theories of secularization. Contemporary evidence is explored to determine the relationship between the social dynamics of modernization and the cultural attitudes of secularity. Final discussion questions the use of "secularization" to explain religion in China.

Historically, the spiritual traditions in eastern cultures have functioned quite differently than has the religious heritage of Christianity in the West. Aware of these differences, scholars today are appropriately cautious in using western-derived categories to describe religious developments in China. Secularization theory provides a case in point.

Among western intellectuals, the secularization model emerged as a dominant explanatory schema more than a century ago, and it continues to provoke energetic debate among both proponents and detractors. This model links the development of modern society with the demise of religion. While different observers give it different emphases, the term generally refers to historical developments that gradually diminished the pervasive cultural influence of the religious worldview.

As commonly described, this secularization process—generated by the advances in scientific knowledge and technological innovation which have fueled modern industrialization—has been at play over several centuries in the West. This historical process is understood to be manifest at the personal level in decreasing participation in formal church activities, in the erosion of religious identity, and in a general diminishment of religious sensitivity.

The secularization debate continues among western religious thinkers and social scientists. Expanded empirical research and interdisciplinary analysis have led to more nuanced expressions of the theory and more limited scope to its claims. But the secularization model still shapes much of the discussion of social modernization in China, among intellectuals and other observers both eastern and western. For this reason it is important to clarify the meaning of several key words that are used in this discussion.

As a conceptual model, secularization theory does not stand alone. Rather it is part of a broader discussion of modernization, or how modern civilizations develop. Therefore to understand the secularization model and to evaluate its claims, we must begin by clarifying the elements of modernization and modernity.

MODERNIZATION AND MODERNITY

Both these terms focus our attention on modern life. But their vantage points are somewhat different. *Modernization* points to changes in the structures of life and work that develop as societies based on rural agricultural economies become more dependent on industrial production. Sociologists are particularly interested in describing these structural changes and tracing their causes and consequences.

Modernity points to the shifts in culture and in personal consciousness that accompany these significant social changes. Social philosophers and social scientists—historians, cultural anthropologists, cultural psychologists—all contribute to a lively ongoing debate about these cultural shifts.

In real life, the structural dynamics identified as elements of modernization and the cultural developments identified as elements of modernity are essentially interrelated. Thus *modernity* and *modernization* provide two perspectives on a common phenomenon. But while these two terms share a common focus, they are not describing exactly the same thing.

Philosopher Charles Taylor helps clarify some of the distinctions between these two ideas. [1] For Taylor, modernization describes a range of social processes that characterize the movement of society from feudal organization toward the institutional forms characteristic of the nation state. This description was originally based on the significant historical events that reshaped Europe between the 17th and 19th centuries. And the concept remains embedded in the history and culture of the West.

Modernity, for Taylor, is a cultural phenomenon. Modernity designates ideas and ideals that have both led to and emerged within the social processes of modernization, and that now characterize the thinking and feeling of most people who dwell in modern societies. Taylor identifies a broad set of understandings about personhood, nature, society and morality that are now widely accepted in many parts of the world. He argues that these elements of modern

Social Processes Associated with *Modernization*

- **industrialization**

  Process through which the economic base of the society becomes increasingly linked to factory-based
  manufacture and centralized distribution of goods.

- **urbanization**

  Processes by which large segments of population
  move from rural areas to expanding cities in pursuit
  of paid employment; this disrupts traditional family-
  based social control and places new demands on urban services.

- **participative political life**

  Process by which political organization moves toward
  increased citizen participation, as more personal forms
  of civic governance (inherited monarchy and land-
  based aristocracy) are replaced by impersonal bu-
  reaucracies.

- **functional differentiation in society**

  Process through which various spheres of social activity—the economy, government, science, education,
  religion, media, the arts—while interrelated, are understood as distinct and function with increasing autonomy.

Figure Two

Cultural Ideas and Moral Ideals Linked with *Modernity*

- **science as source of truth and foundation of progress**

  Widely shared belief that scientific method provides most reliable access to truth and that technological application of its findings offers the best hope for human benefit.

- **instrumental rationality**

  Priority is given to calculating the most efficient means to a given end. Cost-benefit ratio becomes the dominant measure of success. As a result, the economic realm gains greater influence in social and political life and policy.

- **individualism**

  Conviction that people have a right to make choices, based on conscientious personal conviction, across a broad range of political and moral domains; these rights should be defended by political and legal safeguards.

- **universal equality**

  Concept of the state as an instrument designed to serve individuals and intended to serve all interests equally. In principle, all citizens have direct access to political system, which is committed to improving social condition of all.

Figure Three

consciousness have been evoked and sustained in diverse social settings across the globalizing world. So Taylor acknowledges that in the West these ideas and ideals of modernity are historically linked to particular forms of economic organization and political governance. But he warns against seeing these historical links as necessary or inevitable.

Along with a growing number of scholars both East and West, Taylor concludes that there are *multiple modernities*, that is, a variety of historically and culturally distinct paths along which contemporary societies develop. As the changes associated with new patterns of social and economic life affect different societies, each of these "receiving cultures" responds in its own way. And contemporary evidence shows that diverse cultural settings have been able to sustain an industrial economy and to support the development of modern consciousness among their citizenry.

Figures Two and Three may help distinguish between the sociological concept of *modernization* and the cultural concept of *modernity*. [2]

SECULARIZATION

With this understanding of modernization and modernity as a background, we can return to our discussion of secularization theory. American sociologist Peter Berger's definition offers a good place to start: "By secularization we mean the process by which sectors of society and culture are removed from the domination of religious institutions and symbols. "[3]

Emile Durkheim, one of the most influential thinkers among

classic sociological theorists, determined that functional differentiation was the major dynamic in the movement toward modern social organization in the West. Functional differentiation, as we see in Figure Two, describes the emergence of several somewhat autonomous arenas of social organization from an earlier, more organically interrelated whole.

In pre-modern Europe, Catholic Christianity was at the core of society's functioning. Catholic symbols and religious practices animated and often stabilized a web of shifting political allegiances. And the Catholic church, through its organizations and personnel, provided the bulk of the available social services—schools, hospitals, care for the needy, support of the arts, mediation between warring factions. These interwoven cultural and social threads formed the social fabric of medieval Christendom.

In Europe, then, functional differentiation had profound impact on the Catholic (and, later, the Protestant) church. Its political influence was gradually diminished, as new forms of governance no longer looked to the church for validation. Its role as chief provider of social services was undercut, as wealthy individuals and civic organizations took more and more responsibility for education, the arts, and other communal needs. And the religious movements of the Reformation shattered its cultural dominance; no longer speaking in one voice, the churches' moral message was more easily questioned, even dismissed.

It is this European context that provides the background for the sociological term *secularization*. And in the historical developments in western Europe over the past five hundred years we see Berger's definition in action: "the process by which sectors of (European) society and culture are removed from the domination of (both Catholic and Protestant) religious institutions and symbols. "

But in many contemporary discussions of religion, the term secularization has taken on a much broader meaning. No longer used in a descriptive sense, to highlight significant dynamics in western social history in the last millennium, it has expanded into a generalized theory of the role of religion in modern society. In its most simple form, this theory posits a *necessary* relationship between the growth of modern society and the decline of religious institutions; it predicts the inevitable loss of religious faith with the expansion of modern consciousness.

The Secularization Hypothesis. A growing understanding among scholars today suggests that secularization does not qualify as a *theory*, that is, a comprehensive explanation drawn from empirical evidence. More accurately, "secularization" functions as an *hypothesis*, that is, a proposition set out to guide further empirical investigation into questions not yet settled.

The work of sociologist Jose Casanova has been helpful in clarifying the secularization hypothesis. In his influential book *Public Religions in the Modern World*, he first identifies three central arguments that are part of most discussions of secularization. "Only if we separate these three theses analytically," Casanova insists, "can we fully make sense of the complexity of modern historical reality. "[4]

The first proposition is that secularization involves **functional differentiation** in society. Functional differentiation is the process through which different spheres of social activity—the economy, government, science, education, media, the arts—function with increasing autonomy from the religious sphere.

Central Propositions of the Secularization Hypothesis

As commonly understood, *secularization* includes three propositions:

- **secularization as functional differentiation in society**
  Process through which spheres of social activity, such as economy, government, science, education, media, the arts, function with autonomy from the religious domain.

- **secularization as privatization of religion**
  Process through which religion is understood as distinct and specialized activity, removed from public life and focused on private/personal concerns—personal values, moral behavior, family cohesion, subjective well-being.

- **secularization as religious decline**
  As a result of the loss of its public role, religion will be increasingly marginalized in modern societies. Religious institutions will lose membership and religious belief and practice will diminish among individuals.

Figure Four[5]

The second proposition is that secularization involves the **privatizing of religion.** Privatization is the process through which the "religious sphere" is seen as a distinct and specialized activity, increasingly removed from public life and focused on private concerns—personal values, individual moral behavior, family cohesion, the subjective sense of well-being.

The third proposition is that secularization leads to **religious decline.** As religion's public role is lost and its social influence lessens, religious institutions will lose membership and religious belief and practice will diminish among individuals.

Casanova then moves on to examine the findings of current research, to determine if these propositions have been confirmed.

In regard to **functional differentiation,** research evidence is generally supportive. The predicted separation and specialization of institutions in modern societies has been demonstrated in multiple studies. Most modern nation states function through multiple spheres of activity and influence, each somewhat autonomous. And religious institutions often struggle to find their location within this larger field. The struggle is more acute in societies in which a single religious institution once played a dominant cultural role.

But there are exceptions. Several nation states are currently attempting to develop functionally differentiated societies, under an explicit and exclusive religious worldview and ethos. Consider, for example, the role of Islam today in Iran, Saudi Arabia, and other middle eastern nations.

In regard to the **privatization of religion,** research evidence is mixed. In western Europe the churches have been largely relegated to the private sphere. In many other places—for example, some settings in South America, the Middle East, and some Asian countries, as well as in the current debate in the United States—religious institutions have an increasingly public role.

But available research evidence does not support the proposition of **inevitable religious decline**. The often-predicted diminishment of religious identity and personal belief and practice has not happened. In fact, as Casanova reports,

> from a global perspective, since 1950 most religious traditions in most parts of the world have either experienced some growth or maintained their vitality. This has been the case despite the fact that throughout the world there have been rapid increases in industrialization, urbanization, education, and so forth. Religious vitality has been particularly evident in the highly industrialized societies of Japan and the United States. [6]

In fact, as several social analysts have argued, secularization is more often related to the declining influence of religious authorities in public life than to a decline in religious belief or practice.

The connections between religion and modern society, then, are more complex than the over-simplified understanding of secularization often suggests. Across a variety of national settings, evidence does not show a general pattern of the demise of religion as a social institution or a diminishment of religiousness in the lives of individuals. What we do see increasingly (and even here, not without exceptions) is religious institutions that are no longer "embedded" in their host societies, no longer receiving special protection or privileges denied to other social organizations.

SECULARITY

In our earlier section, we discussed modernization in terms of social processes and modernity in terms of culture. It will be useful to make a similar distinction between secularization and secularity: *secularization points to social processes*; *secularity names a cultural perspective*. Casanova's work has clarified the social dynamics commonly associated with secularization. To clarify the cultural dynamics of secularity we will draw again on the work of Charles Taylor, particularly his 1999 Gifford Lectures *Living in a Secular Age*. [7]

Taylor begins with the ideas and ideals that he judges to be central in modern consciousness: personal freedom finds its moral foundation in the autonomous self; the scientific method and instrumental reason are humanity's most certain guides; universal equality is the goal of political life. These ideas have been quickly disseminated throughout the world, not just as repudiations of religious belief. Each is powerfully attractive on its own terms. And humanity has clearly benefited from them all.

In the West, many people who cherish these ideas and ideals of modernity identify themselves as religious and interpret their lives in relation to a transcendent God. But these ideals of modernity have also generated a cultural stance—perhaps even a spiritual outlook—of *secularity*. At its core, secularity is not necessarily an attack on religious faith or religious institutions. But the secular outlook does not need belief in God as the foundation of its world-view. For many people in modern societies, science has proved adequate to give an understanding of nature, making a creator God unnecessary. Social order appears securely based in the instrumental contract among individuals, making God's will unnecessary as a transcendent foundation of the human community. And human benevolence seems an adequate source of moral standards, making the divine law and final judgment of God unnecessary. As a result, much of the basis of traditional theistic belief has been undermined.

This contemporary secular worldview, in Taylor's analysis, includes several characteristic elements: a disenchanted worldview; a self-sufficient humanism; the autonomous self; and religion as a private concern. Figure Five gives a brief description of each of these element. In the remaining chapters of Part Two, several characteristics of the secular worldview will be discussed in greater detail.

Secularity, thus, is one of the ways that the ideas and ideals of modernity are expressed. But the most significant effect of secularity, or secular culture, is not a dramatic loss of faith but a critical change in how faith is realized. Religious conviction today is often accompanied by doubt. Faith is experienced as a continuing quest, more that a confident state of belief. Spiritual commitment is embraced as a personal realization, rather than the substantial core of a shared way of life. This leaves belief in God open to challenge, both from within and from outside the community of believers.

A CONTEMPORARY SECULAR WORLDVIEW

- **disenchantment of the world**

  No mythic understandings or "other-worldly" forces are required to explain the world; in principle, the cosmos can be fully understood through the scientific account of naturalistic dynamics.

- **"exclusive" or self-sufficient humanism**

  Life's ultimate goal—human flourishing—can be a-chieved through common resources of the human community. Political legitimacy and moral order require no further transcendent foundation.

- **image of the autonomous self**

  New view of self as less vulnerable to forces beyond one's control. Personal action is less susceptible to demands of external authority or influence of fate. By using reason alone, the self can reach mastery over passion and emotion.

- **religion as a personal option, not a common cultural resource**

  Spiritual perspective no longer provides a common cultural foundation. Religious beliefs and practices are seen as options among several alternative life-perspectives. Now theism, rather than atheism, requires justification.

Figure Five[8]

SECULARIZATION AND SECULARITY IN CHINAS EXPERIENCE

The social processes and cultural ideals that have been named *modernization* and *modernity* in the West are now worldwide phenomena. While Europe was the setting in which these developments emerged, it is clear that modernity is not limited to the West. Now these processes are at play throughout the world. But modernity takes different shape, depending on the historical background and current circumstances in the receiving culture. So it is possible, even useful, to discuss China's *modernization* and the spread of *modernity* in Chinese culture today. But using *secularization* to explain developments in China is more complicated.

Secularization names the historically-situated social processes involved in the "separation of church and state" in western societies. In western Europe (and societies shaped by this culture, such as Canada, United States, Australia) institutional religion lost its earlier privileged position in national life. Catholic Christianity and Protestant Christianity were no longer formally established as state religions. Churches, then, became less influential; now in public life religious leaders were just one voice among many others. These institutional dynamics of church-state relations are particular to the western experience.

Some analysts see the rise of the Confucian school to prominence in China as an instance of secularization. They point to Confucius' insistence on a "this world" orientation as essentially *secular*. But the historical setting and social processes of Confucius' time were very different that those in Europe in the 17th and 18th centuries. This being the case, it is perhaps better to describe these dynamics in early Chinese history without using the historically-conditioned term *secularization*.

Even in contemporary China, using secularization to describe religious developments may be misleading. Beginning in the late 1970s, the Reform and Opening policy has initiated a period of dramatic economic and social modernization in Chinese society. But this rapid industrialization, stimulated and sustained by the dynamics of market capitalism, does not fit easily into the predictive framework of the secularization hypothesis outlined above. An analysis of religious developments in China today is further complicated by the structures of political oversight under which the registered religious institutions continue to function. On the contemporary scene, then, it is too early to suggest that the dynamics of secularization are irrelevant to Chinese modernization. But it is equally premature to apply this western model of interpretation, without acknowledging the many circumstances that make China's experience unique.

While the relevance of secularization to China's modernization remains an open question, another dynamic of modernity may well find its counterpart in China's recent cultural experience. As we saw above, modern consciousness has emerged in settings where significant economic changes are accompanied by increasing complexity of societal life. This modernity finds expression in the psychological and cultural experience of *disenchantment*. In Chapter Six we explore connections between modernity and disenchantment.

NOTES

[1]Charles Taylor's comprehensive discussion of modernity is found in *Sources of the Self*; for his expanded discussion of modernity and modernization see "Two Theories of Modernity. "

[2] Figures Two and Three in this chapter draw on the analyses of Taylor's position found in Ruth Abbey,*Charles Taylor* and Nicholas Smith, *Charles Taylor*:*Meaning*,*Morals and Modernity*.

[3]Peter Berger,*The Sacred Canopy*,p. 107.

[4]Jose Casanova,*Public Religions in the Modern World*,p. 20.

[5]This chart reflects Jose Casanova's discussion of secularization theory in *Public Religions in the Modern World*.

[6]Casanova,*Public Religions in the Modern World*,p. 27.

[7]Charles Taylor,*Living in a Secular Age* (forthcoming).

[8]Figure Four draws on Ruth Abbey's discussion in *Charles Taylor*, Chapter Five "Sources of Secularity",pp. 195—212.

CHAPTER SIX: MODERNITY AND DISENCHANTMENT

This chapter contrasts the gradual development of the culture of modernity in the West with its more abrupt e-mergence in China. This shift toward modern conscious-ness has led to disenchantment, both in Chinese and west-ern culture.

Modernization, as we saw in the last chapter, identifies a mul-tifaceted social process: historic changes in production (industriali-zation), financial exchange (capitalism) and population density (ur-banization) have altered the way people live and work. The term *modernity*, on the other hand, describes a cultural perspective shaped by the social dynamics of modernization, a shift in con-sciousness that leads people to understand the world in new ways. The social processes of modernization and the cultural perspective of modernity have profoundly influenced the shape of religion in western culture. We will examine the phenomenon of modernity here, with two goals: to better understand the traditional role of Christianity in Europe as the dynamics of modernization unfolded and to understand the attitude toward religion of many Chinese in-tellectuals in the early 20th century.

As a cultural attitude, modernity dawned first in Europe. The

British moral philosopher Bernard Williams remarked that the modern world is " a European creation presided over by the Greek past. "[1] If Europe provided the social setting for the beginning of modernity, the contemporary experience of globalization means that every nation today faces the challenges and opportunities that are part of modernization. We will look first at the appearance of modernity in the West, especially its impact on religion. Then we will examine Chinese culture's different experience of modernity.

THE TIDE OF MODERNITY

We may picture modernity as "a long incoming tide gathering over centuries. "[2] This image describes the gradual appearance of various social and cultural forces that, together, would establish the culture of modernity in the West. This long incoming tide was composed of many waves, each adding its force to the accruing energy that would transform Europe and North America between the 17th and 19th centuries.

Modernity in the West, then, describes not a single event but a sequence of developments—scientific, political, economic, cultural— that grew into a world-changing dynamic. For China the cultural experience of modernity was different. Modern culture arrived in China, along with the foreign gunboats of the Opium war, not with the gradual force of a rising tide but as a sudden tsunami that crashed ashore.

In Europe, an early wave in the tide of modernity was generated by the Copernican revolution, with its startling evidence that the sun rather than the earth stood at the center of the planets' movement. Appearing in the work of Copernicus in the early 16th century and announced more forcefully a century later by Galileo, this realization led to a profound shift in how humans were to understand their position in the universe.

Subsequent discoveries undermined the pre-modern image of the natural world as a numinous cosmos. An earlier sense of the world as alive with sacred energy was replaced by a mechanical image of the universe, as a massive piece of machinery governed by laws of physics and chemistry. In the 17th century with his comprehensive explanation of basic elements of the physical world, such as the force of gravity and the spectrum of light, Newton generated new confidence that all natural phenomena might soon be knowable by human beings. As physicist Alan Lightman remarks, "Newton conquered the notion that some areas of knowledge were inaccessible to the human mind, an idea ingrained in western culture for centuries. "[3]

THE WAVE OF MODERNITY CONTINUES

The second wave in the incoming tide of modernity was the intellectual transformation known as the Enlightenment. Throughout the 18th century, intellectuals in Europe debated questions about the basic elements of human society. By what right did a monarch rule a state or nation? By what right did a religious leader, such as a bishop or pope, exercise public authority? Was human morality rooted exclusively in religious truths? Or might human reason, unassisted by religious guidance, discover reliable principles of good and evil? Characteristic of the Enlightenment was new confidence in the ability of human reason to understand and shape society. Emboldened by this new self-confidence, many intellectuals of this time judged that no divine agency was required as a foundation of moral insight or social stability.

A major legacy of both the scientific revolution and the intellectual perspective of the Enlightenment was a narrowed definition of the human capacity for reflective understanding. Critical reason was given priority over religious reflection in the search for truth; gradually reason was focused even more narrowly on "instrumental rationality"—intellectual activity functioning as a strategy for calculating the most efficient means to achieve a specific end. [4] Other means of gaining insight—such as appreciation or empathy or emotion or artistic imagination—were relegated to inferior status.

The third wave that shaped modernity in the West was the political force of the American Revolution (1776) and the French Revolution (1789), events that challenged the traditional shape of western civilization. A new enthusiasm for equality rooted in citizenship spread quickly, replacing the preferential status of elites such as the aristocracy and the clergy. The traditional authority of the king and of the religious leaders, long a mark of premodern Europe, gave way to new models of political participation and social power. Experiencing a greater range of autonomy, both as citizens and as religious believers, western thinkers identified and defended a range of *rights* as essential to what it means to be human. These rights were understood to be rooted in *human nature* rather than in the decree of kings or the decisions of the state.

THE TIDE OF MODERNITY IN THE
WEST—THREE WAVES

1600	1700	1800	1900

1. The Scentific Revolution(Galileo to Newton; Darwin to Einstein)

   An increasing confidence in reason and its ability to understand and control the world

2. The Philosophical and Humanistic Enlightenment

   An increasing confidence in reason and its ability to understand and control human society

3. The American and French Revolutions

   A new interest in human rights:
   freedom, equality, democracy

Figure Six

The Industrial Revolution that transformed England between 1750 and 1850 offers another instance of the social processes that supported modernity. The amazing inventions of this revolution in technology expanded confidence in human ingenuity and nurtured an expectation of endless progress. Factories sprang up in urban centers, producing new products made possible by technological innovations. The appearance of the steam engine in 1769 triggered a movement of wide-spread urbanization, as people left farms and villages to seek employment in these factories. A culture that had for many centuries been essentially rural was suddenly transformed by the demands and opportunities that came with city life.

MODERNITY AND RELIGION

These overlapping and interdependent social changes were accompanied by institutional religion's loss of its traditional privileged position in European culture. For many centuries the church had provided the basic worldview for understanding the universe and humanity's place within it. While many early modern scientists— such as Galileo and Newton—were themselves religious believers, their new scientific findings challenged and overwhelmed a premodern religious vision.

The church of medieval Europe had likewise supported the doctrine of the monarchy's "divine right" to rule, in return for the monarchy's recognition of a parallel role for religious authorities in moral and spiritual matters. Thus the church and state could cooperate to enforce a single religious belief and punish those who did not comply. As European society gradually experienced dynamics of modernization, Protestant Christianity and Catholic Christianity remained the religions of most Europeans. But many of the essential activities that previously the church had sponsored were taken over by civil governments. Education, health care, even the registering of births, weddings and deaths had been the exclusive domain of the church during the long period that historians identify as Christendom. Now this was beginning to change. As religion scholar Bruce Lincoln comments,

> Equipped···with a social contract theory that derived legitimacy from the people who constitute the nation, rather than from God, the early modern state was freed from its ideological dependence on the church, and increased its power at the latter's expense, assuming an ever larger share of functions that had previously fallen under religious purview: education, moral discipline and surveillance, social relief, record keeping, guarantee of contracts, and so on. [5]

Thus the social and cultural developments identified with modernity gradually undermined a worldview that had prevailed in Europe for centuries. Increasingly, social services belonged to the state and intellectual pursuits were dominated by methods of science. Gradually religious institutions became disengaged from the activities of the laboratory, the market, the factory, and public policy. Religious beliefs and activities gradually retreated into the private realm of personal devotion.

THE MERITS OF MODERNITY

In the judgment of many contemporary analysts, modernity remains an ambiguous achievement. Its many advances—in human freedom and political participation, in medical research and public health, in communication and transportation—are offset by the international conflicts, ethnic tragedies, and economic excesses that stand as its legacy in contemporary life. People in many countries have embraced the modern cultural perspective, happy to move beyond the traditions of their ancestors. Many others see modernity as a force of western cultural hegemony, diluting social identity and threatening cultural heritages of non-western civilizations.

Philosopher David Tracy urges us to recognize both the merits and shortcomings of modernity:

> The achievements of modernity—in science and technology, in democratic politics and cultural pluralism, in human rights to resist evil, in sustainable technologies to relieve suffering—should not be denied and must be defended. [6]

But, he reminds us, these many achievements were accompanied by other, more problematic, consequences:

> The Enlightenment both freed us from the weight of certain oppressive traditions and taught us, as Kant insisted, that we must dare to think for ourselves. But as the dialectic of the Enlightenment unfolded, it became trapped in ever narrower models of what could count as truth and what could count as free action, namely purely autonomous action···Reason retreated into a formal and technical rationality. [7]

THE END OF THE ENCHANTED WORLD

Modernity's multiple advances, particularly in science and philosophy, gradually eroded a long-cherished experience of the world as *enchanted*. In an enchanted worldview, the cosmos is animated. Spirits inhabit mountains and streams; heavenly deities intervene in earthly matters. An eclipse of the sun or a devastating flood, for example, might signal divine displeasure. A child born blind could represent the moral failure in his parents. The enchanted world was a place in which "all nature and experience were suffused with divine significance. "[8]

Jews and Christians find a compelling example of this enchanted world in the biblical story of Noah and the flood, recorded in the Book of Genesis. Seeing that humans were living immorally, the creator God determined to destroy all life with a great flood. "Now the earth was corrupt in God's sight and the earth was filled with violence" (Genesis 6:11). The righteous man Noah convinces God to spare some living things. So Noah and his family build an enormous boat, onto which they bring two of each species of animal. In the devastating flood that follows, the boat with its precious cargo survives. Noah and his descendents return to dry land, bringing with them the animals that will assure human survival. Following this cleansing catastrophe, God determines never again to punish humanity so severely. As sign of this commitment, God places a rainbow in the sky. The appearance of the rainbow after every storm will remind both God and the human race of this divine commitment.

This is the sign of the covenant that I make between me and you and every living creature that is with you, for all future generations. I have set my rainbow in the clouds and it shall be a sign of the covenant between me and the earth. When I bring clouds over the earth and the rainbow is seen in the clouds, I will remember my covenant··· (Genesis 9:12).

Over many centuries Jewish and Christian believers found consolation in the rainbow. This arc of color appearing after a storm was a concrete reminder of God's presence and power. When Newton demonstrated that a refracted beam of light displays a full spectrum of color, the rainbow lost its sacred meaning. Now the rainbow was simply a natural phenomenon, light acting according to physical laws. The rainbow remained a beautiful sight, but now it signaled no special religious meaning.

An enchanted worldview represents what philosopher Paul Ricoeur calls "the immediacy of belief." Here the world is a seamless reality, where spiritual power interpenetrates daily life. There is spiritual meaning and personal significance is every natural event. Ricoeur uses the term *first naiveté*[9] to describe the season of human consciousness that supports such an enchanted worldview. This early cultural consensus did not survive the assaults of modernity.

MODERNITY: A SEASON OF DISENCHANTMENT

With modernity, the cosmos alive with divine power and human purpose was replaced by the mechanical universe driven by impersonal forces. This shift in consciousness resulted in a pervasive cultural mood, a stark rationality that sociologist Max Weber has famously described as *disenchantment*.

Gone was the magical harmony of this world and the divine. Rainbows that had once signaled the Creator's benevolence were now recognized as natural phenomena. Science could demonstrate that a comet was just a comet, not a heavenly signal. Nature apparently operated according to the fixed universal laws of physics and chemistry; no divine creator seemed required to keep this ordered universe in existence. The drama of symbolic stories was replaced by a cool detachment of scientific research.

During these same centuries political changes were on the horizon, strengthened by vigorous intellectual debates. Philosophers and others argued that human societies are not structured according to some underlying natural design. Rather, society functions as a form of contract, based on trade-offs of benefits and needs agreed upon by its members. Political rulers no longer exercised their authority by "divine right" but were subject to the will of the people. Philosophical justification of democracy was developing.

Another development during these centuries was the emergence of the *autonomous self*, a key element in the culture of modernity. As Charles Taylor remarks, "in the enchanted world of 500 years ago, the boundary around the mind was constitutionally porous."[10] Humans were thoroughly imbedded in their communities, identified less as individuals than as members of their family, or tribe, or feudal kingdom. In the shift of consciousness that is a core aspect of modernity, persons became more aware of their individuality. This individual consciousness was "far less vulnerable to forces beyond its control that was the case in an enchanted world of spirits and demons. "[11]

Taylor suggests several ambiguous characteristics of modern self-consciousness. The modern self is more *protected* from external demands—whether arising from external authority or communal obligations. Modern persons understand themselves as more *separate*, since identity is grounded in autonomous individual choice rather than in shared cultural commitments. As a result, modern persons are more likely to experience themselves as *isolated*: distinct from the natural world and unique among other humans, each individual essentially exists alone. In this understanding, *relationships* are not the primary matrix of human consciousness and well-being but "secondary" developments that result from individual decision and action. This modern self is awakened to the frightening responsibility of personal choice.

Disenchantment touched the world of religion as well. Enlightenment thought replaced the loving Creator of biblical religions with a more distant Deism. Belief in God remained, but this Deity functioned in a transcendent realm far removed from daily life. Both Catholic and Protestant theologians, intimidated by the advances of science that often seemed to be at the expense of religious belief, constructed a firewall between faith and reason. To *reason* they ceded the realm of science, the natural world and the public sphere. Religious faith, they claimed, would function in its own autonomous realm of personal salvation and spiritual consolation.

Now religion, safely separated from the natural world and the advance of science, no longer needed to provide rational or philosophic justification for its beliefs. Some apologists for religious faith even returned to the ancient claim of the third-century theologian

Tertullian: "I believe because it is absurd."

Thus Christian faith slipped into a ghetto of its own making. If it could not compete with science, it at least had its own domain of sovereignty. Religion increasingly became a matter of the heart and a haven from a hostile world; private devotion predominated over a formerly more public presence of the church in society.

As the world was emptied of its charm and humans lost the consoling sense of being part of an organic whole, disenchantment became the dominant mood of the time.

MODERNITY AND DISENCHANTMENT IN CHINA

Both the social processes of *modernization* and *modernity's* shifts in consciousness emerged gradually in western cultures. These developments were driven by optimism and confidence. This was not the case in China.

As Yu Ying-shih has observed, what "had taken the West almost two centuries to absorb and digest, arrived in China within a short span of three or four decades."[12] With the Opium War in 1840 China had to face western displays of power that flaunted the advantages of modernization. Suddenly not only Hong Kong but strategic sections of Shanghai, Tianjin and other coastal cities were cordoned off as *concessions* under the control of these western nations. This insulting presence of "modernized" western forces was a painful announcement of the need for China to enter the modern world. A second shock occurred in 1895, as Japan sustained easy victory in its war against China. Here again the Chinese were made aware, in Yu Ying-shih's words, of "the marginalization of China in the world. "[13]

In the first decades of the 20th century China moved quickly to modernize, eager to adopt the mind-set of modernity. Disenchantment with its Confucian heritage and pre-modern bureaucracy led to the demise of the Qing dynastic rule in 1911. The traditional civil service exam had been terminated six years earlier, to be replaced by modern universities designed on European models. Beijing University was established in 1898; Fudan University in Shanghai opened its doors in 1905.

The decision of the Treaty of Versailles in 1919 to cede part of the Shandong peninsula to Germany was an equally traumatic event in China's movement toward modernity. The May Fourth Movement reacted to this humiliating decision, challenging China's leaders and intellectuals to embrace modernity's goal, symbolized in the images of "Mr. Science and Mr. Democracy."

The frantic rush to modernize seemed to demand both widespread embrace of scientific thinking and repudiation of the popular beliefs and rituals of China's past. Hu Shi, Liang Qichao, Feng Youlan and many other intellectuals were convinced that modern China would be a country without religion. Influenced by the rationalist philosophies that dominated post-Enlightenment Europe and United States, these scholars judged that religion was a major obstacle to modernity.

Thus modernization began with enthusiasm in the first decades of the 20th century. But the events that unfolded in the following decades compromised any sustained effort. The Japanese invasion in the 1930s disrupted life, especially in the northeast and along the east coast. The civil war that raged through the 1930s and 1940s made sustained scientific research all but impossible.

1949—A Season of Enchantment. The torturous half-century of China's disenchantment with its own cultural heritage—a series of humiliations suffered from the outside and of frustrations at efforts of modernization inside the country—came to an end in October 1949. With Mao Zedong's Proclamation that "now the Chinese people have stood up," a period of intense re-enchantment began.

Just as the terms "modernization" and "modernity" had quite different nuances in China (where developments were sudden and traumatic rather than gradual, as in the West), so the Chinese experience of enchantment would be unlike the experience in the West. The era of Communism and "Marxism with Chinese characteristics" ushered in a season of intense national pride and a time of rapid efforts of modernization. Chinese intellectuals' call for an end to religion that had been sounded early in the century (aimed especially at Buddhism and Catholic and Protestant Christianity, but including the spiritual practices of Daoism) would at last be realized in the atheistic ideology of Marxism, a mode of modernity itself imported from the West. To better understand the enchantment of the next twenty-five years it may be helpful to turn to the image developed by sociologist Peter Berger nearly forty years ago.

The Sacred Canopy of Marxism. In many societies, Berger suggests, religion functions as a *sacred canopy*. [14] A sacred canopy is a kind of social tent; it both collects a people under one roof and covers them with an all-embracing interpretation of reality.

A sacred canopy protects a group from outside forces, in the way an umbrella protects an individual from a storm. With its authoritative ideology, the sacred canopy also protects people from doubt. But a canopy sometimes blocks the vision of those who dwell under its protective cover. Precisely because one is so well protected under the tent,one cannot see the sky.

For Berger,a sacred canopy has a monopoly of ultimate meaning;it is "the only tent in town. " This common consciousness provides many advantages to a society,but at a high cost. All who dwell within its protective realm must embrace its comprehensive vision. Authority comes to be seen as sacred,since it functions by virtue of "divine right" or ideological imperative.

Sacred canopies reinforce enchanted worlds:they provide the authoritative architecture through which an enchanted world is constantly defended and celebrated. When a sacred canopy is broken, the result is disorienting as well as exhilarating. Individuals lose a consoling if restricting common orientation to the world but gain the opportunity to explore new patterns of thought and choice.

Contemporary sociologists in China and the West have suggested that Chinese culture fell under its own sacred canopy in the year 1949. The Marxism that Mao Zedong preached offered a view of reality that was as all-encompassing as that of Catholic Christianity in medieval Europe. Despite an emphatic atheism and secularizing orientation,its authority was "sacred"—laying claim to explain all reality. With its explanation of the origin of social evil (comparable to the Christian understanding of "sin") and its ideal of a classless society (an earthly "salvation"),Marxism's sacred canopy performed very much like a religion.

Maoist Marxism promised the Chinese people a new worldview and moral compass,a political sacred order. It offered a vision of an eschatological paradise on earth,an ideal that motivated altruism and self-sacrifice. In the following years patriotism flourished;nationalistic fervor took on the aura of religious devotion. Present personal suffering seemed minor compared to the reward that awaited the whole nation in the future. Mao, as the charismatic leader, was recognized as savior of the nation. His "little red book" was a treasured classic; his portrait was an icon of the new China.

The idealism of this season in Chinese history demanded the removal of all religious competitors: Buddhist temples, Daoist shrines, along with Protestant and Catholic churches were razed to the ground. In place of the traditional Confucian tolerance of alternate spiritual movements, Maoism took on an intolerance that was reminiscent of the religious wars in Europe in previous centuries.

Disenchantment: The Death of a Dream. Between the end of the Cultural Revolution in the mid-1970s and Deng Xiaoping's announcement of an Opening and Reform at the end of that decade, a mood of profound disenchantment swept through the culture. The promise of Marxism seemed to have failed. The younger generations who had given themselves to Mao's revolutionary vision felt a deep disappointment. They experienced what can only be called a loss of faith.

The sacred canopy of Maoism was torn open and threatening winds—of despair, of consumerism—rolled through the nation. The ideology of Marxism had dispensed with the traditional wisdom of the China's Confucian heritage; now the new ideals of Maoist/Marxist belief seemed empty. Throughout the culture the sacred canopy lay in tatters. In its place, a spiritual vacuum expanded.

Material success, once a staple of Chinese culture but disparaged under Maoism, again became a worthy goal of life. Suddenly making money was more acceptable. In the frantic consumerism that accompanied this disenchantment, as Ci Jiwei laments, "a spiritually exhausted people found a pursuit in which the spirit did not have to participate. "[15]

Just as modernization and modernity had different meanings in China, so the Chinese experienced disenchantment in very different ways than the West. In Europe, disenchantment accompanied the collapse of the sacred canopy of Christendom; religion no longer played the authoritative role it had previously claimed in the culture. Thus western disenchantment was coupled with secularization. In a secularized western culture, religion was demoted to a much reduced status. The church became one voice among many in the society's search for values.

In China, disenchantment dawned differently. The Chinese people were not disaffected from a religious sacred order; society-wide disappointment of the late 1970s and early 1980s was provoked by a failed political arrangement. As the promise of Marxism eroded, people felt both the disorientation and the exhilaration that come with the collapse of a sacred canopy.

In the early 1980s "culture fever" swept through the country. Chinese people were demanding: what has gone wrong with our country? How has this great culture become so backward? Humiliation and regret for both its deep Confucian heritage and its more recent romance with Marxism fueled a broad-based reexamination of what it means to be Chinese.

At the popular level this cultural dialogue began with an article "Why is Life's Road Getting Narrower and Narrower?" that appeared in May 1980 issue the magazine *China Youth*. Using the pen name Pan Xiao, the author complains of her disillusionment with the Communist ideals that had once motivated her. Her article drew 57,000 responses to the magazine over the next seven months.

At the end of the decade of the 1980s the television series *River Elegy*[16] drew on the central symbols of Chinese culture, the

Yellow River and the Great Wall, to raise similar issues. Its self-lacerating inquiry opposed the color "yellow"—referring to both the river and the Chinese race—to the color "blue" which represented the open and expansive waters of the ocean as well as blue-eyed westerners. The great wall was portrayed not as an honorable bulwark of defense against foreign barbarians, but as a self-defeating barrier that shielded an entire culture from the healthy incursions of modernity.

The disorientation that accompanied this period of disenchantment in China was matched by a mood of exhilaration. In more open philosophical discussion as well as in the renewal of the arts, Chinese culture blossomed in new expressions of the human spirit. At this time, religious interest among Chinese suddenly mushroomed. Buddhist and Daoist temples reopened; Protestant and Catholic churches were restored; training sites for the education of Muslim clergy cautiously opened their doors again. Many other Chinese turned to spiritual practices inherited from traditional Chinese popular religion. When Deng Xiaoping announced the Opening and Reform in 1979, his clearly stated intention was to promote new forms of economic activity. But it soon became obvious that shifting the boundaries of the economy had altered the horizon of the spirit.

The role of religion in China in the twenty-first century remains uncertain. Chapters Nine and Ten will examine the ways in which the citizens of one modern city in China are seeking spiritual renewal.

NOTES

[1]Bernard Williams, *Shame and Necessity*, p. 3.

[2]Michael Gallagher, *Clashing Symbols*, p. 6

[3]Alan Lightman,"Einstein and Newton:Genius Compared," p. 109.

[4]Charles Taylor describes *instrumental reason* as "the kind of rationali-ty we draw on when we calculate the most economical application of means to a given end. Maximum efficiency, the best cost-benefit ratio, is the meas-ure of success"; see his *Ethics of Authenticity*, p. 5.

[5]Bruce Lincoln,"Conflict" in *Critical Terms for Religious Studies*, p. 56.

[6]David Tracy, *Plurality and Ambiguity*, p. 23.

[7]Tracy, *Plurality and Ambiguity*, p. 31.

[8]Michael Pollan, *The Botany of Desire*, p. 34.

[9]Ricoeur, *The Symbolism of Evil*, p. 351; *naïveté* means simple and in-nocent, to be at an early stage of development. Ricoeur uses the term to de-scribe the pre-modern era when many people experienced the world filled with signs and portents.

[10]This statement, taken from Taylor's yet-unpublished 1999 Guifford Lecture, is quoted by Ruth Abbey in *Charles Taylor*, p. 204.

[11]Abbey, *Charles Taylor*, p. 203.

[12]Yu Ying-shih,"The Radicalization of China in The 20th Century," p. 133.

[13]Yu,"The Radicalization of China," p. 135.

[14]Berger discusses his understanding of this term in *The Sacred Canopy*.

[15]Jiwei Ci, *Dialectic of The Chinese Revolution*, p. 11.

[16]For the text of this series, see Xiaokang Su and Luxiang Wang, *Deathsong of the River*.

CHAPTER SEVEN: RELIGION'S PLACE IN A LATE-MODERN WORLD

This chapter traces shifts in the role of Catholic Christi-
anity and Protestant Christianity during the long transi-
tion from pre-modern to late-modern society in the West.
Then two significant openings to religion that are part
of a late-modern world are explored.

The Enlightenment's confident prediction of religion's imminent demise has proved to be wrong. Both the institutional religions of the historic traditions and the search for meaning that is characteristic of popular religion remain alive, often flourishing, throughout the world. But the role of religion in a late-modern world has shifted in significant ways.

First, many religious believers are now more aware of the deep ambiguity in their own histories. Religious traditions are often identified with the admirable virtues of charity, justice and compassion; religious history tells a more complex story. Throughout history and across cultural settings, as institutional religions have gained political leverage there is evidence of intolerance and even violent oppression of those who do not "belong. " As David Tracy has observed,

Any religion, whether past or present, in a position of power surely demonstrates that religious movements, like secular ones, are open to corruption. The impacted memories of religious fanaticism and its demonic history of effects upon all cultures are memories that cannot be erased. [1]

Acknowledging, understanding, and counteracting this tendency that lies at the heart of organized religions remains a challenge for both people of faith and religious scholars today.

Second, in late-modern societies religious traditions—whether Buddhist or Hindu, Catholic or Protestant, Jewish or Islamic—must find a place in a world of plural beliefs and values. Having lost a privileged position in their cultures, these institutional religions are challenged to assume an unfamiliar posture. Each now stands with others in the global public square. Potentially, all are called to membership at a common table.

Religious groups respond differently to these two challenges of late-modern society. The role of religious institutions in the future will be shaped by their responses. Here we will examine religion's changing role as Europe shifted toward late-modern culture.

CHRISTENDOM AND MODERNITY

During the earliest centuries of the common era, the followers of Jesus remained a small minority, a powerless and often persecuted group. With the religious conversion of Emperor Constantine early in the 4th century, Catholic Christianity became the official religion of the realm. Historians use the term Christendom to name the cultural and political developments that resulted from this close (and often antagonistic) relationship between Catholic religion and political rulers in Europe.

The high season of Christendom prevailed between the time of Charlemagne (800ce) and Napoleon (1800ce). Across Europe Catholic Christianity and, after 1500ce, Protestant Christianity as well enjoyed a privileged place. For this thousand year period, religious faith and European culture were profoundly interconnected. With few exceptions (Jews, for example, were found in small numbers throughout Europe; Muslims flourished for several hundred years on the margin of Europe in medieval Spain[2]) the worldview and religious practices of the church dominated the land.

Christendom and Europe's Moral Orientation. During the long season of Christendom, the beliefs and values of the church supplied Europe with its moral foundation. The universities that emerged in the 12th and 13th centuries were staffed by faculties composed of Catholic scholars, most of them clerics of the church. These new institutions of learning—particularly at Bologna and Paris and Oxford—began the systematic study of law, as the basis of church organization and the foundation of social order. The modern discipline of jurisprudence in the West finds its roots here.

Social historians today trace the western heritage of "human rights" to religious convictions that were cherished in this Catholic cultural setting. These early scholars understood valid human laws as reflections of the natural law established by their Creator. Two characteristics of this natural law were identified: the dictates of natural law were discernible to human reason and not simply a matter of religious faith. And the demands of natural law carried an authority that was independent of any human ruler. Centuries later, these initial insights supported an understanding of all human beings as possessing basic privileges and responsibilities, as "endowed by the Creator with certain inalienable rights. "[3] When nation states in Europe and North America later disengaged their legal systems from explicit religious roots, they nevertheless retained the moral orientation to human rights inherited from the legacy of Protestant and Catholic Christianity.

The culture of Christendom offered a welcoming worldview for members of the church. For Jews and Muslims at this time, the culture was less hospitable. Blamed for the death of Jesus centuries before, Jews in Christendom were sometimes tolerated but often persecuted. In the fateful year 1492, as the discoverer Columbus set sail across the Atlantic Ocean in hopes of reaching "a new world," Catholic rulers in Spain expelled both Jews and Muslims from their kingdom. [4]

The End of Christendom. Christendom long served as a sacred canopy for Europe. Charles Taylor describes this cultural arrangement that shaped European culture:

> The project of Christendom: the attempt to marry the faith with a form of culture and a mode of society. There is something noble in the attempt···but as a project to be realized in history, it is ultimately doomed to frustration. [5]

Taylor argues that the very values that the church espouses—the dignity and equality of all humans, the right of individuals to follow personal conscience in religious beliefs—could be realized only with the end of the state-sponsored and privileged religion of Christendom. Only when its spiritual values were severed from secular power was it possible for the church's best hopes to be realized. Modern culture has emerged, Taylor insists, "where the casing of Christendom has been broken open and where no other single philosophy has taken its place. " Late-modern society requires this value pluralism, where "the public sphere has remained the locus of competing ultimate visions. "[6]

In Chapter Six we discussed the waves of modernity that swept European culture, eroding the foundations of Christendom. During the 19th century new nation-states began to assume social responsibilities once seen as the domain of the churches. The church was left, for the first time in many centuries, without direct access to political power. For the Christian churches of the West—both Catholic and Protestant—this transition from a privileged position in Christendom to an apparently "powerless" role of advocate of ultimate values has been traumatic. Only gradually have the churches found a new public role. No longer the authoritative source of ultimate truth, institutional religion is finding its place as one strong moral voice among many in the public square.

NEW OPENINGS FOR RELIGION

In the setting of the late-modern world two developments have provided new openings for religion. These openings, unexpected consequences of late-modern consciousness, serve as opportunities for religion to rejoin the larger cultural conversation about meaning and values. The first of these is an expanded understanding of human reason itself; the second is a reawakened vision of an enchanted world.

An Expanded Understanding of Reason. As the scientific revolution gained momentum in Europe through the 18th and 19th centuries, intellectuals became enamored of the power of scientific thinking. The scientific method, joining controlled observation with precise measurement, seemed capable of achieving so much good for the human community. In time the capacious resources of human reason came to be focused narrowly as instrumental rationality. Increasingly the highest, perhaps exclusive function of reason seemed to be the quantitative analysis of the physical dimensions of the world, and the application of these discoveries in profitable technologies. More qualitative ways of knowing—artistic or poetic or religious—were judged to be less relevant to a modern world. In this new intellectual climate, science and economics rejoiced while religion grieved.

Human reason, honed to this specialized use, has produced extraordinary achievements that continue to improve the human condition: in the medical and pharmaceutical inventions that have dramatically extended human life expectancy; in momentous developments in production and communication and transportation. Yet as the scope of reason narrowed, human inquiry was deprived of other resources. Imagination and emotion, empathy and intuition were disqualified from the serious pursuit of knowledge. By becoming more and more focused on quantitative analysis, human reason had lost much of its humane breadth.

Reclaiming Practical Reason In this season of late-modernity, philosophers and other intellectuals are returning to Aristotle's understanding of practical reason (*phronesis*). As Martha Nussbaum reminds us, Aristotle recognized that reason serves not only in the search for the universal principles yielding certain knowledge (the realm of science, which Aristotle called *episteme*). [7] Reason is also used to make things; this kind of knowledge Aristotle called *techne* (thus, "technology"). Reason is also exercised in the everyday decisions of our lives; this knowledge is the domain of practical reason or *phronesis*.

Practical reason is guided less by general principles and more by the demands of the particular situation. Here reason is challenged not to simply follow general principles, but to discern how to respond well, in the particular circumstances of this time and this place. In each moral decision, a person considers a particular action related to a concrete set of circumstances. General principles and rules may assist our decision-making but do not guarantee an answer about how we should act "here and now." A well-developed sense of practical wisdom is essential for a responsible life in the world.

Practical reason, confronting an imminent decision regarding a particular situation, depends on a kind of improvisation. Alert to the specific context with its concrete possibilities and perils, a person must creatively choose what to do next. Aristotle gave the example of the river boat captain. The captain collects important information about the river he is navigating: how deep is it, what are its currents. Likewise he must be very familiar with his boat: its size, weight and steering ability. But in an actual situation—this particular storm at this exact turn in the river—all his knowledge and experience must flow into a practical decision about immediate action.

Practical reason stands at the heart of moral reflection and religious ethics. Practical wisdom serves as the very core of conscience. Moral reasoning relies on rules and principles, but also on experience; good moral decisions depend on well-cultivated emotions and a trustworthy imagination. Broadening our appreciation of practical reason, we find new openings for religion as a resource in contemporary reflection on moral life.

The Rehabilitation of Emotion. For reason to function well at this practical level it must rely on the information that arises from both the emotions and the imagination. To decide wisely a person must "imagine all the relevant features as well and fully and concretely as possible, holding them up against whatever intuitions and emotions, and plans and imaginings we have brought into the situation or can construct in it. "[8] By doing so, reason expands its potential for guiding a person toward wise and morally responsible action.

In the past quarter century there has been an emphatic return in a number of disciplines (philosophy, psychology, ethics, and brain research) to a respect for the emotions as providing crucial cognitive information in any process of rational reflection. [9] Martha Nussbaum has designated this developmentas"the rehabilitation of emotion in practical reasoning. "[10] Today scholars recognize that emotions are far from being simply biological sensations or hormonal surges; emotions attune humans to their environment and "embody ways of interpreting the world. "[11] In the process of coming to a wise judgment, the information we receive from emotions "is a mark not of irrationality but of rich or complete rationality. "[12]

Aristotle, Nussbaum reminds us, was well aware that emotions "are not always correct…they need to be educated and brought into harmony with a correct view of the good human life. But so educated, they are not just essential as forces motivating to virtuous actions, they are also…recognitions of truth and value. "[13]

Two millennia separate Aristotle's endorsement of emotions

and the contemporary rehabilitation of emotions. During this period philosophers from Plato to Kant disparaged the emotions, judging them to be empty of any cognitive content or reliable information. Again, in Nussbaum's words:

> Plato repudiated emotion and appetite as corrupting influences, insisting that correct practical judgments are reached only by encouraging the intellect to go off 'itself by itself,' free from their influence as far as possible. [14]

This negative evaluation of the emotions continued in the view of philosopher Immanuel Kant: "for Kant, the passions are invariably selfish and aimed at one's own states of satisfaction."[15]

Roberto Unger has offered perhaps the most trenchant defense of the essential role of emotions in human life: "Reason gives us knowledge of the world, but it cannot tell us in the final instance what to want or what to do." That is, reason analyzes and clarifies the information that floods our conscious minds, but accumulated information alone does not provide a compelling basis for moral choice. Further, reason "cannot provide the quality of sustained commitment that we need to pursue our most reasonable goals."[16] In human affairs, motivation and commitment arise from other sources.

With this cultural rehabilitation of the emotions we can recognize that the virtues of loyalty and devotion—so central to religious living—are more than blind attachments. The emotion of anger, when well-tempered, energizes the ethical and religious demand for justice. The powerful feeling of grief, as refined through religious rituals of sorrow and lamentation, assists people in healing their losses. Such emotions sustain humans in pursuit of their highest spiritual values. A new attitude of respect allows back into the late-modern scene the religious emotions of wonder and reverence, awe and gratitude. We see here yet another opening for religion in late-modern cultures.

Cultivating the Moral Imagination. Just as practical reason relies on the insights and motivations that are embodied in the emotions, so it depends on a seasoned imagination. Ricoeur defines this elusive interior resource as "a rule-governed form of invention···the imagination can be considered as the power of giving form to human experience, or···as the power to re-describe reality. "[17]

Imagination, like emotion, has suffered an undeserved bad reputation. The conventional wisdom in western culture, sometimes supported by religious convictions, was that imagination distorts reality, inventing unreal things and conjuring up fantasies and dangerous images. Nussbaum summarizes this culture-wide prejudice:

Imagination is thought to be too often egoistic and self-indulgent, too concerned with particulars and with their relation to the self. One can be (it is thought) correctly motivated by duty without developing imagination; therefore its cultivation is at best a luxury, at worst a danger. [18]

In the past thirty years philosophers, psychologists and religious scholars have come to recognize that the imagination, like the emotions, makes crucial contributions to our recognition of values. Ricoeur describes the imagination's role in moral reflection:

We never tire of exploring new ways of evaluating actions and characters. The thought experiments we conduct in the great laboratory of the imaginary are also explorations in the realm of good and evil. [19]

Nussbaum argues that we cultivate our humanity by developing a moral capacity rooted in mature emotions and seasoned imagination. She traces the development of the moral imagination from its earliest stage in story-telling: the child listening to nursery rhymes is alerted to wonder—"a sense of mystery that mingles curiosity with awe. "[20] Nussbaum continues, "The habits of wonder promoted by storytelling thus define the other person as spacious and deep, with qualitative differences from oneself and hidden places worthy of respect. "[21] Moral emotions of empathy and compassion—essential religious sensitivities—are stirred in the imagination. This inner resource provides sympathetic images of others, motivating virtuous behavior toward them.

Moral philosopher William Spohn traces how the imagination is shaped, morally and religiously, by religious classics. Striking stories of forgiveness and tales of generosity in the Bible, for example, bathe the reader's imagination with compelling values. In Spohn's understanding, "Scripture is seen to have its main moral effect on the imagination···(These stories) become scenarios for action by evoking affective energies in distinctive ways. "[22] The stories in religious classics are not meant to be mere illustrations of moral principles; instead their compelling images and lively emotions suggest how to choose and ways to live. As Spohn notes, "The images (in these biblical stories) do not directly dictate what to do, but they frame perception and encourage certain scenarios. "[23] The forceful and attractive images found in sacred texts "tutor the imagination. "[24]

The rehabilitation of emotions and recovery of moral imagination provide resources for religious reflection in a late-modern world. In this time in human history we are moving from a narrow, rationalistic understanding of human knowing toward recognizing an expanded range of interior resources that illumine and motivate life. This increasing sophistication about human knowing, in turn, opens the door both to religion and to a "second naïveté" that Ricoeur has forecast.

SECOND OPENING FOR RELIGION: THE RETURN TO MYSTERY

With the advent of the scientific revolution and subsequent waves of modernity, a once-enchanted world lost its luster. The cosmos, previously animated with sacred signs and illuminated by comets and rainbows, gave way to mere "nature"—that mass of inanimate matter whirling through space according to laws of physics. Such a universe had little need for God and less space for religion. Mysteries that had previously inspired wonder now became problems to be solved. In Ricoeur's words, the world of enchantment gave way to a desert of criticism.

In the desert of criticism, the physical world and the spiritual realm are split asunder. The desert of criticism took an enormous toll on religion. In Ricoeur's words,

In every way something has been lost, irremediably lost: immediacy of belief. But if we can no longer live the great symbolism of the sacred in accordance with the original belief in them, we can, we modern men, aim at a second naïveté in and through criticism. [25]

A Second naïveté. People in many cultures today—ordinary persons as well as poets and scientists—are recovering a sense of mystery in the world. The planet we inhabit now seems to be more than a machine running according to the rigid rules of Newtonian physics. Reflecting on the events of their own lives, people discover hints of meaning and purpose; more than random chance seems to be involved. This contemporary appreciation differs from the enchantment of pre-modern consciousness. In that earlier era—Ricoeur's "first *naïveté*"—every natural event might signal a spiritual message. The comet in the sky or the river's flood had moral meaning. The arrangement of tea leaves in a cup forecast personal fortune. For most who live in the late-modern world, this level of enchantment is gone forever. What is experienced today is not a pre-scientific appreciation of the cosmos, but a post-scientific reckoning with our mysterious world.

The return of mystery is accompanied by a renewal of wonder. In Chapter One we discussed wonder as a marker of transcendence. Historian Caroline Bynum describes this experience: "We wonder at what we cannot in any sense incorporate, consume, or encompass in our mental categories; we wonder at mystery, at paradox. "[26]

The achievements of the scientific method, along with the acknowledgment of its limits, have returned wonder to late-modern consciousness. A more sophisticated scientific appreciation of the natural world—not available in pre-modern times—provokes wonder at our planet's profound fragility, its extravagant immensity, and its mysterious interconnections.

An initial opening for the return of natural wonder in the West was the appearance in 1962 of environmentalist Rachel Carson's influential book *Silent Spring*. Carson exposed the devastation that poisonous pesticides and other pollutants brought to natural water supplies, resulting in the death of both wildlife and plant species. Her compelling descriptions shocked readers into a new awareness of the earth's fragility. Her reflections on the vital complexity of soil, the intricate balance of chemicals and living organisms that renders the fields fertile, replaced common-sense images of "dirt." Suddenly the planet was re-imagined, no longer a self-sufficient machine but a vulnerable organism. Its very survival depends on human appreciation and action.

Since then astronomers and cosmologists have been describing a universe whose immensity is extravagant and awe inspiring. How do we comprehend a world that embraces millions of galaxies and billions of stars? What does such immensity and extravagance mean? Why is there so much? And, perhaps the deepest wonder, why is there anything at all?

Science today records the startling interconnectedness of all things. The blood that flows in human veins contains the same iron that constitutes the stars and planets; the calcium in human bones is the same calcium found in the ocean. Biophysicist Tyler Volk has written about "the global metabolism" in which the exchange of oxygen and carbon dioxide, through photosynthesis, regulates the planet as a single breathing organism. [27] Other scientists examine the extraordinary coincidences of chemistry that permit life on earth: the constancy of temperature, the abundant availability of liquid water, the level of atmospheric oxygen that remains at 21%— the precise amount required to sustain life. What to make of these "coincidences in our favor"? Appreciation and wonder seem the best response.

The Mystery of Beauty. Beauty, like wonder, serves as a threshold of mystery. Astonished at the beauty that surrounds us we ask: what is beauty for? Critic Elaine Scarey comments, "beauty welcomes us; makes us attentive. " She continues, "It is as though beautiful things have been placed here and there throughout the world to serve as small wake-up calls to perception. "[28]

Beauty expands our attention: " Beautiful things," as Scarey notes, "always carry greetings from other worlds within them. "[29] She adds, "At the moment we see something beautiful, we undergo a radical decentering. "[30] Our attention is drawn elsewhere and "all the space formerly in the service of protecting, guarding, advancing the self (or its 'prestige') is now free to be in the service of something else. "[31]

A frightening fragility, an extravagant immensity, the mysterious interconnectedness: these aspects of our common existence invite a renewal of wonder that allow us to honor again the mystery of the world. [32]

RELIGIOUS FAITH AND A LATE-MODERN WORLD

In the pre-modern world, the sacred texts of classic traditions—Hebrew bible and Buddhist sutras, for example—were often read as literal revelations of religious realities. With the advent of modernity, many people have lost this "first naïveté" of simple religious faith. In its place came a season of disenchantment, what

Ricoeur has called "the desert of criticism." Now, after several centuries of disenchantment, Ricoeur recognizes the emergence of a "second naïveté," alert to the symbolic indicators of a mystery beyond human comprehension. Many reflective people today have begun to craft a style of religious belief that fits a late-modern world.

Ricoeur's image of the desert of criticism points to the tumultuous period in western intellectual history, during which many people abandoned the beliefs and practices of pre-modern religion. Central figures in this desert of criticism were Freud, Marx and Nietzsche. Their positive contribution was to unmask the inferior motives for religious behavior: fear of punishment, childish yearning for guarantees, avoidance of personal responsibility.

Freud understood religion as an illusion, "a compensation for the harshness of life."[33] Marx defined religion as an "opiate of the people." In his evaluation, religion was no more than a sedative: a drug ingested to relieve the harsh symptoms of social injustice, without probing deeper for its underlying cause. The German philosopher Nietzsche criticized Christianity for its tendency to reduce believers to infancy, or worse, to slavery.

From Ricoeur's judgment, the "death of God" that Nietzsche describes is the death of pre-modern religious consciousness: the tendency to experience religion—whether Christian, Buddhist or Islamic—as a defense against the rigors of human life with its unavoidable terrors and tragedies.

The desert of criticism serves as a time of purification, as believers struggled to move beyond "craven fear of a vengeful god and a nostalgia for a god that will guarantee a safe, protected life."[34] The god whose death was celebrated here was a god of retribution, a divinity that required slavish obedience and resentment. The future of religion, in Ricoeur's view, entails "a faith that moves through the shadows, (seeking) a God who would not protect me but would surrender me to the dangers of a life worthy of being called human. "[35] Such a religious faith is "an essentially tragic faith, beyond all assurances and protection. "[36]

The late-modern challenge facing all religious believers, Ricoeur judges, is to re-imagine obedience not as slavish submission to a transcendent law-giver and watchdog, but "a surrender and acceptance of a mature and necessary dependence on other persons and the environment. "[37] The challenge will be for people to find their way to "a dependence and an obedience that is no longer infected with accusation, prohibition and condemnation. "[38]

This late-modern religious faith provides "a form of consolation which depends on no external compensation (a god of guarantees and rewards) and which is equally distant from any form of vengeance (a god of who demands obedience and evokes resentment). "[39]

In the late-modern world, religion has many faces. Many believers today, unexposed to the swirling changes of modernity, still inhabit the enchanted world of the first naïveté. Many contemporary people remain in a desert of criticism, judging every expression of religious consciousness to be unscientific and illusory. But many late-modern people experience the second naïveté, in which the fragility of our shared planet and the extravagance of our universe have awakened a sense of wonder. This emotion of wonder, sometimes embodied as a bow that expresses a religious reverence, serves as a threshold to the sacred and a doorway to religion.

NOTES

[1]David Tracy,*Plurality and Ambiguity*,p. 85.

[2]Maria Rosa Menocal discusses the religious diversity of Spain in her book *Ornament of the World:How Muslims,Jews and Christians Created a Culture of Tolerance in Medieval Spain*.

[3]This phrase is taken from the Declaration of Independence of the United States,initially published in 1776.

[4]Menocal,*Ornament of the World*,p. 260 ff.

[5]Charles Taylor,*A Catholic Modernity*,p. 17.

[6]Taylor,*A Catholic Modernity*,p. 18.

[7]For more on Aristotle's broad understanding of knowledge,see Martha Nussbaum,"The Discernment of Perception:An Aristotelian Conception of Private and Public Rationality" in *Love's Knowledge*,pp. 54—105 and her essay "Non-Scientific Deliberation" in *The Fragility of Goodness*,pp. 290—317.

[8]Nussbaum, *Love's Knowledge*,p. 74.

[9]A short list of these scholars would include philosopher Robert Solomon,*The Passions:The Myth and Nature of Human Emotions*,psychologist James Averill,*Anger and Aggression:An Essay on Emotion*,educator Carol Gilligan,*In A Different Voice:Psychological Theory and Women's Development* and philosopher Roberto Unger,*Passion:An Essay on Personality*.

[10]Nussbaum,*Love's Knowledge*,p. 42,note 76.

[11]Nussbaum,*Therapy of Desire*,p. 369.

[12]Nussbaum,*Love's Knowledge*,p. 100. She adds:"Because the emotions have this cognitive dimension in their very structure,it is very natural to view them as intelligent parts of our ethical agency,responsive to the workings of deliberation and essential to its completion,"p. 40.

[13]Nussbaum,*Therapy of Desire*,p. 96.

[14]Nussbaum,*Love's Knowledge*,p. 76.

[15]Nussbaum,*Love's Knowledge*,p. 76.

[16]Unger,*Passion:An Essay on Personality*,p. 101.

[17]Paul Ricoeur, *Figuring The Sacred*, p. 95.

[18]Nussbaum, *Love's Knowledge*, p. 76.

[19]Ricoeur, *Oneself as Another*, p. 164.

[20]Nussbaum, *Love's Knowledge*, p. 89; see also her essay "Literature and the Moral Imagination" in *Love's Knowledge*, pp. 148-67.

[21]Nussbaum, *Love's Knowledge*, p. 90.

[22]William Spohn, "Jesus and Christian Ethics," p. 104.

[23]Spohn, "Jesus and Christian Ethics," p. 104.

[24]Spohn, "Jesus and Christian Ethics," p. 105.

[25]Ricoeur, *The Symbolism of Evil*, p. 351. Ricoeur understands history, especially in the West, as moving through three stages of evolution: in a "first *naïveté*" people had a simple vision of the world with no distinction between the natural order and the moral order. In "the desert of criticism," ignited by the scientific revolution, many people in Europe lost this simple view of the world and began to understand the world as merely a collection of physical events, without mystery or spiritual significance. In the following pages we will see Ricoeur's explanation of the emerging period of a "second *naïveté*."

[26]Caroline Bynum, *Metamorphosis and Identity*, p. 52.

[27]See Tyler Volk, *Gaia's Body: Toward a Physiology of Earth*.

[28]Scarey, *On Beauty and Being Just*, p. 81.

[29]Scarey, *On Beauty and Being Just* p. 47.

[30]Scarey, *On Beauty and Being Just* p. 111.

[31]Scarey, *On Beauty and Being Just* p. 113.

[32]For a theological reflection on these themes, see Sally McFague, *Super, Natural Christians*. Also see Mary Evelyn Tucker and John Berthrong, eds., *Confucianism and Ecology: The Interrelation of Heaven, Earth, and Humans*. Historian Lynn White was one of the first critics of Christianity's role in the pollution and degradation of nature still so prevalent throughout the world; see his essay, "The Historical Roots of our Ecological Crisis."

[33]Ricoeur, *The Symbolism of Evil*, p. 458.

[34]Ricoeur, *The Symbolism of Evil*, p. 460.

[35] Ricoeur, *The Symbolism of Evil*, p. 455.

[36] Ricoeur, *The Symbolism of Evil*, p. 460.

[37] Ricoeur, *The Symbolism of Evil*, p. 448.

[38] Ricoeur, *The Symbolism of Evil*, p. 449.

[39] Ricoeur, *The Symbolism of Evil*, p. 467.

CHAPTER EIGHT : CHARACTERISTICS OF
LATE-MODERN RELIGIOUSNESS

This chapter examines shifts in religious sensitivity that are part of late-modern consciousness and discusses different motives that support religious participation today.

Robert Bellah, as noted in Chapter One, defines religion as "a set of symbolic forms and acts relating humans to the ultimate conditions of existence."[1] He goes on to identify, across the wide expanse of human existence, several critical stages in the development of these symbolic forms. Bellah notes that he is describing the development of human consciousness about religion, not tracking historical changes in religious institutions. And he adds the caution that his evolutionary model is a conceptual schema to guide further thinking, not an empirical account of all religious phenomena. We will use his model in this chapter to provide background information, helping us to understand cultural shifts that are shaping religiousness today.

In his essay, Bellah emphasizes the importance of the historic wisdom traditions that emerged during the axial age of civilization, between 800bce and 700ce.[2] The origins of Buddhism, Christianity and Islam—along with significant developments in Hinduism, Judaism and Chinese religious traditions—can be traced over these centuries. In the advanced cultures that flourished in many parts of the world at this time, people searched for an ultimate single Power or Being that encompasses all reality. This single transcendent Power was seen as source of universal moral laws, to which all individuals were personally responsible. Dissatisfied with the imperfections and compromises of ordinary life, people sought a more perfect realm of existence, symbolized as the "other world. " And this new comprehensive world-view was expressed in classic texts, intellectual commentaries, and orthodox formulations.

The understanding of religion in western societies has been shaped largely by religious institutions identified with the historic wisdom traditions of Bellah's schema: Judaism, Catholic and Protestant Christianity, and Islam. These classical belief systems of the West have often viewed each other with suspicion. And western history is scarred by the evidence of continuing social discrimination and brutal warfare, arising from—even justified by—perceived religious differences among these faith traditions. But today many religious leaders and ordinary believers in each of these traditions are eager to overcome this sad heritage of mutual antagonism. Contemporary religious scholars, for example, readily acknowledge the common sources and mutual influences among Jews, Protestant and Catholic Christians, and Muslims that are part of the historical record.

While Muslims and Jews, Catholic and Protestants have developed many distinctive symbols and ritual practices, each of these traditions manifests the three characteristics that Bellah identifies as part of the classic religious belief system:

1. *Ultimate Reality*: search for a single principle in terms of which it would be possible to make sense of everything else.

2. *Universalism*: belief that there is one basic truth or set of interrelated truths about all things.

3. *"World-Rejection"*: the classical vision of perfect order and ideal values leads to a dissatisfaction with the highly imperfect order of ordinary life in this world.

In each of these historic traditions, the classic religious vision finds expression in the development of theological explanations of humanity's brokenness or sin, along with a confident expectation of deliverance or salvation to be realized in its fullness beyond this earthly existence. The spiritual resources of these classic religious traditions remain vital throughout the world today, as sources of commitment and consolation for millions of believers.

RELIGION IN LATE-MODERN CONSCIOUSNESS

Bellah's model of religious consciousness moves beyond the axial age to identify distinctive stages emerging within early modern and, now, late-modern societies. These historical shifts have significantly influenced the ways in which human religiousness is explored and expressed today. In the contemporary world, for example, many people who embrace religious faith recognize that religious language is essentially symbolic—images embodied in the familiar stories of classic texts, symbols embodied in the art and gesture of religious ritual. And increasingly the experience and expression of religious consciousness is no longer exclusively the domain of traditional religious institutions.

Building on Bellah's work, philosopher of religion Michael Barnes examines the dynamics of contemporary religious consciousness. Barnes describes late-modern religiousness this way:

> There is, however, a religiousness that is thoroughly modern in that it has come to terms with scientific world-views, has a secular orientation which focuses on the issues and concerns of contemporary society, promotes responsible autonomy, and lives by an openness to new ideas and changes. This late-modern religiousness will never entirely replace earlier forms, but it will continue to influence them as well as draw from their heritage. [3]

This new religious consciousness is emerging among many people living in the highly complex and interdependent societies that encompass today's world. In these settings, ordinary people experience increasing cross-cultural contact and are personally confronted by the challenges of global pluralism. With a profound appreciation of personal autonomy, contemporary religious consciousness resists attempts to make all people follow the same single spiritual path. And the absolute doctrines of the historic religions are seen as open to further discussion and debate.

Here we will examine several characteristics of this late-modern religiousness:

1. Greater awareness of the ultimate mystery of human experience.
2. Increased recognition that all knowledge is limited.

3. Heightened appreciation of the spiritual significance of ordinary life.

4. Genuine openness to religious pluralism and value diversity.

Greater Awareness of the Ultimate Mystery of Human Experience. In late-modern religious consciousness, mystery is more prominent than belief. For many people today, religious awareness is not based primarily on an acceptance of certain theological doctrines. Instead, their spirituality reflects a greater mindfulness of the enduring questions that surround the experience of human life and of all existence. Orthodox expressions of theological concepts are often respected, but seldom regarded as exempt from questioning or criticism. Personal experience of life and critical reflection become more important in the process of evaluating religious statements.

This late-modern religiousness is often shaped by the conviction that there is a mysterious Presence at the heart of our experience of the world. This presence comes as gift, with a power that creates, sustains, reconciles and heals. It is a power that engages humans personally, drawing them into fuller participation in life beyond narrow self-interest. This sacred presence is elusive, but real. Its reality defies conceptual definition; it cannot be adequately expressed in the language of discursive rationality.

Late-modern religiousness draws on plural sources of spiritual nourishment. The diverse wisdom traditions of the world are recognized as rich storehouses of spiritual insight. Using the symbolic language of myth and poetry and image and gesture, these multiple traditions expand and deepen humanity's relationship with this mysterious Reality.

Increased Recognition that all Knowledge is Limited. People in late-modern societies have access to multiple sources of information and explanation. Science and the scientific method have expanded tremendously the frontiers of human knowledge; yet by definition all current scientific understanding remains tentative and open to correction. Philosophy and the humanities, religious faiths and political ideologies—all claim to provide essential insight into "the way things are" and "the way things should be. " Yet today there is heightened awareness that these explanations, too, leave much that is unexplained. Increasing numbers of people recognize that knowledge is socially constructed: understanding necessarily arises in particular settings and truth can only be expressed from a particular perspective or point-of-view.

In the contemporary world, many people who embrace religious faith recognize that religious language, too, is necessarily limited. The sacred texts of the historic religious traditions reflect the cultural milieu in which they were crafted. Theology, the disciplined reflection on religious classics and their implications for the life of believers and for the larger society, is necessarily involved in the interpretation and re-interpretation of these religious symbols. Today theologians, along with ordinary believers, recognize that the sacred books of classical religions are not intended to provide scientific information or historical documentation. Their gift to the human community is insight into the meaning of life. Many traditional religious symbols have enduring significance. But for their spiritual power to be available to people within contemporary societies, these symbols must be reclaimed—both purified and renewed.

Among theologians, this awareness is registered in an increasing modesty. This comes with recognition that traditional formulations of religious belief have, perhaps, claimed to know too much: their concepts are too full, too clear, too certain. In late-modern theological work, the doctrines of traditional religious thought are re-examined and restated, often with acknowledgment that any statement about the ultimate dimensions of human experience will be partial and thus must remain tentative. Theologian Paul Lakeland gives voice to the theological modesty of late-modern religiousness. He notes that the Christian worldview is "a vision of the universal, but not a universal vision."[4]

Heightened Appreciation of the Spiritual Significance of Daily Life. The religious traditions emerging from the classical axial age were shaped by a passion for perfection beyond this world. But in late-modern religiousness, this focus on an "other-world" is challenged.

Many people today—those formally committed to religious faith and others as well—are searching for a "this world" spirituality, one deeply responsive to the genuine beauty as well as the less-than-perfect ambiguities of the world as we find it. The fast-paced lifestyles and electronic environments of global culture leave many people spiritually empty. They hunger for a more profound connection with the natural world, for more genuine relationships with family and friends. They are eager to reconcile their deeply held values with the daily demands of their work life.

A this-world spirituality recognizes ordinary life, with its joys and responsibilities, as both sacred space and call to service. It is here, in our daily interactions of love and work and civic participation, that the gracious mystery of life is encountered. It is here, too, that life's misery and suffering call human beings to respond. Late-modern religious consciousness seeks ways to engage this world, through both appreciation and critique: to raise up the simple pleasures that carry authentic delight, and to face up to the complex issues that carry the value agenda of our own time.

Daimund O'Murchu sees the "this world" perspective of late-modern religiousness as refocusing theology's work. Theological exploration, he suggests, "may no longer begin with God and work downward; rather it will originate in the human experience of searching and seeking and move outward to embrace every wider horizons of life and reality. " With this new focus, he continues, "the spiritual landscape rather than the religious tradition has become the task of the theologians. "[5]

Openness to Religious Pluralism and Value Diversity. Religious pluralism and value diversity are defining characteristics of contemporary culture. Classic religious sensitivity, with its commitment to single theological orthodoxy, identifies pluralism as a problem to be overcome. Contact with other religions is minimized, even forbidden, lest the purity of true belief be put at risk. This orientation supports an atmosphere of competition and mutual suspicion among religious groups. Such an atmosphere defeats any efforts by these groups to work together for common cause.

Late-modern religious sensitivity often sees pluralism as a resource. The diverse religious traditions of the world, with their core moral convictions and value commitments, offer resources for healing and hope. Late-modern religiousness recognizes that the problems confronting humanity are too complex for any single group to solve. Therefore religious people must seek ways to cooperate across traditions, and beyond formal religions, in the search for shared bases for global response and responsibility. Interfaith collaboration here is not aimed at theological agreement but at moral solidarity—working together in practical and effective ways, to respond to the needs of the world.

The Parliament of the World's Religions, mentioned in Chapter Three, offers a useful example of this shared search for a global moral response. The Parliament has become more than an interfaith spiritual gathering; its participants are vitally concerned with the pressing issues of the contemporary world. This concern was reflected in the statement "Toward a Global Ethic" prepared for and promoted by the 1993 Parliament gathering. This statement does not establish a new set of ethical norms. Rather it recognizes many commonalities among the moral values embraced by the world's religions, and—based on these shared moral commitments—attempts to address practically some of the critical issues facing the world community. Now a Global Ethics Foundation has been established, to support collaborative responses to many challenges that face the world.

This global effort links people of different faiths with others who embrace no religion. The success of such collaboration demands a new stance for committed religious believers. As people of faith approach those of different religious traditions or those with no religious beliefs, a conscious transformation is required. In these settings, Lakeland suggests, believers must appreciate that their cherished religious convictions stand "behind" them rather than "in front." Behind them—motivating, supporting, sustaining their personal commitment to the arduous tasks of collaborative action for social change. Rather than "in front"—as a barrier forcing other people to adopt this religious vision. In late-modern consciousness, religious faith is "the background out of which we operate," not a "blueprint for history or a program for the reform of the world. "[6]

DIVERSE RELIGIOUS MOTIVATIONS TODAY

Research in the psychology of religion provides another perspective on contemporary religious consciousness. Attempting to understand the motives that lead people to participate in religious activities today, scholars have identified three sets of reasons.

Instrumental religious motives are largely utilitarian. Here a person seeks religious identification or church membership because this is useful in reaching other goals. Membership in a prestigious church, for example, may raise a family's social standing. Or religious practices may seem to provide an almost magical safety shield, protecting the believer from life's problems. A religious group that reinforces conventional ideas and moral values usually makes few demands for personal conversion or social transformation; thus some people join this kind of religious group in order to find support for their current values and way of life. In each of these examples, religious participation has more to do with immediate personal benefit than with a transforming encounter with sacred mystery.

Intrinsic religious motives involve a deep sense of personal commitment to a particular religious tradition. People of intrinsic faith seek a personal relationship with sacred reality (whether named as God or the higher Reality identified in other faith traditions) and draw strength and support from this relationship. They consider their religious faith to be a guiding force in their lives, the major determinant in their view of the world. The values and moral code of this particular religious heritage have practical impact on their decisions and behavior, moving believers toward personal and social transformation. The effort to overcome self-centeredness is embraced as a spiritual goal. Believers hold themselves accountable to religious ideals of altruistic behavior and moral rectitude, even when adherence is difficult. Psychological benefits—hope, consolation, sense of purpose, joy—are welcomed as gifts of faith but are not the primary goal of religious belief and practice.

This description of intrinsic faith fits the experience of many believers in the contemporary world who strongly identify with classic religious traditions, such as Buddhism, Judaism, Catholic and Protestant Christianity, and Islam. There is much to admire in the resolute commitment and self-sacrificing behavior that characterize intrinsic faith. Both individuals and societies have benefited from such wholehearted embrace of a particular religious tradition. But critics note that this intrinsic faith commitment can also support a rigid approach to religious truth that judges other faith traditions harshly.

Researchers today report a different set of motives at play in late-modern religiousness. Psychologist of religion Daniel Batson and his colleagues have named this perspective a *quest orientation*. [7] People on the spiritual quest are conscious that religious awareness is an ongoing process. Suspicious of simple solutions proposed for complex problems, they remain open to new religious ideas and willing to reexamine orthodox beliefs. Tentativeness and doubt are companions on their spiritual journey. As a result, they display a healthy skepticism toward many of the claims of traditional religion.

Nevertheless, many people with a quest orientation see themselves as committed participants in a particular religious tradition. But their commitment is expansive not limiting: grateful for the spiritual insights received from their own spiritual heritage, they value the symbolic resources of other wisdom traditions as well. Some committed believers today prefer to acknowledge their multiple allegiance, identifying themselves—for example—as Confucian Christians or Catholic Buddhists.

In regard to spirituality, the quest orientation challenges the dichotomies that have been part of conventional religious understanding. Intrinsic faith, especially in the West, has often defined the spiritual life in antagonistic terms. Spiritual development was understood as a process of overcoming the desires of the body. The supernatural realm was recognized as distinct from the natural world of ordinary experience. Spirituality was interpreted as the practice of sacred activities, undertaken in order to counteract the distractions and temptations of secular life.

People with a quest orientation express a more integrated religious consciousness. Sacred mystery, self-development, and social compassion are recognized as essentially interconnected. Their spiritual awareness is rooted in personal and communal experience, more than in the authority of received tradition. Their spiritual practices are focused more on transformation—of self as well as society—than on self-denial and self-control.

People with a quest orientation seek out settings that can sustain the value conversation, not just transmit or defend a particular moral code. They are eager to be part of honest discussion of what is of value in our lives, where we experience these values, what we can do to safeguard these values, and how we can express our values in the real circumstances of our lives.

Evidence from the social sciences continues to record decline in the membership of institutional religions in many late-modern societies. But along with others, Robert Bellah insists that secularization is not the best explanation of this contemporary decline of institutional affiliation. He suggests that religious individuation—consciousness that persons must work out their own ultimate solutions and take personal responsibility for values that shape their lives—plays the defining role in late-modern religiousness. For those on the spiritual quest, religious institutions are not the final destination. Instead, the role of the established religions is to provide a favorable environment for the continuing personal search. [8]

NOTES

[1] Robert Bellah, *Beyond Belief*, p. 21.

[2] Various historical times are offered by different scholars, to circumscribe the period of the *axial age*. Karl Jaspers, who is widely credited with introducing this term into the modern discussion, suggests the year 800bce as initiating a thousand-year transformation in human consciousness. In his article, Bellah does not give precise dates for the emergence of what he calls the "historic religions," but his inclusion of Islam justifies the broader end-limit we offer here. For further reflections on the significance of the axial age, see James D. Whitehead and Evelyn Eaton Whitehead, "From Consciousness to Conscience: Reflections on the Axial Age."

[3] Michael Barnes, *In the Presence of Mystery: An Introduction to the Story of Human Religiousness*, p. 309.

[4] Paul Lakeland, *Postmodernity: Christian Identity in a Fragmented Age*, p. 91.

[5] Daimund O'Murchu, *Quantum Theology*, p. 21.

[6] Lakeland, *Postmodernity*, p. 102.

[7] In *Religion and the Individual*, Daniel Batson, Patricia Schoenrade

and Larry Ventis provide theoretical background and empirical findings on the function of these different religious motives；see especially pp. 155—164.

[8]Bellah, *Beyond Belief*, p. 44.

PART THREE
RELIGION CHINA AND THE FUTURE

PART THREE
RELIGION CHINA AND THE FUTURE

CHAPTER NINE: CHINA'S RELIGIOUS HERITAGE AS MORAL CAPITAL

This chapter examines ideals and images from the rich heritage of Chinese popular religion being embraced in contemporary China. The focus is provided by research among middle-class residents in Shenzhen, a rapidly expanding city designated as Special Economic Zone. [1]

The city of Shenzhen, an hour's train ride from Hong Kong, was not long ago a sleepy fishing village. In 1979 as part of his program of Opening and Reform, Deng Xiaoping declared this village and a vast track of surrounding territory as a Special Economic Zone. During the 1980s a first wave of immigrants, predominantly unskilled laborers and recruits from the Peoples Liberation Army, arrived to supply needed construction and factory workers. In the 1990s a second wave of immigrants, including many middle-class Chinese, came to fill the demand for management personnel or to start their own businesses. With generous tax incentives in place for foreign investment, the city has exploded into a rough-edged metropolis of seven million, of whom several million are temporary workers or "floating residents" who labor in various jobs without the benefits of legal residency.

In many ways the city of Shenzhen is unique in China: more

than 90% of its inhabitants were born elsewhere; the average age of current residents is less than thirty years. Social and psychological forces here differ dramatically from those that still prevail in the interior regions where most Chinese live. The speed of change in Shenzhen has outpaced even the rapidly modernizing urban metropolises along China's eastern coast.

But while this free economic zone is not typical of China today, it may hold significant clues to this country's future. With the dynamics of globalization cast here in such sharp relief, Shenzhen presents a compelling site for examining the impact of social change on religious consciousness.

The Shekou Incident. In January of 1988 two Chinese political supervisors arrived in the Shekou district of the burgeoning new free economic zone of Shenzhen. They came to lecture a youth assembly, which included university students and industrial workers along with other young adults. Their instruction addressed a theme familiar in such compulsory gatherings: the revolutionary ideals of party and state that must guide Chinese young people. The lecture was routine, but the response it generated was not.

While the officials were still speaking, a young worker arose in protest. In tone and terms that were startlingly direct, he challenged their message as empty propaganda, words that no longer carried meaning in Shenzhen. Here workers did not need to depend on the state-controlled work unit (*danwei*) for their jobs, he asserted. Here workers could seek and find employment on their own; fired from a factory one day, a laborer could easily find work by the next. In this exploding economic arena, he announced, party directives and government control were irrelevant. And the gathered workers cheered his audacious announcement.

Reports of this act of public defiance—the "Shekou Incident"—spread quickly. People living in this economic free zone were embarked on a new adventure. The laissez-faire atmosphere of Shenzhen's economic frontier offered options that promised release from dependence on the all-providing, all-controlling institution of the *danwei*. Opportunities for individual choice quickly expanded beyond the economic realm. With the wider range of options came an increased awareness of personal responsibility. Where to live, what life-style to pursue, what values to adopt—now these decisions had to be made on one's own. Among these industrial migrants—no longer embedded in the values of family and village life, no longer limited by the constraints of the work unit—the taste of personal responsibility developed an appetite for personal freedom. For some residents of Shenzhen this new opportunity raised questions of religious meaning and purpose.

In summer 1998 sociologist Lizhu Fan began an eighteen-month field study in the Shenzhen special economic zone, to investigate personal and communal coping strategies being used in response to Chinese modernization. [2] She interviewed women and men who had moved to Shenzhen in the past decade. All were part of Shenzhen's emerging middle-class of white-collar employees and small business owners. Having met the strict educational and economic criteria for permanent residence status, all these respondents reported that they intended to remain in Shenzhen.

In the course of her interviews in Shenzhen, a common vocabulary begin to emerge. To explain their struggles and successes in this challenging urban setting, these residents turned repeatedly to themes and images deeply rooted in the traditions of China's popular religion.

CHINA'S MORAL CAPITAL

Judith Berling employed the term moral capital in her exploration of a 17th century novel, *The Romance of the Three Teachings*. The novel, published in Nanjing between 1612 and 1620, addressed the tension between financial profit and moral goodness in the last years of the Ming dynasty. The novel was set in what Berling describes as "the competitive urban environment" of the area near Nanjing during a period of great social change, a social context curiously similar to Shenzhen today.

The novel argues that a virtuous life amounts to the accumulation of moral capital. A person's meritorious actions of honesty and compassion are "saved" just as money might be saved. These accrued virtues become the spiritual inheritance that funds the next generation. A person who squanders these spiritual resources in his own life has nothing to hand on to his children. In a typically Chinese fashion, the novel insists that moral capital (accumulated merit) is just as important a legacy for one's descendents as land or money. In fact, the successful long-term management of property depends on the management of moral capital; "the two cannot be separated. "[3]

Berling concludes: "religion as the management of moral capital thus involves taking responsibility: learning to manage one's life and human relationships so as not to exhaust moral collateral. " Thus, she argues, "we see here the seeds of a religiously based work ethic not unlike the Calvinist ethic in the West. "[4]

As Berling has explored the image of moral capital in Chinese history, the influential moral philosopher Alasdair MacIntyre has examined how the virtues of individuals in a society contribute to the economic well-being of the group. "Virtue is a form of capital, a storing within a single individual of a moral capital of a tradition, without which productive capital could not be found. "[5]

Religions and cultures often imagine their heritage in terms of a patrimony of moral goodness and spiritual achievements that represent the group's accumulated worth. This heritage functions as an endowment to be cherished and conserved, as well as an asset to be invested in the future. When a religion or culture squanders these reserves it jeopardizes its social identity and risks spiritual bankruptcy.

FROM SOCIAL CAPITAL TO MORAL CAPITAL IN THE WEST

In recent years social scientists Robert Putnam and Francis Fukuyama have popularized the notion of social capital as describing the human resources that a society relies on for its flourishing. Fukuyama defines social capital as "a society's stock of shared values⋯which is principally manifested in trust. "[6] For Putnam social capital refers to the connectedness that people feel with one another and the trust that this relatedness engenders.

The core idea of social capital is that social networks have value⋯Whereas physical capital refers to physical objects and human capital refers to properties of individuals, social capital refers to connections among individuals—social networks and the norms of reciprocity and trustworthiness that arise from them. [7]

By identifying the human resources of trustworthiness as social capital, both authors refer to more than the societal well-being that these vital resources produce. Social capital implies the community's ability to invest this capital, the danger of going into debt when trust is not met by an ethical response, and even the specter of moral bankruptcy when this mutual trust has been depleted.

If social capital describes the human resources currently available in a particular society, the question arises: where do these resources originate? What is their origin or wellspring? Fukuyama has suggested that these valuable resources spring from "certain pre-modern cultural habits. "[8] Later in his book, he attempts to clarify this suggestion: the trust at the core of social capital has "its origins in ···phenomena like religion and traditional ethics. "[9]

Trustworthiness—generally identified as a personal virtue or moral dynamic—can also be understood as an inherited reserve of social cohesion. At the core of social cohesion is the shared recognition of promises made and kept, of reliability that has been established over many transactions. This communal confidence can be understood as a resource that accrues like other capital; it can be both accumulated and invested in the future. Moral capital may also be depleted: as when a society continues to draw on its inherited moral reserves without replenishment.

Thus in western societies, now sometimes described as "post-Christian," national policies and social norms often depend on a communal ethos rooted in a religious worldview that no longer claims the active allegiance of many of its citizens. The risk here is that such a society is living, as it were, beyond its moral means—drawing on a moral capital that is not being actively replenished. Similarly, in a post-Confucian and post-Marxist China, officials often appeal to ideals of personal sacrifice and common benefit to which even few policy makers appear personally committed. Fuku yama comments on the dire result of such a scenario: "Once social capital has been spent, it may take centuries to replenish, if it can be replenished at all. "[10]

MANAGING MORAL CAPITAL IN SHENZHEN

The concept of social capital explicitly links contemporary societal behavior with inherited religious values. Lizhu Fan's research in Shenzhen traces the spiritual resources—the moral capital—upon which contemporary middle-class Chinese residents draw, as they cope with social and economic transformations in this rapidly modernizing special economic zone. Discussing the challenges they faced, respondents characteristically used the religious imagery and moral vocabulary of Chinese popular religion.

Wondering About His Fate (*ming yun*). Mr. Zhou grew up in rural Anhui Province, during a time when popular beliefs were under attack and all religious rituals were prohibited. Several years into his career as a middle school teacher, he began planning for marriage and a family. When his fiancée rejected him for a richer suitor, Mr. Zhou left the area in shame and despair. After several mishaps along the way, he eventually arrived in Shenzhen. Initially he found only menial jobs available. Three years later he had saved enough to start his own small printing business, producing mailing envelopes, deposit slips and receipt books. The business grew rapidly, in pace with Shenzhen's expanding economy. Mr. Zhou found himself suddenly wealthy, with sufficient financial resource to purchase a new home and even a private automobile.

Mr. Zhou recalls years of poverty and struggle during which he was untroubled by larger questions of meaning or purpose. Only recently has he begun to reflect on his success: why had this good fortune been his, while others—equally hardworking—continue to struggle with little reward? Before these issues arose for him as personal questions, he remembers laughing at his parents' Daoist beliefs. Now for the first time, Mr. Zhou reports, he is confronted by the question of personal destiny. Does his unexpected good fortune point to something more? Is it, perhaps, part of a deeper design for his life? Uncertain about how to safeguard his good fortune, he has turned his attention to a nearby Buddhist temple. He has donated a large sum of money to this religious site; he has also asked his wife to attend celebrations there just in case this might help their fate. Mr. Zhou has also begun to visit the temple itself for the peaceful setting it offers when he finds himself angry or exhausted.

The Chinese, as those in other cultures, have long recognized the dual aspect of personal destiny; it is acknowledged as both pre-established and as susceptible to manipulation. Human fate is both fixed and flexible. As discussed in Chapter Three, the Chinese word *ming yun* captures this duality. *Ming* alludes to ancient convictions concerning heaven's mandate (*tian ming*), pointing to the aspects of fate experienced as fixed: parental genes and the accidents of one's time and place in history. [11] *Yun* refers to those circumstances and opportunities that emerge, providing options that give flexibility to life. [12]

In the pre-Confucian era in China, as Cynthia Brokaw writes, "*ming* ··· might refer ··· to the original, predetermined fate a person received at birth ···" But even in this early period *ming* referred, ambiguously, both to "a set, unchangeable destiny ··· and the success or failure earned through personal moral effort." The moral effort dimension of personal fate was raised to prominence in the thought of Confucius and Mencius as they stressed "man's responsibility to do good for its own sake."[13]

The Doctrine of the Mean had distinguished a virtuous posture of "awaiting fate" from reckless adventurism: "The mature person lives peacefully and at ease, awaiting his fate, while the immature person walks in dangerous paths, hoping for good luck" (*Zhong Yang*, 14.4). Mencius likewise believed that one must await his fate, but added the need to actively "establish his destiny." More than close attention to a ready-made destiny was called for; a person must also perform his fate. And Mencius saw this assertive response to the challenge of fate as superior to other aspects of fate, such as an early death or longevity: "Whether he is going to die young or to live to a ripe old age makes no difference to his steadfastness of purpose, and he awaits whatever is to befall him. This is the way he establishes his destiny" (7A:1). But Mencius was also aware of the many ways humans undercut their own best interests: he warned the person who was eager to establish his own best destiny "to avoid standing under a wall that is about to collapse."

The tension of a fate provided and a destiny to be performed came to special focus in the Ming dynasty. As Cynthia Brokaw relates, the young scholar Yuan Huang was troubled by a fortune teller's prediction that he would die at age fifty-four, without a male heir. He sought the advice of a Buddhist monk who, quoting Mencius, assured him that his fate was not so fixed. Virtuous behavior could alter this predicted destiny. So Yuan set about performing virtuous acts and recording them in a ledger, with the goal of accumulating enough merit to alter his fate. At play here is the conviction that moral capital—this personal accumulation of merit—can influence one's personal destiny. As we shall see below in the discussion of moral reciprocity (*bao ying*), the prudent accumulation of moral capital can also support future generations.[14]

In contemporary Shenzhen, with its rapidly developing economic climate and multiple employment possibilities, residents often speak of "grasping their fate" (*bawo sizide ming yun*). No longer does a person depend on the state's "iron rice bowl" or expect the *danwei* to provide for the future. Instead, personal destiny is something to be seized.

Journalist Peter Hessler describes another Shenzhen resident who set out to grasp her fate. This young woman had been a student in the teachers' college in Sichuan Province where Hessler taught. Upon graduation, all students were guaranteed jobs as teachers in their home provinces; a last vestige of the "iron rice bowl." Only one young woman in the graduating class refused an appointment. She made the risky decision to travel alone to Shenzhen in search of a career. Later she discussed her choice with Hessler. Becoming a teacher in the familiar setting of her home province, she observed, "could have been a very comfortable life. But, if it is too comfortable, I think it's like death."[15] Eager to seize and shape her own destiny, she preferred to take her chances in the city of Shenzhen.

Questioning Apparent Coincidence (*yuan fen*). Ms. Wang was born in Tianjin just prior to the Cultural Revolution. Entering adulthood without religious belief or practice herself, she carried memories of her grandmother—a devout Buddhist—attempting to conceal her prayers and rituals from the watchful eye of neighborhood informers. After graduating the university in economics, Ms. Wang found a promising position in Tianjin and later moved to a new job in Hainan Province.

While she was working in Hainan, Ms. Wang's beloved grandmother died. The shock of this death triggered for her new questions about the purpose of her own life. She decided to return to Tianjin where, for the first time, she began to practice Buddhism.

Subsequently she received an opportunity to advance her career through a period of study in England. But in a distant city on the eve of her departure for London, she fell victim to a robbery. All her belongings—passport, cash, visa, scholarship papers—were lost. Unsuccessful in her attempts to remedy this unfortunate turn of events, Ms. Wang traveled to Shenzhen to seek the solace of her boyfriend, who had himself just moved to that city. But he refused to see her or offer any help.

Deeply disappointed but determined, she remained in Shenzhen and eventually found a position in an accounting firm. As the business grew, she was frequently promoted and soon occupied a senior position with a very good salary. Now in her early forties, she is well-satisfied in her work and financially secure. Reflecting on her life in Shenzhen, Ms. Wang recalls the series of painful events that led her to this city where she has flourished. Perhaps, she mused, those troubling chance events were more than simple chance. Perhaps there is a hidden logic in life's events, a guiding pattern revealed only in careful reflection. If so, how can she cooperate more fully with this force, whatever its source? These reflections led Ms.

Wang toward more public religious behavior; she frequently joins pilgrimages to nearby temples and shrines and annually helps to organize a local ritual of releasing animals (*fang sheng*) as a commitment to social compassion.

A second theme recorded repeatedly in Shenzhen was the experience of *yuan fen* as chance event or apparent coincidence. This phrase is commonplace in contemporary Chinese life, serving as a rough equivalent to the English phrase "good luck. " Chinese today are likely to describe any happy coincidence—a chance meeting of a good friend in a public market, for example—as *yuan fen*. The term is also used to describe unfortunate events, what in English one might name "an unlucky break. "

In Shenzhen Ms. Wang struggled to understand her own life. Her current economic well-being seemed dependent on circumstances that remained mysterious to her. She often reflected on the painful events in her past—a failed romantic relationship, the theft that defeated her plan to study abroad. But now she recognizes that these negative experiences—her bad *yuan fen*—contributed to her present good fortune. As did Mr. Zhou, Ms. Wang drew on the vocabulary of a deep cultural heritage to describe her contemporary life.

In the course of this reflection, Ms. Wang's interpretation of *yuan fen* has undergone transformation. She reports that now this traditional image no longer refers to simple coincidences or everyday chance events. Instead she assigns to the traditional term *yuan fen* a richer significance, seeing these "fateful coincidences" as somehow linked in ways that shape the direction of her life. For Ms. Wang, *yuan fen* has shifted from a cultural cliché to a meaningful marker of a purposeful life.

The notion of *yuan fen*, common currency in the moral capital of Chinese culture, resonates with the Buddhist concept of *karma*. In orthodox Buddhist belief, the universe is profoundly moral; personal life events follow upon one's virtue or vice. In this karmic worldview there are no coincidences. The devout believer discerns purpose and intent in every happening, however accidental it may seem. What may appear as a chance occurrence—the coincidental meeting of the person one will later marry or an unexpected absence from the office site on the day of a devastating fire—in fact results from a person's moral past and in turn determines the shape of the person's destiny.

K. S. Yang and David Ho have discussed the psychological advantages of this traditional belief. By "external attribution" or assigning causality of negative events to *yuan fen*—which is beyond personal control—groups are able to "soothe relationships, reduce conflict, and promote social harmony."[16] Similarly, when positive events are seen to result primarily from *yuan fen*, personal credit is not directly assigned—thus reducing pride on one side of the relationship and envy and resentment on the other.

Moral Reciprocity (***bao ying***)[17]. Ms. Shen was born in Shandong Province, into a military family strongly opposed to any religious expression. Her first job was as middle manager at the local airport. With encouragement from state officials, she and her husband moved to Shenzhen in 1992 to fill management positions at this city's new airport.

Divorcing her husband some years later, Ms. Shen began an affair with a married man who held a high position at the Shenzhen airport. His early promise to seek a divorce himself so that they might marry was postponed again and again. Frustrated by this situation she began to pray—somewhat randomly—to a variety of gods and spirits, hoping this might bring solace in her distress. Ms. Shen acknowledges that her family upbringing and subsequent education had taught her that such practices were mere superstition, but she was desperate enough to continue praying. In the midst of this turmoil, Ms. Shen left her position at the airport to become manager of an advertising firm. Here she threw herself wholeheartedly into making money, ready to cheat both colleagues and clients in pursuit of greater profit.

Some months later Ms. Shen accepted a friend's invitation to attended a public lecture offered by a Buddhist monk who was touring mainland China. There she was struck by his statement, "if you are meant to have something it will be yours." This sentence returned to her consciousness again and again, compelling her to question her own acquisitiveness. Gradually she came to see her business pursuits in a new light; she determined to end her deceitful activities and to conduct her business in a more honest fashion. The monk's observation now guides her behavior beyond the business realm, as well. Sensitive to the possibility of a broader plan at play in her life, Ms. Shen reports a new sense of purpose.

The theme of *bao ying* or moral reciprocity appeared repeatedly in the Shenzhen interviews. This belief in a moral universe in which no action, good or bad, goes unrewarded is woven deep into the fabric of Chinese culture. Browkaw notes the importance of *bao ying* as a

belief in a supernatural or cosmic retribution, a belief that has been a fundamental, at times the fundamental, belief of Chinese religion since the beginning of recorded history…

Brokaw defines this belief as

> the faith that some force—either a supernatural force like
> heaven or the gods, or an automatic cosmic reaction—inevita-
> bly recompensed human behavior in a rational manner：it re-
> warded certain "good" deeds, be they religious sacrifices, acts
> of good government, or upright personal conduct, and punished
> evil ones. [18]

The belief at the heart of moral reciprocity, as with fateful co-incidence, is that the universe is moral：good actions have enduring consequences and personal virtue contributes to improving the world. This belief is also the engine that fuels virtuous practices—the Chinese tradition of doing good or *shan*.

Brokaw traces the evolution of the belief in moral reciprocity in Chinese history. One of the earliest statements of this moral princi-ple is found in the *Classic of History*："On the doer of good, heaven sends down all blessings, and on the doer of evil, he sends down all calamities. " Basic here is the assumption of "the existence of a heaven or a group of spirits fully conscious of human actions and vigorously active in their punishment or reward. "[19]

By the Han dynasty a new interpretation of *bao ying* had ap-peared：

> Retribution was not necessarily dependent on a morally con-
> scious and actively judgmental heaven or group of spirits.
> Rather the cosmos responded automatically and naturalistically
> to human actions through the movements of *qi*, the subtle and

pervasive pneuma that constituted all things. [20]

In yet a third stage of development during the eastern Han, Brokaw describes the Huang-Lao cult of immortality that practiced "a variety of charitable acts—the feeding of orphans, the repair of roads and bridges, and so forth—in their quest for eternal life. "[21]

Finally, with the advent of Buddhism in China, the traditional notion of *bao ying* was joined to that of Buddhist *karma* to further reinforce the conviction that good begets good and evil results in e-vil. By the early medieval period "the major Chinese schools of be-lief—Confucianism, the immortality cult, and Buddhism—all shared ···a basic faith in some form of cosmic retribution. "[22]

For Chinese people, the moral cultivation implied in such reci-procity has always been much more than a personal affair. The in-fluence of good actions affects not only the future life of the individ-ual, but spreads through one's family and community. The Ming dy-nasty scholar Yuan Huang believed that those who pass the civil service examination did so because of the store of merit accumula-ted by their forebears. He likewise interpreted his own ledger of good and bad deeds as a joint account with his wife. [23] The merit accumulated by such efforts constituted a spiritual reservoir and moral capital to fund the future.

Yang Liansheng has documented the continuing popularity in China, into the 20th century, of good books (*shan shu*) which con-tained explanations of the principles of *bao ying*. [24] The frequent reference to *bao ying* made by Shenzhen residents confirms Yang's findings. In fact, Brokaw's comments on the function of *bao ying* in the Ming dynasty seem appropriate to Shenzhen today. She notes, for example, that "good books" were valued as sources of moral guidance "during a time of high mobility, shifting values, and uncertain beliefs. "[25] The ambiguous challenge that *bao ying* raised for Chinese in the Ming dynasty is similar to one confronted by modern citizens in Shenzhen:"If the belief that a man could create his own moral and material fate gave the individual a power and a freedom he had not possessed before, it imposed as well a crushing responsibility. "[26]

Chinese concepts of destiny, fateful coincidences and moral reciprocity are closely interrelated. Coincidences, small and great, influence the shape and fortune of each person's destiny. But recognizing that some chance events may be more than coincidence can motivate a person to take advantage of every coincidence. In addition, belief that the universe is—at its core—moral links the concepts of *yuan fen* and *bao ying*. Virtuous deeds are not only recorded in ledgers; they are also related to the apparent coincidences of daily life.

The concept of moral capital links connectedness (*guanxi*) and moral reciprocity (*bao ying*). Anthropologist Yan Yunxiang sees *guanxi* as "the very matrix in which one learns to be a social person. " Yan traces the role of *guanxi* and *renqing* (human feelings) as part of the "moral economy" of Chinese culture. [27] Anthropologist Mayfair Yang finds links between the tradition of *guanxi* and the moral capital of Chinese society. Examining the emerging market economy in China, Yang argues that the deep cultural instincts of *guanxi* may be able to balance the acquisitive and accumulative forces of capitalism. "When *guanxi* is adapted to capitalism, money loses its independence because money itself must be mediated by symbolic capital, which is only gained through generosity. "[28] Yang is optimistic that the symbolic capital of *guanxi*, with its roots in a traditional sense of generosity and mutual indebtedness, may continue to fund the interactions of Chinese, even in the face of the daunting financial forces of global capitalism.

In Shenzhen today, economic opportunities and political freedom provide the context for a new generation of Chinese to confront the perennial questions of meaning and purpose. In this contemporary social setting, modern Chinese have turned to ancient categories retrieved from their common past. Beliefs and practices adopted from the moral capital of their tradition now help them adapt them to the present circumstances of their lives.

NOTES

[1]An earlier version of this chapter appeared as "Fate and Fortune: Popular Religion and Moral Capital in Shenzhen," *Journal of Chinese Religions* .

[2]See Lizhu Fan, "A Study of Modern Chinese Religious Beliefs—The Case of Shenzhen Economic Zone," Occasional Paper # 12, Centre for the Study of Religion and Chinese Society.

[3]Judith Berling, "Religion and Popular Culture," p. 208.

[4]Berling, "Religion and Popular Culture," p. 218.

[5]Quoted in John Gunnemann, "Capital Ideas," p. 3.

[6]Francis Fukuyama, *Trust: The Social Virtues and the Creation of Prosperity*, p. 3.

[7]Robert Putnam, *Bowling Alone*, p. 5.

[8]Fukuyama, *Trust*, p. 11.

[9]Fukuyama, *Trust*, p. 325.

[10]Fukuyama, *Trust*, p. 324.

[11]For a fuller discussion of *ming* see Christopher Lupke, ed. , *The Magnitude of Ming: Command, Allotment and Fate in Chinese Culture*.

[12]T'ang Chun-I comments on this aspect of *ming yun*: "any circumstances we encounter may reveal to us what we ought to do; it is up to us to handle the circumstances in accord with our duty; " see his essay "The Heav-

enly Ordinance (*Tien-ming*) in Pre-Ch'in China. "

[13]Cynthia Brokaw, *The Ledgers of Merit and Demerit*, p. 53.

[14]Brokaw discusses Yuan Huang in Chapter Two of *The Ledgers of Merit and Demerit*.

[15]Peter Hessler, "Boomtown Girl: Finding a New Life in the Golden City," p. 119.

[16]K. S. Yang and David Ho, "The Role of *Yuan* in Chinese Social Life: A Conceptual and Empirical Analysis," p. 270.

[17]Cynthia Brokaw, along with many other scholars, usually translates *bao ying* as "moral retribution. " She does, however, use the word "reciprocity" on some occasions in *The Ledgers of Merit and Demerit*, see, for example, p. 28. Since the term "retribution" carries primarily negative nuances in English language, using this term to translate *bao ying* suggests that the Chinese term characteristically points to punishment. In our judgment, the term reciprocity better expresses the distribution of both reward and punishment. "

[18]Brokaw, *The Ledgers of Merit and Demerit*, p. 28.

[19]Brokaw, *The Ledgers of Merit and Demerit*, p. 29.

[20]Brokaw, *The Ledgers of Merit and Demerit*, p. 29.

[21]Brokaw, *The Ledgers of Merit and Demerit*, p. 30.

[22]Brokaw, *The Ledgers of Merit and Demerit*, p. 31.

[23]Brokaw, *The Ledgers of Merit and Demerit*, p. 87.

[24]Yang Liansheng, "*Zhongguo wenhua bao , bao, bao de yisi.* "

[25]Brokaw, *The Ledgers of Merit and Demerit*, p. 3.

[26]Brokaw, *The Ledgers of Merit and Demerit*, p. 119.

[27]Yan Yunxiang, *The Flow of Gifts: Reciprocity and Social Networks in a Chinese Village*, p. 222.

[28]Mayfair Yang, "The Resilience of *Guanxi* and its New Deployments: A Critique of Some New *Guanxi* Scholarship," p. 475.

CHAPTER TEN: ADOPTING AND ADAPTING CHINA'S RELIGIOUS HERITAGE

This chapter reports the continuing vitality of popular religious practices in the contemporary urban setting of Shenzhen. Comparisons with traditional practices reveal both similarities and differences in the new cultural expression of Chinese religiousness. [1]

It is Saturday in Shenzhen, the bustling free economic zone an hour's train ride from Hong Kong. At noon one of the city's largest vegetarian restaurants is crowded with families gathering for a leisurely meal together and shoppers stopping in for a quick snack before returning to their weekend errands. All the tables in the restaurant's several large rooms are filled and a waiting line begins to form in the large lobby entrance.

There is something different about this restaurant. While waiting for a table, many people browse through the impressive array of books that line the lobby's long bookshelf. Here they find titles on a range of practical and moral themes—achieving peace of mind in today's complex world, honesty in personal and business relationships, understanding problems in marriage and family life, and life-strategies to improve physical and emotional health. Others glance through the posters and notices listing upcoming lectures and workshops offered by Chinese and international figures, many with Buddhist or other religious affiliation. Once seated, the customers are greeted by attentive young restaurant servers and welcomed to move toward the central buffet. The selection of hot and cold vegetarian dishes is plentiful, with tempting aromas and attractive presentations adding to the appeal.

The steady traffic to and from the buffet area is not the only movement among the gathered diners. Regularly one or two members of a dining party will leave the table and make their way through the kitchen area and beyond the storage rooms. In a narrow hall an older Chinese woman sits beside a closed door. As patrons approach, she opens the door and gestures them to join those who have already found a place to sit on the floor of this medium-size room, typical of a modern Shenzhen commercial building. At the front of the room a small religious shrine has been set up for this occasion; the room holds no other furnishings.

Over the course of several hours, five traditionally garbed young Buddhist monks engage in a series of ritual activities—paying homage to several Buddhist images with bowing and incense, chanting aloud, and reading the sutras. Restaurant patrons come and go during this time, some joining the monks in ritual gestures but most simply sitting attentively for a period of time before returning to the restaurant area and continuing on their day's activities.

At one point, a middle-aged monk enters the room, to be greeted respectfully by some members of the seated crowd and by the younger monks. Quickly the room fills to capacity, leaving many disappointed people in the hall outside. Quiet falls as the older monk begins to speak. After his lengthy lecture the crowd disperses, the ritual objects are packed, and the monks depart. The room returns to its commercial uses···until the next occasion.

What is going on here? A religious ritual, to be sure, but of what kind? This location is a restaurant—part of the regular economic life of Shenzhen, not a sacred site registered with the local religious affairs bureau. The ritual forms here are Buddhist, and monks have played important roles in the event. But the monks are not the initiators of this gathering and few of those in attendance identify themselves as Buddhists. The session's host is Mr. Yang, the restaurant's owner. Mr. Yang understands this commercial setting—with its appealing vegetarian menu, its array of morally uplifting books, its up-to-date information about local spiritual resources, and its frequent opportunity for simple ritual participation—as part of his own spiritual practice.

Here, on the border between mainland China and Hong Kong, the dynamics of modernization interact with the search for spiritual meaning. Middle-class residents in Shenzhen draw selectively on perennial elements from China's indigenous cultural tradition to support a personal quest. But in this new religious milieu, traditional elements are readily adapted to suit new life circumstances. And in this rapidly developing urban setting, the spiritual search is characterized by a new emphasis on personal choice.

THE SPIRITUAL SEARCH IN SHENZHEN

The metropolis of Shenzhen boasts new and refurbished worship sites of each of the five religions officially recognized by law in the People's Republic of China—Daoism, Buddhism, Islam, and Protestant and Catholic Christianity. And while accurate numbers are difficult to determine, membership in these registered religious groups is on the rise here as well as elsewhere throughout mainland China. But evidence from Shenzhen reveals another, often overlooked, dynamic of Chinese modernization. One of the most significant—and surprising—developments has been the extent to which the urbanized Chinese in Shenzhen adopt and adapt elements of these traditional ritual practices as part of an intentional spiritual search.

In her Shenzhen research, Lizhu Fan found urbanized Chinese, all children of the revolutionary generation, embracing elements of traditional belief and practice as part of a personal spiritual awakening. Confronted by new questions of meaning and purpose, these residents did not turn to the now-approved religious institutions of Buddhism or Christianity. Instead they gave very personal expression to their spiritual search in the age-old idiom of China's common spiritual heritage. Despite determined opposition over the past two hundred years—from state Confucianism, from Christian missionary efforts, from the westernizing efforts of Chinese intellectuals, and from Maoist-Marxist political philosophy—this spiritual sensitivity survives in the mainland today.

The continuing vitality of this common religious heritage in rural areas of mainland China has been convincingly documented in contemporary field studies. [2] To date, the influence of traditional beliefs in city settings has received less attention. Our findings in Shenzhen suggest that the values and practices of China's common spiritual heritage continue to energize contemporary Chinese caught up in the dynamics of urbanization.

But while many urban dwellers now enthusiastically embrace elements of China's traditional heritage, their experience of these beliefs and practices does not simply repeat the patterns of China's rural past. In the experiences of Shenzhen people, we see both continuities with China's common spiritual heritage, and differences. Continuities include (a) the practical nature of spiritual concerns, (b) an open or, as Daniel Overmyer describes it, "non-sectarian"[3] attitude, which draws freely from plural sources of spiritual nourishment, and (c) the predominance of lay initiative over formal religious leadership. Differences include (d) the broader range of spiritual options currently available, (e) new settings for communal support and spiritual formation, and (f) the heightened awareness of personal decision in spiritual belief and practice.

RELIGIOUS CONTINUITIES IN SHENZHEN

Practical Nature of Spiritual Concerns. As is characteristic of traditional Chinese spirituality, the beliefs and practices of today's Shenzhen respondents are located in the midst of everyday life and focused on life's daily problems—health and healing, hope for good fortune, smoothing troubled relations. Ms. Shi, for example, is a news commentator at a local television station. Growing up during the Cultural Revolution, she had little direct experience of religious practice. Now in her apartment in one of the modern housing complexes that surround the city of Shenzhen she has set up a small altar. A statue of Guanyin, the Buddhist figure widely venerated among Chinese, figures prominently here. Ms. Shi places fresh fruit on the altar for a time, and then offers this as a gift to friends who are suffering from bad health or family problems. Her sense is that this fruit now carries special power (*ling*) that will bring healing and consolation to these friends. In the midst of her busy professional life, she tries to spend time daily in meditation and in reading morally uplifting books. While Ms. Shi insists that she is not a Buddhist, she finds the prayerful reading of Buddhist texts to be especially consoling. Ms. Shi acknowledges that her daily practices are part of a search for a calm life and peaceful heart, in the midst of a complex and confusing world. She embraces these activities as significant in her life and necessary for her spiritual well-being.

Spiritual Practices Drawn from Plural Traditions. Outsiders might also be struck by the eclectic range of Ms. Shi's devotions; her home altar displays items of ritual significance in Daoism and in Buddhism as well as some with uniquely personal meanings. On the one hand, this creative assembly of images may be seen as a reflection of modern consciousness, with its commitment to personal relevance and individual choice. But the openness and selectivity we see here also resonate with deeper cultural dynamics.

Historically, Chinese religiousness has drawn upon plural sources of spiritual nourishment. Resources separately identified with China's three great traditions—Confucianism, Daoism, and Buddhism—have been combined freely in local religious practice, without troubling considerations of denominational distinction or ritual orthodoxy. This characteristic openness, too, reflects the practical bias of China's common spiritual heritage.

For centuries the common ritual activities of China's peoples have existed symbiotically with the more formalized traditions of Confucianism, Daoism and Buddhism. As we noted in Chapter Four, Chinese popular religion developed with no need to create its own distinct rituals, elaborate doctrines, or full-time professional leaders such as monks or priests. Chinese have traditionally borrowed beliefs and ceremonies originally developed within the "great traditions" of Taoism, Confucianism, and Buddhism, adapting these to suit local conditions. Yet the underlying worldview remains that of the common spiritual heritage.

Another word may be helpful here regarding the role of Buddhism. The cultural heritage of Chinese Buddhism has served as a significant source of spiritual activities through much of China's history. But the beliefs and practices Shenzhen respondents today find spiritually nourishing are not experienced as distinctively or exclusively "Buddhist."

For example, many of Dr. Fan's respondents participate—along with thousands of other Shenzhen residents—in the annual pilgrimage to a Buddhist temple to join in the festive celebration of Guanyin's birthday. And several, like Ms. Shi, describe their personal devotion to this important Buddhist figure. But the Buddhism we see here is neither orthodox doctrine mediated through an officially designated guru nor disciplined practice overseen by a temple master. It is rather the popular expression of Buddhism's centuries-old spirituality, now thoroughly woven into the fabric of Chinese culture.

So while many Shenzhen respondents embrace spiritual understandings and practices that can be traced, historically or theologically, to Buddhist sources, most do not understand themselves as having "become" Buddhists. Few Shenzhen residents are interested in undergoing the formal initiation ceremony of "taking refuge in the Buddha," with its attendant ritual and financial responsibilities. In fact, some—like Ms. Shi herself—want to make it clear that they are not Buddhists. Even for Ms. Zhang who, as we shall see later, identifies herself as a lay Buddhist, this designation does not carry the exclusivist sense that religious identity commonly carries in the West.

Lay Leadership Predominates. China's local religious traditions, as Overmyer reminds us, "are characterized by their location in the midst of everyday life and their focus on practical aid and results···. Though clergy may be involved, for the most part these traditions are led, organized, and continued by the people themselves. "[4] The demands of rural village life did not permit the emergence of a group of specialists, freed from the demands of daily work and dedicated to religious activities. Such a division of labor was beyond the resources of the rural hamlet or small village. And since the ritual activities were so intimately woven into the patterns of daily life, it was natural that those who carried out the ordinary village responsibilities would play the significant roles in village rituals.

In Shenzhen, lay leadership continues to characterize the informal gatherings and larger communal activities. Lay people call on monks to conduct rituals, but they are in charge. For example, a loose network associated with one of the vegetarian restaurants has adopted a Buddhist ritual as part of a larger social concern. Annually they undertake a symbolic freeing of animals (*fang sheng*) to cultivate mercy and compassion in the world.

Notice of the time and place of the *fang sheng* is distributed by flyers, e-mail, and word-of-mouth. Individuals—many of them previously unknown to the planners—bring cages of small birds and turtles purchased at the local market. A monk from the nearby registered monastery is hired to read the appropriate sutras and to guide the ritual activities releasing the animals from their cages. But the ordinary people are clearly the initiators and the hosts of this gathering.

In Shenzhen, these lay leaders are not local village leaders as in rural tradition. Leadership comes from the initiative of assertive personalities and from successful immigrants who have financial resources to expend. As part of her own spiritual practice, for example, Ms. Zhang takes responsibility for many details in organizing these rituals. She is also active in inviting monks from elsewhere to Shenzhen, to meet informally with interested people. A wealthy man often hosts these visiting religious specialists in his home.

In this urban setting, the religious professional is not the center of the loose network of practitioners; instead this person is an invited guest. Persons who gather to welcome this religious figure usually provide a financial donation to compensate the visitor for his time and teaching. Individuals may ask personal questions or seek spiritual advice. But allegiance to a single religious master is not expected. Instead, different religious masters will be welcomed to join the group at other times.

This discussion of continuities between the rural spiritual heritage and its urban re-appropriation has already hinted at some emerging differences. Here we will examine more explicitly three of these differences.

RELIGIOUS ADAPTATIONS IN SHENZHEN

Broader Range of Spiritual Options Available. In Shenzhen, some people's practice involves simply the regular repetition of prayer formulas. But most respondents reported seeking deeper understanding by reading texts or commentaries on religious classics (Daoist stories, Buddhist sutras, works of Confucius and Mencius) or morally up-lifting contemporary books. An extraordinary range of authors and titles is now available, resulting from both the loosening of editorial restrictions on mainland publishing houses and the burgeoning interest in new ideas and foreign views that has accompanied this city's globalization. As a result, more sources of spiritual nourishment are available in Shenzhen, and more personal choice is required.

Expanded media sources have played a crucial role in the spiritual revival in Shenzhen. Local bookstores abound with titles providing alternative life perspective and moral advice. A steady stream of Buddhist and Christian television and Internet programming arrives from Taiwan and North America. Local and international religious entrepreneurs promote programs for health and healing and peace of mind, even as state propaganda urges a return to now-discredited Communist ideals and values. And images and icons of western popular culture flood the local media. Confronted by this vast array of possibilities, Shenzhen residents need to, and want to, find for themselves the sources of spiritual nourishment that suit their own situations and temperaments.

New Communal Settings—Role of Vegetarian Restaurants. Many in Shenzhen sense themselves to be without the supports and constraints that were once provided by extended family or local village life. And most respondents cherish this new psychological freedom. But hunger for a sense of belonging continues—for some, even intensifies—in this modernizing city. Here, through personally chosen participation in a loosely organized social network, spiritual seekers sustain one another in a new level of consciousness and reinforce an emerging spiritual identity.

Shenzhen brings together people from many different areas of

China. This mobility and heterogeneity of population has affected the experience of this common religious heritage. While most Shenzhen respondents resist formal identification with any particular religious institutions, the communal dimensions of spiritual practice remain strong. But in this new urban setting, the communal practices of Chinese religiousness are organized differently.

Many respondents assemble regularly with fellow searchers. These gatherings function as a loosely organized network, more than a formally constituted membership group. Vegetarian restaurants are frequent settings for these gatherings. In addition to the large restaurant depicted earlier, several others serve as important locations for those on the spiritual search.

Another example: a small storefront restaurant nestled in a downtown high-rise building comfortably accommodates perhaps thirty people at its several round tables. Open to the general public, the restaurant welcomes passers-by along with more regular customers. A book shelf stretches along one wall, stocked with a selection of spiritually-oriented books that the restaurant owner makes available to patrons for loan or purchase. At one end of the room a video screen continuously displays a series of calming nature scenes, interspersed with brief readings and recitations from spiritual texts. In another corner, a small altar has been set up and many patrons stop on their way in or out of the shop to offer a gesture of respect. A notice board lists activities in which people may be interested—a lecture in the area, a ritual gathering planned for the future, an ecological project inviting volunteers.

The restaurant was not established by a religious organization and exists without any outside investment. The manager, a lay man without formal religious training or membership, indicates that operating this restaurant is part of his own spiritual practice. Several respondents gather here regularly to share a vegetarian meal and to discuss their spiritual reading and practices. Sometimes the restaurant owner will invite a local monk or a visiting international author to make a brief presentation. More often the discussion develops informally, as customers linger after their meal to share concerns and speak about their spiritual practices. Respondents report that their discussion often centers on traditional Chinese themes—*ming yun* (personal destiny), *yuan fen* (fateful coincidences) and *feng shui* (orientation to nature's energy). The patrons' interest is seldom in the historical development or orthodox understanding of these themes. Instead they speak of the impact of these spiritual insights and ritual activities in their own lives. Often newcomers will be invited to join the meal, as a way of introducing them to this wider network and offering them support in their personal search.

The motives for these gatherings seem to include people's need for encouragement and mutual support in life's daily struggles as well as in religious practice, a hunger to experience the sense of transcendence that comes from the fellowship and the rituals that are frequently part of the group's gathering, and a desire to improve the world by spreading information about these sources of spiritual awareness among others in Shenzhen.

Heightened Awareness of Personal Agency in Belief and Practice. In these self-selected gatherings we may have evidence of a new dynamic in the relationship between individual and group, one that characterizes a shift toward modern consciousness. In China's rural past, entire families or villages lived within a shared spiritual perspective. Commonly-held values served as the screen through which personal experience was filtered. The group thus provided and secured the meaning system for its members. Embedded in this surrounding culture, there was neither need nor opportunity for intentional spiritual choice.

At this new stage in China's historical experience, middle-class Chinese are consciously endeavoring to interpret their lives for themselves. No longer embedded in the assumptive world of village life, less subject to constraints of family network and work unit, these people are finding for themselves sources of spiritual nourishment appropriate to their lives and temperaments. As one respondent asserted, "What I believe is nobody's business but my own."

In Shenzhen, as is typical of rural China, most respondents do not join an established religious group or identify exclusively with a single sect or master. But respondents here gave personal reasons to justify their eclectic approach. Some suspected that the officially registered religions remain too close to the government, too susceptible to party control. Having only recently escaped the all-encompassing control of the state-sponsored work unit, they resisted affiliating with another institution that seems to depend on government approval.

But most offered another explanation. For the people in Shenzhen, a dominant feature of life is the exhilaration of personal choice. In the realm of spirit, as in much of the rest of their lives, personal choice has become the standard. Respondents wanted to make clear that their new moral convictions and ritual practices, too, represented personal decisions. These decisions are personal because these were not limited by the social pressures exerted by family and village life. Their religious choices are personal because these were not coerced by government control or political orthodoxy.

For many in Shenzhen today, spiritual practice is a matter of conscious choice. And their choices are made with keen awareness that these are both intentional and voluntary. But the selectivity manifested here is not the religious individualism more evident in North America. In Shenzhen, the personalized quality of spirituality is less a private journey of the interior life and more a heightened awareness of personal responsibility.

Personal choice based on selective criteria that are available to reflective awareness—this stands as evidence of a basic shift in consciousness among middle-class residents in Shenzhen. While many now enthusiastically embrace elements of China's traditional heritage, their experience of these beliefs and practices is not traditional. Rather they experience traditional beliefs and practices as a source (and only one source among several) from which they will construct a personally meaningful interpretation of their own lives. Shenzhen residents are *choosing what to believe*. Based on the characteristically Chinese criteria of practicality—"what works"—they select symbolic forms and spiritual practices that offer tangible results in healing, health, and peace of mind. And, in this most secular of Chinese cities, they are *choosing to believe*—aware that personal faith of any kind remains open to development and doubt. In these choices, the vitality of China's common spiritual heritage is being reaffirmed, now as a resource for China's future.

NOTES

[1] An earlier version of this chapter appeared in "The Spiritual Search in Shenzhen: Adopting and Adapting China's Common Spiritual Heritage," *Nova Religio*.

[2] See, for example, Robert P. Weller, *Unities and Diversities in Chinese Religion* and Kenneth Dean, "Local Community Religion in Contemporary Southeast China."

[3]Daniel Overmyer, "Gods Saints, Shamans, and Processions: Comparative Religion from the Bottom Up," p. 7.

[4]Overmyer, "Gods Saints, Shamans, and Processions," p. 4.

CHAPTER ELEVEN:CIVIL SOCIETY,RELIGION AND THE COMMON GOOD

This chapter introduces two concepts important in the current discourse on late-modern culture:"civil society" and the "common good." A discussion of these concepts suggests areas for unique contributions by institutional religions today.

Pluralism is a constitutive characteristic of late-modern cultures. No single religion or philosophy dominates the intellectual scene;sacred canopies are no more. In this new environment,institutional religions struggle to find authentic ways to witness to humane values and minister to societies' needs. Jose Casanova describes this challenge as "the relocation of religion from a pre-modern form of publicness to the public sphere of civil society."[1] Both Catholic Christianity and Protestant Christianity have lost their positions of privilege in European nation states, for example. Now both must struggle to enter the public sphere again. This will require,in Casanova's view, religion's transformation from "a state-oriented to a society-oriented institution."[2]

    This is institutional religion's challenge in the 21st century: to image new ways to participate in,and contribute to,the public life of the societies in which they are located. Help in responding to this challenge may come in a deeper understanding of the common space that social analysts, following philosopher Jurgen Habermas,[3] have named the public sphere. The public sphere is a creation of modern democracy with its value pluralism. As an arena of free expression, the public sphere sustains "a form of life in which authority is accountable to common norms based on widespread, open, rational discussion among citizens. "[4] These norms are not mandated by the government nor validated by a single privileged religious institution; instead, they arise in public discussion and are clarified through ongoing debate.

Other western social theorists link this free public discourse with civil society, the many kinds of social organization in contemporary life that fall outside the formal control of governmental or economic organizations. In the West, private educational institutions, the popular media, and the free press are part of civil society. Civil society also includes voluntary groups that bring together people with similar interests. For example: professional associations of doctors or lawyers or teachers; informal organizations whose members raise money to support cultural life—museums, art exhibits, music performances; people who gather regularly to offer assistance to each other with special problems or concerns, such as parents of seriously ill children, people trying to overcome addictions, new immigrants to the country. Sociologist Richard Madsen defines civil society as "a sphere of life concerned not with the fulfillment of traditional loyalties but with the reciprocal meeting of needs. "[5]

In a pluralist democratic society, any individual or group is welcome to participate in this public "free zone. " And in many nations, religious institutions are finding their place in civil society. Although the voice of religion is only one among many in this public conversation, its unique role may be to raise questions of meaning and morality that other aspects of the society would prefer to ignore. Casanova describes this particular contribution: "by entering the public sphere and forcing the public discussion…of certain issues, religions force modern societies to reflect publicly and collectively upon their normative structures. "[6]

CIVIL SOCIETY: ARENA FOR THE CONVERSATION ABOUT MEANING

What is civil society? Civil society or the public sphere occupies the middle ground between government and the private sector. Civil society is the realm of society's life that is identified neither with the bureaucratic structures of the state nor with the productivity demands of the economic marketplace. Civil society " is not where we vote and it is not where we buy and sell, " remarks social analyst Benjamin Barber, rather "it is where we talk with neighbors …plan a benefit for the community school, discuss how our church …can shelter the homeless… "[7] Barber concludes his description: "civil society is thus public without being coercive, voluntary without being privatized. "

Civil society, as social ethicist Alan Wolfe observes, "brings us into contact with people in such a way that we are forced to recognize our dependence on them. "[8] Many different kinds of groups are active in civil society: neighborhood associations that take steps to keep local playgrounds safe for children; volunteers who offer help to AIDS patients at the local hospital; young people who gather voluntarily to repair their recreation center.

What does civil society accomplish? In pluralist modern socie-ties, no single religious tradition stands as guardian and guarantee of social norms. Instead the citizenry itself must become responsible for moral obligations. It is in the intermediate space of civil society that members of modern societies discern and describe their shared values. It is here that citizens craft their morality, both learning to appreciate different moral perspectives and developing the deman-ding skills of the contemporary craft of compromise.

A unique feature of civil society is that people move beyond the old boundaries of "my" ethnic heritage and "my" religious tradi-tion, to approach fellow citizens who bring with them other values and different cultural heritages. Alan Wolfe comments that it is here we learn "the social practices that enable us to empathize with others, even with strangers and future generations. "[9]

Wolfe also notes that discussions in this civic realm "do not operate according to the logic of free markets but according to *an old moral logic* that predated capitalism. "[10] Thus, in such gather-ings questions of value are not automatically resolved according to the economic criteria of the marketplace. Here other markers of val-ue and worth may be invoked. What is friendship worth? What is the value of social solidarity—the sense of "belonging to one anoth-er" that is forged in the diversity of civic participation? These value judgments are not determined by financial benefits; rather it is a question of *moral worth* that the group must determine and defend.

Richard Madsen emphasizes a communal dynamic in civil socie-ty: "To the extent that the moral dimension of civil society is cruci-al, the associations of civil society are not just interest groups, but communities. "[11] Through the broader conversations that are often part of civic participation, even a group that begins with a narrow

focus on self-interest may develop into a community more concerned with deeper values that support a common benefit. And,
Wolfe adds, we give our time and energy to common projects in civil
society because these intermediate institutions "give people realistic
hope that action in common ·produces results worth working
for. "[12]

THE COMMON GOOD:FOCUS OF THE CONVERSATION ABOUT MEANING

Action in common that supports a common benefit—this
phrase connects the modern concept of civil society with an older
tradition in western social theory, the *common good*. In the long
philosophical tradition of Catholic Christianity, the *common good* is
seen as the goal and responsibility of good governance. At the heart
of the notion of the common good is the understanding that there
are "goods" or benefits of human life that are neither private nor individual. Instead, these goods should be publicly available and commonly enjoyed. Seen in this perspective, there are crucial benefits of
human society—such as political freedom, universal education,
available health care—that are not properly understood as "individual rights. " While these benefits should be available to all in society, they cannot be achieved individually or preserved privately.
These are common goods—"goods that we hold as public and agree
to pursue in common. "[13]

Beginning in the discussions of medieval philosophers, Catholic
social thought has recognized that the pursuit of the common good
is an essential task of every valid form of human society. Upon this

goal both human dignity and societal flourishing depend. Continuing this discussion today, the Catholic church has defined the common good as "the sum total of those conditions of social living whereby men and women are enabled more fully and readily to achieve their well-being. "[14] The Catholic moral tradition also links the common good with the vitality of civic participation.

In the European era of Christendom, the common good was often identified with the values and norms of the dominant religious worldview. The pluralism of late-modern societies has enlarged the understanding of common good to include a much wider range of needs and values.

Criticism of the Common Good. This communal interpretation of society's goal challenges the individualism still prevalent in western societies today. Many secular critics insist that modern societies are too diverse for the concept of the common good to have any meaning. Social life today is fragmented into different groups expressing different values. Citizens in the same society embrace very diverse cultural and moral convictions. These critics fear that, in the context of such pervasive pluralism, it is only governmental coercion that can enforce agreement on any single vision of the common good.

Other critics affirm the instrumental view of society that still dominates western social theory. This perspective understands that human society exists "to provide security and prosperity, without interfering with individuals and their liberties and rights. "[15] In this worldview there is no natural solidarity that might serve as the foundation of the common good. Instead, society is made up of competing factions that may, at times, be forced to compromise for purposes of personal security and their increased private prosperity.

Criticism of the concept of the common good arises from some conservative Christians as well. Distressed by governmental corruption and a decline in public morality, these Christians thinkers display "an increased suspicion that the public realm of law, politics, and policy is not susceptible to moral transformation. " Among such believers, "the emphasis on personal conversion takes precedence over the call to social transformation. " To some of these religious believers it seems that "outside the Christian community Christian values are simply incomprehensible" and that "civic virtue is an illusion for Christian ethics to dispel. "[16]

Other Christian thinkers dispute this disheartened turn away from civic involvement. Theologian Robin Lovin insists that the very virtues that are "learned in the Christian community require this engagement with a civic community despite the hypocrisy, self-interest, and moral blindness that are present there. " Lovin shares the conviction of many contemporary Christians—Catholic and Protestant alike—that "we live our lives more completely and more truly in the image of God when we step out into public with confidence than when we closet ourselves in segregated communities. "[17]

The Common Good , Human Rights and Religion. The contemporary notion of human rights may open the way to a broader appreciation of the common good. The concept of human rights is, to be sure, a development of modernity. The Declaration on Human Rights issued by the United Nations in 1948 inaugurated a broader understanding of the basic rights common to all humans. "The category of human rights is the first universally agreed upon moral category in human history. "[18]

The concept of human rights has evolved along with the progress of modernity itself. In the course of the 19th century modern states recognized certain economic rights of citizens, such as the right to own property and to buy and sell goods. These were judged to be "material conditions necessary for human flourishing."[19] "Cultural rights" basic to group identity and self-determination emerged in the discussions of the 20th century. The 21st century confronts questions of moral freedom, that is, the right of each individual to form and follow personal conscience.[20]

The concept of universal human rights balances the Enlightenment's understanding of human society as no more than a contractual arrangement. As philosopher Mary Midgley notes, this Enlightenment ideal itself had the positive effect of overcoming the outmoded concept of the king's "divine right" to rule.[21] But when taken to an extreme, the social contract theory suggests that society was held together only by means of agreements among individuals, agreements that are made—ultimately—in pursuit of individual self-interests. In this perspective morality, too, is seen as created by and solely dependent on the free agreement among individuals. In such a society, there can be no compelling call of duty toward others, particularly no responsibility toward any who live outside the social arrangements of one's own nation.

Recognition of universal human rights restores a public morality that transcends the self-interest of individual persons and societies. As philosopher Alasdair MacIntyre has observed, "each of us achieves our good only if and insofar as others make our good their good⋯"[22]

The Catholic intellectual heritage was significant in the development of the concept of the common good. But the church was slow to endorse the concept of universal human rights. A number of historical factors contributed to this hesitance. Medieval philosophy's position that" error has no rights" led many religious leaders to judge that those who were not Catholic were not free to hold beliefs that contradicted the religious truths honored by the church. Later, the violence and anti-clericalism that were part of the demand for individual political rights during the French Revolution further frightened the church. Here again, human rights seemed to conflict with religious values and with the privileges that religious institutions enjoyed at this time. As sociologist John Coleman has commented, in much of its history the church was better at "caring for human need" than attending to human rights. [23]

The common good is a good pursued in common. In latemodern democracies, free citizens—in their multiple gatherings and many associations—must examine their own values and craft the shared moral vision that offers the best possibility for the whole community to flourish. Here religions may find another opening for participation in the public world of late modernity. Each religious tradition carries a rich heritage of moral conviction, especially sensitive to the essential values of justice and compassion, of personal commitment and mutual responsibility. By bringing these values and convictions into the public sphere, not as sectarian demands but as ideas and ideals worthy of common consideration, religious institutions may secure their respected place in civil society.

RELIGION, CIVIL SOCIETY AND
THE COMMON GOOD

What transformations are required, if institutional religions are to assume a public role in late-modern societies? Richard Madsen's recent research on Buddhist and Taoist groups in Taiwan offers some clues.

Madsen has examined several trends in religiousness that reflect the dynamics of modernization in Taiwan. Since the mid-1980s Taiwan has experienced rapid economic growth and cultural transformation. In 1987 the end of martial law resulted in "a springtime for Taiwan's civil society. "[24] Buddhist and Daoist organizations took advantage of this new openness, consciously adapting many religious practices to make these more appealing to the growing middle class.

Prior to this transformation, religion institutions in Taiwan tended to be "parochial, particularistic, habit-driven. " Their focus was on "rituals for bringing personal good fortune and a happy afterlife. "[25] After Taiwan's disastrous earthquake in 1999, the Buddhist Compassion Relief Association mobilized 100,000 volunteers to help with rescue, cleanup and reconstruction. The leader of the Dharma Drum Mountain Buddhist Temple appeared frequently on television, encouraging Taiwanese "not to think of the disaster as the result of bad *karma* for previous sins but as an important opportunity to make Taiwan safer and better for future generations. "[26] We see here a shift in practices, from an internal focus toward a broader social concern. And religious thinking here shifted from a focus on personal punishment to a recognition of social opportunity.

A second example: at a hospital and medical school established by the Buddhist *Ciji gongde hui* organization, many autopsies are performed as part of the required training of medical students. The dissecting of human cadavers is strictly forbidden in traditional Buddhism. Nevertheless this modern medical procedure is practiced regularly at this Buddhist-sponsored institution. But here it is practiced in an explicitly religious ambience: "Before students dissect the human cadavers used in the class, they pray for the souls of the deceased. On the walls of the classroom, they post biographies of the cadavers they are working on, and students write essays expressing their gratitude toward the person who donated his or her body. "[27] Thus in the context of the "ordinary" mystery of human death, modern medical practice meets traditional Buddhist beliefs.

Madsen concludes his informative essay with the optimistic judgment

> Buddhism and Daoism have the capacity both to adapt to modernity and to humanize the modern world. It shows that globalization can help lead to a kind of religious renaissance that leads to dialogue among civilizations rather than clashes between them. [28]

But Madsen acknowledges that this kind of dialogue among civilizations, stimulated by renewal within institutional religion, is not guaranteed. Many factors stand in the way of both religious renewal and intercultural dialogue. Yet Madsen remains hopeful: "our analysis also shows that these positive outcomes require a good measure of luck or, from the Buddhist point of view, fate (*yuan fen*), or from the Christian point of view, the grace of God. "

CIVIL SOCIETY, NON-GOVERNMENT ORGANIZATIONS AND RELIGION

In the new social space of civil society, both institutional religions and non-government organizations (NGOs) have come forward, eager to contribute to the common good. NGOs—a social phenomenon distinct to late-modern societies—have arisen in many countries, in response to needs in areas of health care, education, environmental protection, and more. Some NGOs have explicit ties with religious groups. The Buddhist association, *Ciji gongde hui*, for example, continues to make extraordinary contributions in Taiwan and elsewhere. [29] For many years the Amity Foundation, a group with Christian roots now headquartered in Nanjing, has responded generously to social needs throughout China. [30] And *Beifang Jinde*, a Catholic social service agency, has recently been established as an NGO in Shijiazhuang.

In China, non-government groups are also identified as nonprofit groups or NPOs. As these groups develop in China, observers recognize several ways in which they differ from counterparts in the West. In the introduction to a study of NGOs in Asia, Robert Weller points out that in Asian countries civil associations are often "based on older communal ties of kinship and village. "[31] They are less voluntary and more related to family than are the NGOs in the West. Similarly, Asian NGOs are more closely linked with the government itself, while NGOs in the West often adopt an antagonistic attitude toward the state. Weller offers the example of NGO-like associations in Vietnam, where "retired veterans' associations and Buddhist groups of old women," are "loosely organized and very local groups," yet "provide concrete mechanisms to mobilize local social ties. "[32]

Acknowledging these East-West differences, we might ask how religious values can enrich the work of NGOs in Chinese society in the future. Some NGOs, like *Ciji gongde hui* and *Beifang Jinde*, will incorporate the moral values of the Buddhist or Catholic traditions. In Chapters Nine and Ten we noted the continuing vitality of China's common spiritual heritage in contemporary Chinese consciousness. These beliefs and values of Chinese popular religion support the moral ideals and behavior of many people in China today. Scholars have suggested that the tradition of doing good for others (*shan*), which is so deeply embedded in China's popular religion, will soon motivate the formation of NGOs "with Chinese characteristics. "

In recent years both national and international conferences have begun to explore the future possibilities for NGOs in China. The role of religion-based NGOs in China is still unclear. But the civic goals and flexible structures of NGOs may become an important context through which institutional religions may contribute to the common good in China.

NOTES

[1]Jose Casanova, *Public Religions in the Modern World*, p. 222.

[2]Casanova, *Public Religions in the Modern World*, p. 220; he judges that only as an institutional religion has successfully responded to the critique of the Enlightenment may it "contribute to the revitalization of the modern public sphere," p. 233.

[3]See the discussion in Jurgen Habermas, *Structural Transformation of the Public Sphere*.

[4]Richard Madsen,"The Public Sphere, Civil Society and Moral Community," p. 186.

[5]Madsen,"The Public Sphere, Civil Society and Moral Community," p. 186.

[6]Casanova, *Public Religions in the Modern World*, p. 228.

[7]Quoted in Dionne, "Faith, Politics, and the Common Good," p. 2.

[8]Alan Wolfe, *Whose Keeper? Social Science and Moral Obligation*, p. 18.

[9]Wolfe,*Whose Keeper?*,p. 104.

[10]Quoted in Dionne,"Faith,Politics,and the Common Good," p. 2;our emphasis.

[11]Madsen,"The Public Sphere,Civil Society and Moral Community," p. 192.

[12]Dionne,"Faith,Politics,and the Common Good," p. 2.

[13]John Coleman,"Pluralism and the Retrieval of a Catholic Sense of the Common Good," Commonweal Spring 2000 Conference,p. 10;for discussion of Asian concepts of the common good,see Theodore De Bary,*Nobility and Civility:Asian Ideals of Leadership and the Common Good*.

[14]Coleman,"Pluralism and the Retrieval of a Catholic Sense of the Common Good," p. 8.

[15]Coleman,"Pluralism and the Retrieval of a Catholic Sense of the Common Good," p. 4.

[16]Robin Lovin,"Civil Rights,Civil Society,and Christian Realism," p. 6.

[17]Lovin,"Civil Rights,Civil Society,and Christian Realism," p. 6.

[18]John Haughey,"Responsibility for Human Rights," p. 755.

[19]Haughey,"Responsibility for Human Rights," p. 765.

[20]See Alan Wolfe,"The Final Freedom," p. 48.

[21]See Mary Midgley,*The Myths We Live By*,p. 8.

[22]Alasdair MacIntyre,*Dependent Rational Animals*,p. 107.

[23]Quoted in Haughey,"Responsibility for Human Rights," p. 783.

[24]Madsen,"Religious Renaissance and Taiwan's Transition to Democracy," p. 44.

[25]Madsen,"Religious Renaissance and Taiwan's Transition to Democracy," p. 8.

[26]Madsen,"Religious Renaissance and Taiwan's Transition to Democracy," p. 7.

[27]Madsen,"Religious Renaissance and Taiwan's Transition to Democracy," p. 36.

[28]Madsen,"Religious Renaissance and Taiwan's Transition to Democ-

racy. " p. 59.

[29]See Julia Huang,"Global Engagement and Transnational Practice:A Case Study of the Buddhist Compassionate-Relief Foundation in Taiwan. "

[30]See Katrina Fiedler's essay,"We Change Society,Society Changes Us - The Example of the Amity Foundation. "

[31]Robert Weller,"Civil Institutions and the State," p. 4.

[32]Weller,"Civil Institutions and the State," pp. 7 and 17.

CHAPTER TWELVE:CHINA AND THE FUTURE OF RELIGION

This chapter examines the re-evaluation of religion tak-ing place in China today. The continuing contribution of religion to culture is discussed, especially its function in providing moral orientation. The chapter concludes with a reflection on religion and the ideal of human flourish-ing.

"Religion is certainly not withering away. "[1] Yue Pan, deputy head of the State Council's Office for the Reform of the Economic System in Beijing, offers this observation in his re-evaluation of the place of religion in China's socialist system. He acknowledges that secularization theory's prediction that modernity would bring the demise of religion has proved to be false. Now, at the beginning of the 21st century, religion is recognized as a perennial element in cul-ture. The challenge for China's governing party, as Pan indicates, is to recognize religion's positive value and ensure that its presence in China contributes to the goals of a socialist society.

Pan puts forward three positive aspects of religion that suggest its potential contribution to society's well-being. Religion's *psycho-logical function* is to bring consolation to people in the midst of distress and suffering. This aspect of religion should no longer be judged simply as illusion, he cautions, but as a genuine service to a society and its people. Religion's second contribution comes through its *moral function*. Pan notes for his Chinese readers that in the midst of the upheavals of the Industrial Revolution in Europe, it was the Protestant ethic that "propped up and restored the western moral character. "[2] Chinese leaders today are keenly aware of the need for moral values as their society experiences the sudden shift to a market economy and an accompanying absorption in consumerism and the personal accumulation of wealth. Religion's third contribution to society is its *cultural function*. Just as the images and values of Catholic Christianity and Protestant Christianity have molded the culture of the West, Chinese culture is replete with values and images that register the influence of Buddhism and Daoism.

Pan opens his article with the observation that religion " belongs to the category of faith" and that it "explores the world of meaning. "[3] This acknowledgement appears to be a major shift in Chinese Communist perspective. No longer evaluating religion as essentially superstition, this new view recognizes developments in the academic study of religion. Increasingly, scholars understand religious faith as rooted in the human capacity to use language and other symbols in the search for meaning.

Daniel Overmyer has recently compiled a review of research on religion that was undertaken in the 1990s by mainland scholars. [4] Overmyer found new and more open approaches to religion among these scholars. He cites, for example, the preface to *Chinese Popular Beliefs* which praises religious beliefs as having "the power to unite the people, to incite their courage and nourish their moral values. "[5] Tao Yang, the author of the preface, then observes that religions "still have a social function. To issue orders to prohibit them is not a wise policy; just like other attempts to wipe out religion, it will not succeed. "[6] As committed Marxists, both Tao Yang and the book's author Wu Bingan accept that religions will, in time, become superfluous and "extinguish themselves. "[7] But, they argue, until that time Chinese leaders should recognize the benefits that religions can offer.

In his analysis of religion in China today, Yue Pan explains the new tolerance among Chinese leaders. The Communist Party, he notes, has moved from an initial revolutionary stage when "fomenting of revolution was its main duty" to a new era in which it is called upon to administer a stable society. Now, recognizing its "main purpose as consolidating its social base, "[8] the Party should view religion not as its sworn enemy, but as a partner in contributing to Chinese society's well-being.

WHAT IS RELIGION'S PURPOSE?

In a late-modern world religion has refused to "wither away. " Yet its proper role in society continues to be questioned. *What* does religion contribute to a culture's well-being and *how* will this contribution best be made?

Sociologist Jose Casanova observes: "When secular ideologies appear to have failed or lost much of their force, religions return to the public arena as a mobilizing and integrating normative force. "[9] But as societies struggle to adapt to the dynamics of globalization they risk losing contact with the historical memories and cultural symbols that constitute their distinctive social identity. Philosopher Paul Ricoeur identifies the cultural malaise that results: "Our individual and corporate worlds remain underdeveloped and impoverished because we no longer have a public symbolic language that speaks both to the brokenness and the intimations of transcendence in our lives. "[10] Ricoeur believes that religion,which has as its ultimate purpose "to aid our efforts to exist with integrity, "[11] can assist a culture in developing "a public symbolic language" with which to discuss these deepest values.

Xinping Zhuo, Director of the Center for the Study of World Religions at the Chinese Academy of the Social Sciences, has emphasized the link between religious traditions and a culture's moral life: "As the source of the cultural tradition of humanity,morality is rooted in and is manifested by the various religions of the world. "[12] Religion,in his estimation,is not a phenomenon added to a culture's life, but "religion and its moral resources are an important part of human cultural and spiritual tradition. "[13] The morality that Zhuo refers to here is more than the lists of rules and commandments found in a specific religion; it includes the deeper moral orientation that guides one's life in the world.

ORIENTATION:MAKING OUR WAY
IN THE LATE-MODERN WORLD

A characteristic of late modernity is "the breakdown in previously fundamental coordinates of experience: time, space, and order. "[14] Put more directly: in this time of profound transitions many people feel disoriented. The Copernican revolution deprived humans of their sense of being at the center of the universe; Darwin's theory of evolution demoted humans from their privileged position in the natural world; disillusionment with modernity´s myth of endless progress has undermined humanity's hope in the future. This world-wide questioning of moral values is deeply unsettling both for individuals and for societies as a whole. The late-modern world is left with few reliable signposts.

Philosopher Robert Neville remarks that confidence in a universal and stable human nature has been lost. "The late-modern view on human identity is that we must be wary of essences, for any attempt to define the essence of human nature is bound to reflect the biases of our own class and social position. "[15] But, Neville insists, "if there is no essence of humanness on which we can at all times rely, there is something very like it ··· There are norms that shape our obligations···and *an orientation*. "[16]

In place of an earlier over-confident western analysis, Neville suggests a more Chinese approach. He recommends remembering that "we have orientations to the world and can develop ways of behaving properly and keeping our balance, existing in harmony with the Dao. "[17] In this approach, the moral self develops less by looking inward for stable criteria of individual conscience, and more by looking outward to the world and its many, shifting environments.

Orientation, for Neville, is a question of harmonizing ourselves with a variety of environments—our network of relationships with family and friends; the immediate environment of our natural world; and the ultimate environment of our humane and religious purposes.

Neville defines his terms: "By orientation is meant the way in which we comport ourselves in some part or dimension of existence that has its own characteristic nature and rhythms. " He adds: "Orientations involve emotional attitudes as well as habits of perception and response⋯"[18] Thus a proper orientation to the universe will include emotions of wonder and respect. And our orientation to one another will, expectably, include responses of gratitude and generosity.

"Poise," for Neville,"is the virtue of balancing these orientations in practical life while we perceive and respond to various things in constant flux that do not fit neatly together. "[19]

Religions offer beliefs and practices that assist people in establishing fundamental orientations—toward one another, toward the world, and toward their ultimate environment. Religious traditions do this by creating enduring symbols, classic stories and rituals that serve as signposts to assist persons and communities in finding their way.

Orienting Ourselves in the Late-Modern World. The image of disorientation encompasses both a literal meaning (arriving in an unfamiliar city, a person turns in the wrong direction and becomes lost) and a metaphorical sense (a person is overwhelmed by the range of choices or possibilities in life and is unsure "which way to turn"). The charm of the metaphor *orientation* is that it combines a sense of landscape—a terrain that is provided for us, an environment we do not ourselves create—and the opportunity to decide where we fit in and how we are to proceed. This metaphor alerts us to the value of maps, astrolabes, global positioning satellites and other instruments of navigation.

The classics of western culture—the early Greek tale of the Odyssey, for example, and the books of the Bible—include stories of dangerous voyages and liberating treks. Their tales recount both the perils of getting lost and the consolations of new discovery. These classics describe a world where constant re-orientation is demanded and where poise is the virtue of keeping one's balance in the midst of these changes.

Religions address issues of orientation—in time and space, in the face of both stability and change. The worldview of medieval Catholic Christianity created a sacred cosmology of heaven "above" and hell "below. " Poet Robert Browning expresses this consoling spiritual orientation when he writes: "God is in his heaven and all is right with the world. " Muslims daily orient themselves—both geographically and spiritually—toward Mecca, as they bow in prayer five times each day. In the Chinese heritage, *feng shui* provides a practice of physical orientation that links humanity's immediate and ultimate environments.

Religious traditions likewise provide orientations in time. Invoking the biblical account of the seven days of creation, Jews celebrate each Saturday as the Sabbath, as a weekly day of rest. Protestant and Catholic Christians continue this ritual orientation to time, but move the observance to Sunday, the Lord's Day. Muslims have designated Friday as their weekly holy day. This religious practice now structures the calendar—if not always the actual lifestyle—of people throughout the world.

Religions develop rituals to support a spiritual orientation. Ceremonies of grieving and lamentation give order to the chaos of loss. The slow-paced ritual of a funeral service provides a rhythm that balances, in some small but meaningful way, the disorientations of grief. In Catholic Christianity, rituals of reconciliation provide opportunity for acknowledgment of failure and sin and for seeking the solace of forgiveness. Every religious heritage celebrates blessings received and bounty enjoyed—feasts at the yearly harvest, festivals at the beginning of the New Year, public recognitions of marriages and births. Celebrations like these shape human consciousness. By orienting participants to beauty and goodness in the world, feasting nurtures gratitude and generosity.

In the world of late modernity, many of these ritual orientations have been muted. The cosmology of heavenly abode and fiery hell now seems quaint. Shopping malls, athletic fields and movie theaters absorb the time once freed for Sabbath rest. Yet the search for life orientation continues.

Moral Orientations. Recent discussions in ethics have taken up the concept of humans "orienting themselves" in the world. Theologian William Schweiker observes: "in moral reflection we do not simply discover or discern anything moral about the world, rather *we try to orient ourselves* in the world. "[20] Moral life is not a question of finding the detailed ethical map that will outline every step for us to follow; contemporary morality requires a more quick-witted judgment of where we stand and in what direction to turn. William Spohn expands on this metaphor: "the religious dimension of life helps to organize the self by relating it to an ordering environment; it *orients the self* by sustaining participation in the world; and it motivates the self by engendering dispositions to appreciate the world. "[21]

The traditional Christian orientation toward "a heaven above" is today replaced by the recognition of "a horizon out there⋯" Charles Taylor argues that humans have a capacity for evaluating some goods as more worthy than others. Taylor describes this "strong evaluation" as an intuitive discernment aided by mature e-motions and life experience. Some goods command our respect because we recognize their intrinsic value. Examples here are the recognition of the inherent dignity of persons or the need to reach out in compassion to an injured individual. We experience such values as "making calls or demands on individuals. "[22]

This human capacity to recognize essential values is exercised in moral judgments. These judgments, in turn, create "moral frameworks or horizons" which "*orient people* in moral space. "[23] Taylor reminds us there are many such moral frameworks. Both Marxism and feminism, for example, are moral orientations that guide the choices of people in today's society. Similarly today's cultural pessimists, who judge that globalization leads the world into a new "dark age," use this negative image as a moral framework for decision and action.

In a stable period in society, the moral horizon is familiar and steady. Thus people hardly notice the value orientations that guide their choices. But the disorienting experience of significant social change forces people to question the established moral framework. This often threatening experience serves also as an opportunity for responsible choice. In seasons of change we are compelled to make choices about the values that will shape our lives. In so doing, we regain our poise in the moral universe.

Orienting ourselves in our world is an exercise in meaning-making. Meaning-making, as discussed in Chapter One, becomes explicitly religious when people open themselves to questions about an "ultimate environment" (the universe and its purpose) and limit questions: What is my life's purpose? What values are worth living for? Are there values worth dying for? Many contemporary people explore these questions of ultimate meaning by drawing on resources in philosophy or science, in nature or the arts. But evidence indicates that for increasing numbers of people worldwide, the spiritual traditions of institutional religions—such as Buddhism, both

Catholic and Protestant Christianity, Jvoaism, and Islam—provide the basis of both social identity and moral orientation.

RELIGION AND HUMAN FLOURISHING

Further insight into the role of religion in late-modern society comes in reflecting on the ideal of *human flourishing*. Across cultures, this ideal represents the "more" of transcendence: the desire to move beyond the boundaries of personal limits and social divisions into a fuller existence for all. While this ideal is shared broadly, the practical shape of human flourishing remains contested today.

In western culture, Aristo-tle was among the first to discuss this ideal in detail. He wrote that society is at its best only when each person experiences fullness of life (*eudaimonia* in Greek). With the individualistic bias of modern western thought, the Greek word *eudaimonia* or "flourishing" has often been interpreted to mean "personal happiness." That individualistic reading of Aristo-tle is being strongly challenged today. Philosopher Martha Nussbaum, for example, describes the broader context of Aristotle's ideal of human flourishing:"the best human life is a life rich in attachments to people and things outside the self—friendships, family, possessions, and property."[24] Humans do not flourish alone. It is only in relationships of trust and companionship, of mutual help and forgiveness, that human life can thrive.

Moral philosopher Alasdair MacIntyre reminds us of the interconnectedness of human society, manifest in the basic relationships of family, neighborhood, and civic life:"the good of each cannot be pursued without also pursuing the good of all those who participate in those relationships. "[25] He adds: "each of us achieves our good *only if and insofar as others make our good their good* by helping us through periods of disability to become ourselves ⋯ "[26] Paul Ricoeur states this communal aspect in a more philosophical framework, defining human flourishing as "a good life with and for others, in just institutions. "[27] At our best, humans live not only *with* others but *for* them. But these best intentions may well be defeated, without the support of just institutions.

From a global perspective of contemporary society, Aristotle's social vision of human flourishing still seems dangerously narrow. The flourishing civic life that he envisioned did not include the participation of women or children; it excluded slaves as well as the "barbarians" who lived outside the Greek culture. This narrowness of vision was corrected, to some extent, by the Stoic philosophers who were Aristotle's contemporaries in Greece. Their goals for humanity moved beyond the geographic limits of the Greek city-state. Acknowledging that political states cannot thrive either in isolation or in violent opposition to one another, the Stoics urged the ideal of becoming "citizens of the world. " As many people recognize today, genuine human flourishing entails global consciousness.

Flourishing in a Modern World. This ideal of human flourishing has come under considerable criticism in recent years. One critique is that there are so many culturally different goals of flourishing that the ideal itself becomes meaningless. In addition, one important dimension of human flourishing—such as participating in activities that seek justice for all—may be incompatible with another ideal—such as seeking to live a peaceful life without disturbance.

A more significant criticism arises from the horrors of the 20ᵗʰ century. Wars, terrorism, genocide—do not these historical realities defeat any notion of human flourishing? Furthermore, Freud has shown the extent to which human consciousness is plagued by illusions and self-deception; what, then, is the basis of humanity's efforts to pursue ideals? British psychologist Adam Phillips sums up the disillusionment of many modern people. In today's world, says Phillips, "we are not in search of wholeness… progress or self-knowledge. " These goals, which shaped the Enlightenment, now seem out of reach. Instead many contemporary people settle for something more mundane: "we are in search of good ways of bearing our incompleteness (tragedy is when we are ruined by our insufficiency, comedy is when we can relish it). "[28]

Suffering:Religion and Flourishing. The universal experience of suffering serves as the final focus in the discussion of religion's contribution to modern cultures. In a superficial view, the ideal of human flourishing may well seem to exclude suffering. To have a full life and truly flourish,it would seem,one must avoid pain; suffering and flourishing appear to be incompatible. A more experienced reflection recognizes that genuine human flourishing does not avoid suffering,but finds ways to incorporate the mystery of suffering into a meaningful existence. It is here that religions may bring their resources of wisdom and ritual.

Religions provide services of compassion and sponsor the pursuit of justice. Religiously affiliated hospitals and hospices are found across the world; orphanages and clinics, sponsored by religious institutions,serve poor and rich countries alike. In the pursuit of justice,religious groups often challenge host cultures to examine and reform their own institutions. Through this dual focus—including both compassion and justice—religious organizations display two responses to the mystery of human suffering.

Religions pronounce a loud "no" to the human suffering that is not necessary. In many places humans have accepted suffering as simply fate; it could not be avoided. Today there is greater recognition that much suffering—such as the diseases spread by polluted water and poor nutrition—is preventable. In the 21st century, millions need not die each year from malnutrition and dysentery. To much suffering in human societies, religions can join the voices that say "no."

But the wisdom traditions of the world acknowledge the mysterious suffering of human life is not always avoidable. Born mortal, humans move inevitably toward death—often along paths of pain and suffering. To face the suffering that cannot be avoided, religions have honed rituals of grieving and lament, practices to help people embrace this mysterious reality in life.

The Jewish tradition of lamentation is especially rich in this regard. In the midst of his great distress, the biblical figure Job prayed, "Since I have lost all taste for life, I will give free rein to my complaints; I shall let my embittered soul speak out. I shall say to God, do not condemn me but tell me the reason for your assault" (Job 10:1). This anguished response in prayer, like the masterpieces of tragedy in art and drama, holds pain in a way that consoles those who suffer. Their suffering can then be integrated into a life story, a life that flourishes even in the face of sorrow and death.

Earlier in this book we recalled the intimations of transcendence in Socrates and Mencius. Their wisdom—profoundly human and close to the heart of religion—recognizes values both worth living for and even worth dying for. For these sages, human flourishing did not exclude suffering. The spirituality of late-modern religiousness is committed to human flourishing in the practical existence of this life. But religious consciousness remains open, in the words of Charles Taylor, to the

> insight that we can find in suffering and death—not merely negation, the undoing of fullness and life, but also a place to affirm something that matters beyond life. [29]

NOTES

[1] Yue Pan, "The Marxist View of Religion Must Keep Up with the Times," p. 7.

[2] Pan, "The Marxist View of Religion," p. 8.

[3] Pan, "The Marxist View of Religion," p. 5. Later in his essay, Pan offers the orthodox Marxist understanding of religion: "The illusory nature of religion derives from the fact there are still many questions, which science is, for the time being, unable to explain, and material needs which cannot be completely satisfied" (p. 9). In this understanding, religion remains an illusion and exists only until science clears up the remaining mysteries about life, suffering and death. Pan then makes a nuanced addition: "Atheism is a requirement for the theoretical purity of Communist Party members, but it is not a requirement so far as the masses are concerned" (p. 9).

[4] Daniel Overmyer, "From 'Feudal Superstition' to 'Popular Beliefs': New Directions in Mainland Chinese Studies of Chinese Popular Religion.

[5] Overmyer, "From 'Feudal Superstition' to 'Popular Beliefs,'" p. 114.

[6] Quoted in Overmyer, "From 'Feudal Superstition' to 'Popular Beliefs,'" p. 115.

[7] Quoted in Overmyer, "From 'Feudal Superstition' to 'Popular Beliefs,'" p. 116.

[8] Pan, "The Marxist View of Religion," p. 8.

[9]Casanova, *Public Religions in the Modern World*, p. 227.

[10]Paul Ricoeur, *Figuring the Sacred*, p. 15.

[11]Ricoeur, *Figuring the Sacred*, p. 14.

[12]Xinping Zhuo, "Religion and Morality in Contemporary China," p. 5.

[13]Zhuo, "Religion and Morality in Contemporary China," p. 9.

[14]Paul Lakeland, *Postmodernity: Christian Identity in a Fragmented Age*, p. 2.

[15]Robert Neville, *Religion in Late Modernity*, p. 2.

[16]Neville, *Religion in Late Modernity*, p. 44.

[17]Neville, *Religion in Late Modernity*, p. 40.

[18]Neville, *Religion in Late Modernity*, p. 180.

[19]Neville, *Religion in Late Modernity*, p. 180.

[20]William Schweiker, "Understanding Moral Meaning," p. 87.

[21]William Spohn and Thomas Byrnes, "Knowledge of Self and Knowledge of God: A Reconstructed Empiricist Interpretation," p. 124.

[22]See Ruth Abbey's discussion of Taylor's approach to morality, in *Charles Taylor*, p. 26.

[23]Abbey, *Charles Taylor*, p. 33-34.

[24]Martha Nussbaum, *The Therapy of Desire*, p. 42.

[25]Alasdair MacIntyre, *Dependent Rational Animals*, p. 107.

[26]MacIntyre, *Dependent Rational Animals*, p. 108. MacIntyre argues here that "communal flourishing will include those least capable of independent rational reasoning, the very young and the very old, the sick, the injured, and otherwise disabled···"

[27]Paul Ricoeur, *Oneself as Another*, p. 172.

[28]Adam Phillips, *Terrors and Experts*, p. 95.

[29]Charles Taylor, *A Catholic Modernity?*, p. 20.

BIBLIOGRAPHY

Abbey, Ruth. *Charles Taylor*. Princeton: Princeton University Press, 2000.

Anderson, E. N., "Flowering Apricot: Environmental Practice, Folk Religion, and Daoism. " In *Daoism and Ecology: Ways Within a Cosmic Landscape*, edited by N. J. Girardot, James Miller and Liu Xiaogan, 157—83. Cambridge: Harvard University Press, 2001.

Averill, James. *Anger and Aggression: An Essay on Emotion*. New York: Springer Verlag, 1982.

Barnes, Michael Horace. *In the Presence of Mystery: An Introduction to the Story of Human Religiousness*. Mystic, Conn. : Twenty-Third Publications, 2003.

Batson, Daniel, Patricia Schoenrade, and Larry Ventis. *Religion and the Individual: A Social Psychological Perspective*. New York: Oxford University Press, 1993.

Bell, Catherine, "Religion and Chinese Culture: Toward an Assessment of Popular Religion," *History of Religions* 29. 1 (1989): 35—57.

Bellah, Robert. *Beyond Belief: Essays on Religion in a Post-Traditional World*. New York: Harper & Row, 1970.

_____. *The Broken Covenant*. New York: Seabury, 1975.

Berling, Judith. "Religion and Popular Culture: The Management of Moral Capital in *The Romance of the Three Teachings*." In *Popular Culture in Late Imperial China*, edited by David Johnson, Andrew Nathan, and Evelyn Tawski, 188—218. Berkeley: University of California Press, 1985.

Berger, Peter, ed. *The Desecularization of the World: Resurgent Religions and World Politics*. Grand Rapids, Mich: Eerdmans, 1999.

_____. *The Sacred Canopy: Elements of a Sociological Theory of Religion*. New York: Doubleday, 1969.

Berthrong, John. *All Under Heaven: Transforming Paradigms in Confucian-Christian Dialogue*. Albany: State University of New York Press, 1994.

Brokaw, Cynthia. *The Ledgers of Merit and Demerit*. Princeton: Princeton University Press, 1991.

Brown, Peter. *Body and Society: Men, Women, and Sexual Renunication in Early Chistianity*. New York: Columbia University Press, 1988.

Bynum, Caroline. *Metamorphosis and Identity*. Cambridge: MIT Press, Zone Books, 2001.

Buruma, Ian. *Bad Elements: Chinese Rebels from Los Angeles to Beijing*. New York: Random House, 2001.

Carmody, Denise. "Women and Religion: Where Mystery Comes to Center Stage. " In *The Study of Women: Enlarging Perspectives of Social Reality*, edited by Eloise C. Snyder, 262—95. New York: Harper and Row, 1979.

Carson, Rachel. *Silent Spring*. Boston: Houghton Mifflin, 1962.

Casanova, Jose. *Public Religions in the Modern World*. Chicago: University of Chicago Press, 1994.

Ci, Jiwei. *Dialectic of the Chinese Revolution: From Utopianism to Hedonism*. Stanford: Stanford University Press, 1994.

Coleman, John. "Pluralism and the Retrieval of a Catholic Sense of the Common Good. " Paper presented at the Commonweal Spring 2000 Colloquium. This text is available at www. catholicinpublicsquare. org (3/31/2004).

Concise Columbia Encyclopedia. Edited by Judith S. Levey and Agnes Greenhill. New York: Columbia University Press, 1983.

Connolly, Peter, ed. *Approaches to the Study of Religion*. London: Cassel, 1999.

Cotter, Holland. "The Jade of China, Alive with Meaning Yet Glossily Elusive." *The New York Times*, August 6, 2004, 31.

De Bary, Theodore. *Nobility and Civility: Asian Ideals of Leadership and the Common Good*. Cambridge: Harvard University Press, 2004.

De Bary, William, ed. *Sources of Indian Tradition*. New York: Columbia University Press, 1958.

Dean, Kenneth. " Local Community Religion in Contemporary Southeast China, "*China Quarterly* 174(2003): 338—58.

Dionne, A. J. , "Faith, Politics, and the Common Good, " *Religion and Values in Public Life* 6. 2 (Spring, 1998): 2—3. (A Harvard Divinity School publication.)

Ellwood, Robert. *Introducing Religion from Inside and Outside*. 3rd Edition. Englewood Cliffs, N. J. : Prentice Hall, 1993.

Fan, Lizhu. "The Cult of the Silkworm Mother as a Core of Local Community Religion in a North China Village, " *China Quarterly* 174 (2003): 359—372.

————. *Dang dai zhongguoren zongjiao xinyang de bianqian— Shenzhen minjianzongjiao xintu de tianye yanjiu.* Taipei: Weber Culture Press, 2005.

————. "Popular Religion in Contemporary China. " *Social Compass* 50. 4 (2003): 449—57.

————. " A Study of Modern Chinese Religious Beliefs—The Case of Shenzhen Economic Zone. " Occasional Paper 12. The Centre for the Study of Religion and Chinese Society, Chinese University of Hong Kong, 2003.

————, ed. *Quanqiu hua xiade shehui bianqian yu fei zhengfu zuzhi* (*NGO*). Shanghai: Shanghai Peoples' Press, 2003.

————, Evelyn Eaton Whitehead, and James D. Whitehead. "Adopting and Adapting China's Common Religious Heritage," *Nova Religio 9. 2* (*2005*): 50-61.

————, James D. Whitehead, and Evelyn Eaton Whitehead. "Fate and Fortune: Popular Religion and Moral Capital in Shenzhen," *Journal of Chinese Religions* 32 (2004): 83—100.

Fiedler, Katrina. "We Change Society, Society Changes Us—The Example of the Amity Foundation. " In *Quanqiu hua xiade shehui bianqian yu fei zhengfu zuzhi* (*NGO*), edited by Lizhu Fan, 382—97. Shanghai: Shanghai Peoples' Press, 2003.

Field, Stephen. "In Search of Dragons: The Folk Ecology of *Feng-shui.*" In *Daoism and Ecology: Ways Within a Cosmic Land-scape*, edited by N. J. Girardot, James Miller and Liu Xiao-gan, 185—200. Cambridge: Harvard University Press, 2001.

Fowler, James. *Faithful Change: The Personal and Public Chal-lenges of Postmodern Life.* Nashville: Abingdon Press, 1996.

_____. *Stages of Faith: The Psychology of Human Develop-ment and the Quest for Meaning.* New York: Harper and Row, 1981.

Freud, Sigmund. *The Future of an Illusion.* Trans. W. D. Robson-Scott. New York: Doubleday, 1957.

Fukuyama, Francis. *Trust: The Social Virtues and the Creation of Prosperity.* New York: Free Press, 1995.

Gallagher, Michael. *Clashing Symbols: An Introduction to Faith and Culture.* New York: Paulist Press, 1998.

Geertz, Clifford, *Available Light: Anthropological Reflections on Philosophical Topics.* Princeton: Princeton University Press, 2000.

_____. *The Interpretation of Cultures.* New York: Basic Books, 1973.

Gilligan, Carol. *In a Different Voice: Psychological Theory and Women's Development*. 2nd edition. Cambridge: Harvard University Press, 1992.

Greeley, Andrew. *Religion as Poetry*. New Brunswick: Transaction Publishers, 1995.

Gunnemann, John. "Capital Ideas," *Religion and Values in Public Life* 7. 1 (Fall, 1998): 3—4. (A Harvard University Divinity School publication.)

Habermas, Jurgen. *Structural Transformation of the Public Sphere*. Cambridge: MIT Press, 1989.

Haughey, John. "Responsibility for Human Rights," *Theological Studies* 63 (2002): 764—85.

Heaney, Seamus. *The Redress of Poetry*. New York; Farrar, Strauss & Giroux, 1995.

Hessler, Peter. "Boomtown Girl: Finding a New Life in the Golden City," *The New Yorker*, May 28, 2001, 109—19.

Hick, John. *An Interpretation of Religion: Human Responses to the Transcendent*. 2nd Edition. New Haven: Yale University Press, 2004.

Huang, Julia. "Global Engagement and Transnational Practice: A

Case Study of the Buddhist Compassionate Relief Foundation in Taiwan. " In *Quanqiu hua xiade shehui bianqian yu fei zhengfu zuzhi*, edited by Lizhu Fan, 496-515. Shanghai: Shanghai Peoples' Press, 2003.

James, William. *The Varieties of Religious Experience*. New York: Modern Library, 1999.

Lakeland, Paul. *Postmodernity: Christian Identity in a Fragmented Age*. Minneapolis: Augsburg Fortress, 1997.

Legge, James. *The Works of Mencius*. New York: Dover, 1970.

Li Peiliang. "Shehui kexue yu bentu guannian: li yiyuanwei lie. " In *Shehui ji xingwei kexue yanjiu de zhongguo hua*, *yan tao hu*, edited by Yang Guoshu, 361-380. Taipei: Academia Sinica, 1982.

————. "Zhongguo wenhua de suming zhuyi yu nengdong quxiang. " In *Zhongguoren de guannian yu xingwei*, edited by Qian Jian, 240—52. Tianjin: Tianjin Peoples' Press, 1995.

Lightman, Alan. "Einstein and Newton: Genius Compared, " *Scientific American*, September, 2004, 108—110.

Lincoln, Bruce. "Conflict. " In *Critical Terms for Religious Studies*, edited by Mark Taylor, 55—69. Chicago: University of Chicago Press, 1998.

Lovin, Robin. "Civil Rights, Civil Society, and Christian Realism," *Religion and Values in Public Life* 6. 2 (Spring, 1998): 6—7. (A Harvard University Divinity School publication.)

Lupke, Christopher, ed. *The Magnitude of Ming : Command, Allotment and Fate in Chinese Culture*. Honolulu: University of Hawaii Press, 2004.

MacIntyre, Alasdair. *After Virtue*. Notre Dame, Ind: University of Notre Dame Press, 1981.

_____. *Dependent Rational Animals : Why Human Beings Need the Virtues*. Chicago: Open Court, 1999.

Madsen, Richard. " The Public Sphere, Civil Society and Moral Community," *Modern China* 19 (1993): 183—98.

_____. "Religious Renaissance and Taiwan's Transition to Democracy. " Paper for Globalization and Chinese Popular Culture Conference, Shanghai, September 16—18, 2003.

_____, William Sullivan, Ann Swidler, and Steven Tipton, eds. *Meaning and Modernity : Religion, Polity and Self*. Berkeley: University of California Press, 2002.

Marx, Karl, and Friedrich Engles. *Marx and Engles on Religion*. New York: Schocken Books, 1964.

McFague, Sally. *Super, Natural Christians*. Minneapolis: Fortress Press, 1997.

Menocal, Maria Rosa. *Ornament of the World : How Muslims, Jews and Christians Created a Culture of Tolerance in Medieval Spain*. New York: Little Brown, 2002.

Midgley, Mary. *The Myths We Live By*. London: Routledge, 2004.

Naquin, Susan. *Peking: Temples and City Life, 1400-1900*. Berkeley: University of California Press, 2000.

Neville, Robert. *Religion in Late Modernity*. New York: State University of New York Press, 2002.

Ning, Chen. "The Concept of Fate in Mencius," *Philosophy East & West* 47. 4 (1997): 495—520.

_____. "The Genesis of the Concept of Blind Fate in Ancient China," *Journal of Chinese Religions* 25 (1997): 141—167.

Nussbaum, Martha. *The Fragility of Goodness*. Cambridge: Cambridge University Press, 1986.

_____. *Love's Knowledge*. New York: Oxford University Press, 1990.

_____. *Therapy of Desire*. Princeton: Princeton University Press, 1994.

O'Murchu, Daimund. *Quantum Theology: Spiritual Implications of the New Physics*. New York: Crossroad Books, 1997.

Overmyer, Daniel. "Chinese Religions—The State of the Field, Part II," *Journal of Asian Studies* 54 (1995):314—395.

_____. "From 'Feudal Superstition' to 'Popular Religion': New Directions in Mainland Chinese Studies of Chinese Popular Religion," *Cahiers d' Extrême-Asie* 12 (2001): 103—126.

_____. "Gods, Saints, Shamans, and Processions: Comparative Religion from the Bottom Up," *Criterion*, Autumn, 2002, 2—9, 34. (A University of Chicago Divinity School publication.)

_____. *Religions of China*. New York: Harper & Row, 1986.

Pan, Yue. "Marxist View of Religion Must Keep Up with the Times," *China Study Journal* 18. 2 (2002):5—18.

Phillips, Adam. *Terrors and Experts*. Cambridge: Harvard University Press, 1995.

Pollan, Michael. *The Botany of Desire*. New York: Random House, 2002.

Putnam, Robert. *Bowling Alone : The Collapse and Revival of A-merican Community*. New York: Simon & Schuster, 2000.

Rahner, Karl. "Christian Humanism." Vol. IX. *Theological Investigations*. New York: Seabury Press, 1976.

Rappoport, Roy. *Ritual and Religion in the Making of Humanity*. Cambridge: Cambridge University Press, 1999.

Ricoeur, Paul. *Conflict of Interpretations*. Chicago: Northwestern University Press, 1974.

_____. *Essays in Biblical Interpretation*. Philadelphia: Fortress Press, 1980.

_____. *Figuring the Sacred*. Minneapolis: Augsburg-Fortress Press, 1995.

_____. *Freud and Philosophy*. New Haven: Yale University Press, 1970.

_____. *Oneself as Another*. Chicago: University of Chicago Press, 1992.

_____. *The Symbolism of Evil*. Boston: Beacon Press, 1967.

Scarey, Elaine. *On Beauty and Being Just*. Princeton: Princeton University Press, 1999.

BIBLIOGRAPHY

Schipper, Kristofer. *The Taoist Body*. Trans. Karen Duval. Berkeley: University of California Press, 1993.

Schreiter, Robert. *The New Catholicity*. New York: Orbis Press, 1997.

Schwartz, Benjamin. "The Age of Transcendence," *Daedalus* 104. 2 (1975): 1—7.

_____. "Transcendence in Ancient China," *Daedalus* 104. 2 (1975): 57—68.

_____. *The World of Thought in Ancient China*. Cambridge: Harvard University Press, 1986.

Schweiker, William. "Understanding Moral Meanings: On Philosophical Hermeneutics and Theological Ethics." In *Christian Ethics: Problems and Prospects*, edited by Lisa Sowle Cahill and James F. Childress, 76—92. Cleveland: Pilgrim Press, 1996.

Smart, Ninian. *Worldviews: Crosscultural Explorations of Human Beliefs*. New York: Scribner, 1983.

Smith, Nicholas. *Charles Taylor: Meaning, Morals and Modernity*. Cambridge: Polity Press, 2002.

Smith, Wilfred Cantwell. *Faith and Belief*. Princeton: Princeton University Press, 1979.

————————. *The Meaning and End of Religion*. New York: Macmillan, 1963.

Solomon, Robert. *The Passions: The Myth and Nature of Human Emotions*. New York: Doubleday, 1983.

Spohn, William. "Jesus and Christian Ethics," *Theological Studies* 56 (1995): 92—107.

————————, and Thomas Byrnes. "Knowledge of Self and Knowledge of God: A Reconstructed Empiricist Interpretation. " In *Christian Ethics: Problems and Prospects*, edited by Lisa Sowle Cahill and James F. Childress, 119—33. Cleveland: Pilgrim Press, 1996.

Su, Xiaokong, and Luxiang Wang. *Deathsong of the River*. Translated by Richard Bodman and Pin Wan. Ithaca: Cornell University Press, 1991.

Swensen, Donald. *Society, Spirituality, and the Sacred: A Social Scientific Introduction*. Orchard Park, N. Y. : Broadview Press, 1999.

Tang, Chun-I, "The Heavenly Ordinance (*Tien-ming*) in Pre-Ch'in China," *Philosophy East and West* 12. 1 (1962): 29—49.

Taylor, Charles. *A Catholic Modernity*? James Heft, ed. Oxford: Oxford University Press, 1999.

BIBLIOGRAPHY

_____. *The Ethics of Authenticity*. Cambridge: Harvard University Press, 1992.

_____. "Living in a Secular Age. " The 1999 Gifford Lectures (forthcoming).

_____. *Sources of the Self : The Making of the Modern Identity*. Cambridge: Cambridge University Press, 1989.

_____. " Two Theories of Modernity," *Public Culture* 11. 1 (1999): 153—74.

Tracy, David. *The Analogical Imagination*. New York: Crossroad, 1981.

_____. *Plurality and Ambiguity*. New York: Harper & Row, 1987.

Tucker, Mary Evelyn, and John Berthrong, eds. *Confucianism and Ecology : The Interrelation of Heaven, Earth, and Humans*. Cambridge: Harvard University Press, 1998.

Unger, Roberto. *Passion : An Essay on Personality*. New York: Free Press, 1984.

Volk, Tyler. *Gaia's Body : Toward a Physiology of Earth*. New York: Copernicus, 1997.

Weller, Robert. "Civil Institutions and the State. " In *Civil Life*, *Globalization, and Political Change in Asia : Organizing Between Family and State*, edited by Robert Weller, 1—25. London : Routledge, 2005.

————. *Unities and Diversities in Chinese Religion*. Seattle : University of Washington Press, 1987.

————. "Worship, Teachings, and State Power in China and Taiwan. " In *Realms of Freedom in Modern China*, edited by William Kirby. Palo Alto, CA : Stanford University Press, 2004.

Whaling, Frank. "Theological Approaches. " In *Approaches to the Study of Religion*, edited by Peter Connolly, 226—274. London, 1999.

White, Lynn. "The Historical Roots of Our Ecological Crisis. " *Science* 155 (1967) : 1203—07.

Whitehead, James D. , and Evelyn Eaton Whitehead. "From Consciousness to Conscience : Reflections on the Axial Age," *Fudan Journal (Social Science)* 3 (2001) : 132—38.

Williams, Bernard. *Shame and Necessity*. Berkeley : University of California Press, 1993.

Wolfe, Alan. "The Final Freedom. " *The New York Times Magazine*, March 18, 2001, 40—8.

BIBLIOGRAPHY

‖◆‖‖

_____. *Whose Keeper? Social Science and Moral Obligation*. Berkeley: University of California Press, 1989.

Yan, Yunxiang. *The Flow of Gifts: Reciprocity and Social Networks in a Chinese Village*. Stanford: Stanford University Press, 1996.

Yang, C. K. *Religion in Chinese Society*. Berkeley: University of California Press, 1962.

Yang, K. S., and David Y. F. Ho. "The Role of Yuan in Chinese Social Life: A Conceptual and Empirical Analysis. " In *Asian Contributions to Psychology*, edited by Anand C. Paranjpe, David Y. F. Ho and Robert W. Rieber, 262—81. New York: Praeger, 1988.

Yang, Liansheng. *Zhongguo wenhua bao, bao, bao de yisi*. Beijing: Chinese University Press, 1987.

Yang, Mayfair Mei-Hui. *Gifts, Favors and Banquets: The Art of Social Relationships in China*. Ithaca: Cornell University Press, 1994.

_____. "Spatial Struggles: Postcolonial Complex, State Disenchantment, and Popular Reappropriation of Space in Rural Southeast China," *Journal of Asian Studies* 63. 1 (2004): 719—55.

_____. "The Resilience of *Guanxi* and Its New Deployments: A Critique of Some New *Guanxi* Scholarship", *China Quarterly* 170 (2002): 459—76.

Yoshinori, Takeuchi, ed. *Buddhist Spirituality*. New York: Crossroad, 1995.

Yu, Ying-shih. "The Radicalization of China in the 20th Century," *Daedalus* 122 (1993): 125—50.

Zhuo, Xinping. "Religion and Morality in Contemporary China," *China Study Journal* 15 (1999): 5—10.

About the Authors

Lizhu Fan is a sociologist of religion who holds the Ph. D. from Chinese University of Hong Kong. A native of Tianjin China, she is currently Associate Professor in the Department of Sociology and Executive Secretary of the Center for Social Development at Fudan University in Shanghai. In addition to her ethnographic work on contemporary expressions of Chinese traditional religious heritage, Dr. Fan's research interests include the role of NGOs/NPSs in China's modernization. She has published widely in both Chinese and international journals, and edited several volumes of cross-cultural and cross-disciplinary research papers. Her most recent publication is *The Transformational Patterns of Religious Belief Systems in Contemporary China: Case Study of Popular Believers in Shenzhen*.

James D. Whitehead is a historian of religion and Christian theologian; he earned the Ph. D. from Harvard University, where his research focused on Buddhism's entry into Chinese culture. Currently his research interests include the role of religion in late modern society and the dynamics of cross-cultural religious dialogue. Dr. James Whitehead is Distinguished Fellow of the EDS-Stewart Chair of the Ricci Institute for Chinese-Western Cultural History at the University of San Francisco. Since 1998, with his colleague Evelyn Eaton Whitehead, he has traveled annually to China to offer lecture series and semester courses at universities in Shanghai, Hangzhou, Nanjing,Beijing,and Hong Kong.

Evelyn Eaton Whitehead is a social psychologist; she holds the Ph. D. from University of Chicago, with a concentration in comparative human development. Her current research focuses on cultural and developmental dynamics in religious consciousness. With her colleague James D. Whitehead, she has co-authored more than a dozen volumes on topics relating to contemporary religious life and spiritual practices; several of these titles are now available in Chinese language translation. Dr. Evelyn Eaton Whitehead is Distinguished Fellow of the EDS-Stewart Chair of the Ricci Institute for Chinese-Western Cultural History at the University of San Francisco.

作者简介

范丽珠,宗教社会学家,香港中文大学博士,现为复旦大学社会学系副教授、复旦大学社会发展研究中心秘书长。长期以来通过田野调查方式对中国民间信仰的现代价值做了大量深刻的研究,并致力于通过对中国宗教的阐释来丰富宗教社会学领域。著述颇丰,在中国国内和国际期刊上发表了大量论文,并主持编写了多部跨文化、跨学科领域的学术论文集。最新出版的著作是:《当代中国人宗教信仰的变迁:深圳民间宗教信徒的田野研究》。

James D. Whitehead,宗教历史学家、基督教理论家,哈佛大学博士。在哈佛期间,主要研究佛教是怎样进入中国文化的。目前的研究兴趣包括宗教在近、现代社会中所扮演的角色、宗教跨文化对话的内在动力。James D. Whitehead 博士是旧金山大学利玛窦中西文化历史研究所(EDS—Stewart Chair)的资深研究员。从1998年开始,每年都与 Evelyn Eaton Whitehead 博士一道来中国讲学。他们已访问过中国上海、杭州、南京、香港等地的多所大学,他们为大学生们举办系列讲座、开设学期课程。

Evelyn Eaton Whitehead,社会心理学家,芝加哥大学博士。在芝加哥大学期间,主要进行人类发展的比较研究。目前主要研究宗教意识中文化和发展的内在动力。与合作者 James D. Whitehead 博士一起出版了大量著作,内容涉及当代宗教生活和精神实践,他们的大部分著作都已有中文译本。Evelyn Eaton Whitehead 博士是旧金山大学利玛窦中西文化历史研究所(EDS—Stewart Chair)的资深研究员。

图书在版编目（CIP）数据

当代世界宗教学/范丽珠等著. —北京：时事出版社，2006
ISBN 7－80009－968－7

Ⅰ．当… Ⅱ．范… Ⅲ．宗教－研究－世界 Ⅳ．B928.1

中国版本图书馆 CIP 数据核字（2006）第 159800 号

出 版 发 行：时事出版社
地　　　址：北京市海淀区万寿寺甲 2 号
邮　　　编：100081
发 行 热 线：（010）88547590　88547591
读者服务部：（010）88547595
传　　　真：（010）68418647
电 子 邮 箱：shishichubanshe@sina. com
网　　　址：www. sspublish. com
印　　　刷：北京百善印刷厂

开本：787×1092　1/16　印张：29.25　字数：380 千字
2006 年 3 月第 1 版　2006 年 3 月第 1 次印刷
定价：58. 80 元